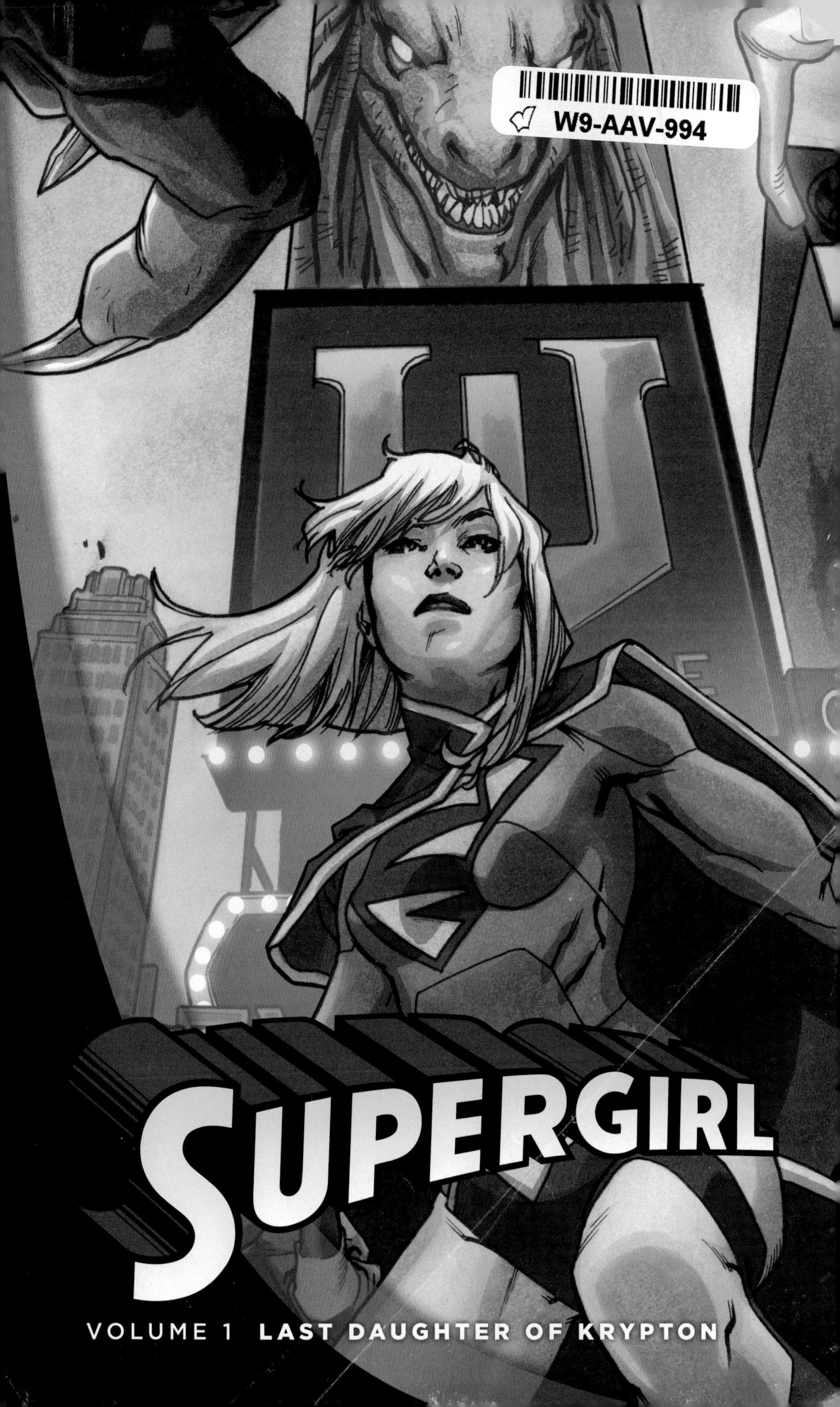

SUPERGIRL

VOLUME 1 LAST DAUGHTER OF KRYPTON

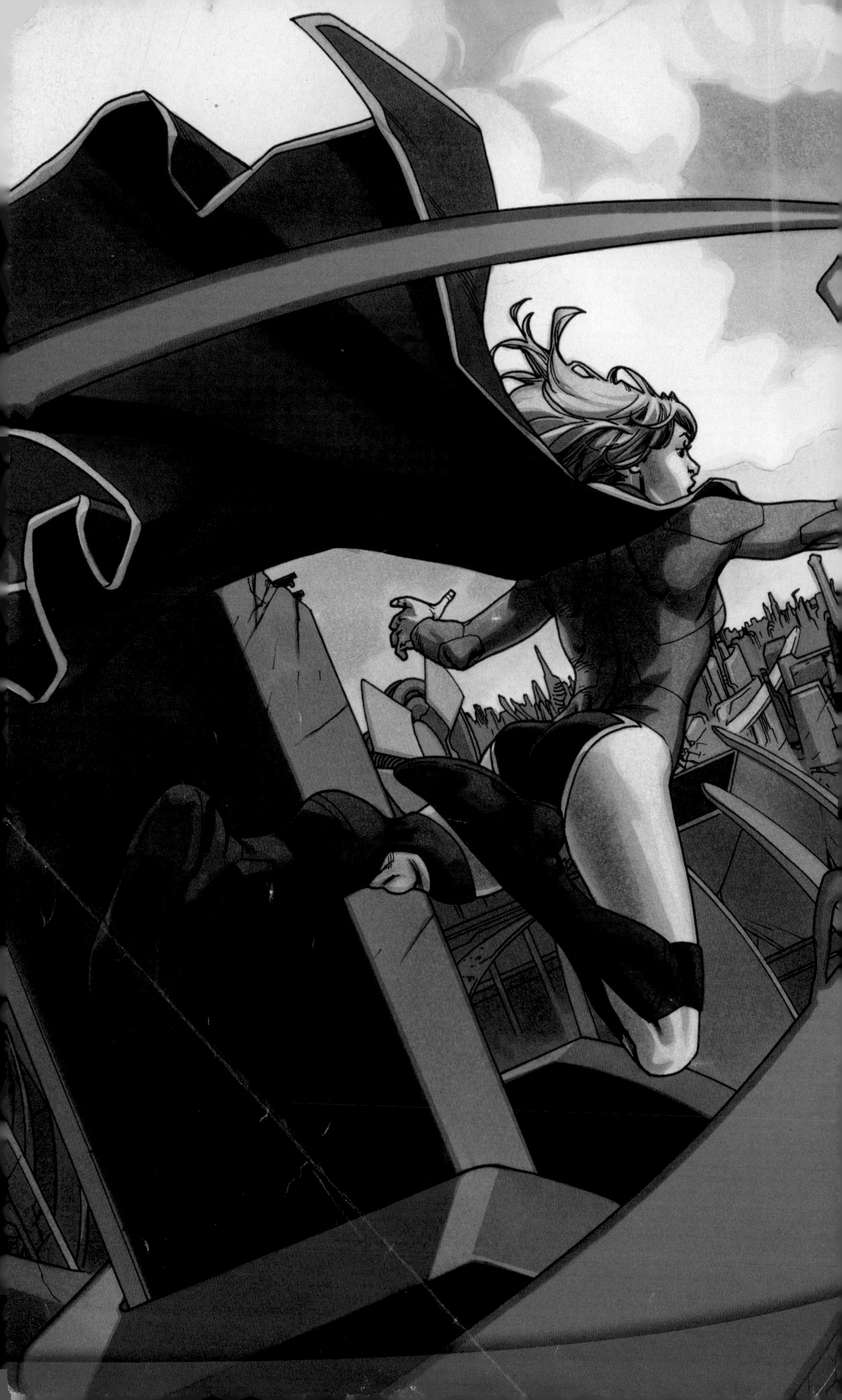

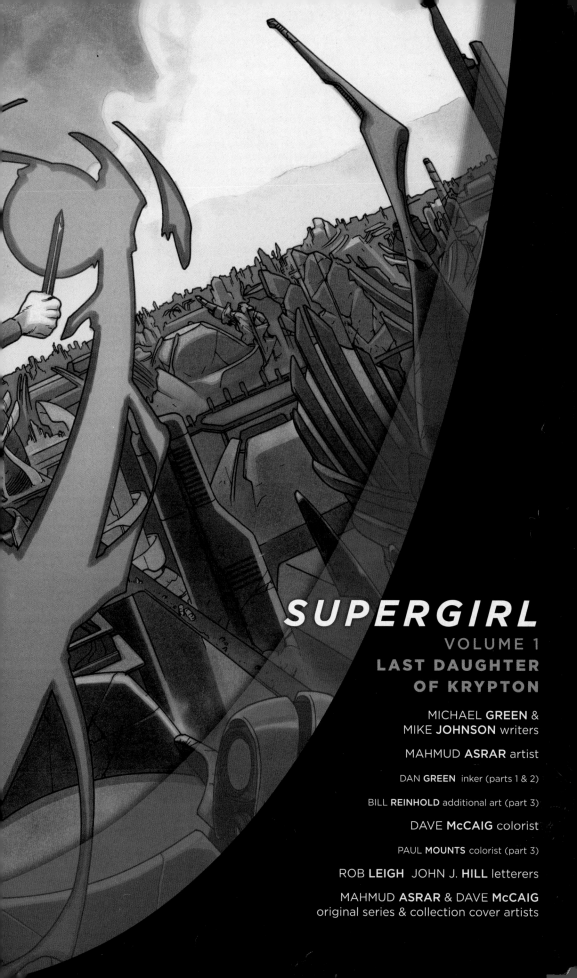

SUPERGIRL

VOLUME 1
LAST DAUGHTER
OF KRYPTON

MICHAEL **GREEN** &
MIKE **JOHNSON** writers

MAHMUD **ASRAR** artist

DAN **GREEN** inker (parts 1 & 2)

BILL **REINHOLD** additional art (part 3)

DAVE **McCAIG** colorist

PAUL **MOUNTS** colorist (part 3)

ROB **LEIGH** JOHN J. **HILL** letterers

MAHMUD **ASRAR** & DAVE **McCAIG**
original series & collection cover artists

WIL MOSS Editor – Original Series ROBIN WILDMAN Editor
ROBBIN BROSTERMAN Design Director – Books ROBBIE BIEDERMAN Publication Design

BOB HARRAS Senior VP – Editor-in-Chief, DC Comics

DIANE NELSON President DAN DIDIO and JIM LEE Co-Publishers
GEOFF JOHNS Chief Creative Officer
JOHN ROOD Executive VP – Sales, Marketing and Business Development
AMY GENKINS Senior VP – Business and Legal Affairs NAIRI GARDINER Senior VP – Finance
JEFF BOISON VP – Publishing Planning MARK CHIARELLO VP – Art Direction and Design
JOHN CUNNINGHAM VP – Marketing TERRI CUNNINGHAM VP – Editorial Administration
ALISON GILL Senior VP – Manufacturing and Operations HANK KANALZ Senior VP – Vertigo and Integrated Publishing
JAY KOGAN VP – Business and Legal Affairs, Publishing JACK MAHAN VP – Business Affairs, Talent
NICK NAPOLITANO VP – Manufacturing Administration SUE POHJA VP – Book Sales
COURTNEY SIMMONS Senior VP – Publicity BOB WAYNE Senior VP – Sales

SUPERGIRL VOLUME 1: LAST DAUGHTER OF KRYPTON

DC Comics, 1700 Broadway, New York, NY 10019
A Warner Bros. Entertainment Company.
Printed by RR Donnelley, Salem, VA, USA. 9/20/13. Third Printing.

ISBN: 978-1-4012-3680-9

Library of Congress Cataloging-in-Publication Data

Green, Michael, 1943-
Supergirl volume 1 : last daughter of Krypton / Michael Green, Mike Johnson, Mahmud Asrar.
p. cm.
"Originally published in single magazine form in Supergirl 1-7."
ISBN 978-1-4012-3680-9
I. Johnson, Mike. II. Asrar, Mahmud A. III. Title.
PN6728.S89G74 2012
741.5'973–dc23
2012022436

SUSTAINABLE
FORESTRY
INITIATIVE

Certified Chain of Custody
At Least 20% Certified Forest Content
www.sfiprogram.org
SFI-01042
APPLIES TO TEXT STOCK ONLY

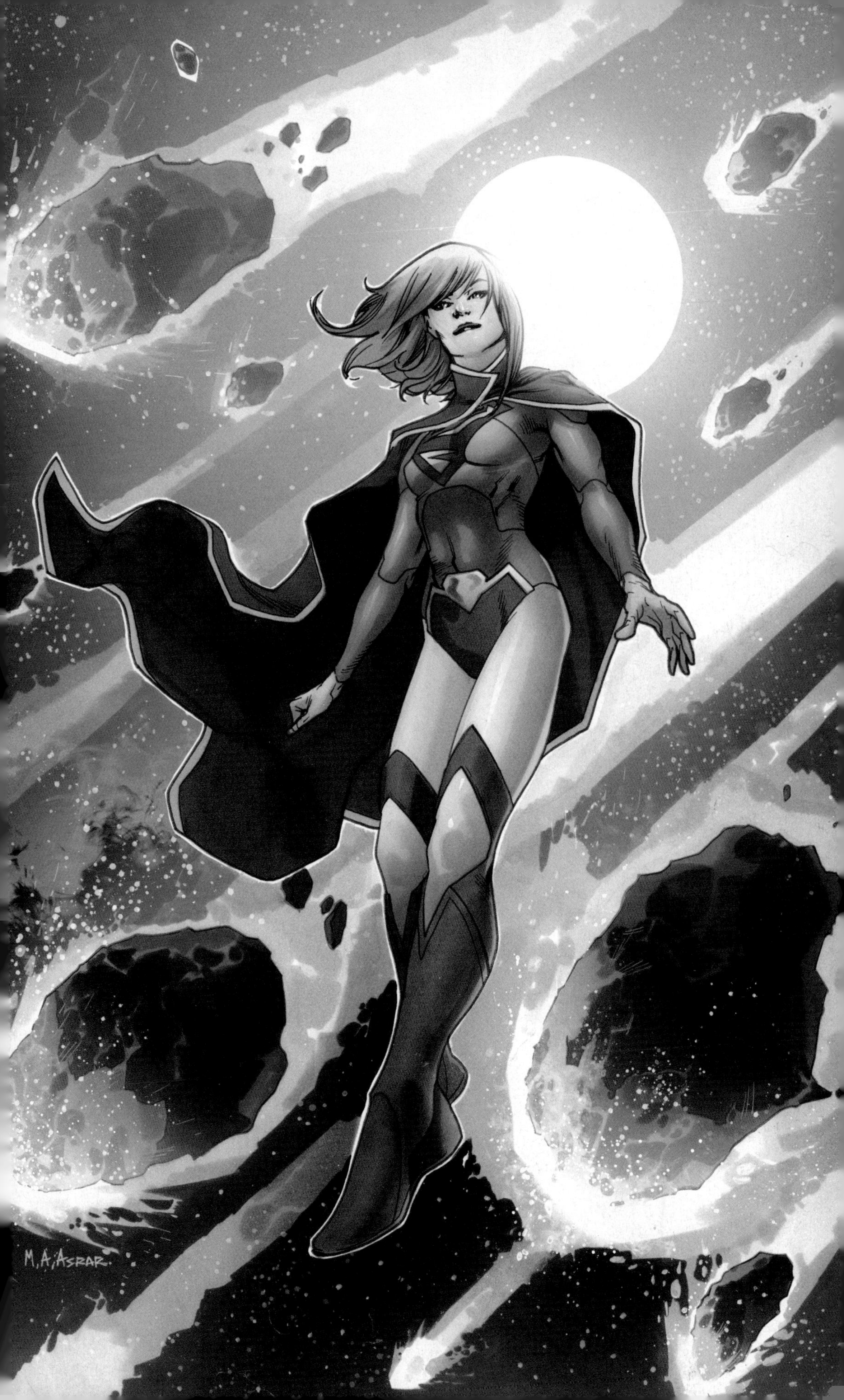
M.A.Asrar.

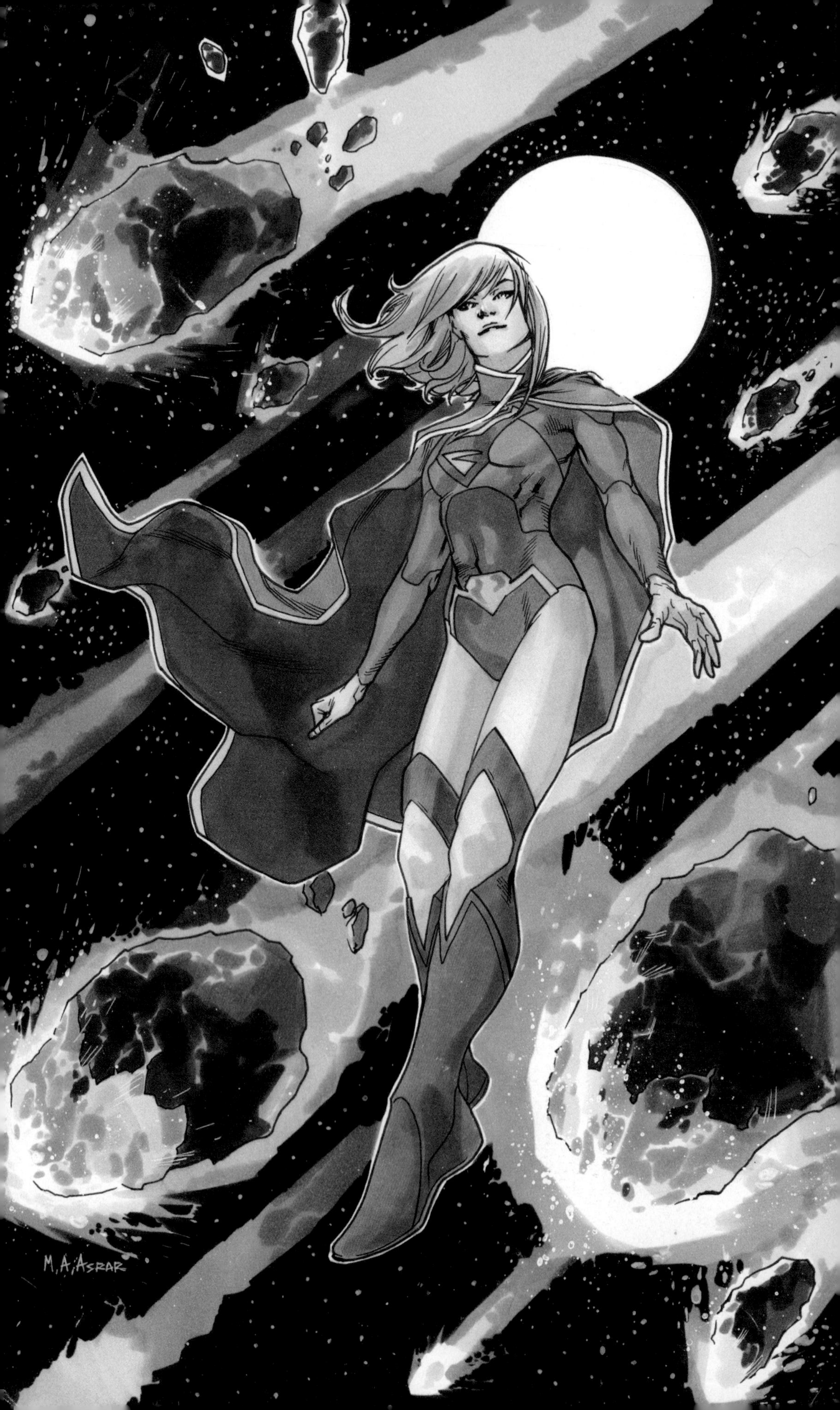
M.A. Asrar

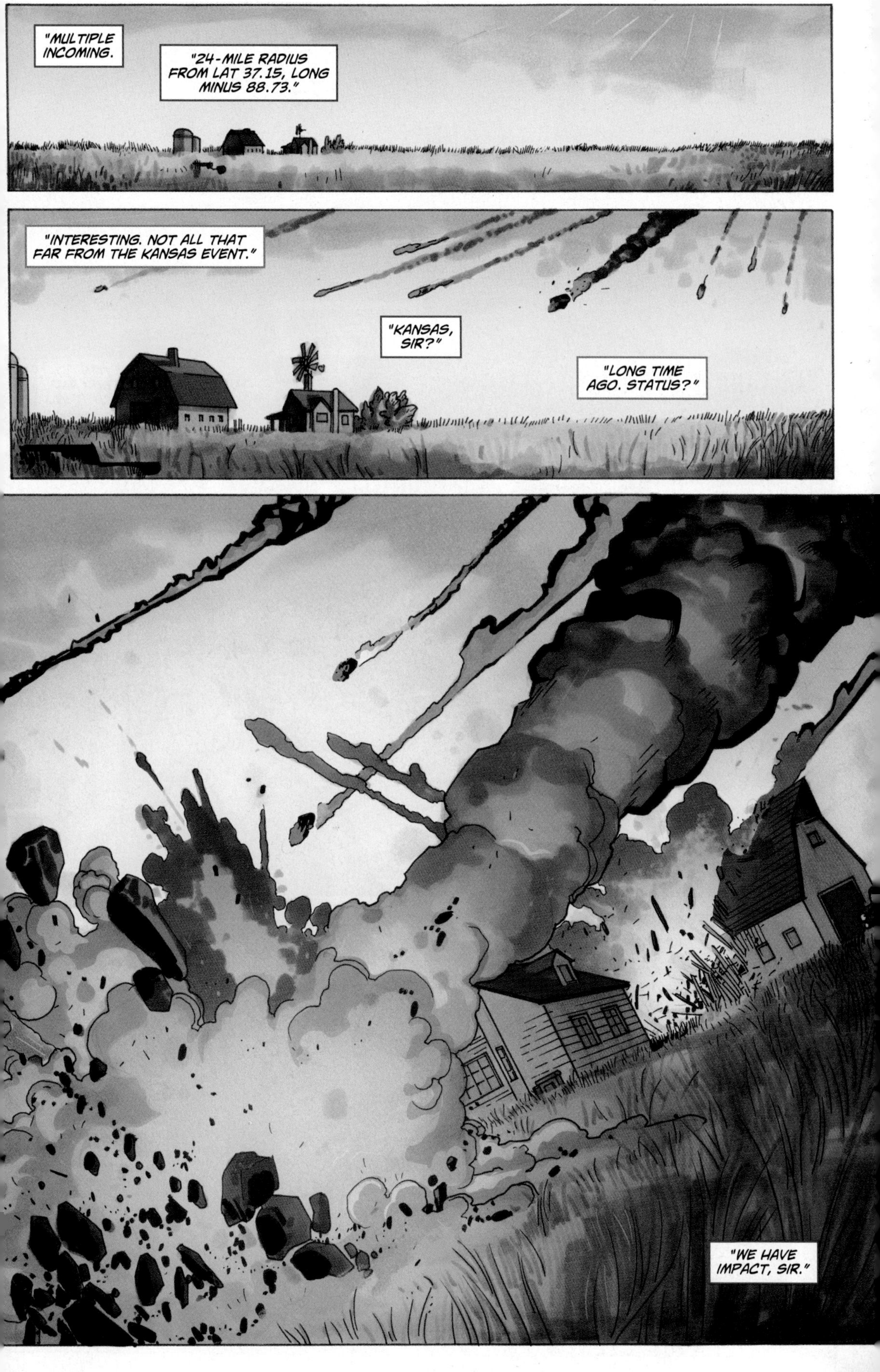
"MULTIPLE INCOMING.
"24-MILE RADIUS FROM LAT 37.15, LONG MINUS 88.73."
"INTERESTING. NOT ALL THAT FAR FROM THE KANSAS EVENT."
"KANSAS, SIR?"
"LONG TIME AGO. STATUS?"
"WE HAVE IMPACT, SIR."

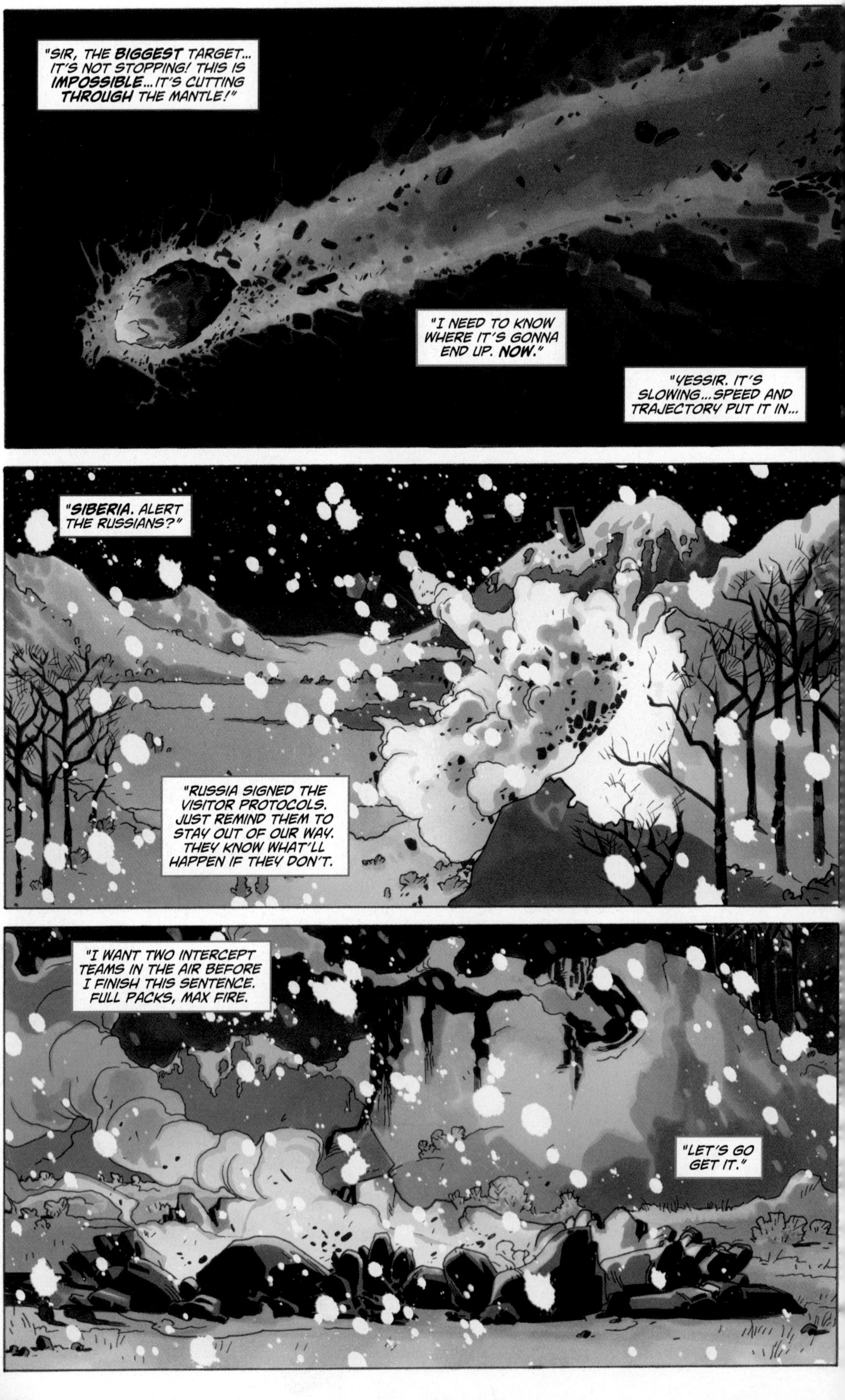
"SIR, THE BIGGEST TARGET... IT'S NOT STOPPING! THIS IS IMPOSSIBLE...IT'S CUTTING THROUGH THE MANTLE!"
"I NEED TO KNOW WHERE IT'S GONNA END UP. NOW."
"YESSIR. IT'S SLOWING...SPEED AND TRAJECTORY PUT IT IN...
"SIBERIA. ALERT THE RUSSIANS?"
"RUSSIA SIGNED THE VISITOR PROTOCOLS. JUST REMIND THEM TO STAY OUT OF OUR WAY. THEY KNOW WHAT'LL HAPPEN IF THEY DON'T.
"I WANT TWO INTERCEPT TEAMS IN THE AIR BEFORE I FINISH THIS SENTENCE. FULL PACKS, MAX FIRE.
"LET'S GO GET IT."

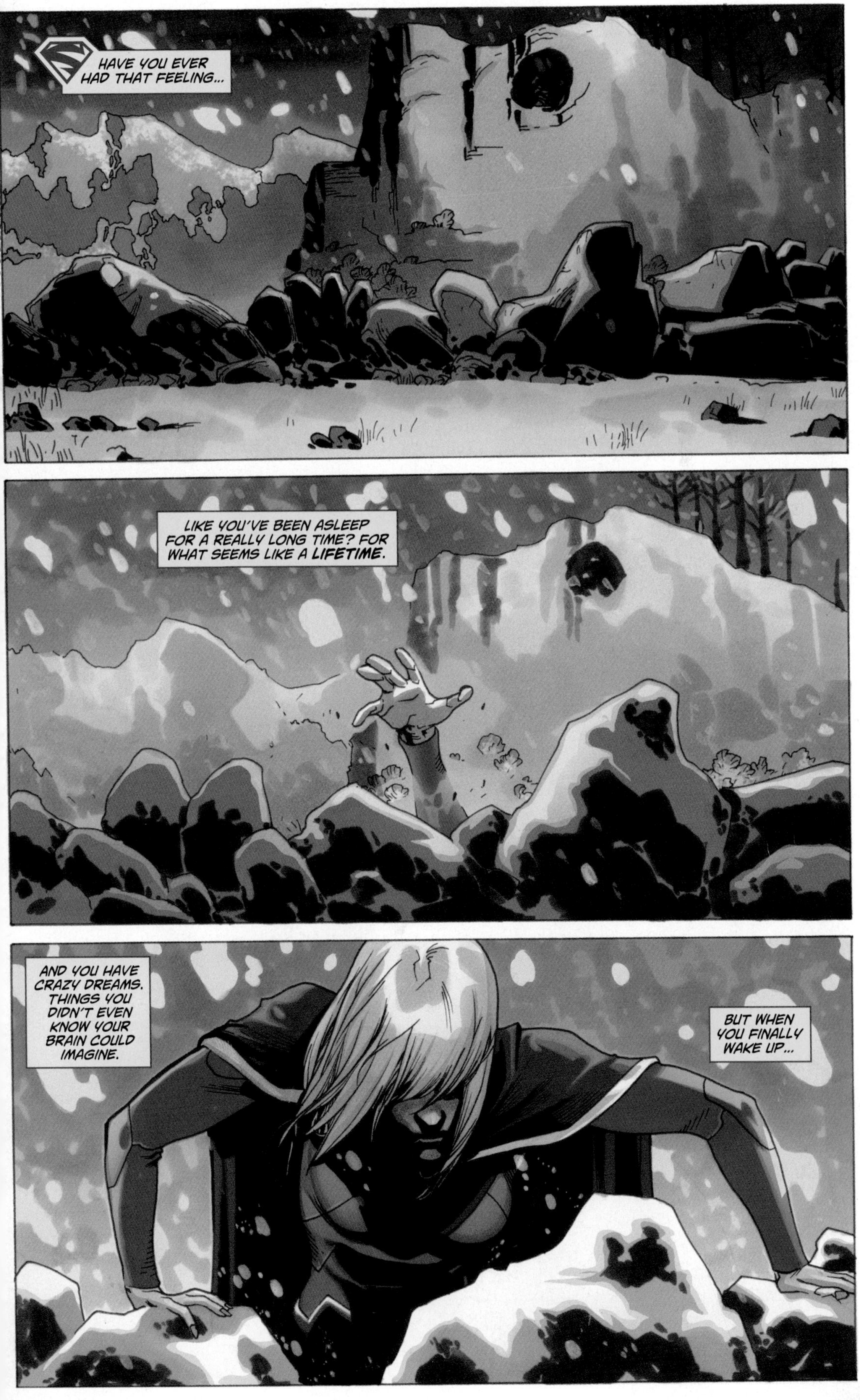
HAVE YOU EVER HAD THAT FEELING...
LIKE YOU'VE BEEN ASLEEP FOR A REALLY LONG TIME? FOR WHAT SEEMS LIKE A **LIFETIME**.
AND YOU HAVE CRAZY DREAMS. THINGS YOU DIDN'T EVEN KNOW YOUR BRAIN COULD IMAGINE.
BUT WHEN YOU FINALLY WAKE UP...

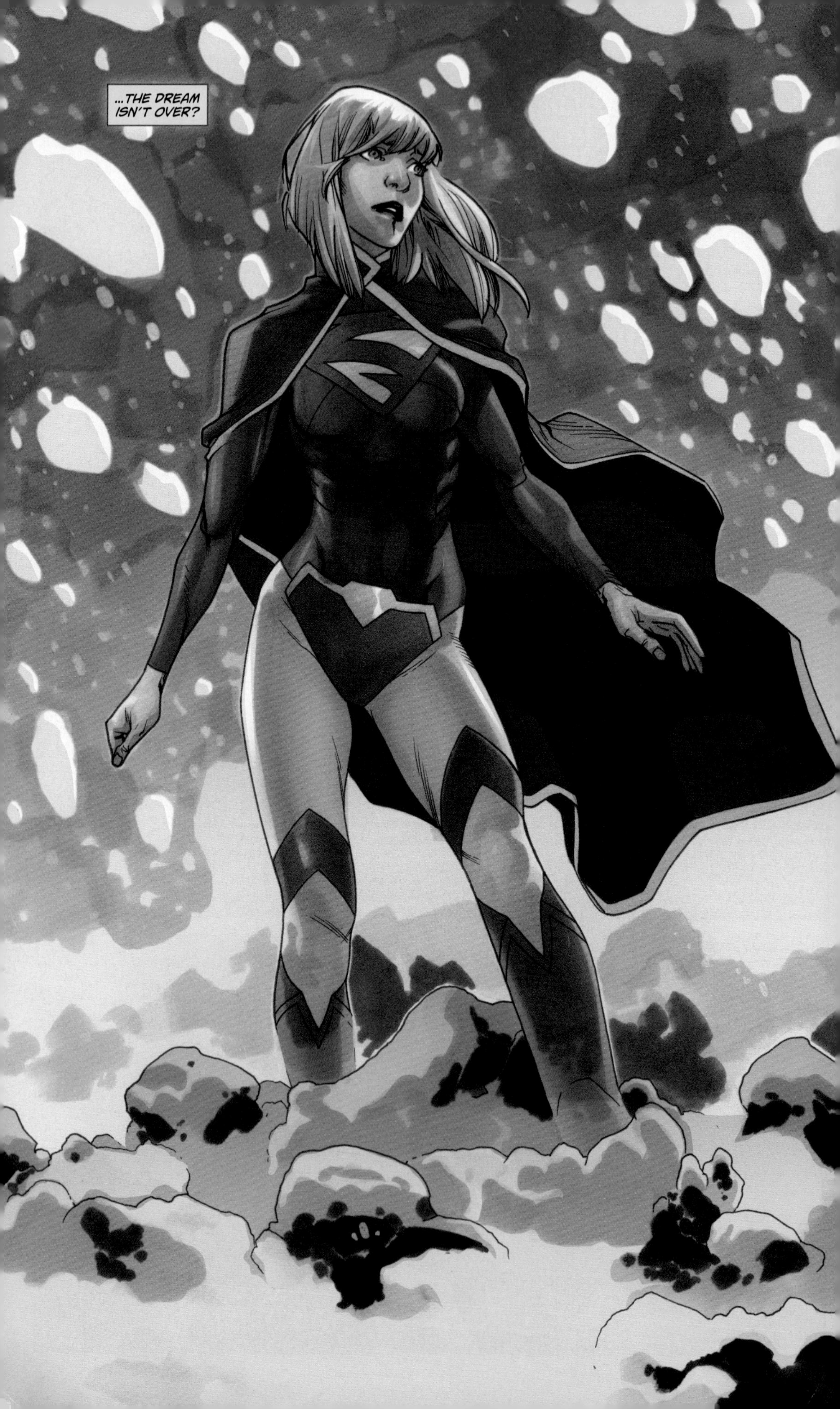
...THE DREAM ISN'T OVER?

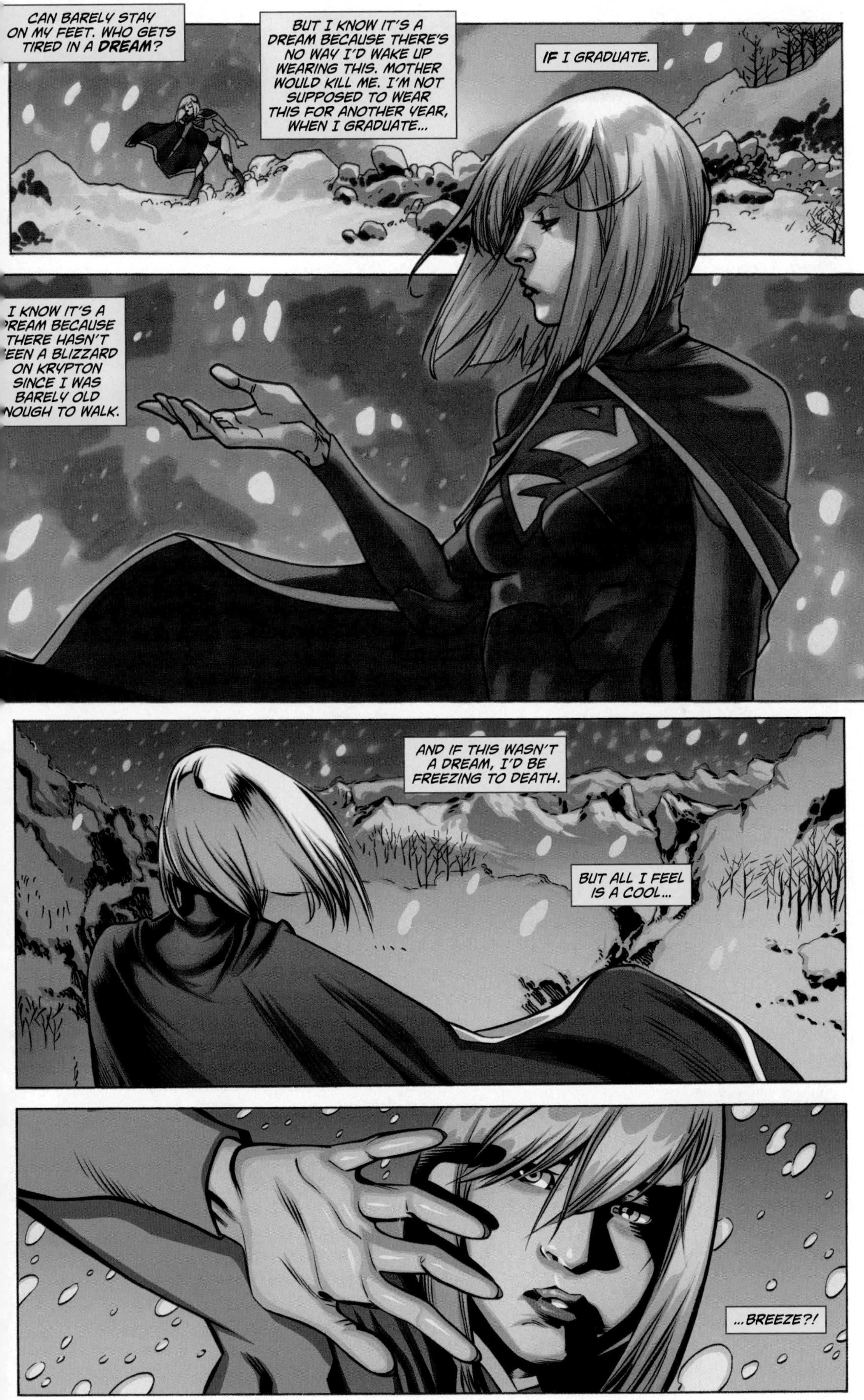
CAN BARELY STAY ON MY FEET. WHO GETS TIRED IN A DREAM?
BUT I KNOW IT'S A DREAM BECAUSE THERE'S NO WAY I'D WAKE UP WEARING THIS. MOTHER WOULD KILL ME. I'M NOT SUPPOSED TO WEAR THIS FOR ANOTHER YEAR, WHEN I GRADUATE...
IF I GRADUATE.
I KNOW IT'S A REAM BECAUSE THERE HASN'T EEN A BLIZZARD ON KRYPTON SINCE I WAS BARELY OLD NOUGH TO WALK.
AND IF THIS WASN'T A DREAM, I'D BE FREEZING TO DEATH.
BUT ALL I FEEL IS A COOL...
...BREEZE?!

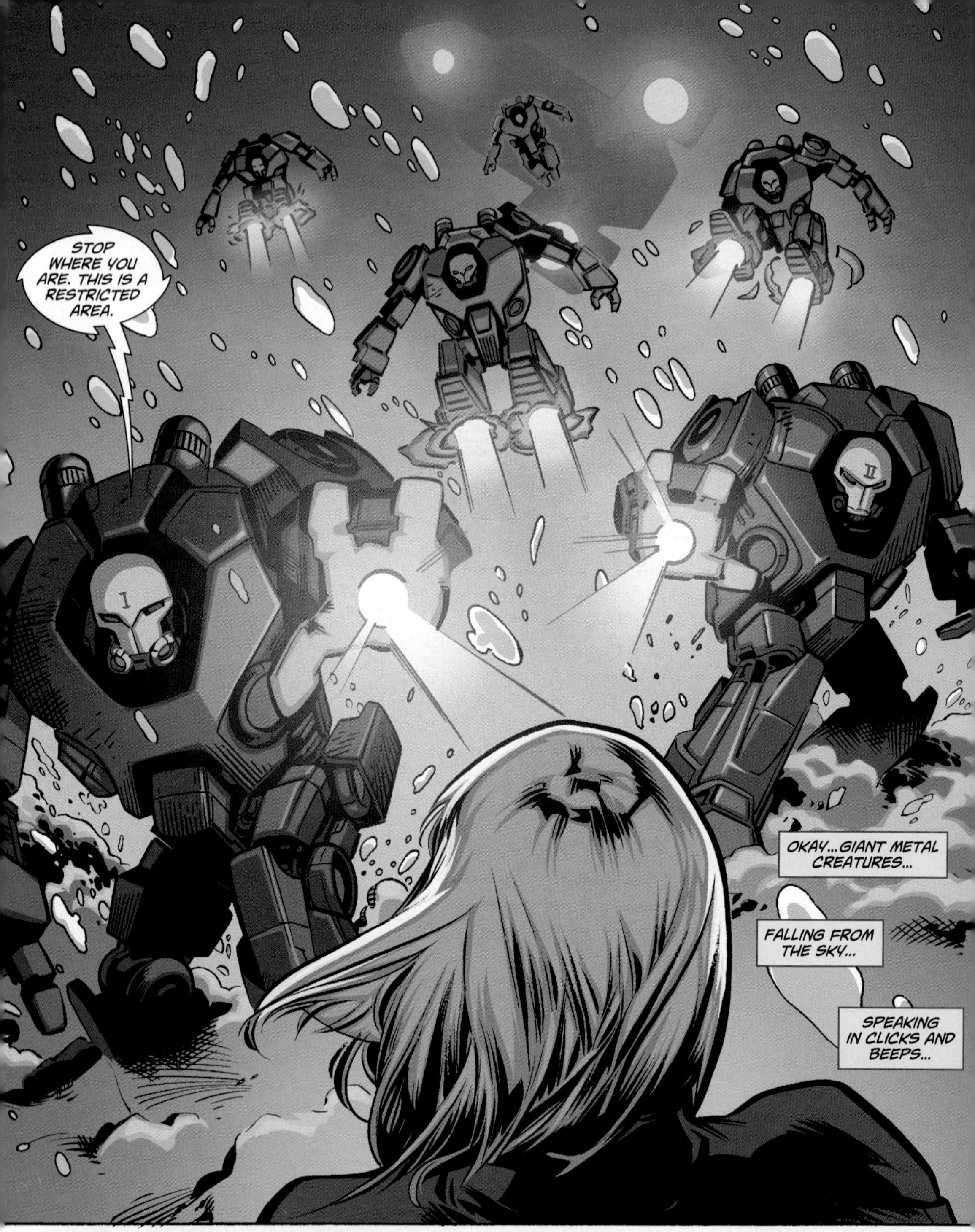
STOP WHERE YOU ARE. THIS IS A RESTRICTED AREA.
OKAY...GIANT METAL CREATURES...
FALLING FROM THE SKY...
SPEAKING IN CLICKS AND BEEPS...

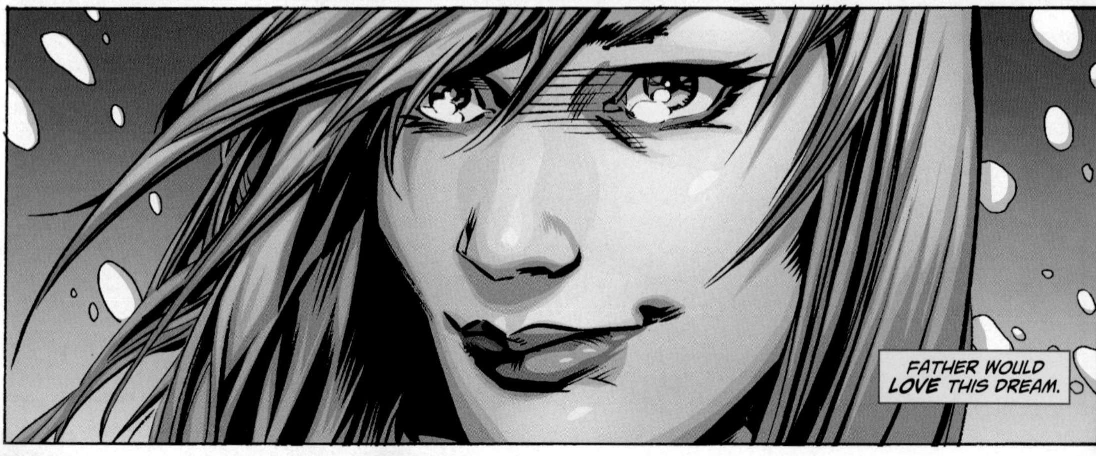
FATHER WOULD LOVE THIS DREAM.

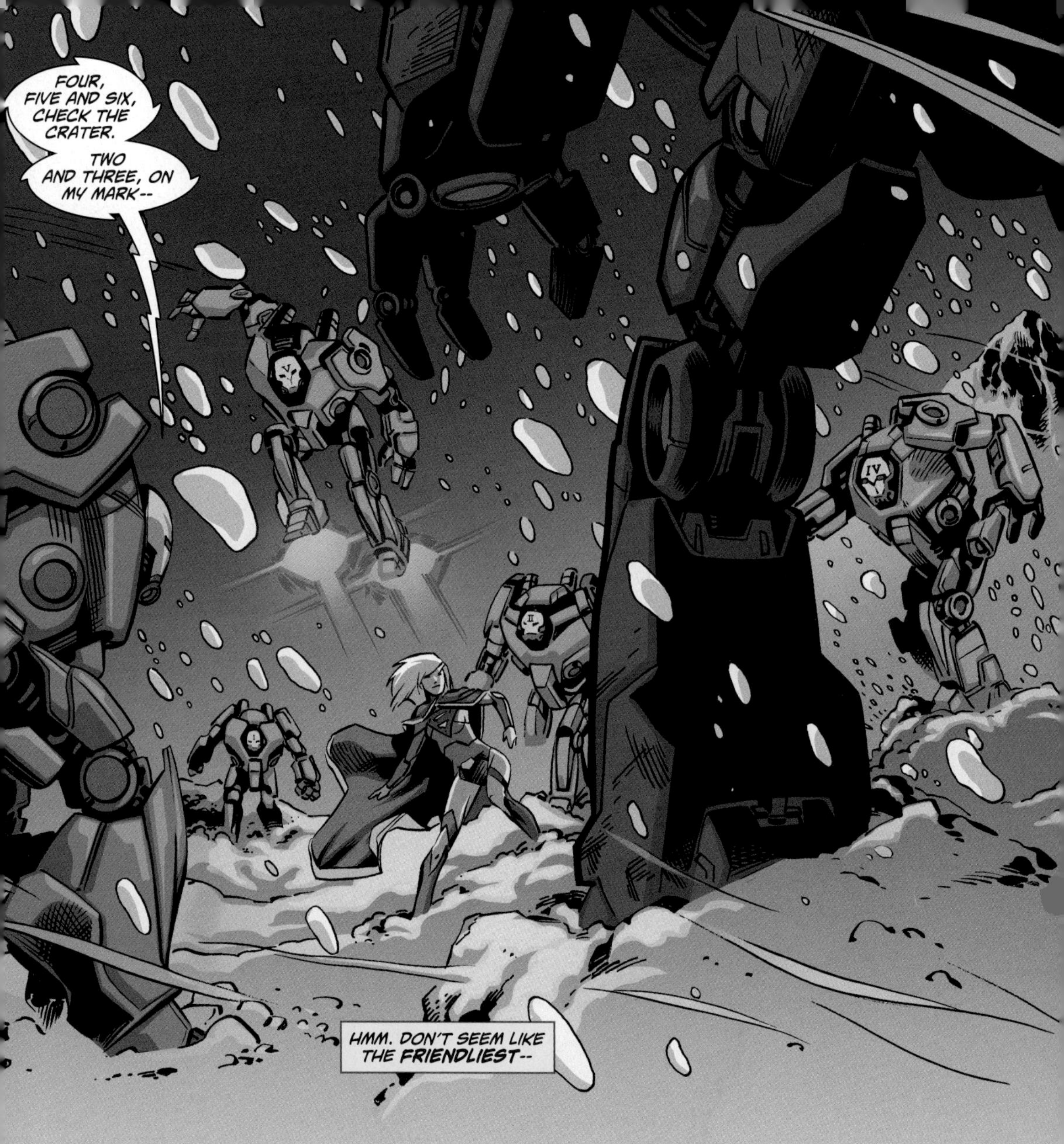
FOUR, FIVE AND SIX, CHECK THE CRATER.
TWO AND THREE, ON MY MARK--
HMM. DON'T SEEM LIKE THE FRIENDLIEST--

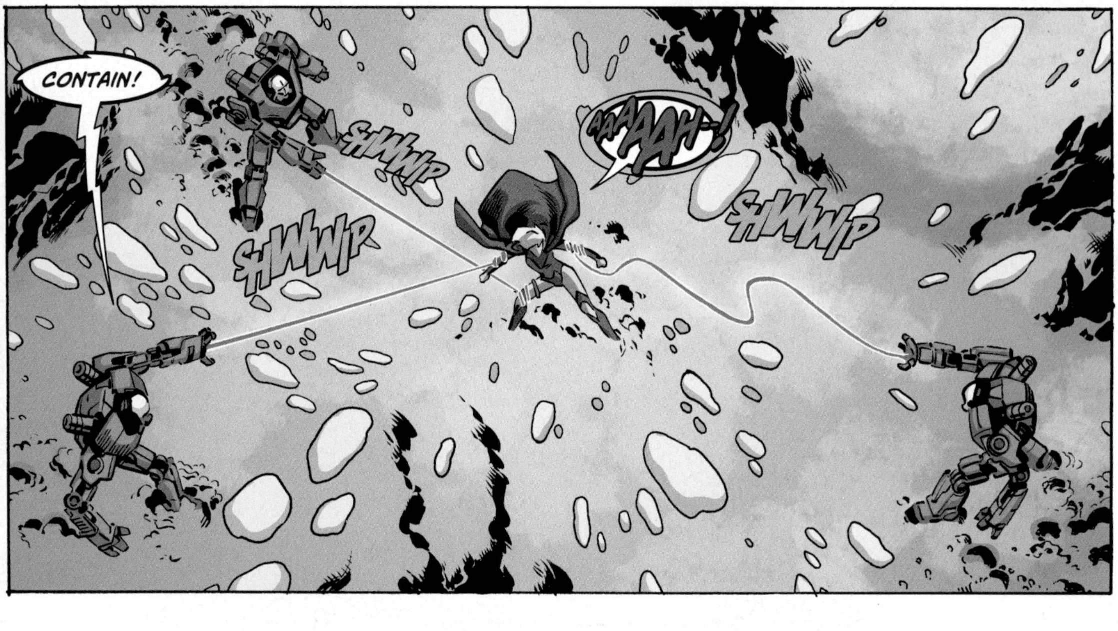
CONTAIN!
SHWWIP
AAAAAH!
SHWWIP
SHWWIP

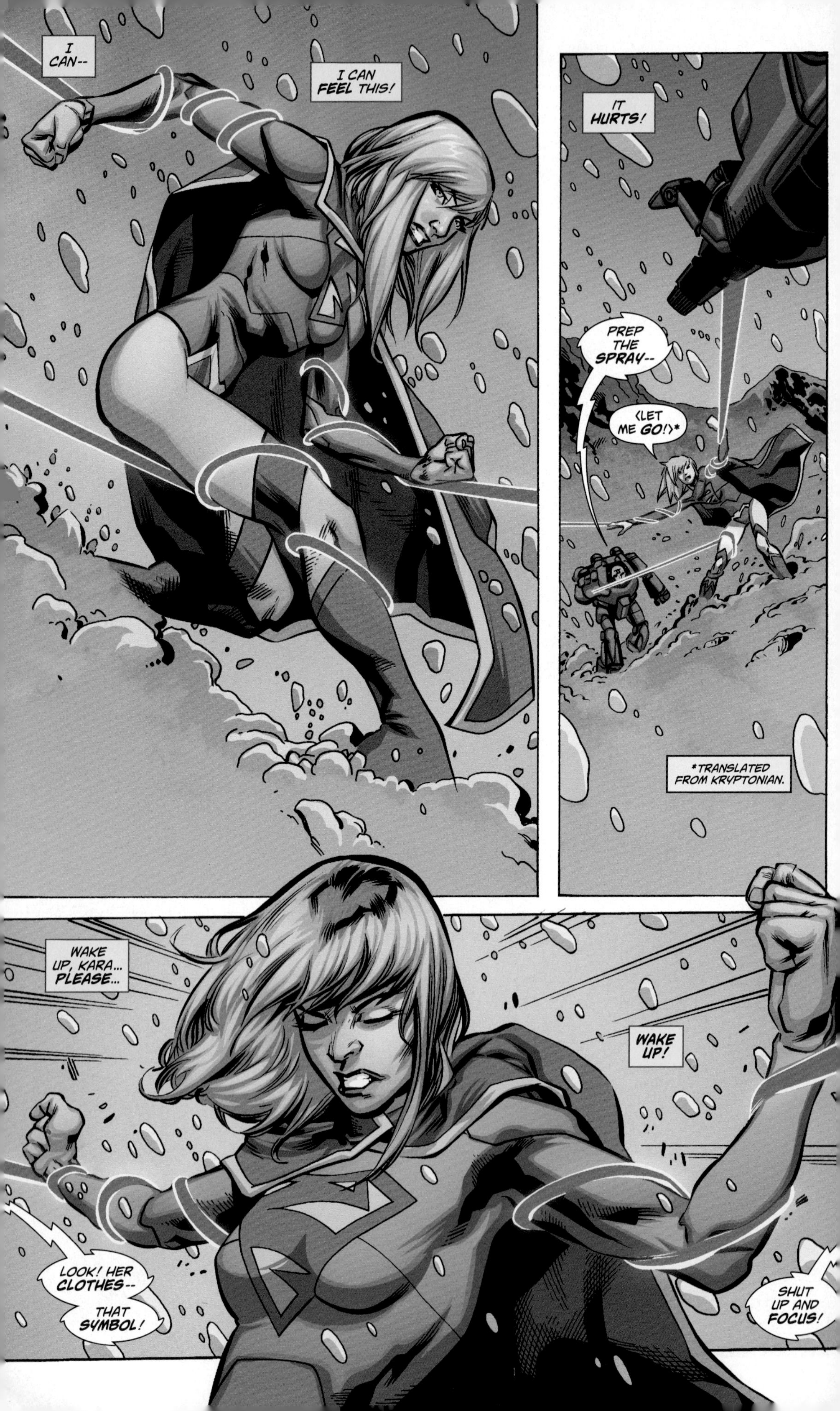
I CAN--
I CAN FEEL THIS!
IT HURTS!
PREP THE SPRAY--
<LET ME GO!>*
*TRANSLATED FROM KRYPTONIAN.
WAKE UP, KARA... PLEASE...
WAKE UP!
LOOK! HER CLOTHES--
THAT SYMBOL!
SHUT UP AND FOCUS!

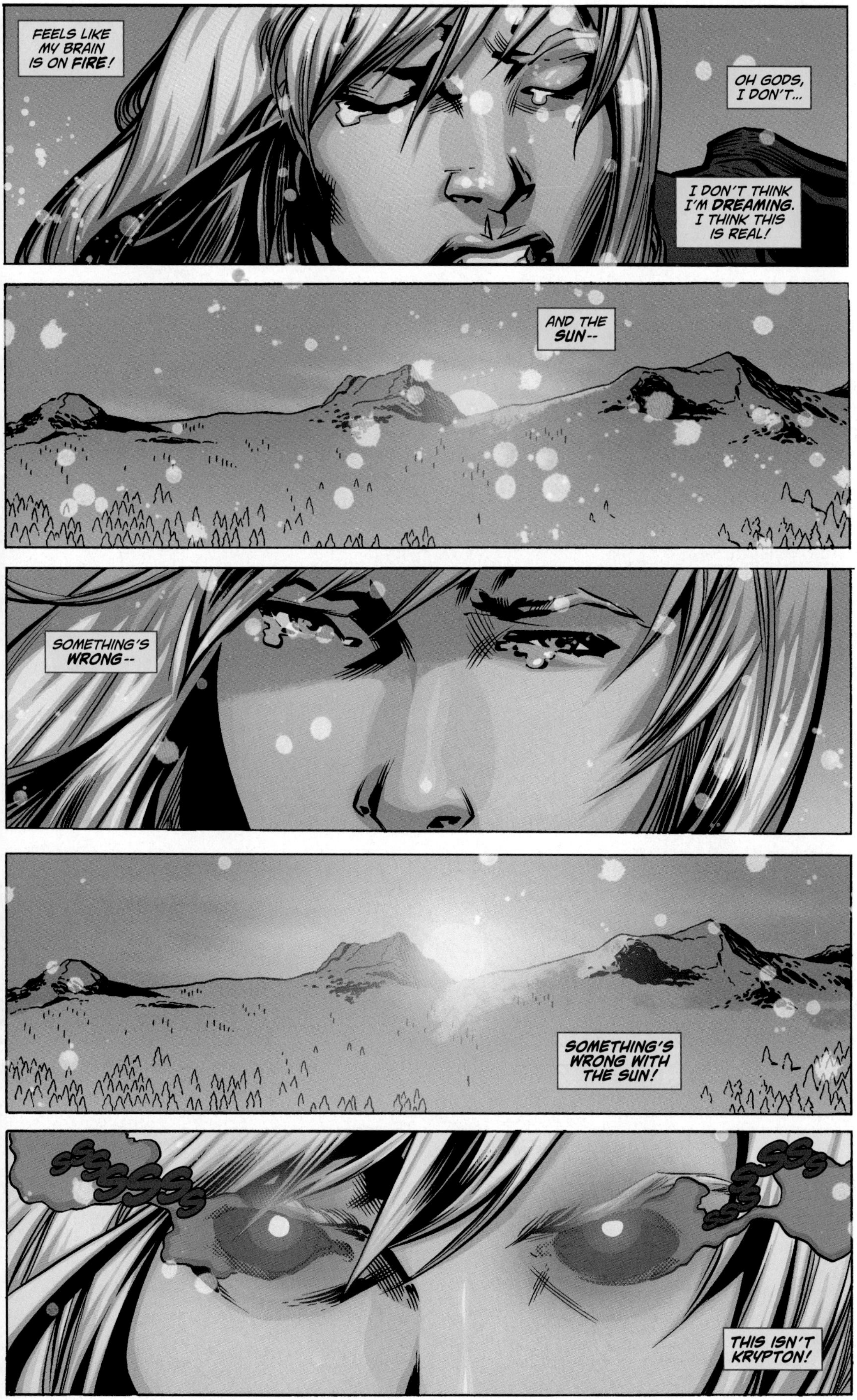
FEELS LIKE MY BRAIN IS ON FIRE!
OH GODS, I DON'T...
I DON'T THINK I'M DREAMING. I THINK THIS IS REAL!
AND THE SUN--
SOMETHING'S WRONG--
SOMETHING'S WRONG WITH THE SUN!
SSSSSSSS
SSSSSSS
THIS ISN'T KRYPTON!

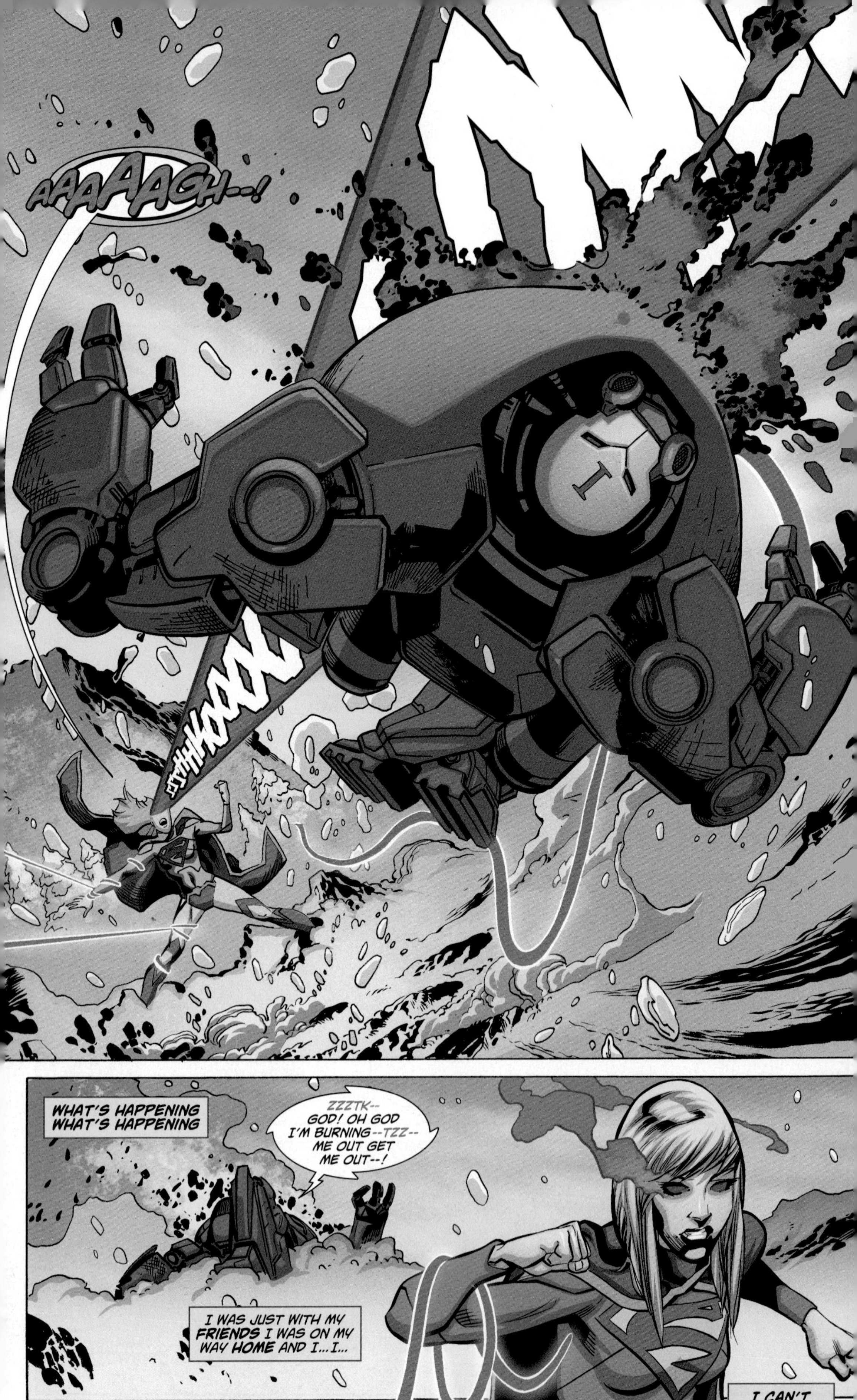
AAAAAGH--!
WHAT'S HAPPENING WHAT'S HAPPENING
ZZZTK-- GOD! OH GOD I'M BURNING--TZZ-- ME OUT GET ME OUT--!
I WAS JUST WITH MY FRIENDS I WAS ON MY WAY HOME AND I... I...
I CAN'T REMEMBER!

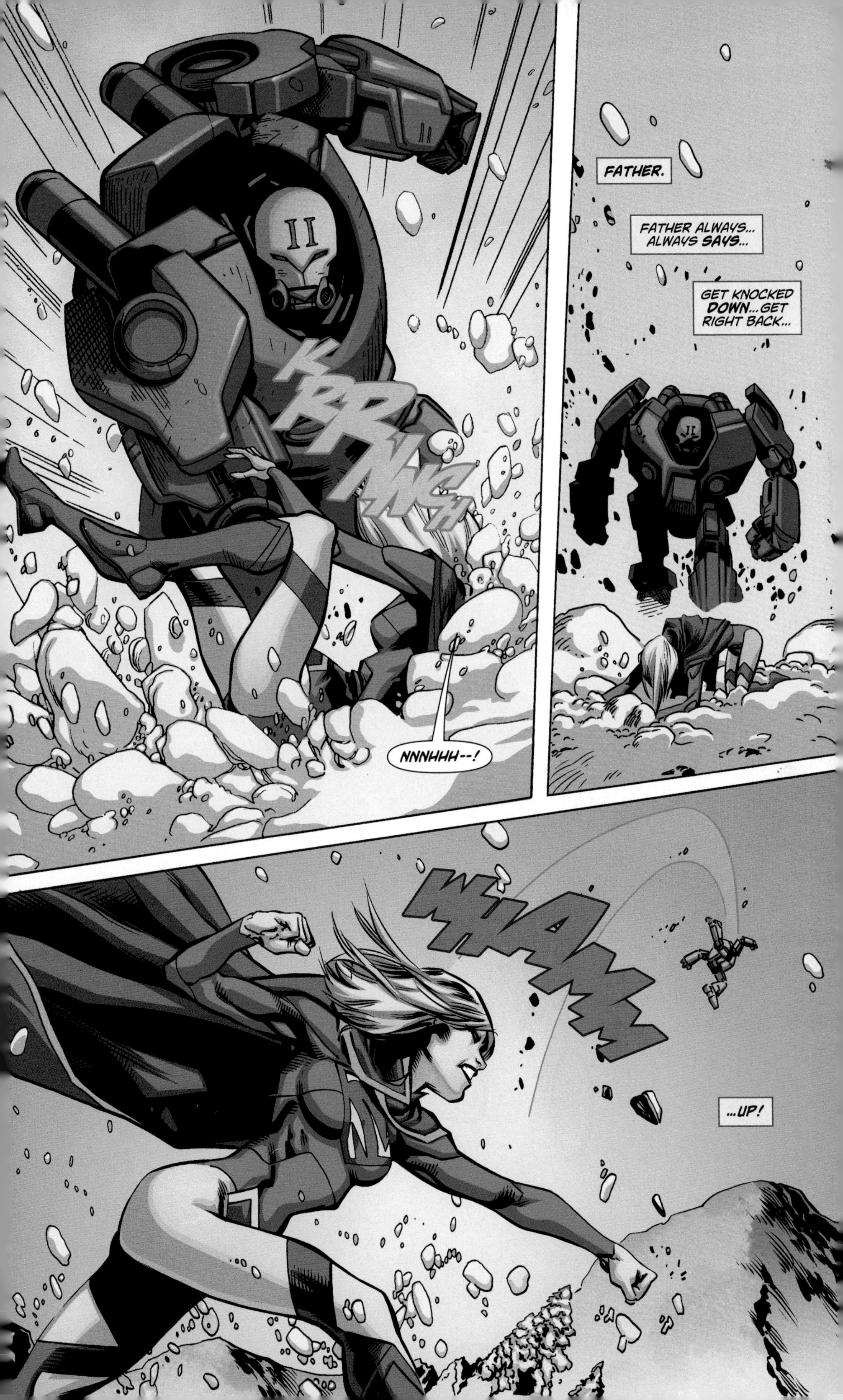
KRRNNCH
NNNHHH--!
FATHER.
FATHER ALWAYS... ALWAYS SAYS...
GET KNOCKED DOWN...GET RIGHT BACK...
WHAMM
...UP!

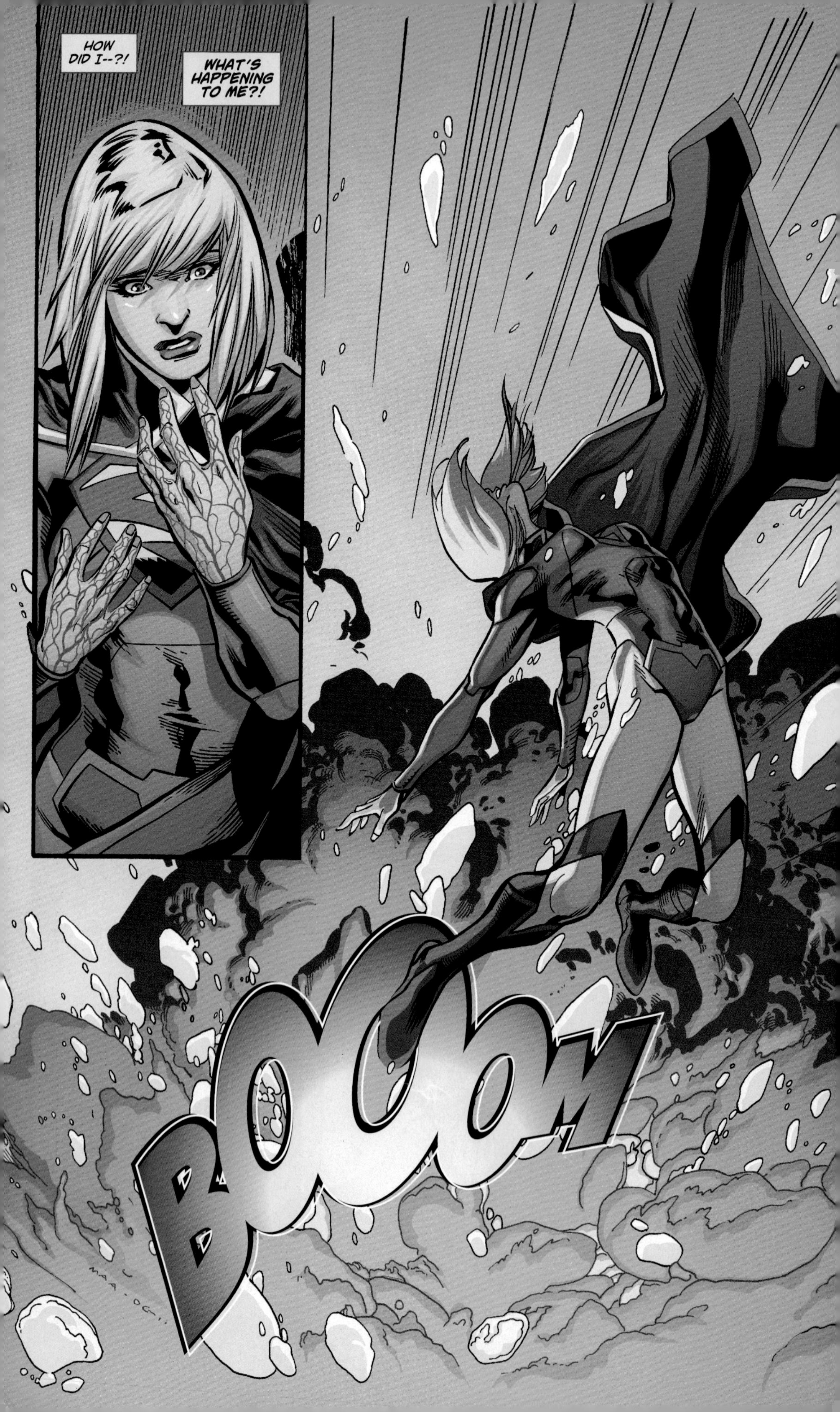
HOW DID I--?!
WHAT'S HAPPENING TO ME?!
BOOOM

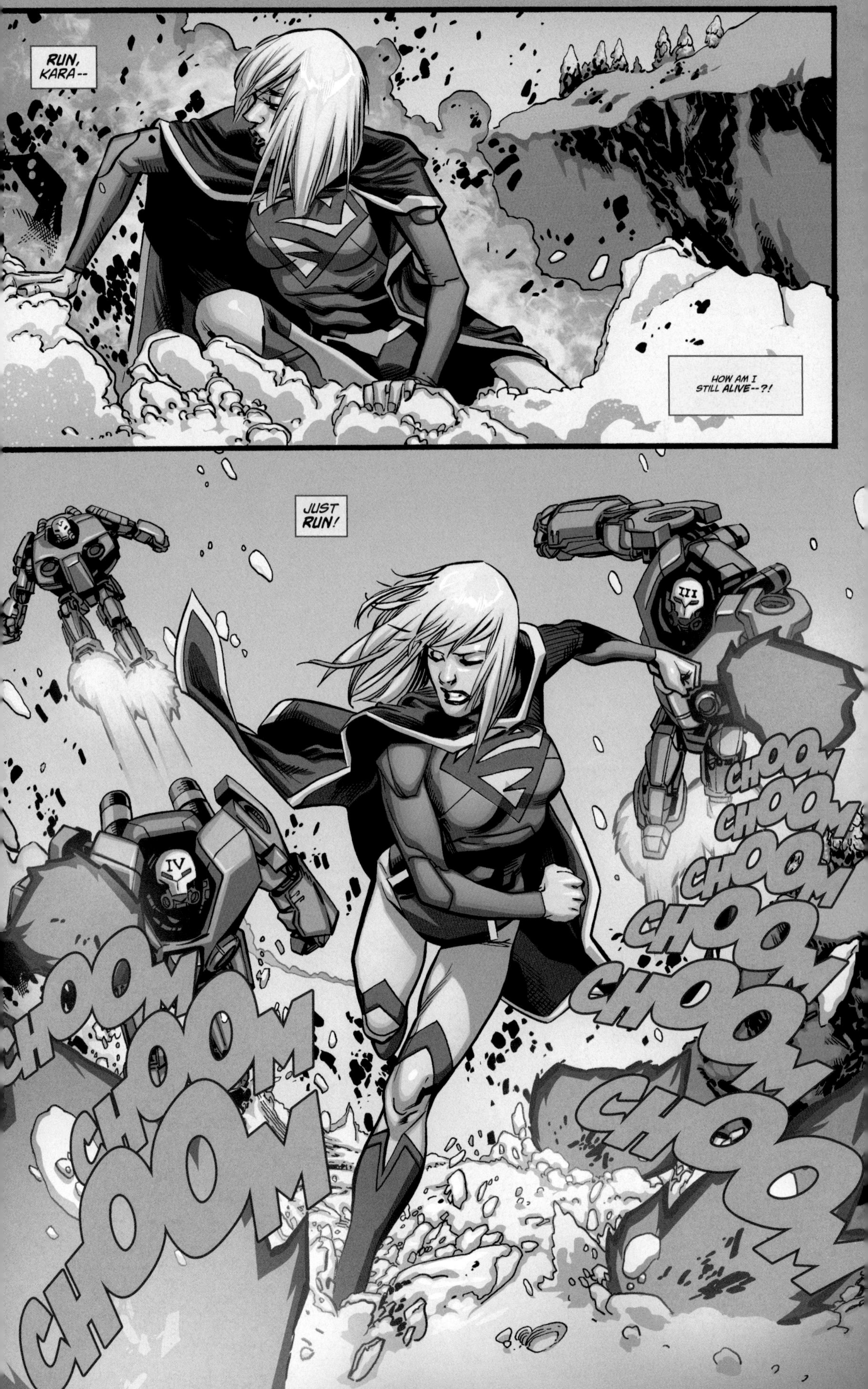
RUN, KARA--
HOW AM I STILL ALIVE--?!
JUST RUN!
CHOOM
CHOOM
CHOOM
CHOOM
CHOOM
CHOOM
CHOOM
CHOOM
CHOOM

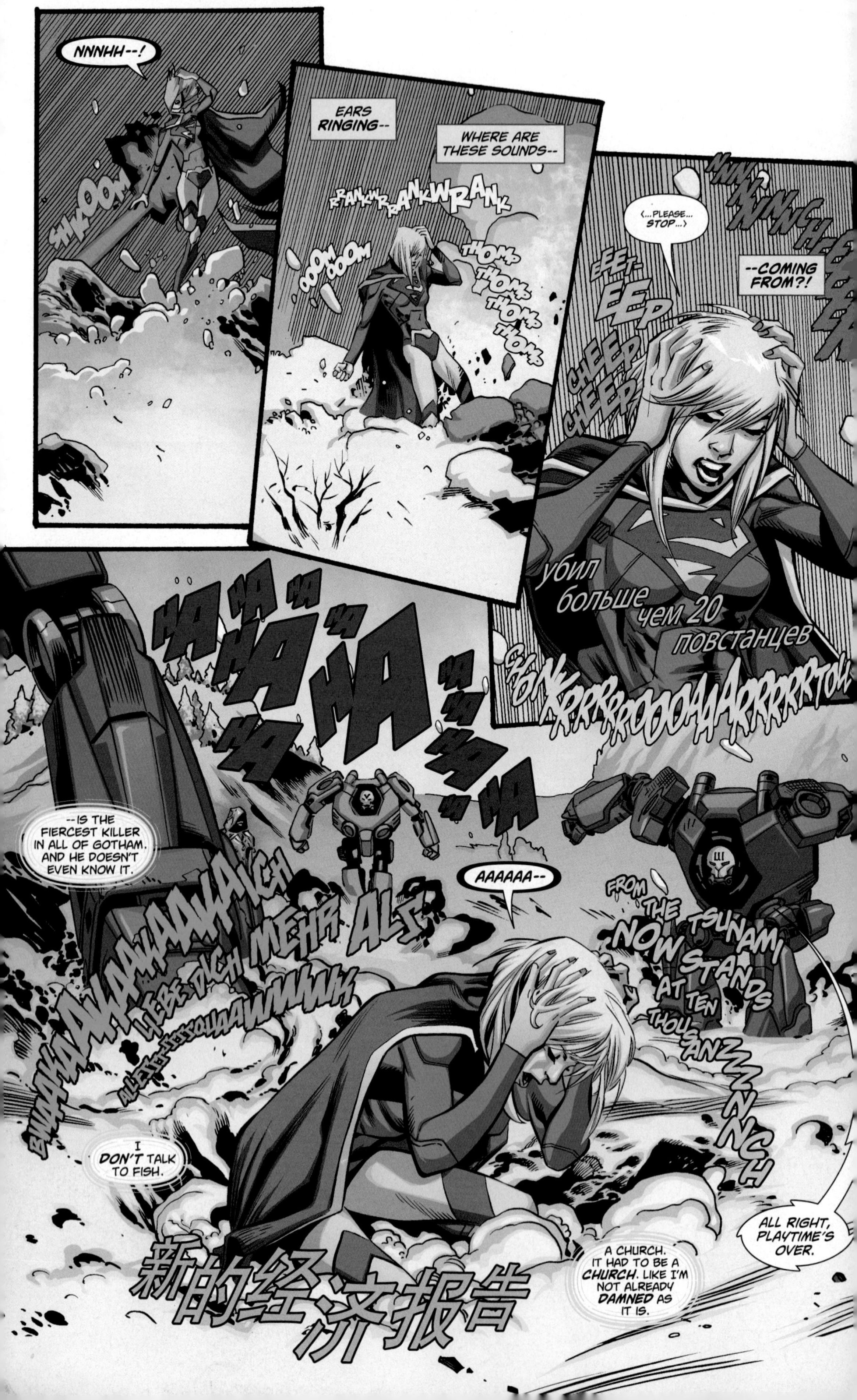
NNNHH--!
SHKOOM
EARS RINGING--
WHERE ARE THESE SOUNDS--
RANKWRANKWRANKWRANK
OOOM OOOM
THOMP THOMP THOMP THOMP
‹...PLEASE... STOP...›
EEEP- EEP
CHEEP CHEEP
--COMING FROM?!
убил больше чем 20 повстанцев
HA HA HA HA HA HA HA HA HA HA HA HA HA
--IS THE FIERCEST KILLER IN ALL OF GOTHAM. AND HE DOESN'T EVEN KNOW IT.
AAAAAA--
LIEBE DICH MEHR ALS
FROM THE TSUNAMI NOW STANDS AT TEN THOUSANZZZNNCH
I DON'T TALK TO FISH.
新的经济报告
A CHURCH. IT HAD TO BE A CHURCH. LIKE I'M NOT ALREADY DAMNED AS IT IS.
ALL RIGHT, PLAYTIME'S OVER.

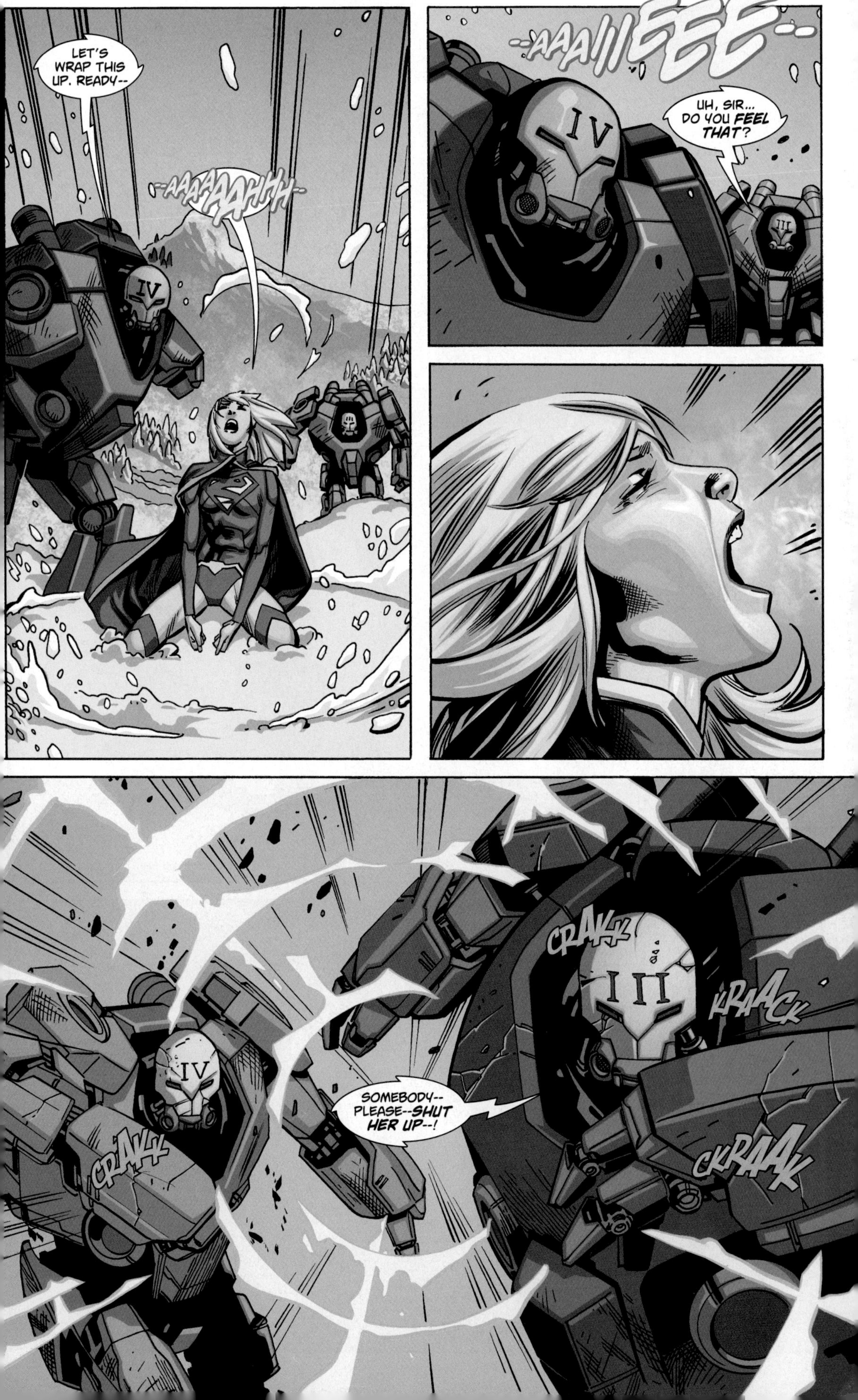
LET'S WRAP THIS UP. READY--
--AAAAAAHHH--
--AAAIIIEEE--
UH, SIR... DO YOU FEEL THAT?
CRAKK
KRAACK
SOMEBODY--PLEASE--SHUT HER UP--!
CRAKK
CKRAAK

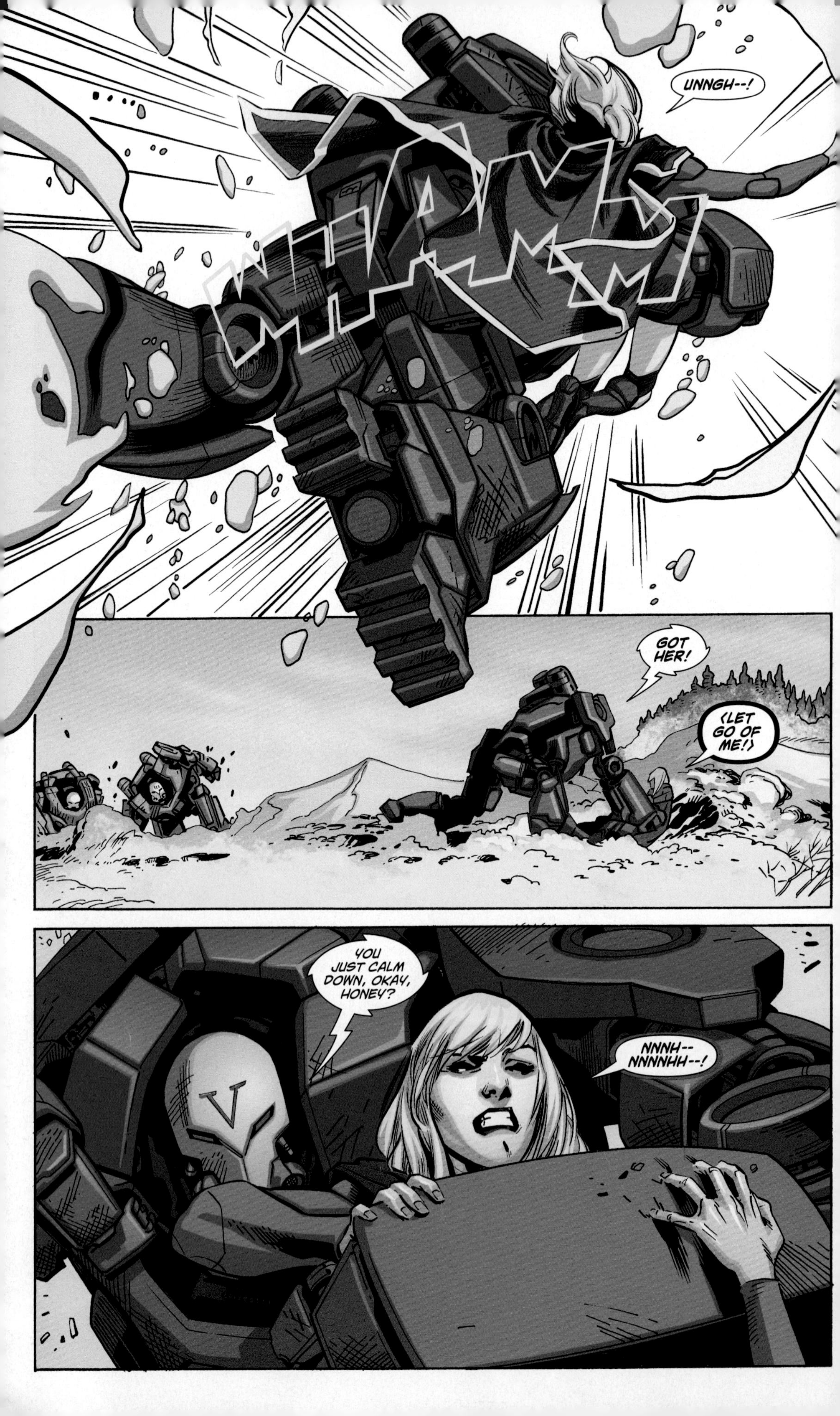
UNNGH--!
WHAM
GOT HER!
‹LET GO OF ME!›
YOU JUST CALM DOWN, OKAY, HONEY?
NNNH-- NNNNHH--!

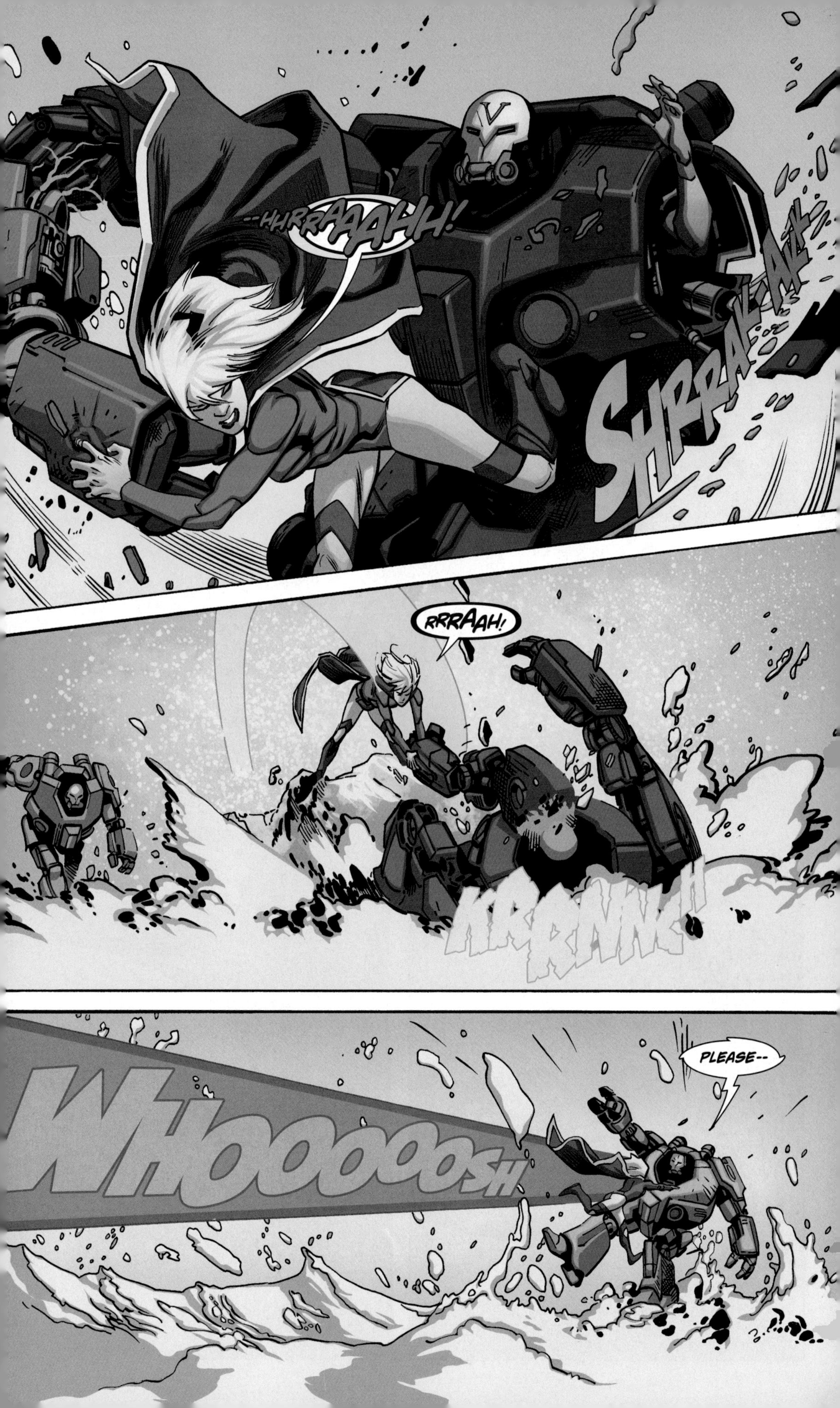
--HHRRAAAHH!
SHRRAK-AKK
RRRAAH!
KRRNNCH
WHOOOOOSH
PLEASE--

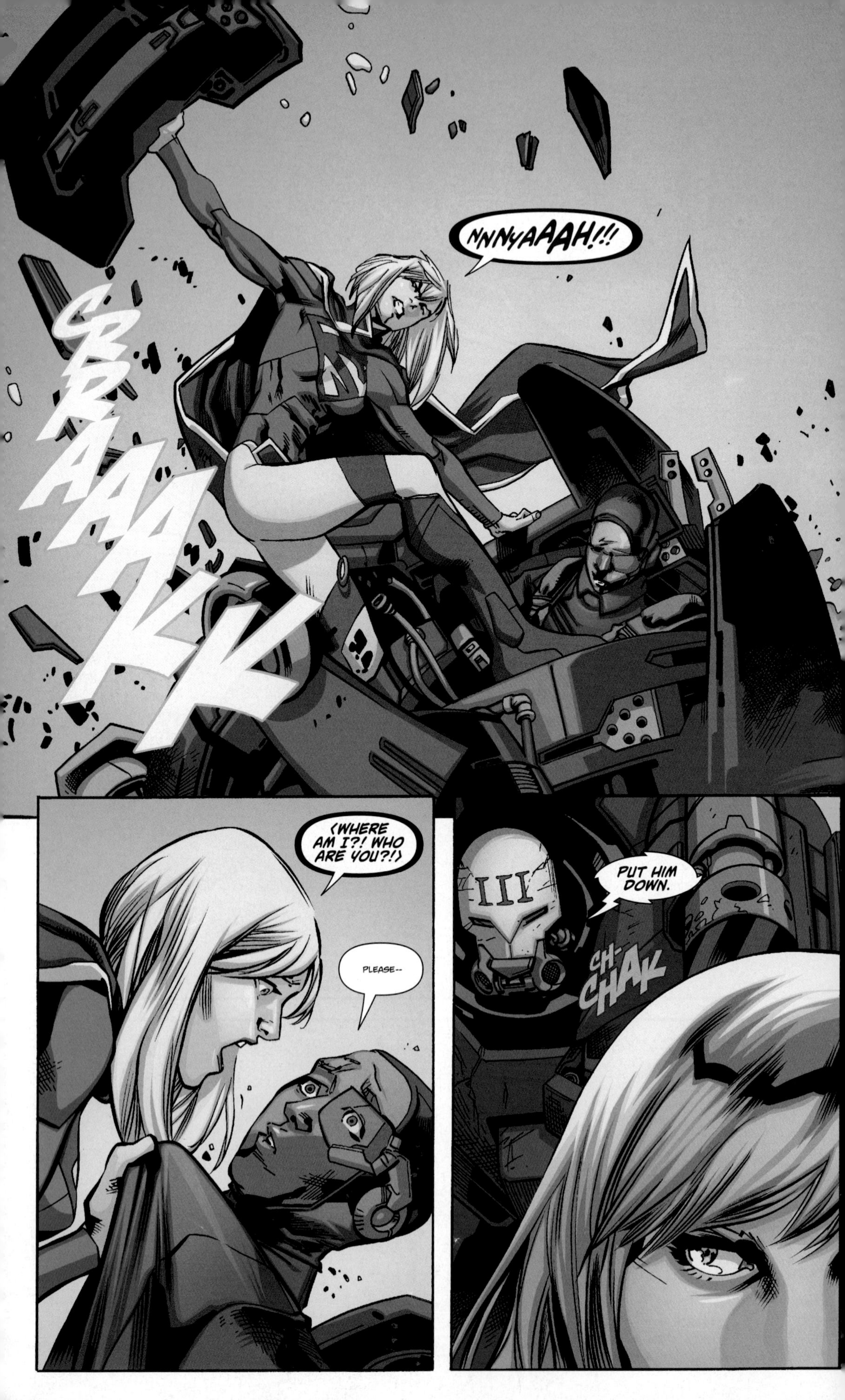
NNNyAAAH!!!
CRRAAAKKK
‹WHERE AM I?! WHO ARE YOU?!›
PLEASE--
PUT HIM DOWN.
CH-CHAK

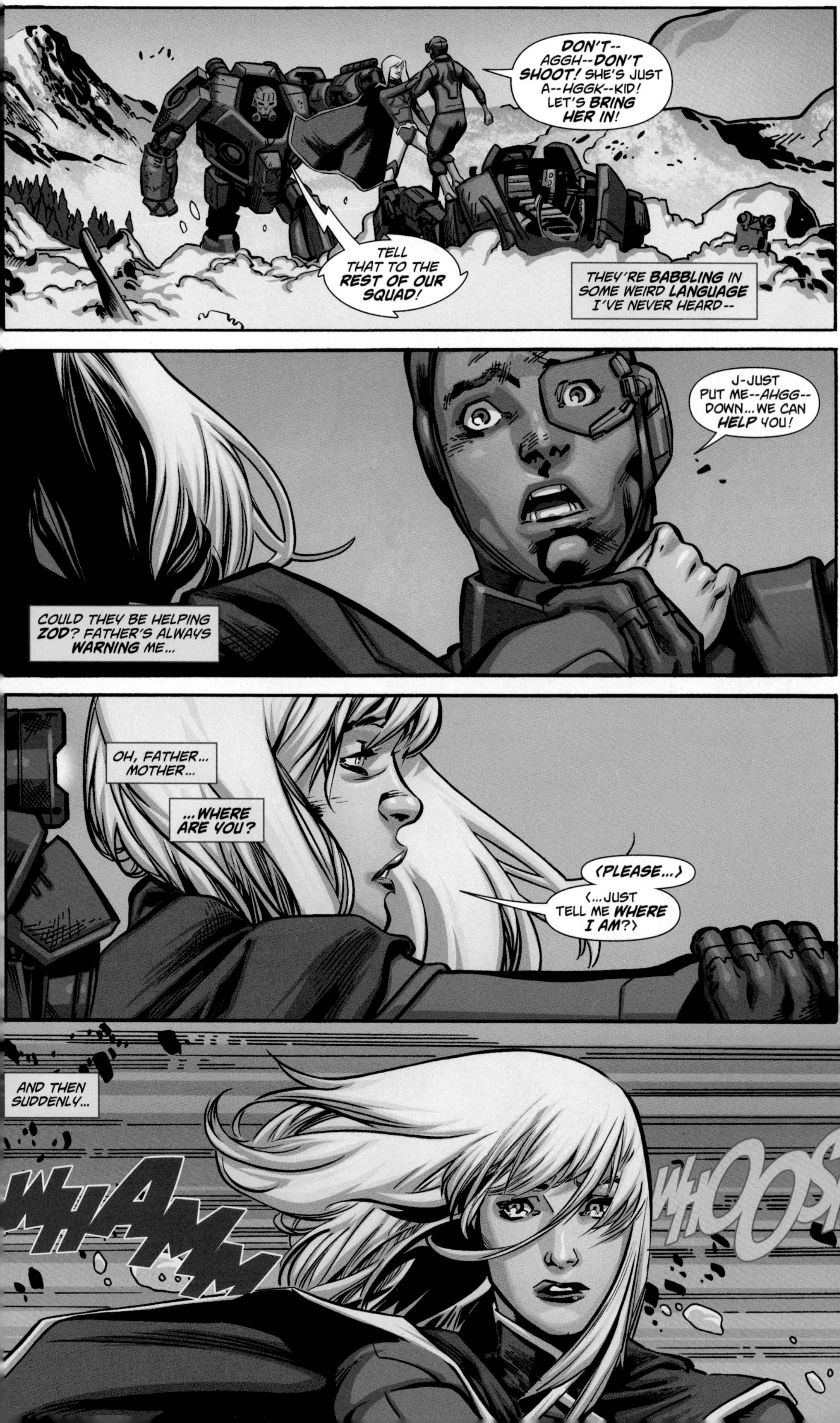
DON'T--AGGH--DON'T SHOOT! SHE'S JUST A--HGGK--KID! LET'S BRING HER IN!
TELL THAT TO THE REST OF OUR SQUAD!
THEY'RE BABBLING IN SOME WEIRD LANGUAGE I'VE NEVER HEARD--
J-JUST PUT ME--AHGG--DOWN...WE CAN HELP YOU!
COULD THEY BE HELPING ZOD? FATHER'S ALWAYS WARNING ME...
OH, FATHER... MOTHER...
...WHERE ARE YOU?
‹PLEASE...›
‹...JUST TELL ME WHERE I AM?›
AND THEN SUDDENLY...
WHAM
WHOOSH

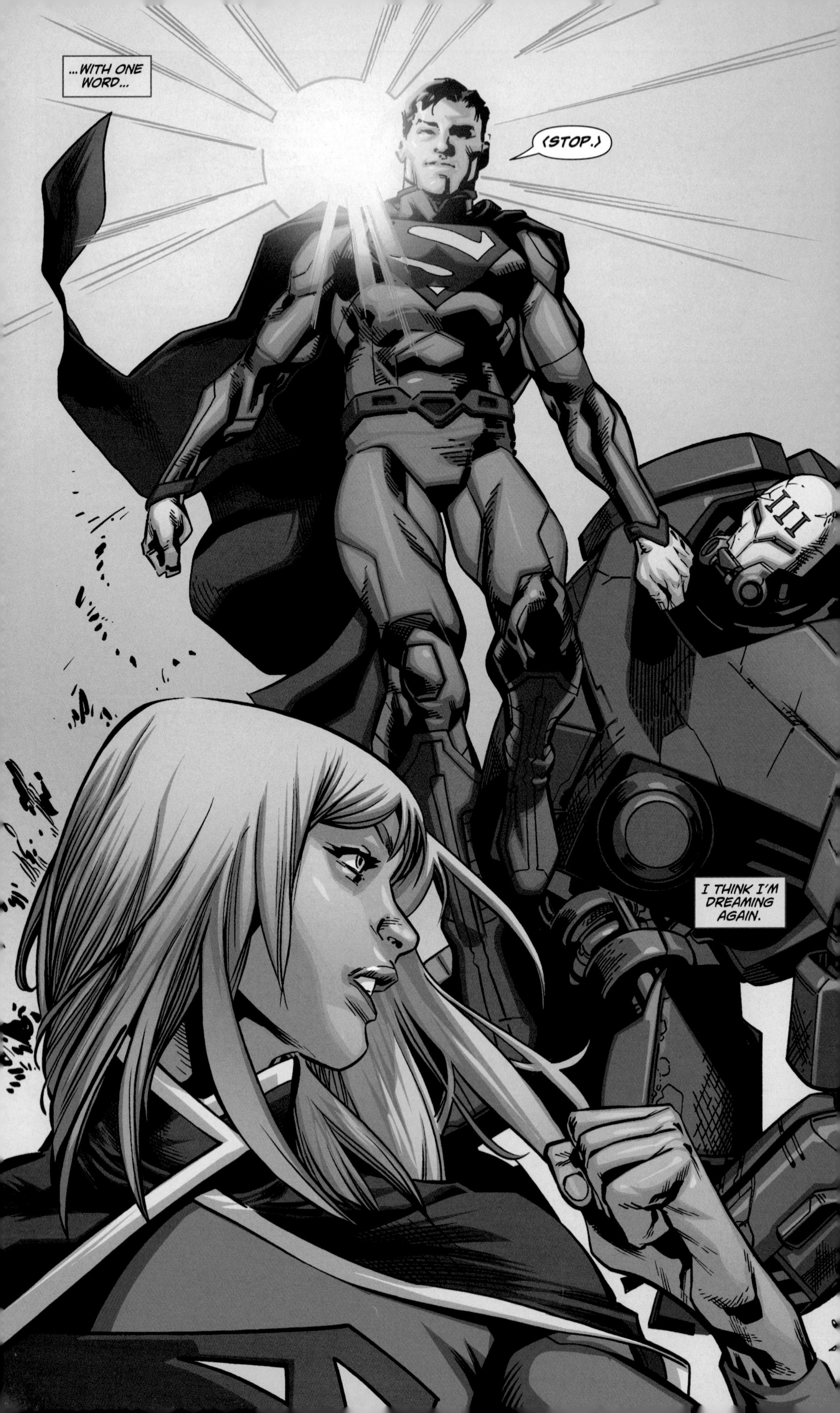
...WITH ONE WORD...
‹STOP.›
I THINK I'M DREAMING AGAIN.

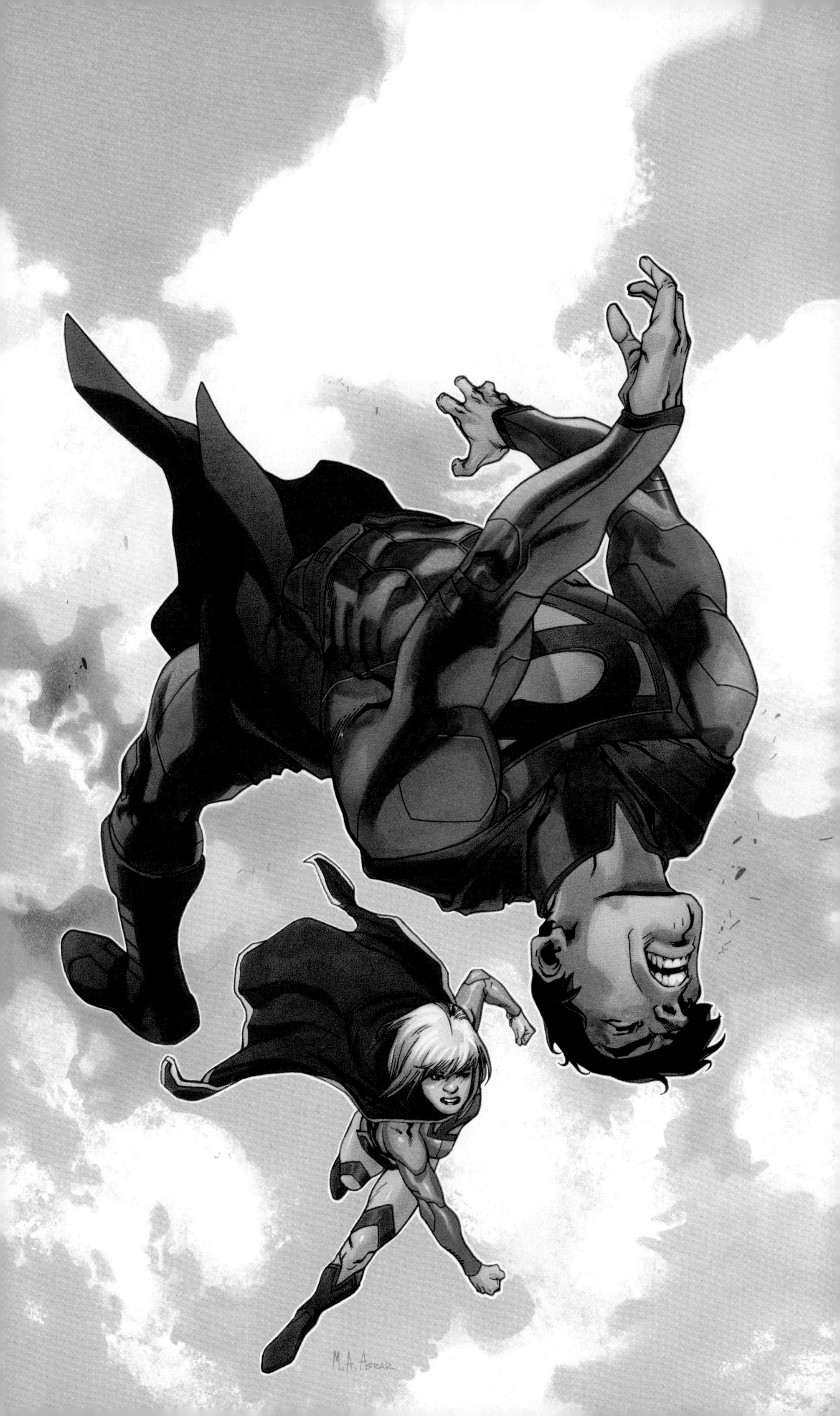
M.A. Asrar

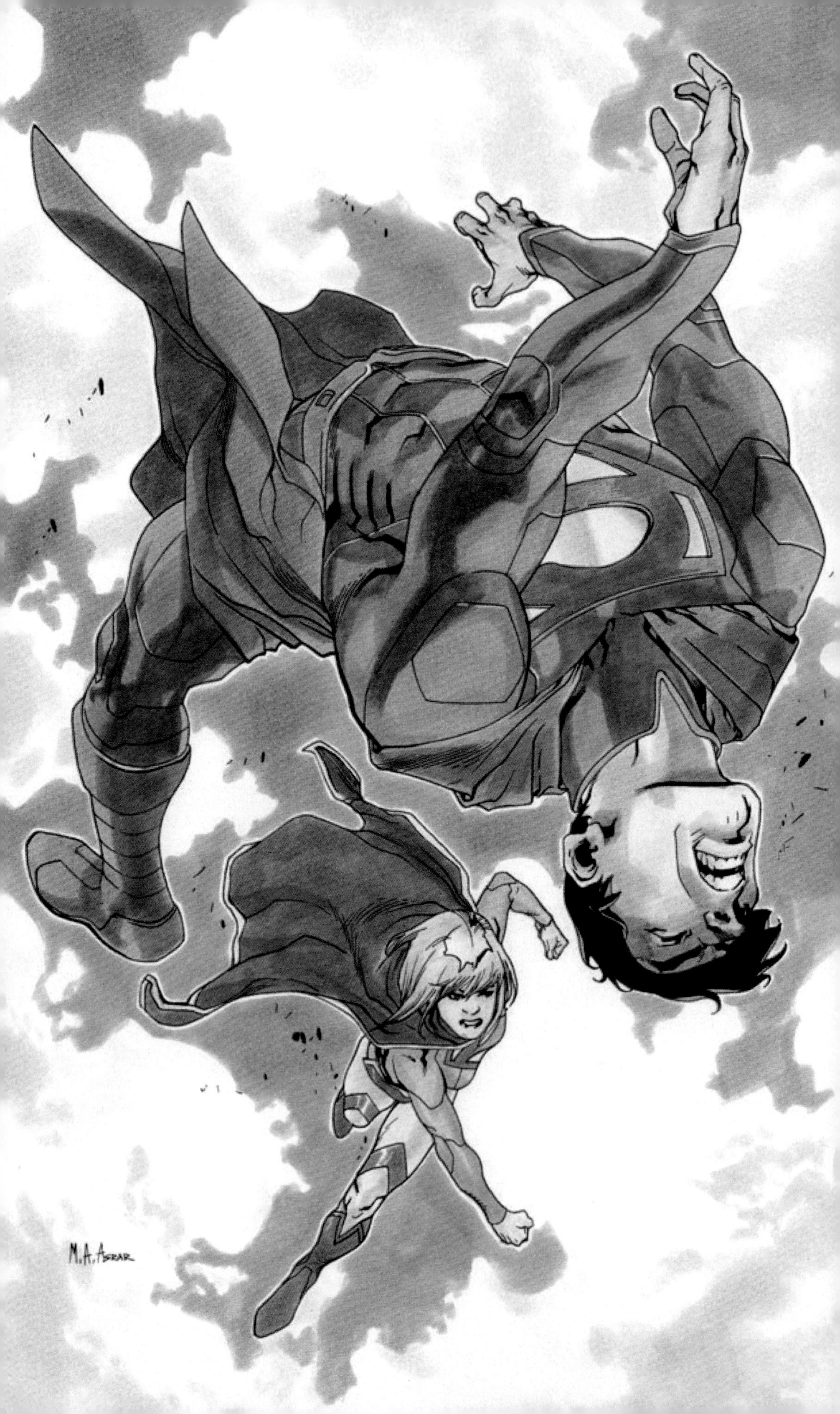
M.A. Asrar

THREE DAYS AGO.

I SHOULD BE STUDYING FOR THE FINAL TRIALS. INSTEAD I'M TAKING CARE OF MY BABY COUSIN, KAL-EL.

I TELL MYSELF I'M HERE OUT OF FAMILY DEVOTION, NOT PROCRASTINATION. NOT TRYING TO AVOID THE INEVITABLE.

EH... EH...

PASSING THE TRIALS MEANS I FINALLY GET TO WEAR THE FAMILY CREST, AND TAKE ON ALL THE RESPONSIBILITIES THAT COME WITH IT.

EH... WAAAAAA--

SHHH... SHH...

HARD TO BELIEVE IT NOW, BUT SOMEDAY KAL WILL DO THE SAME.

GOOD BOY...

WEH... EH...

I JUST DON'T WANT HIM TO GROW UP TOO FAST.

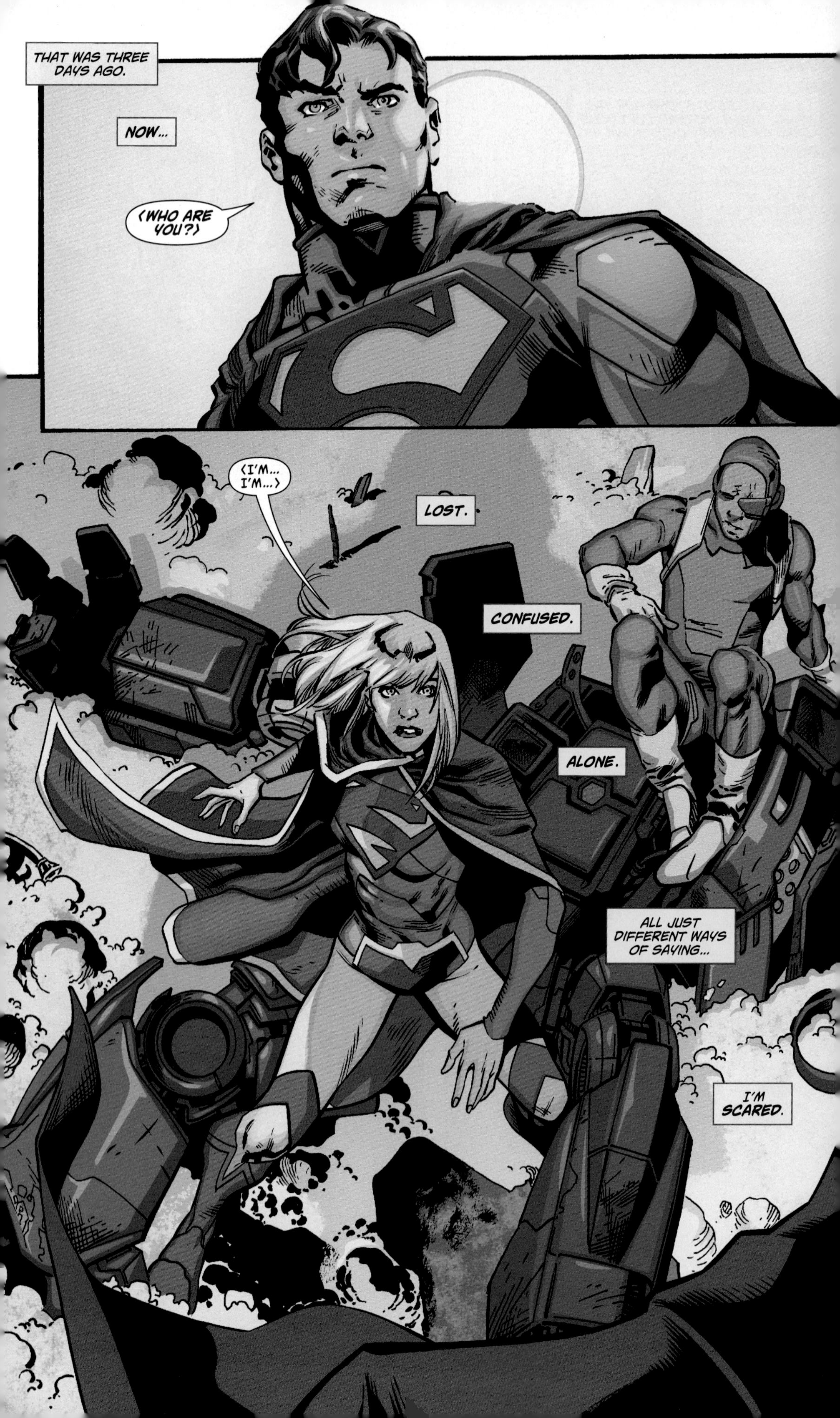
THAT WAS THREE DAYS AGO.
NOW...
‹WHO ARE YOU?›
‹I'M... I'M...›
LOST.
CONFUSED.
ALONE.
ALL JUST DIFFERENT WAYS OF SAYING...
I'M SCARED.

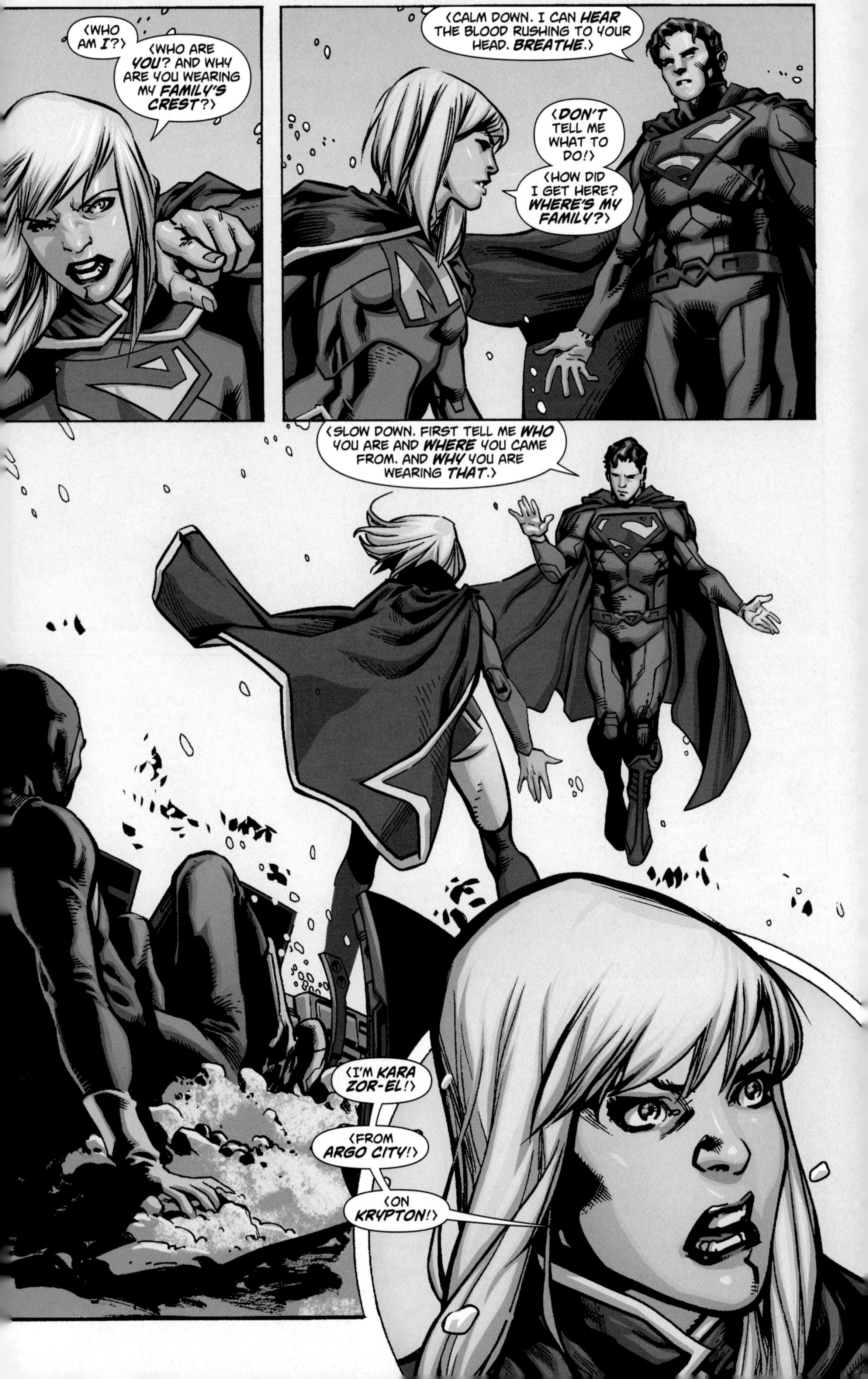
‹WHO AM I?›
‹WHO ARE YOU? AND WHY ARE YOU WEARING MY FAMILY'S CREST?›
‹CALM DOWN. I CAN HEAR THE BLOOD RUSHING TO YOUR HEAD. BREATHE.›
‹DON'T TELL ME WHAT TO DO!›
‹HOW DID I GET HERE? WHERE'S MY FAMILY?›
‹SLOW DOWN. FIRST TELL ME WHO YOU ARE AND WHERE YOU CAME FROM. AND WHY YOU ARE WEARING THAT.›
‹I'M KARA ZOR-EL!›
‹FROM ARGO CITY!›
‹ON KRYPTON!›

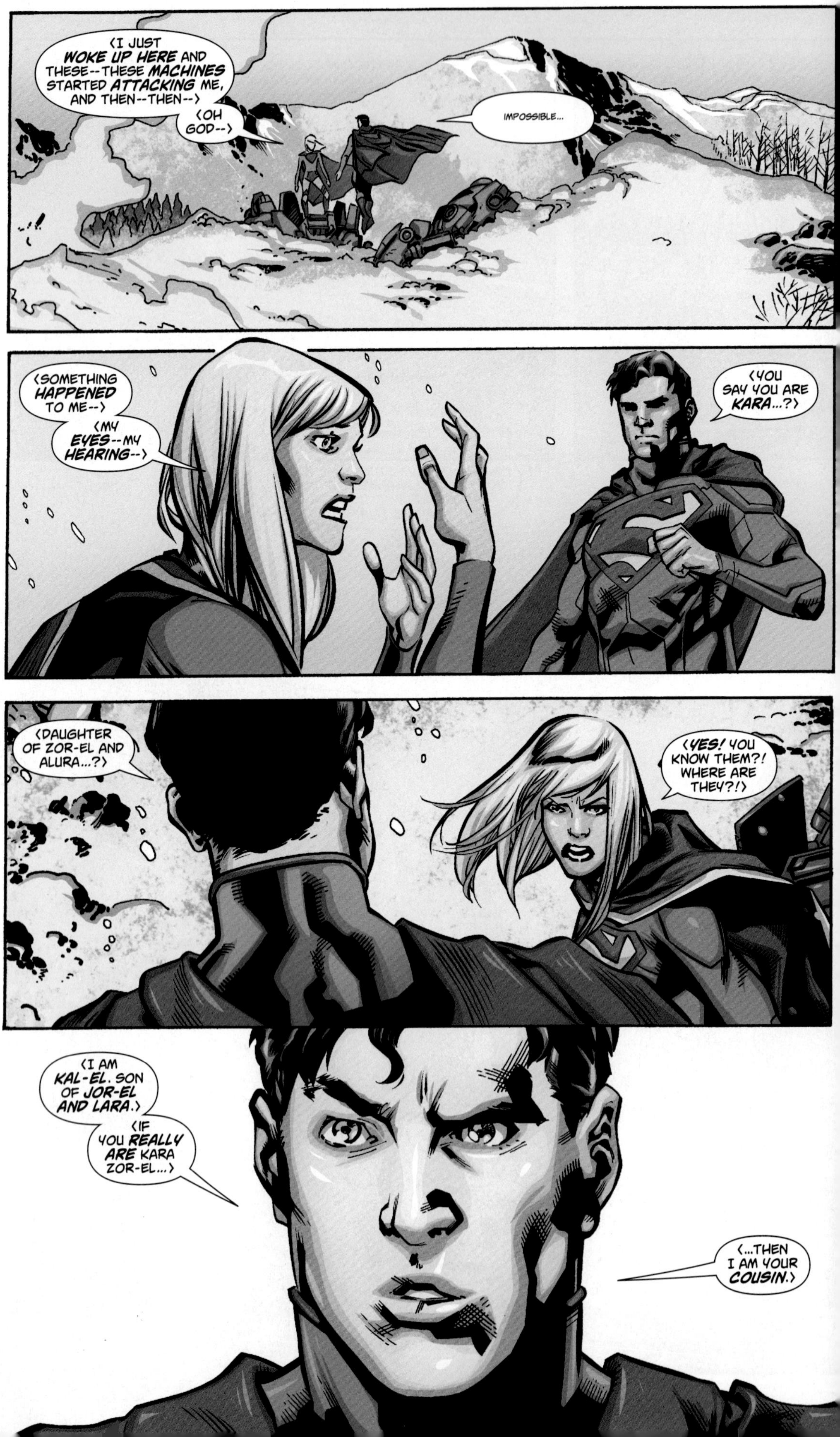

〈I JUST WOKE UP HERE AND THESE--THESE MACHINES STARTED ATTACKING ME, AND THEN--THEN--〉
〈OH GOD--〉
IMPOSSIBLE...
〈SOMETHING HAPPENED TO ME--〉
〈MY EYES--MY HEARING--〉
〈YOU SAY YOU ARE KARA...?〉
〈DAUGHTER OF ZOR-EL AND ALURA...?〉
〈YES! YOU KNOW THEM?! WHERE ARE THEY?!〉
〈I AM KAL-EL. SON OF JOR-EL AND LARA.〉
〈IF YOU REALLY ARE KARA ZOR-EL...〉
〈...THEN I AM YOUR COUSIN.〉

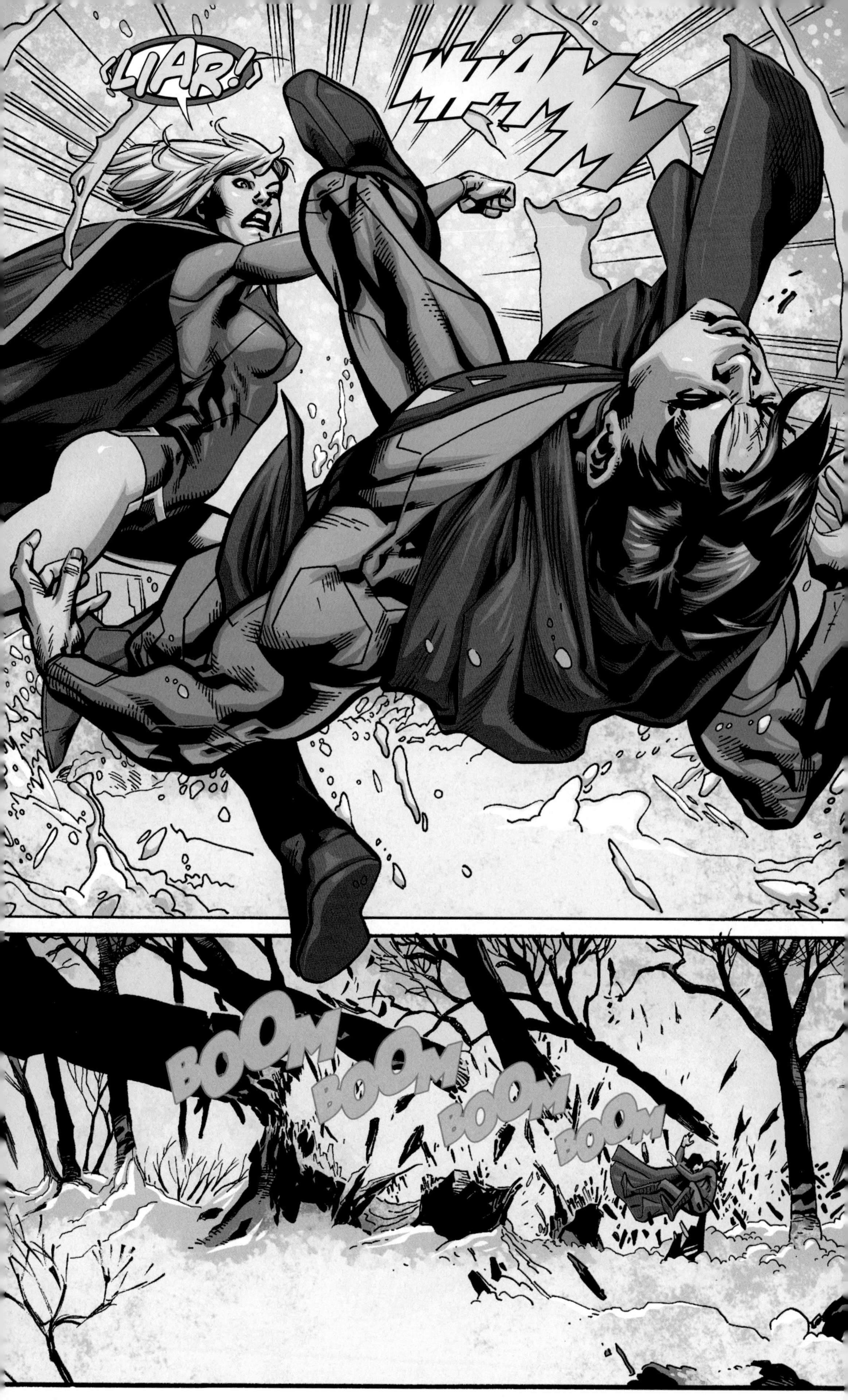
LIAR!
WHAM
BOOM
BOOM
BOOM
BOOM

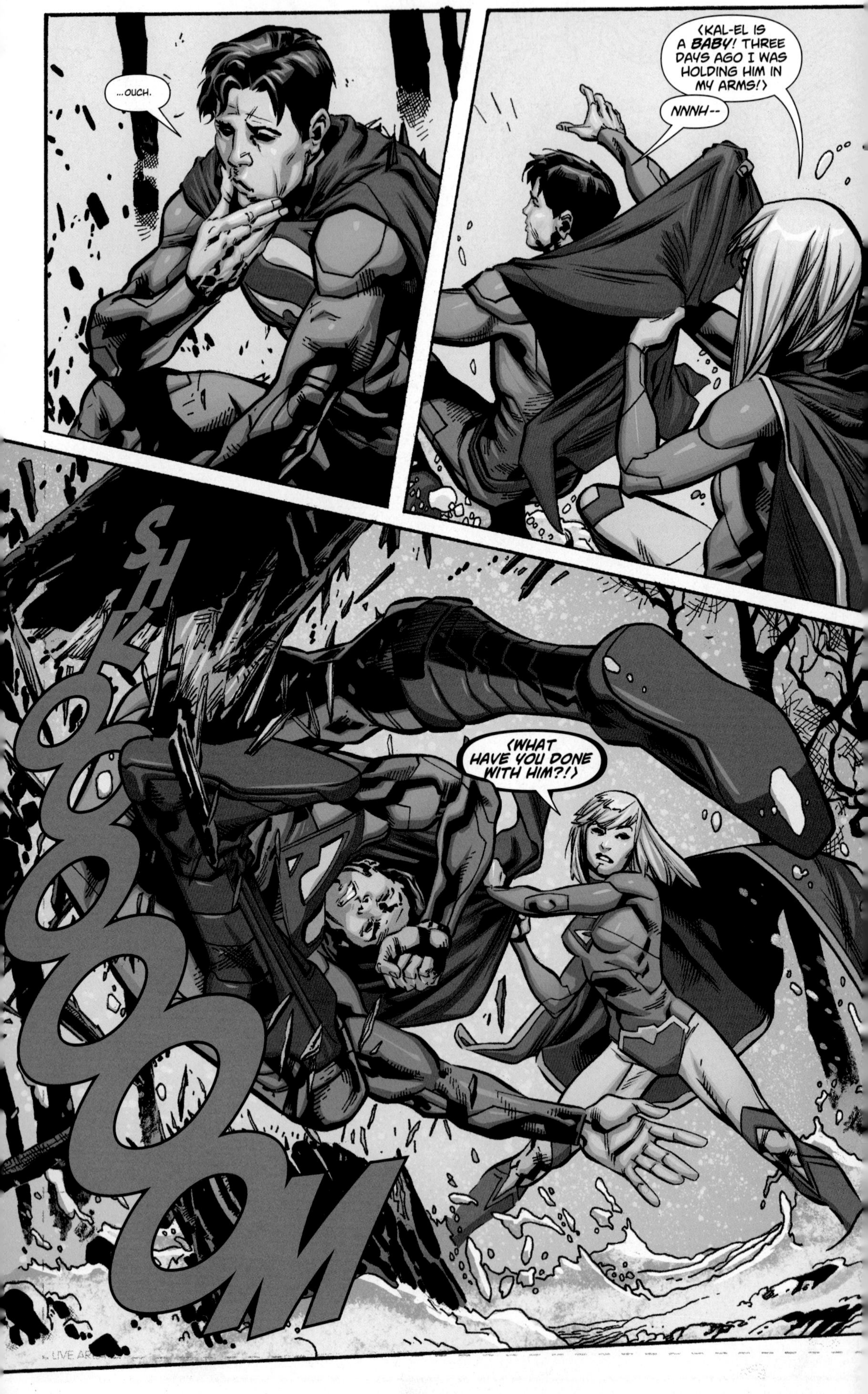
...OUCH.
<KAL-EL IS A BABY! THREE DAYS AGO I WAS HOLDING HIM IN MY ARMS!>
NNNH--
SHKOOOOOOM
<WHAT HAVE YOU DONE WITH HIM?!>

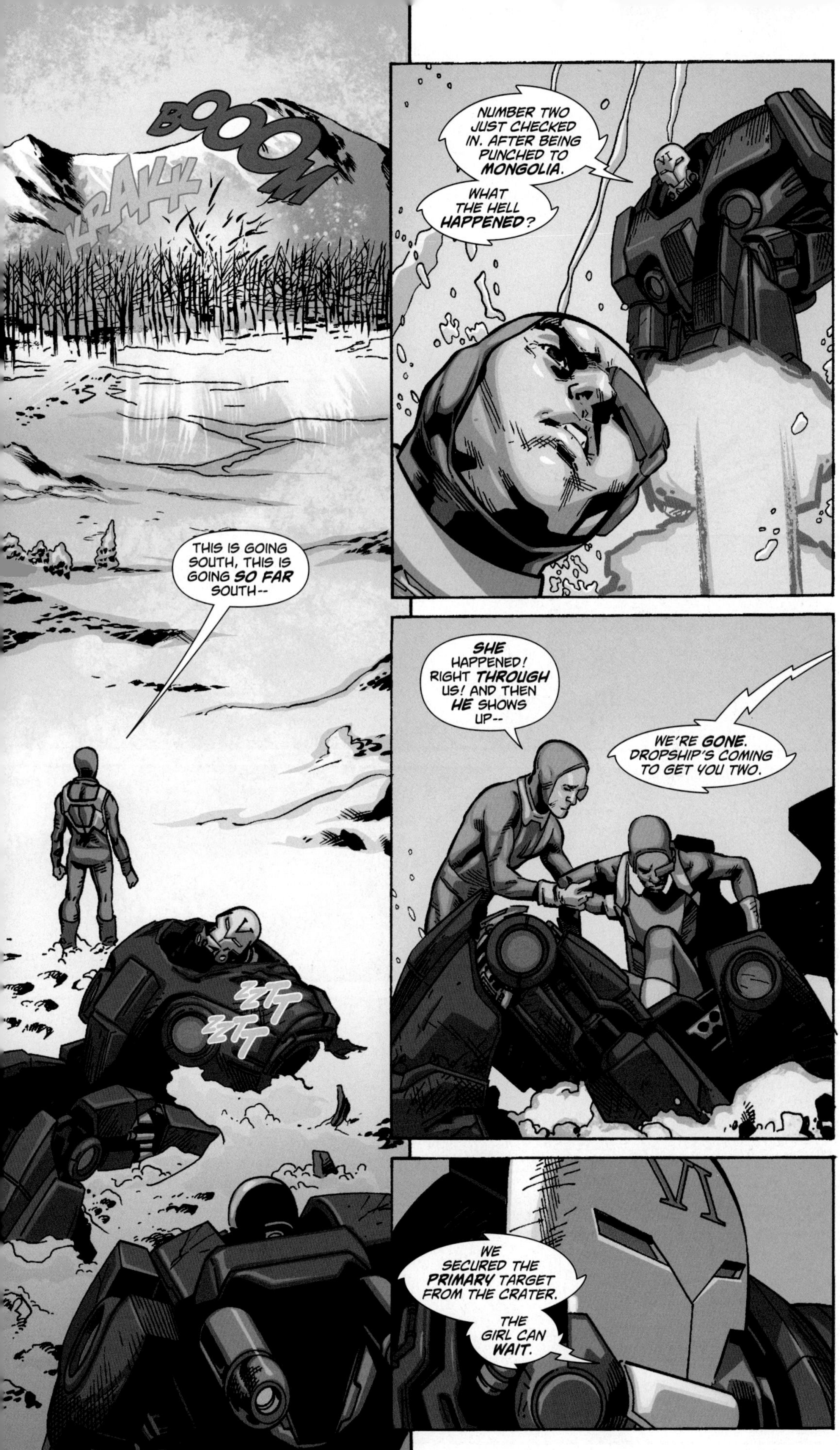
BOOOM
KRAKK
THIS IS GOING SOUTH, THIS IS GOING SO FAR SOUTH--
ZZTT
ZZTT
NUMBER TWO JUST CHECKED IN. AFTER BEING PUNCHED TO MONGOLIA.
WHAT THE HELL HAPPENED?
SHE HAPPENED! RIGHT THROUGH US! AND THEN HE SHOWS UP--
WE'RE GONE. DROPSHIP'S COMING TO GET YOU TWO.
WE SECURED THE PRIMARY TARGET FROM THE CRATER.
THE GIRL CAN WAIT.

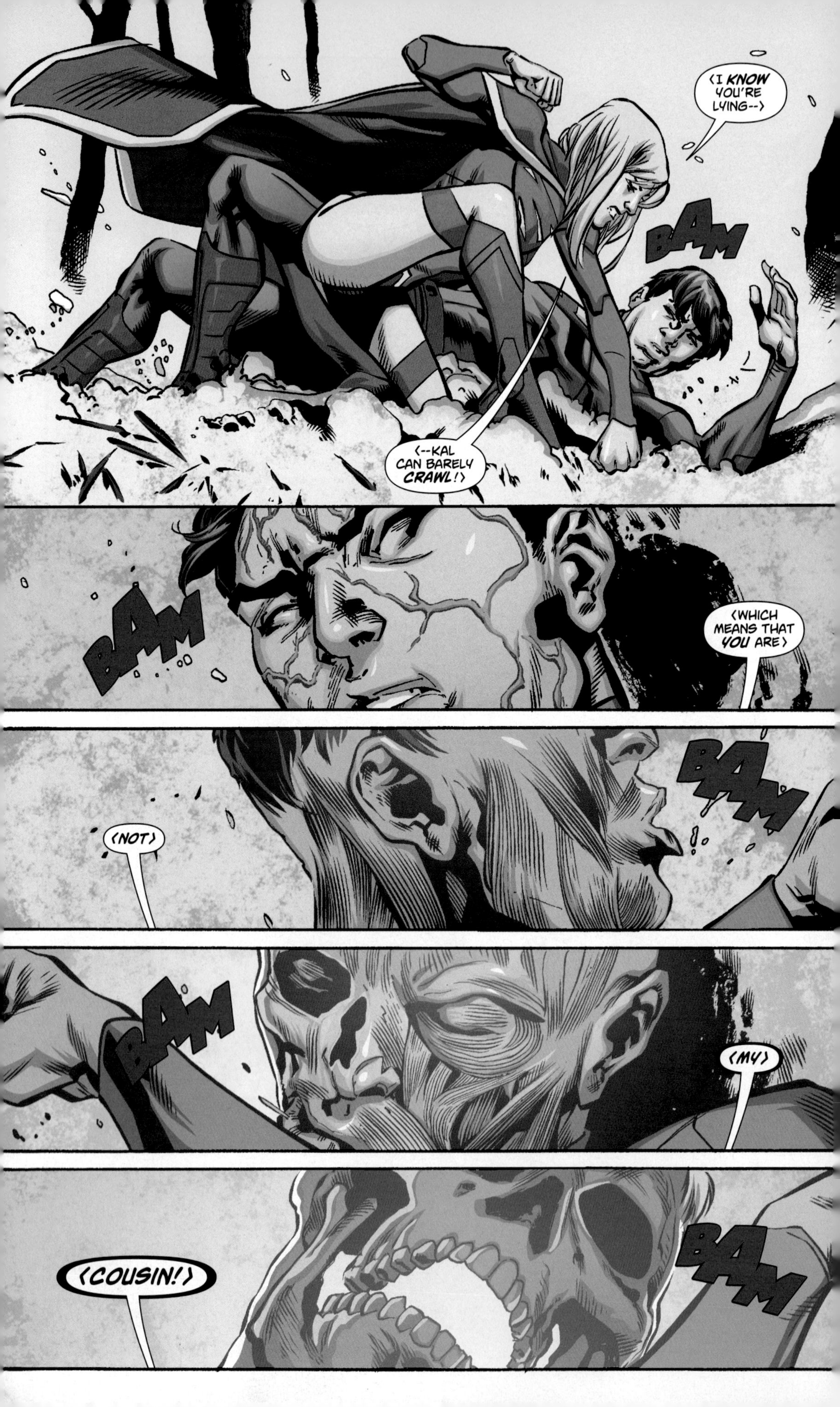
‹I KNOW YOU'RE LYING--›
BAM
‹--KAL CAN BARELY CRAWL!›
BAM
‹WHICH MEANS THAT YOU ARE›
BAM
‹NOT›
BAM
‹MY›
BAM
‹COUSIN!›

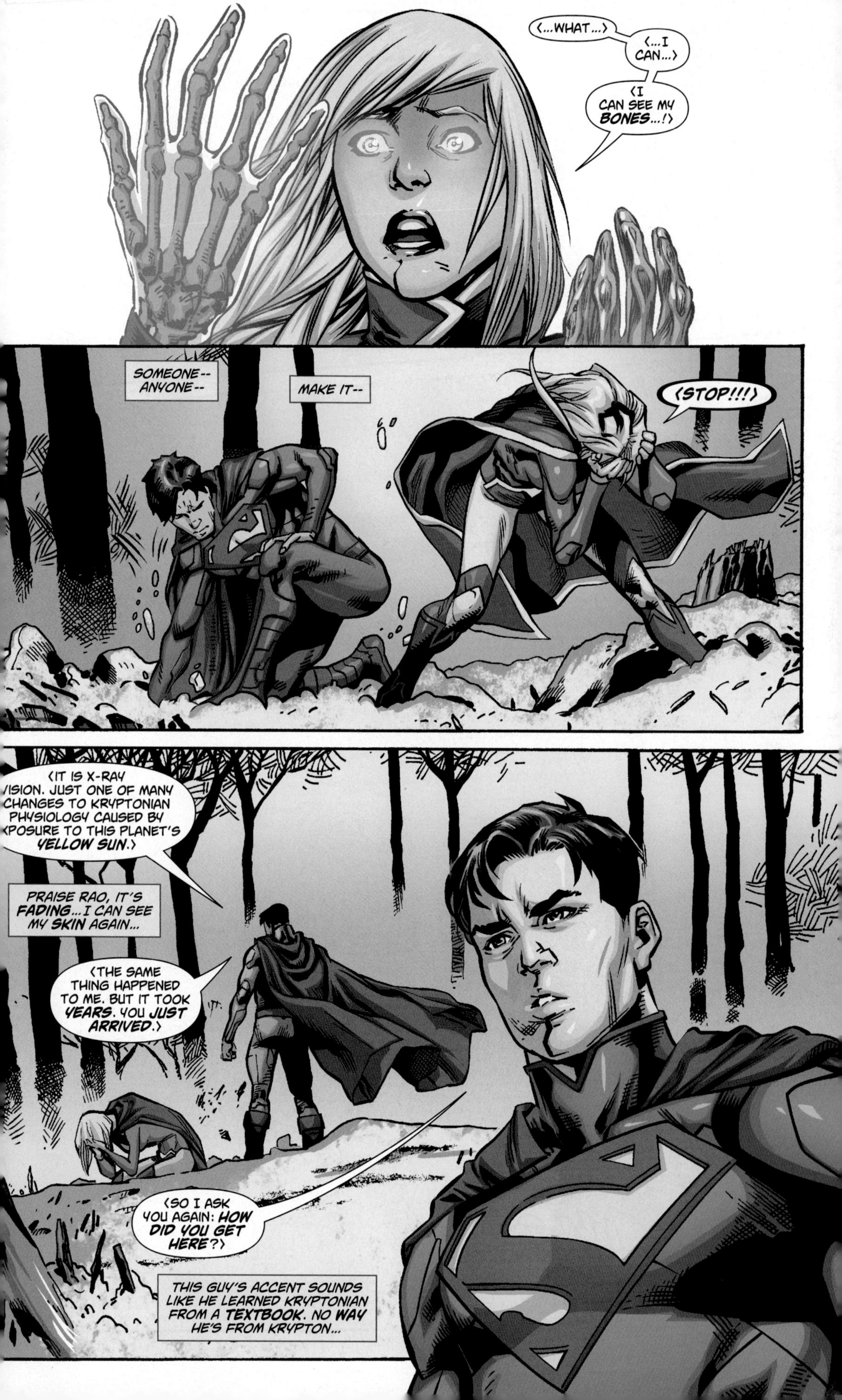
‹...WHAT...›
‹...I CAN...›
‹I CAN SEE MY BONES...!›
SOMEONE-- ANYONE--
MAKE IT--
‹STOP!!!›
‹IT IS X-RAY VISION. JUST ONE OF MANY CHANGES TO KRYPTONIAN PHYSIOLOGY CAUSED BY EXPOSURE TO THIS PLANET'S YELLOW SUN.›
PRAISE RAO, IT'S FADING...I CAN SEE MY SKIN AGAIN...
‹THE SAME THING HAPPENED TO ME. BUT IT TOOK YEARS. YOU JUST ARRIVED.›
‹SO I ASK YOU AGAIN: HOW DID YOU GET HERE?›
THIS GUY'S ACCENT SOUNDS LIKE HE LEARNED KRYPTONIAN FROM A TEXTBOOK. NO WAY HE'S FROM KRYPTON...

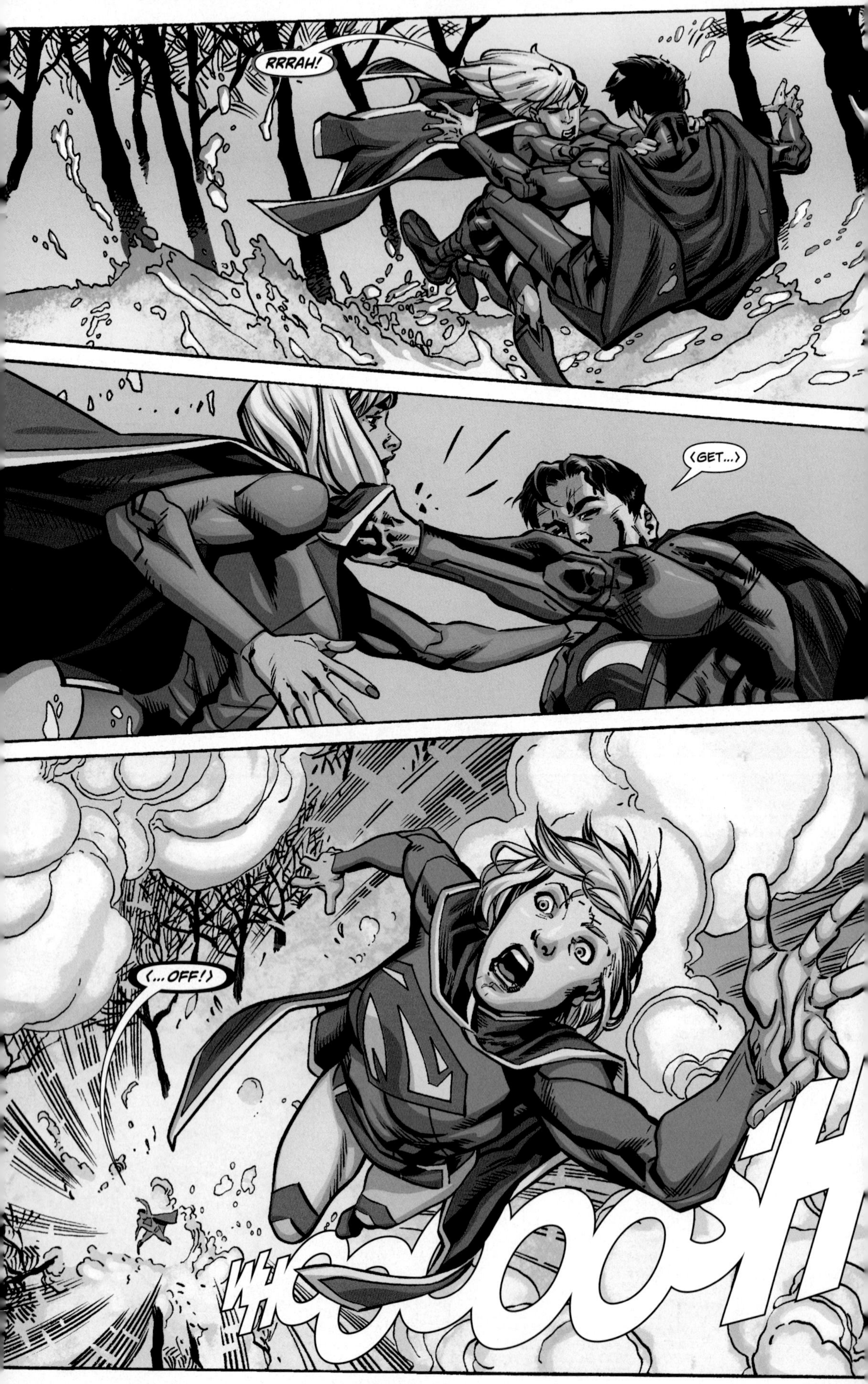
RRRAH!
‹GET...›
‹...OFF!›
WHOOOOOOH

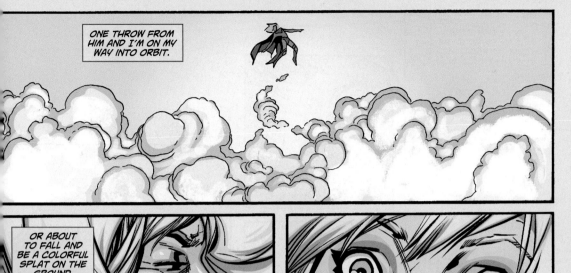

ONE THROW FROM HIM AND I'M ON MY WAY INTO ORBIT.

OR ABOUT TO FALL AND BE A COLORFUL SPLAT ON THE GROUND.

AND THEN SUDDENLY--

--IMPOSSIBLY--

--I'M SOMEWHERE IN BETWEEN.

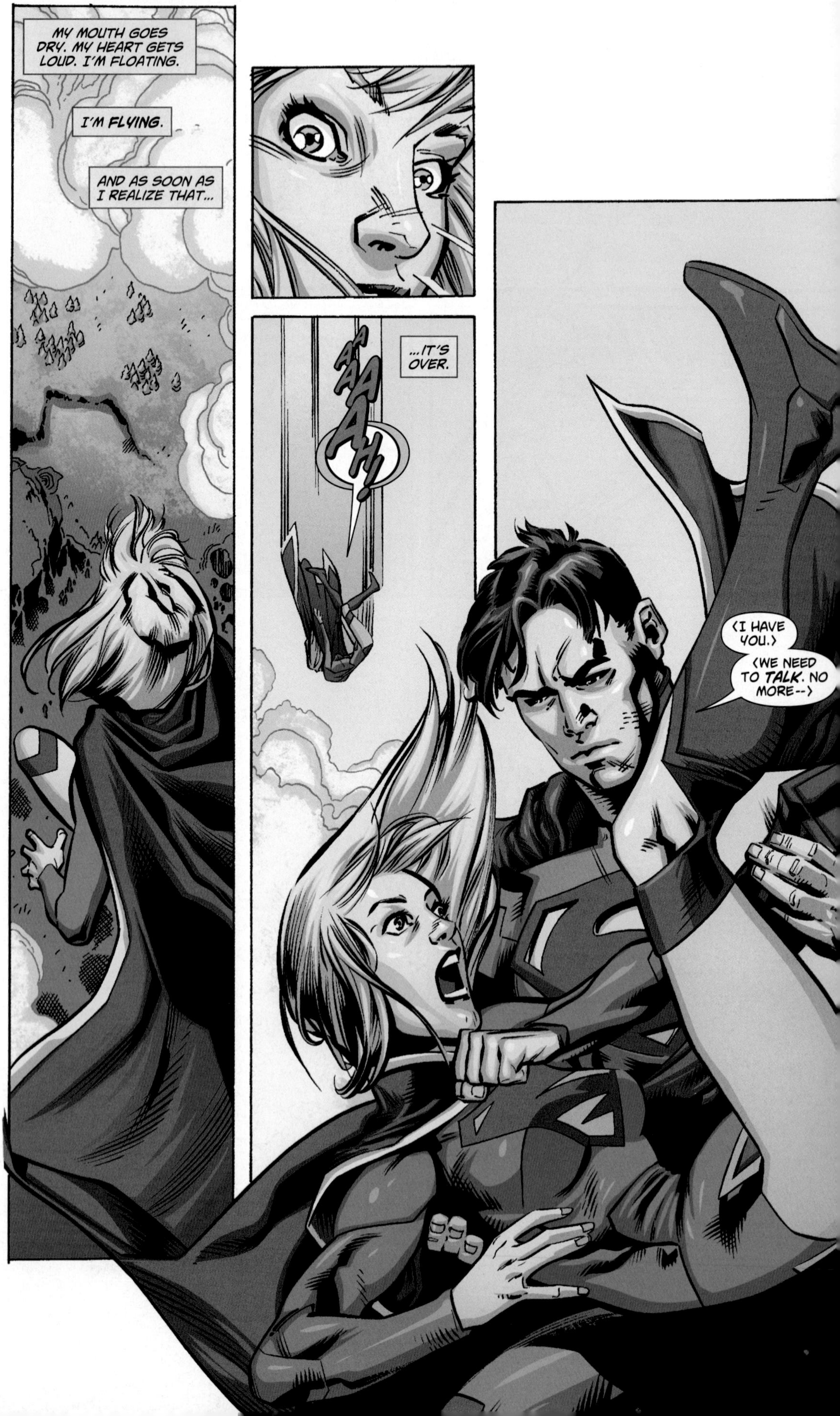
MY MOUTH GOES DRY. MY HEART GETS LOUD. I'M FLOATING.
I'M FLYING.
AND AS SOON AS I REALIZE THAT...
AAAAH!
...IT'S OVER.
<I HAVE YOU.>
<WE NEED TO TALK. NO MORE-->

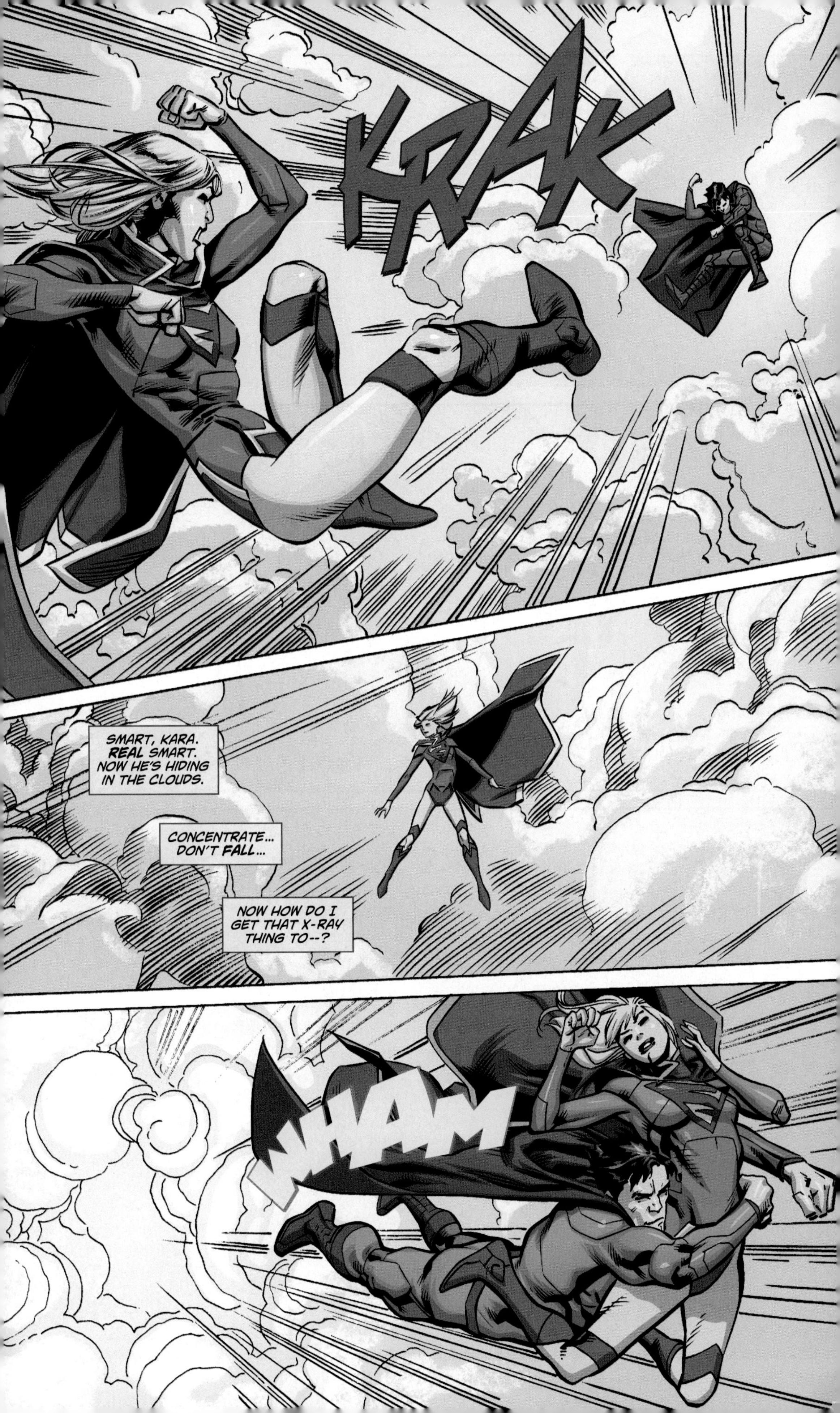
KRAK
SMART, KARA. **REAL** SMART. NOW HE'S HIDING IN THE CLOUDS.
CONCENTRATE... DON'T **FALL**...
NOW HOW DO I GET THAT X-RAY THING TO--?
WHAM

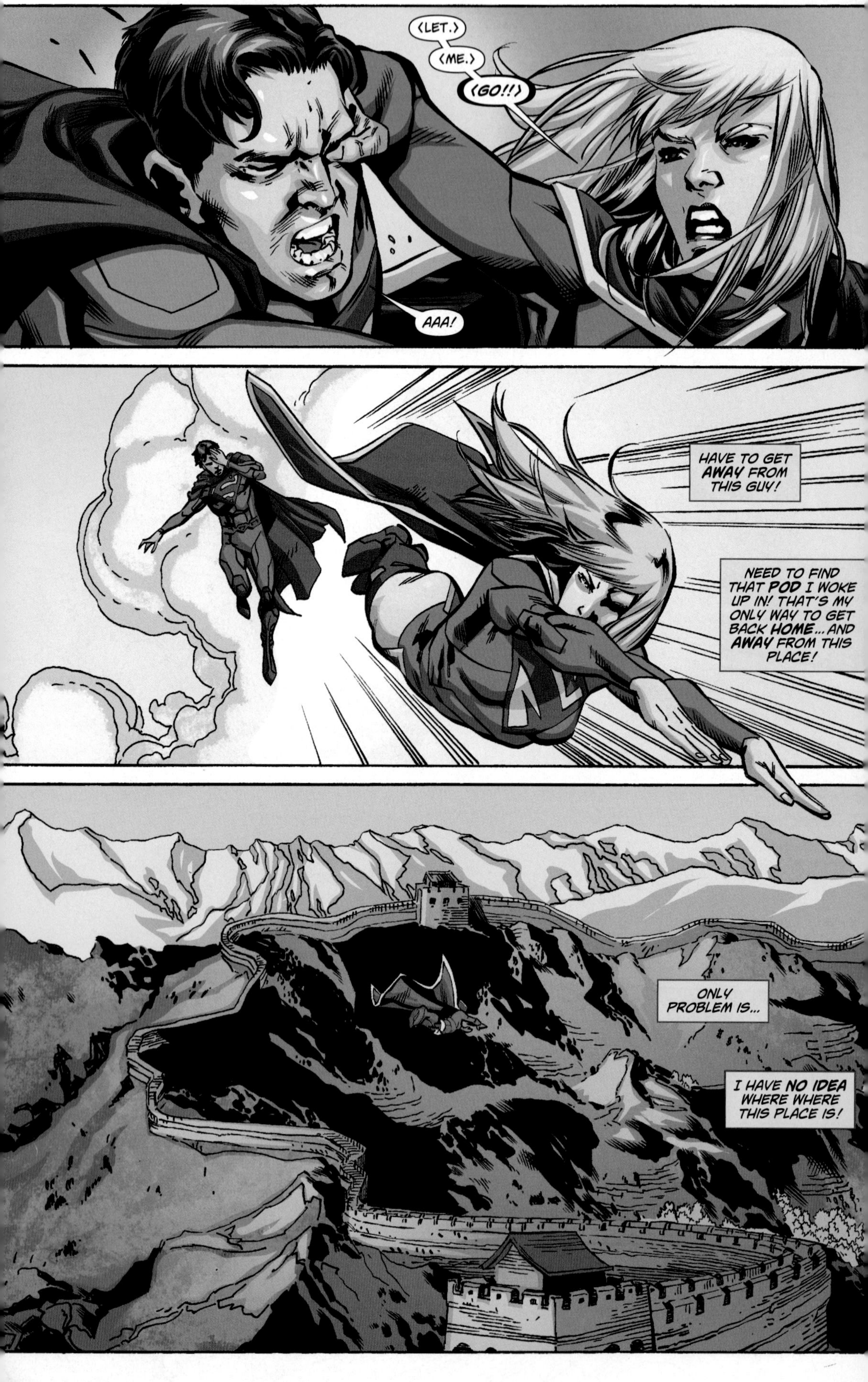
<LET.>
<ME.>
<GO!!>
AAA!
HAVE TO GET **AWAY** FROM THIS GUY!
NEED TO FIND THAT **POD** I WOKE UP IN! THAT'S MY ONLY WAY TO GET BACK **HOME**... AND **AWAY** FROM THIS PLACE!
ONLY PROBLEM IS...
I HAVE **NO IDEA** WHERE WHERE THIS PLACE IS!

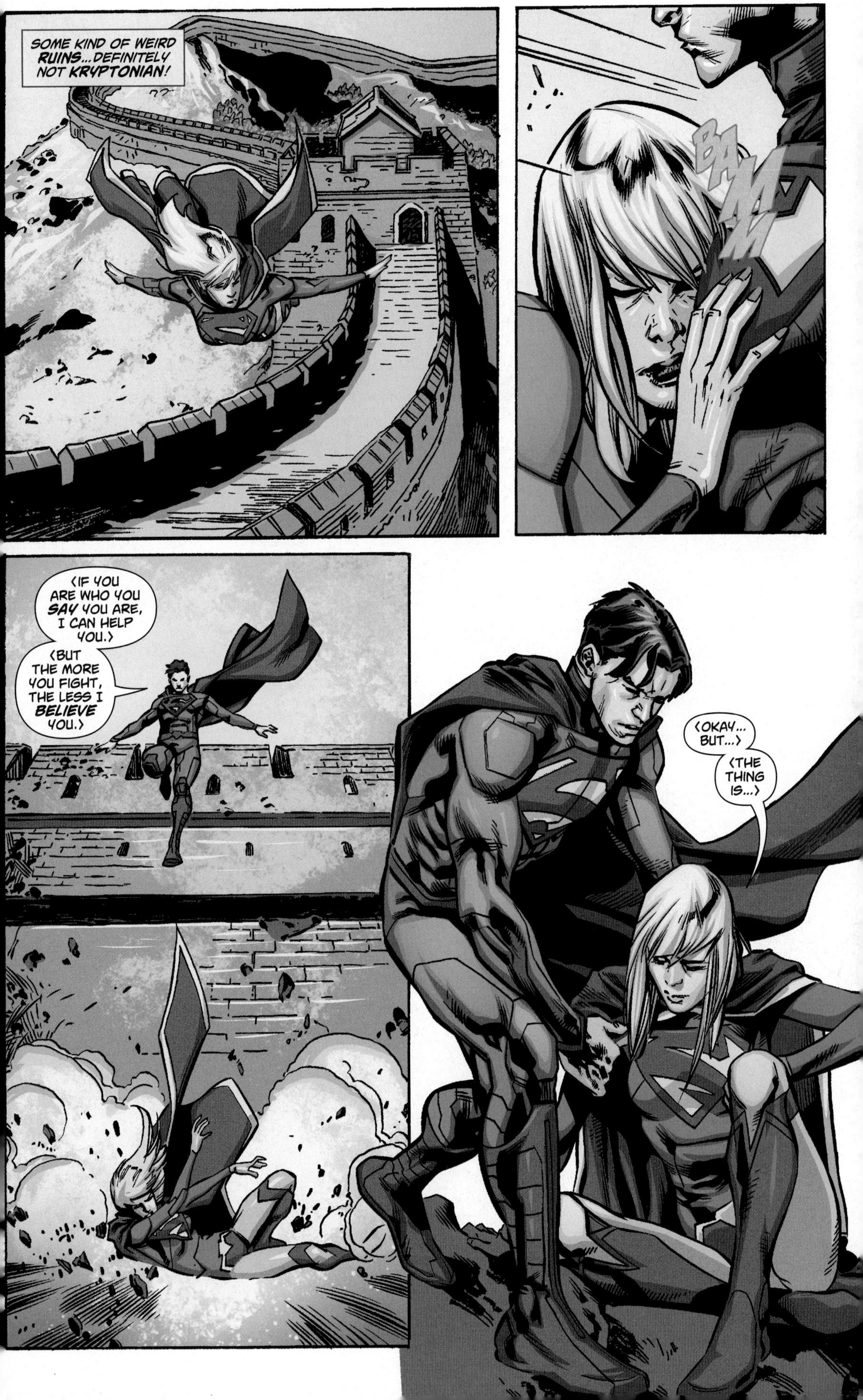
SOME KIND OF WEIRD RUINS... DEFINITELY NOT KRYPTONIAN!
BAM
‹IF YOU ARE WHO YOU SAY YOU ARE, I CAN HELP YOU.›
‹BUT THE MORE YOU FIGHT, THE LESS I BELIEVE YOU.›
‹OKAY... BUT...›
‹THE THING IS...›

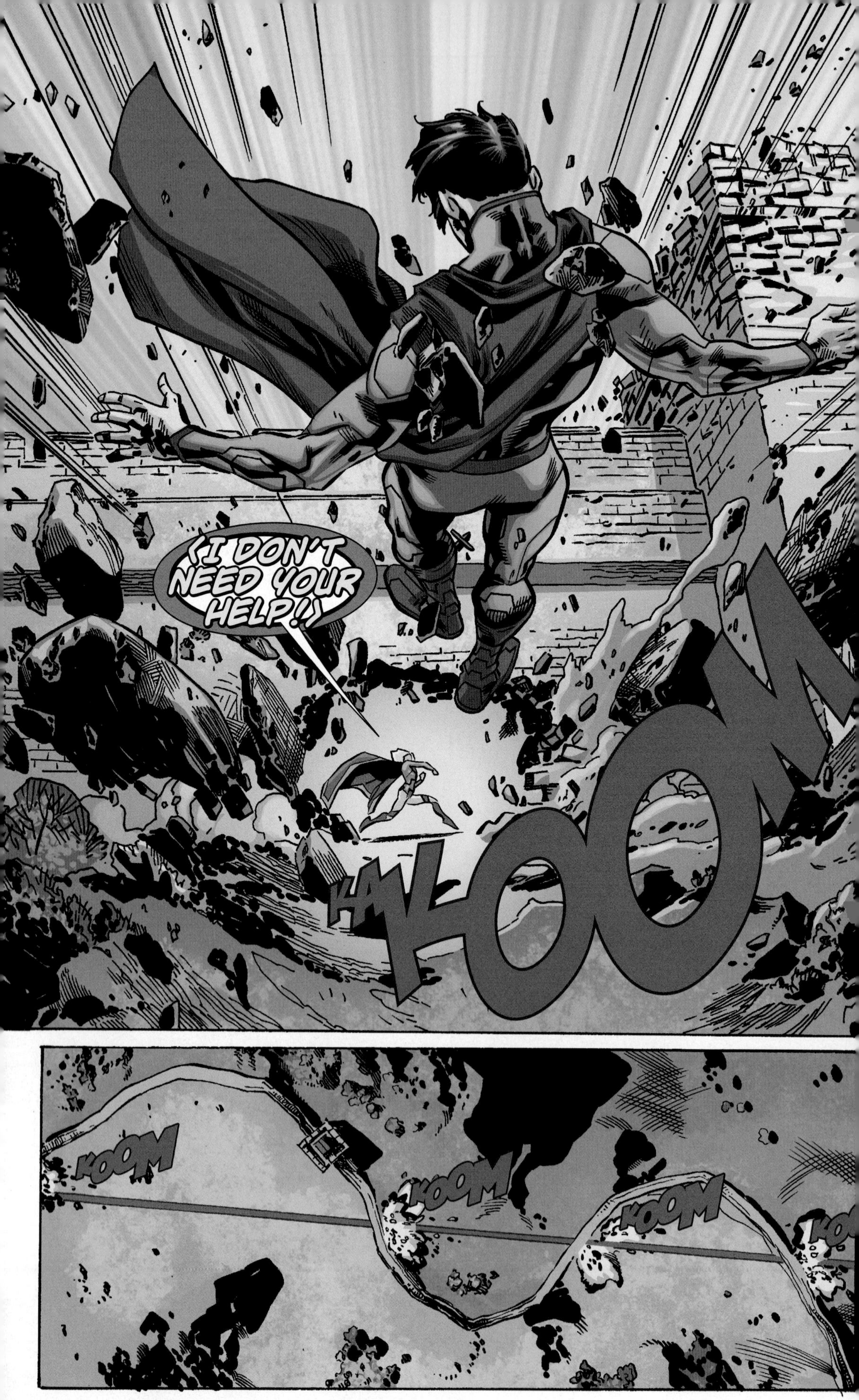
⟨I DON'T NEED YOUR HELP!⟩
KA
KOOM
KOOM
KOOM
KOOM

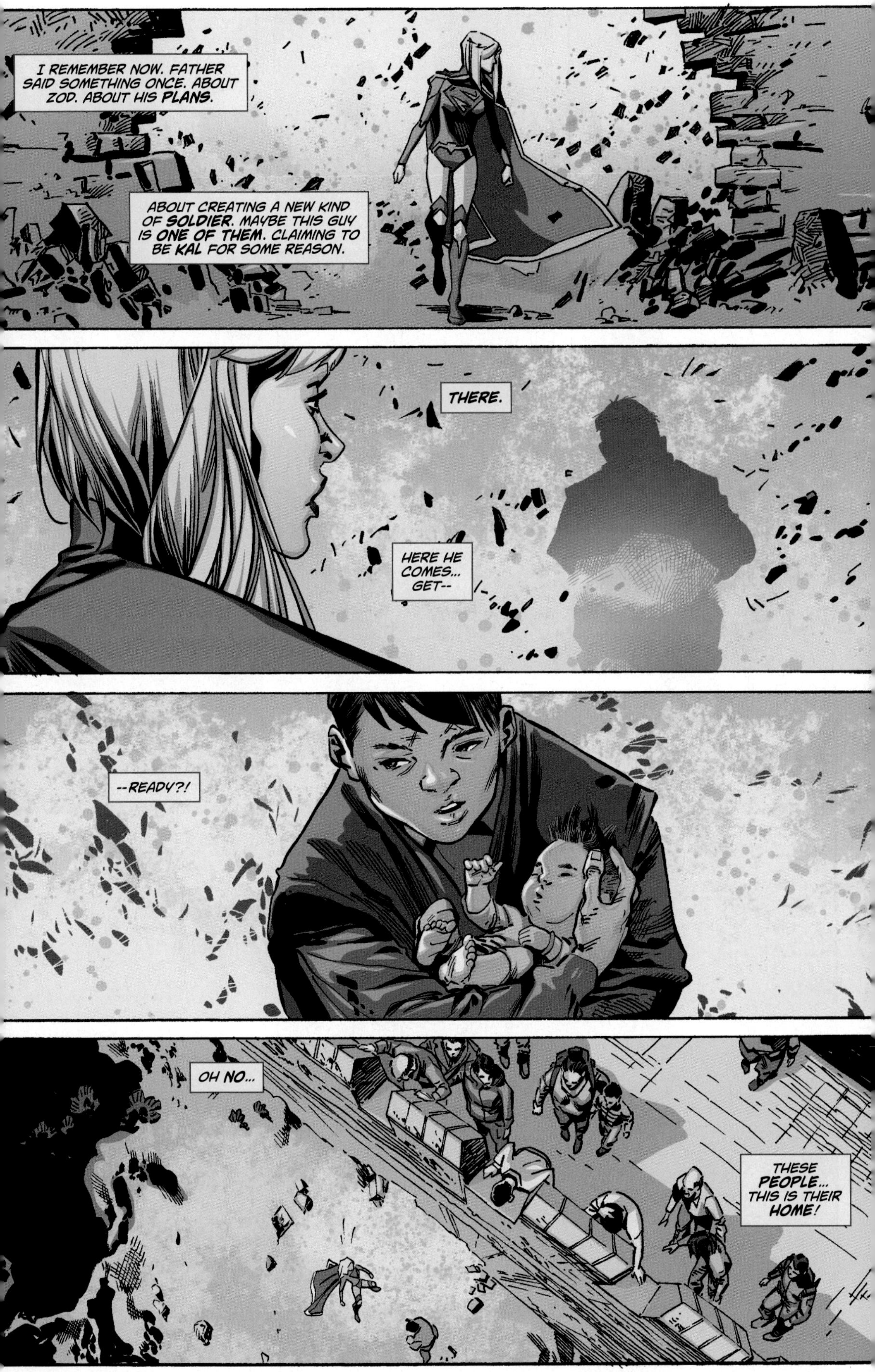
I REMEMBER NOW. FATHER SAID SOMETHING ONCE. ABOUT ZOD. ABOUT HIS PLANS.
ABOUT CREATING A NEW KIND OF SOLDIER. MAYBE THIS GUY IS ONE OF THEM. CLAIMING TO BE KAL FOR SOME REASON.
THERE.
HERE HE COMES... GET--
--READY?!
OH NO...
THESE PEOPLE... THIS IS THEIR HOME!

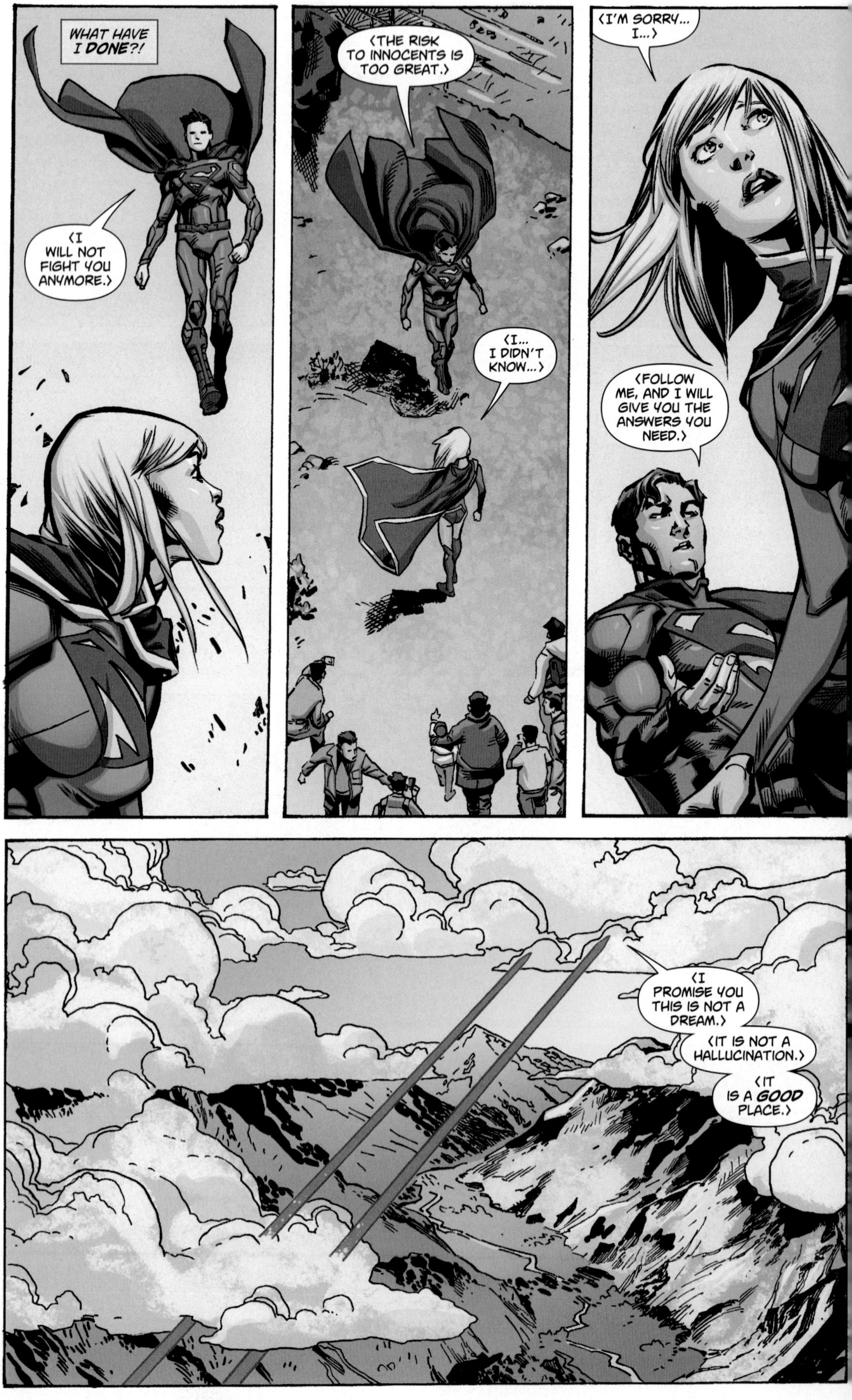
WHAT HAVE I DONE?!
‹I WILL NOT FIGHT YOU ANYMORE.›
‹THE RISK TO INNOCENTS IS TOO GREAT.›
‹I... I DIDN'T KNOW...›
‹I'M SORRY... I...›
‹FOLLOW ME, AND I WILL GIVE YOU THE ANSWERS YOU NEED.›
‹I PROMISE YOU THIS IS NOT A DREAM.›
‹IT IS NOT A HALLUCINATION.›
‹IT IS A GOOD PLACE.›

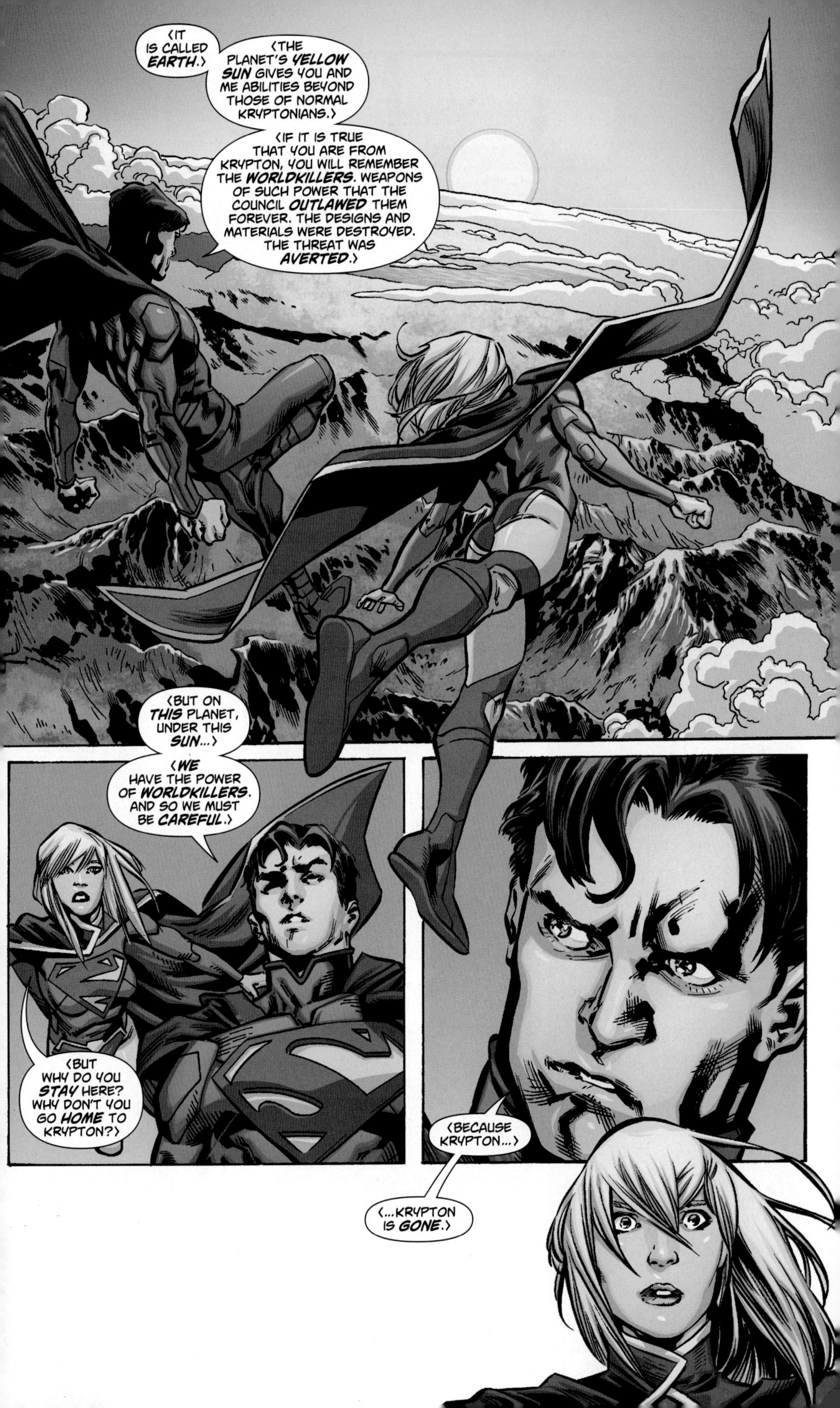

‹IT IS CALLED EARTH.›
‹THE PLANET'S YELLOW SUN GIVES YOU AND ME ABILITIES BEYOND THOSE OF NORMAL KRYPTONIANS.›
‹IF IT IS TRUE THAT YOU ARE FROM KRYPTON, YOU WILL REMEMBER THE WORLDKILLERS. WEAPONS OF SUCH POWER THAT THE COUNCIL OUTLAWED THEM FOREVER. THE DESIGNS AND MATERIALS WERE DESTROYED. THE THREAT WAS AVERTED.›
‹BUT ON THIS PLANET, UNDER THIS SUN...›
‹WE HAVE THE POWER OF WORLDKILLERS. AND SO WE MUST BE CAREFUL.›
‹BUT WHY DO YOU STAY HERE? WHY DON'T YOU GO HOME TO KRYPTON?›
‹BECAUSE KRYPTON...›
‹...KRYPTON IS GONE.›

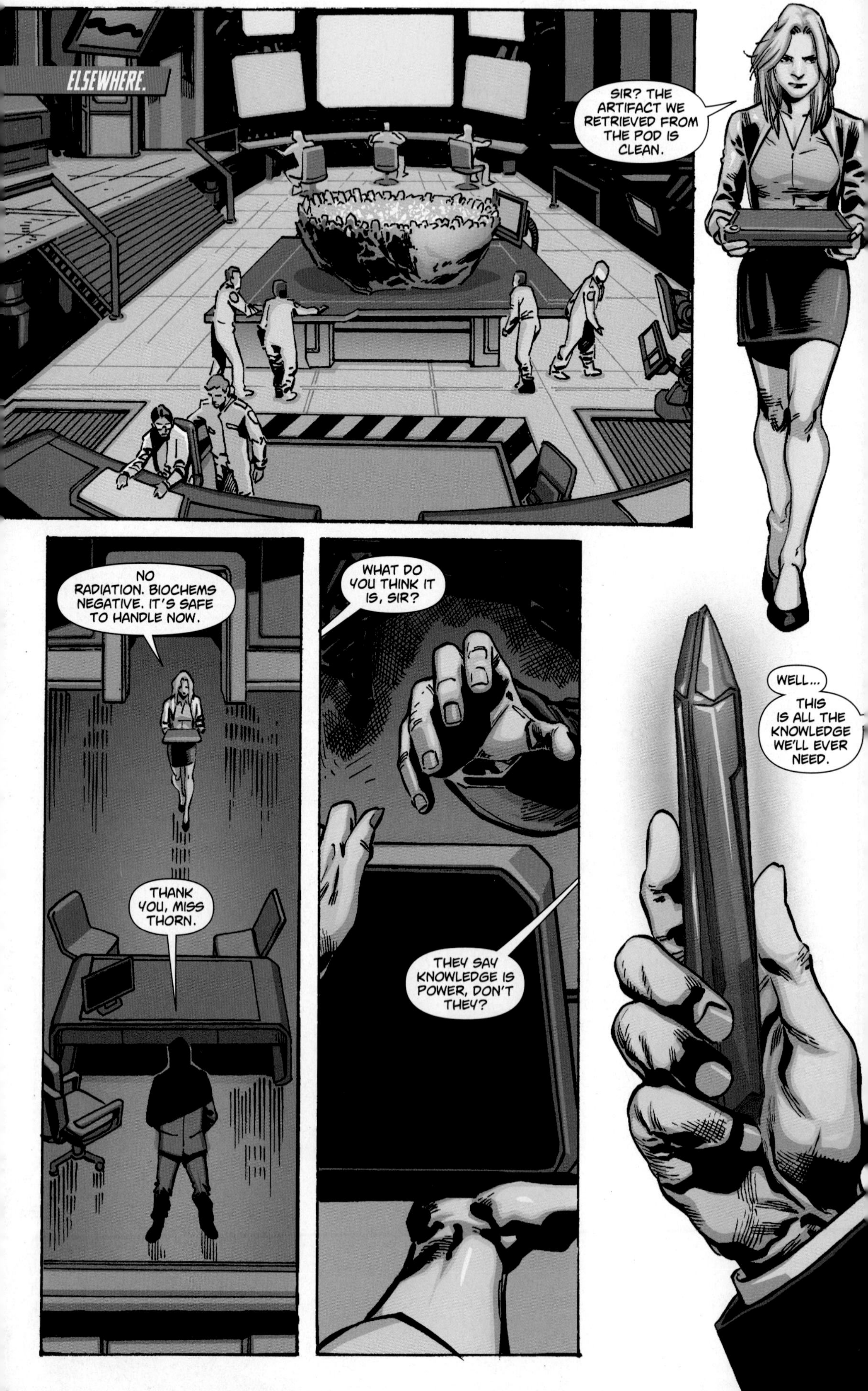
ELSEWHERE.
SIR? THE ARTIFACT WE RETRIEVED FROM THE POD IS CLEAN.
NO RADIATION. BIOCHEMS NEGATIVE. IT'S SAFE TO HANDLE NOW.
THANK YOU, MISS THORN.
WHAT DO YOU THINK IT IS, SIR?
THEY SAY KNOWLEDGE IS POWER, DON'T THEY?
WELL...
THIS IS ALL THE KNOWLEDGE WE'LL EVER NEED.

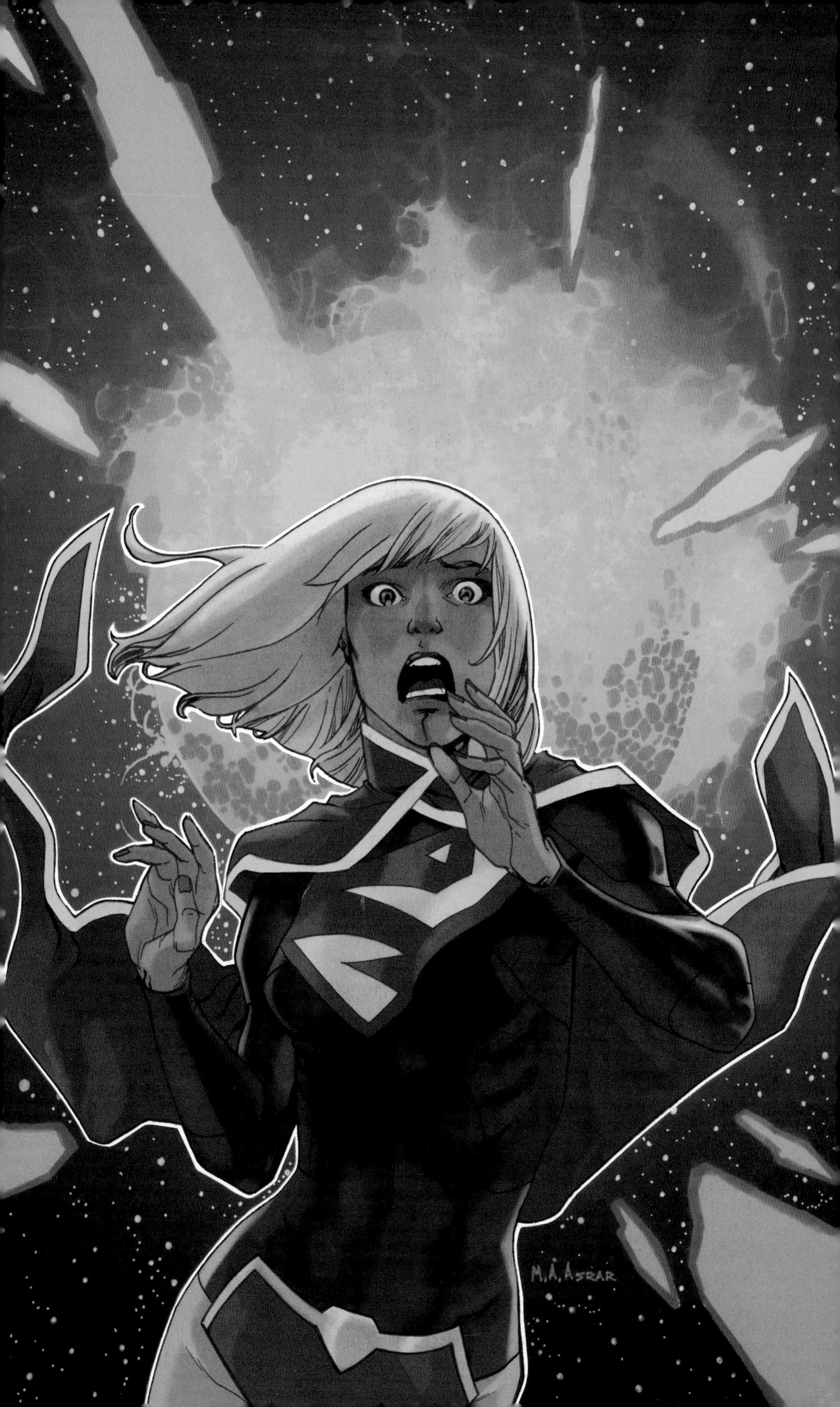
M.A. ASRAR

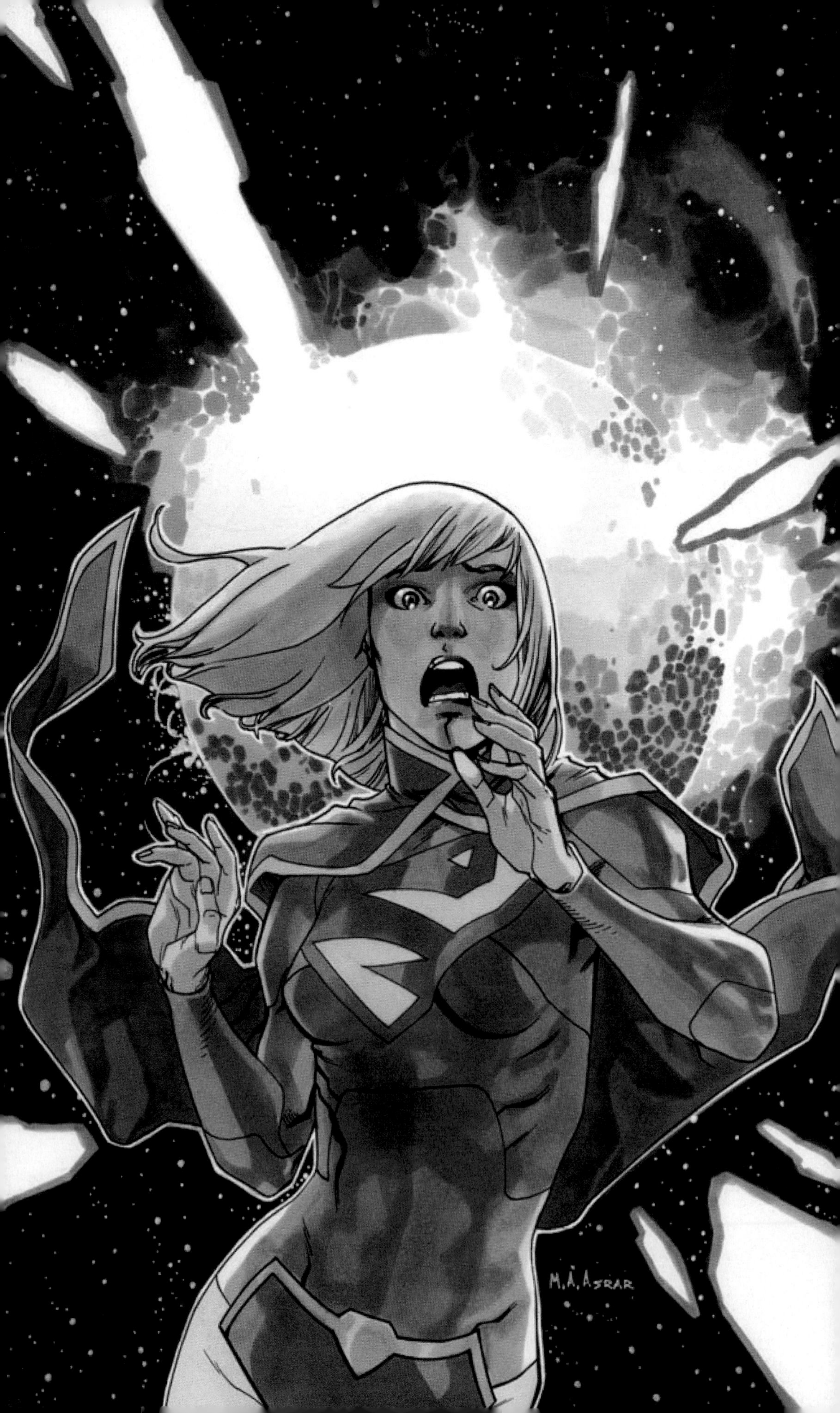
M.A. Asrar

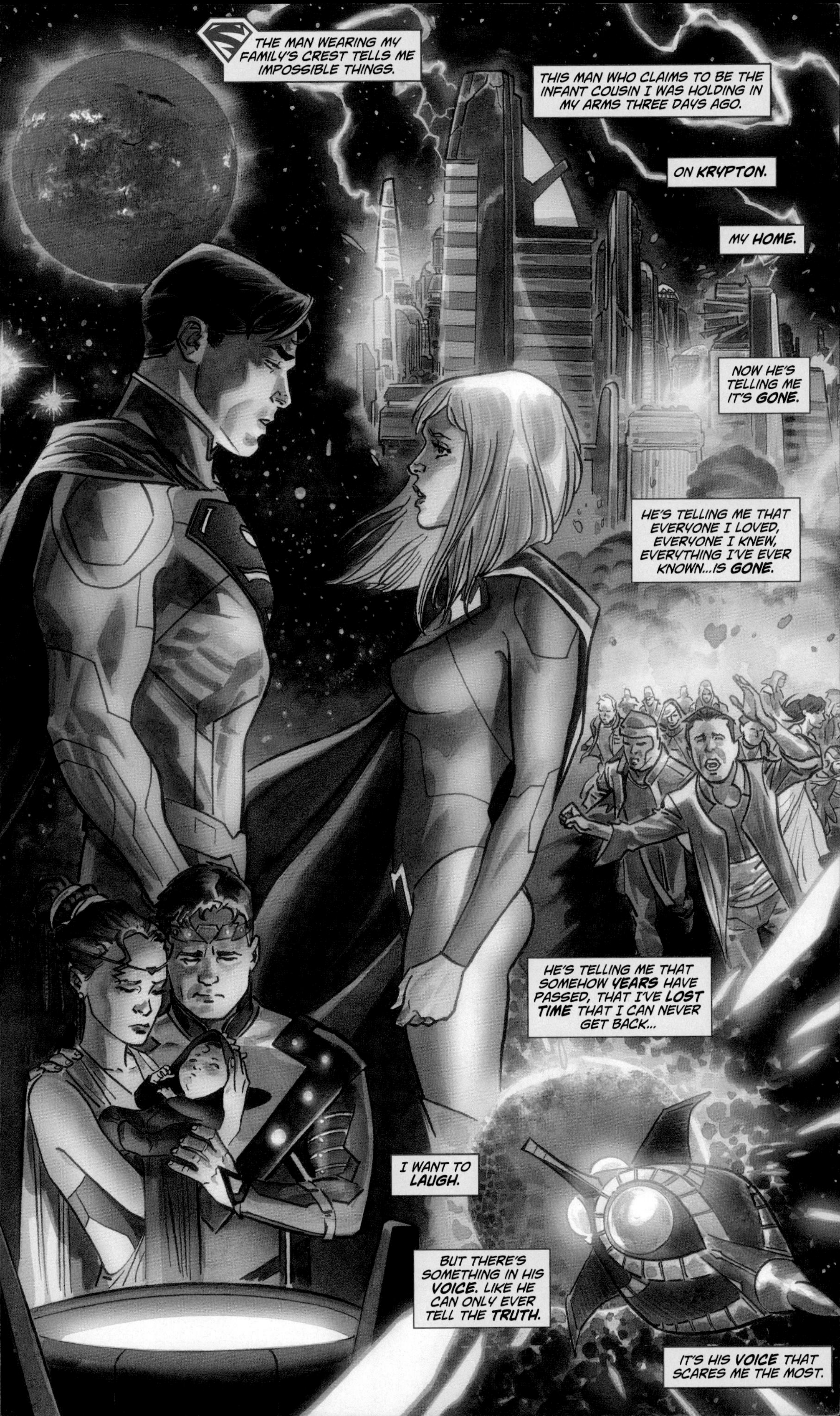
THE MAN WEARING MY FAMILY'S CREST TELLS ME IMPOSSIBLE THINGS.
THIS MAN WHO CLAIMS TO BE THE INFANT COUSIN I WAS HOLDING IN MY ARMS THREE DAYS AGO.
ON KRYPTON.
MY HOME.
NOW HE'S TELLING ME IT'S GONE.
HE'S TELLING ME THAT EVERYONE I LOVED, EVERYONE I KNEW, EVERYTHING I'VE EVER KNOWN...IS GONE.
HE'S TELLING ME THAT SOMEHOW YEARS HAVE PASSED, THAT I'VE LOST TIME THAT I CAN NEVER GET BACK...
I WANT TO LAUGH.
BUT THERE'S SOMETHING IN HIS VOICE. LIKE HE CAN ONLY EVER TELL THE TRUTH.
IT'S HIS VOICE THAT SCARES ME THE MOST.

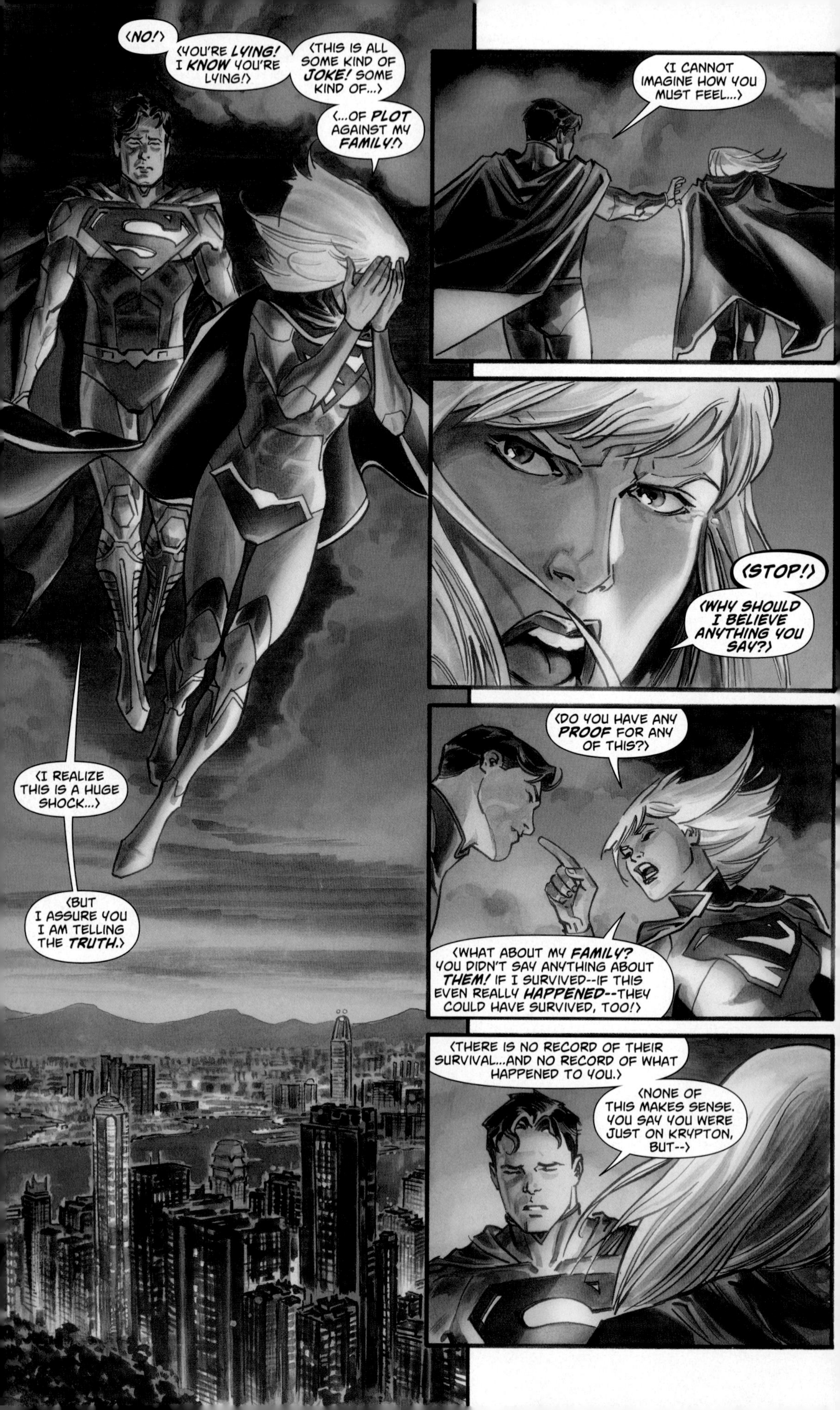
‹NO!›
‹YOU'RE LYING! I KNOW YOU'RE LYING!›
‹THIS IS ALL SOME KIND OF JOKE! SOME KIND OF...›
‹...OF PLOT AGAINST MY FAMILY!›
‹I REALIZE THIS IS A HUGE SHOCK...›
‹BUT I ASSURE YOU I AM TELLING THE TRUTH.›
‹I CANNOT IMAGINE HOW YOU MUST FEEL...›
‹STOP!›
‹WHY SHOULD I BELIEVE ANYTHING YOU SAY?›
‹DO YOU HAVE ANY PROOF FOR ANY OF THIS?›
‹WHAT ABOUT MY FAMILY? YOU DIDN'T SAY ANYTHING ABOUT THEM! IF I SURVIVED--IF THIS EVEN REALLY HAPPENED--THEY COULD HAVE SURVIVED, TOO!›
‹THERE IS NO RECORD OF THEIR SURVIVAL...AND NO RECORD OF WHAT HAPPENED TO YOU.›
‹NONE OF THIS MAKES SENSE. YOU SAY YOU WERE JUST ON KRYPTON, BUT--›

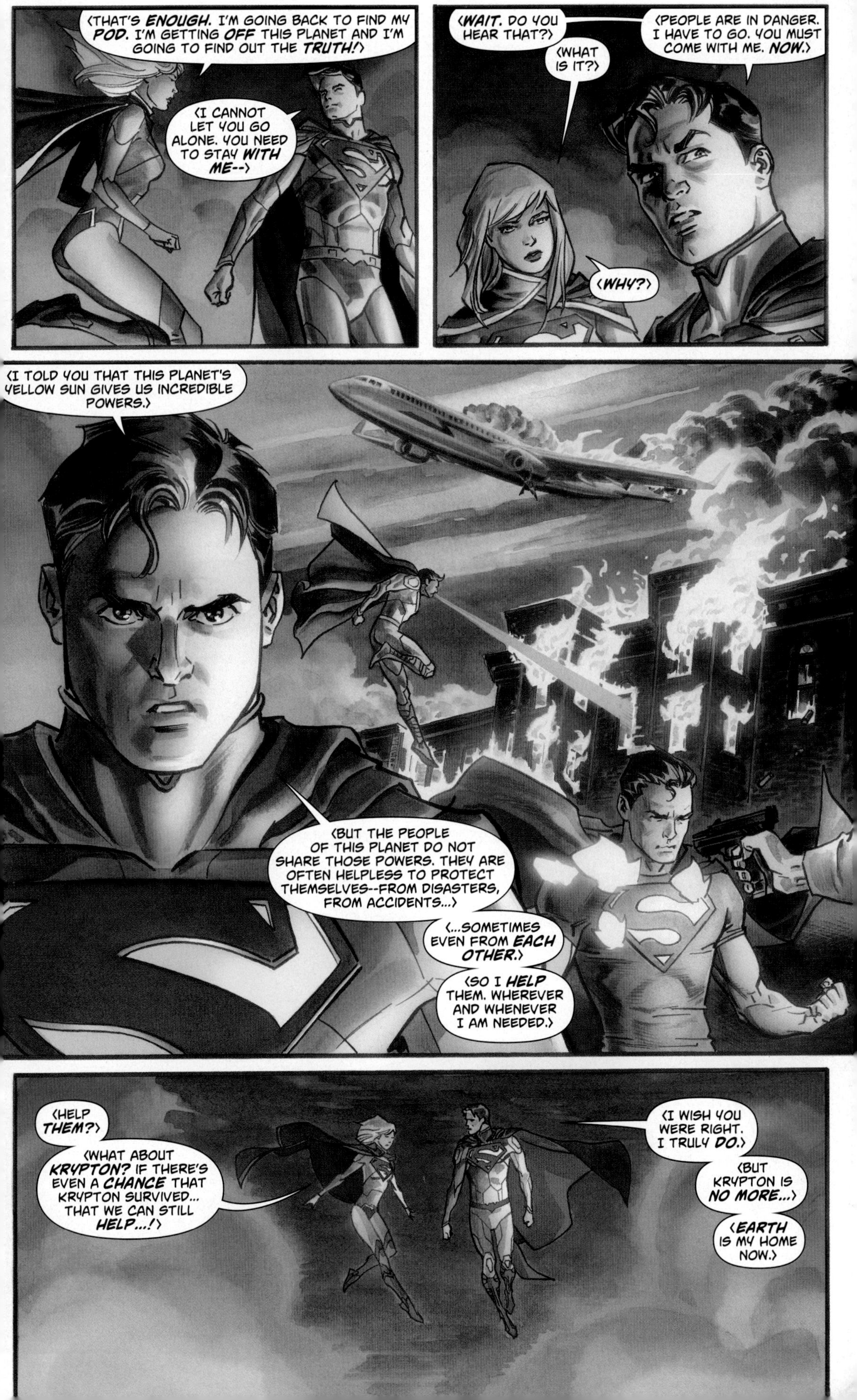

⟨THAT'S ENOUGH. I'M GOING BACK TO FIND MY POD. I'M GETTING OFF THIS PLANET AND I'M GOING TO FIND OUT THE TRUTH!⟩
⟨I CANNOT LET YOU GO ALONE. YOU NEED TO STAY WITH ME--⟩
⟨WAIT. DO YOU HEAR THAT?⟩
⟨WHAT IS IT?⟩
⟨PEOPLE ARE IN DANGER. I HAVE TO GO. YOU MUST COME WITH ME. NOW.⟩
⟨WHY?⟩
⟨I TOLD YOU THAT THIS PLANET'S YELLOW SUN GIVES US INCREDIBLE POWERS.⟩
⟨BUT THE PEOPLE OF THIS PLANET DO NOT SHARE THOSE POWERS. THEY ARE OFTEN HELPLESS TO PROTECT THEMSELVES--FROM DISASTERS, FROM ACCIDENTS...⟩
⟨...SOMETIMES EVEN FROM EACH OTHER.⟩
⟨SO I HELP THEM. WHEREVER AND WHENEVER I AM NEEDED.⟩
⟨HELP THEM?⟩
⟨WHAT ABOUT KRYPTON? IF THERE'S EVEN A CHANCE THAT KRYPTON SURVIVED... THAT WE CAN STILL HELP...!⟩
⟨I WISH YOU WERE RIGHT. I TRULY DO.⟩
⟨BUT KRYPTON IS NO MORE...⟩
⟨EARTH IS MY HOME NOW.⟩

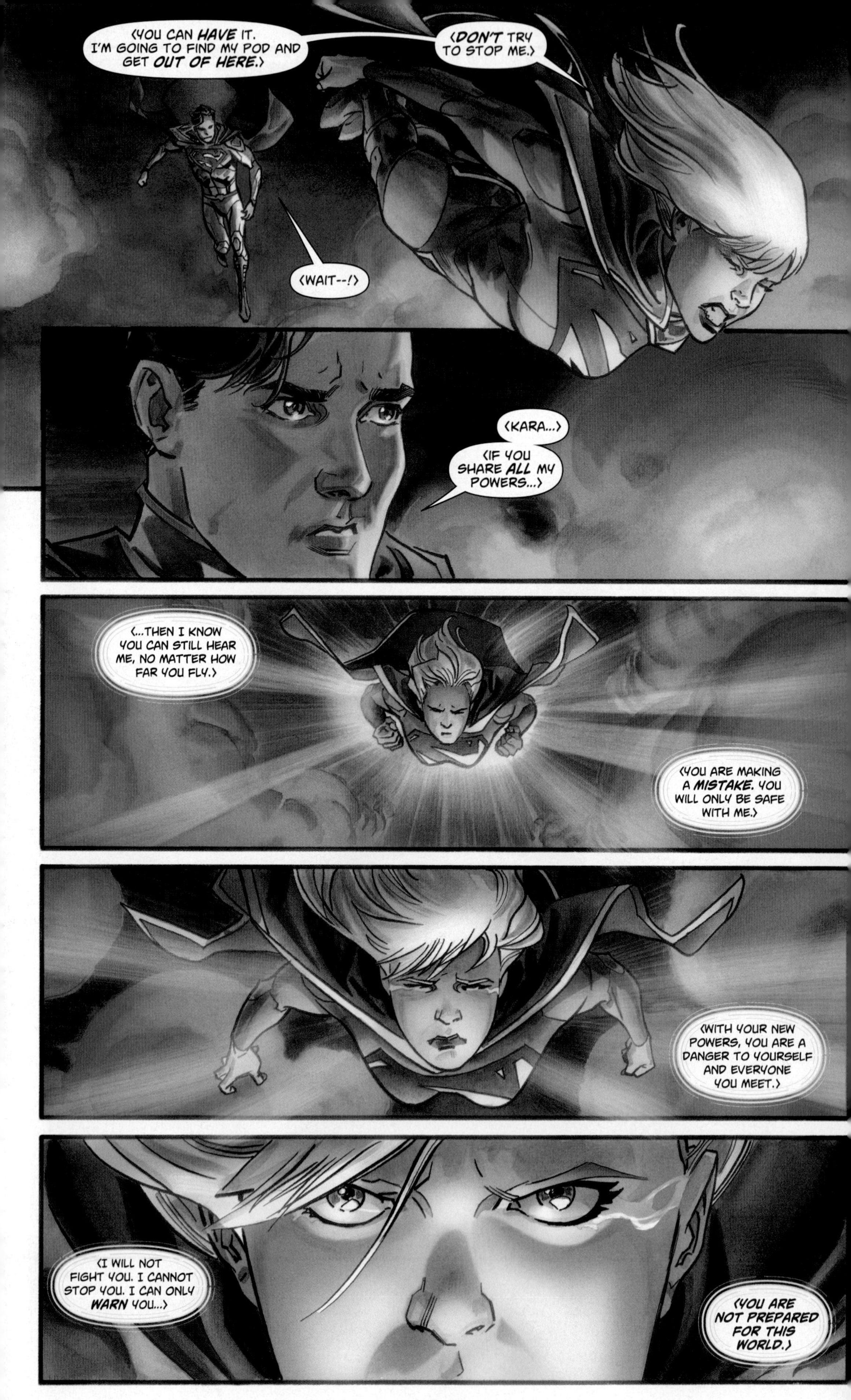
‹YOU CAN HAVE IT. I'M GOING TO FIND MY POD AND GET OUT OF HERE.›
‹DON'T TRY TO STOP ME.›
‹WAIT--!›
‹KARA...›
‹IF YOU SHARE ALL MY POWERS...›
‹...THEN I KNOW YOU CAN STILL HEAR ME, NO MATTER HOW FAR YOU FLY.›
‹YOU ARE MAKING A MISTAKE. YOU WILL ONLY BE SAFE WITH ME.›
‹WITH YOUR NEW POWERS, YOU ARE A DANGER TO YOURSELF AND EVERYONE YOU MEET.›
‹I WILL NOT FIGHT YOU. I CANNOT STOP YOU. I CAN ONLY WARN YOU...›
‹YOU ARE NOT PREPARED FOR THIS WORLD.›

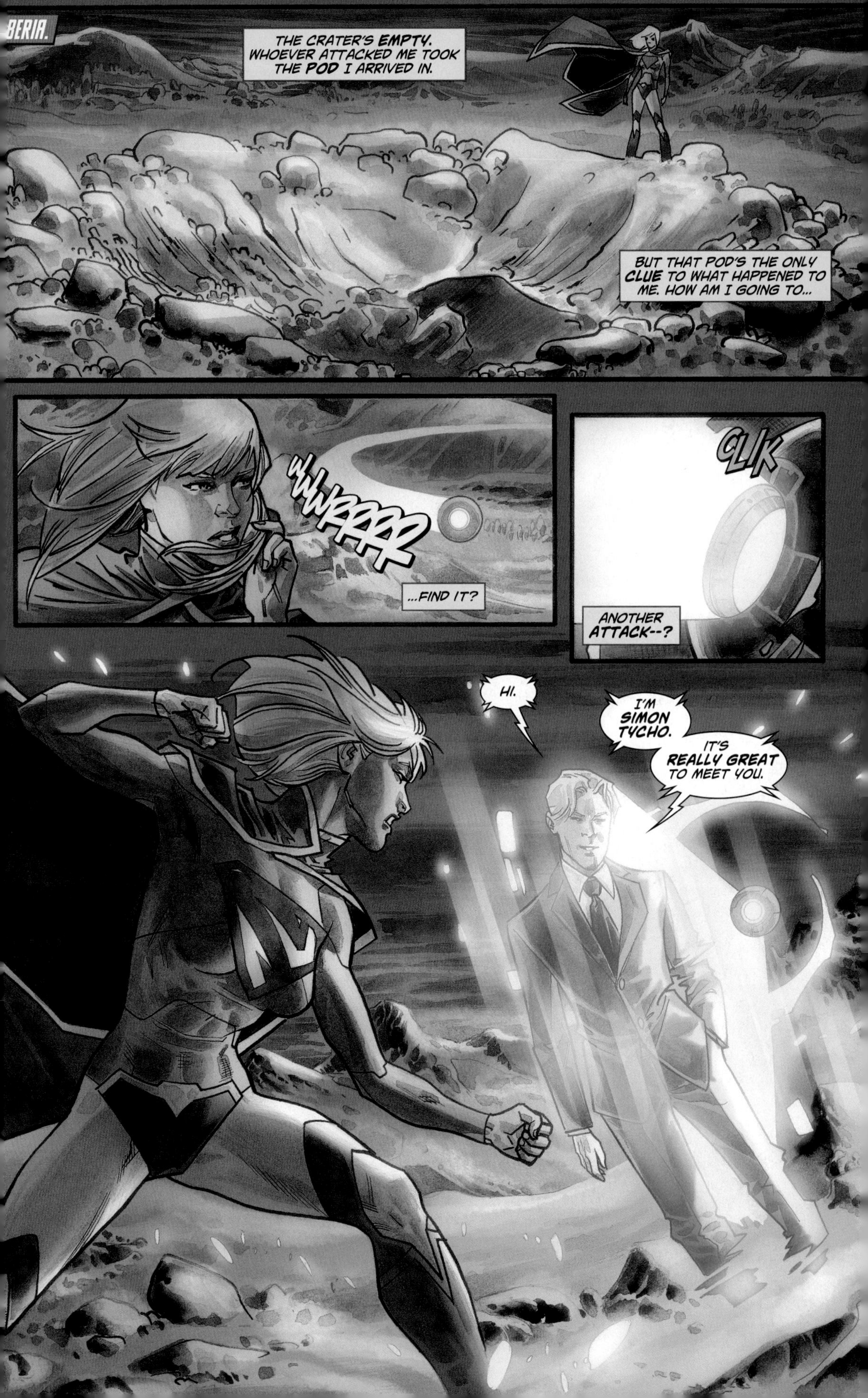
BERIA.
THE CRATER'S EMPTY. WHOEVER ATTACKED ME TOOK THE POD I ARRIVED IN.
BUT THAT POD'S THE ONLY CLUE TO WHAT HAPPENED TO ME. HOW AM I GOING TO...
WWRRRR
...FIND IT?
CLIK
ANOTHER ATTACK--?
HI.
I'M SIMON TYCHO.
IT'S REALLY GREAT TO MEET YOU.

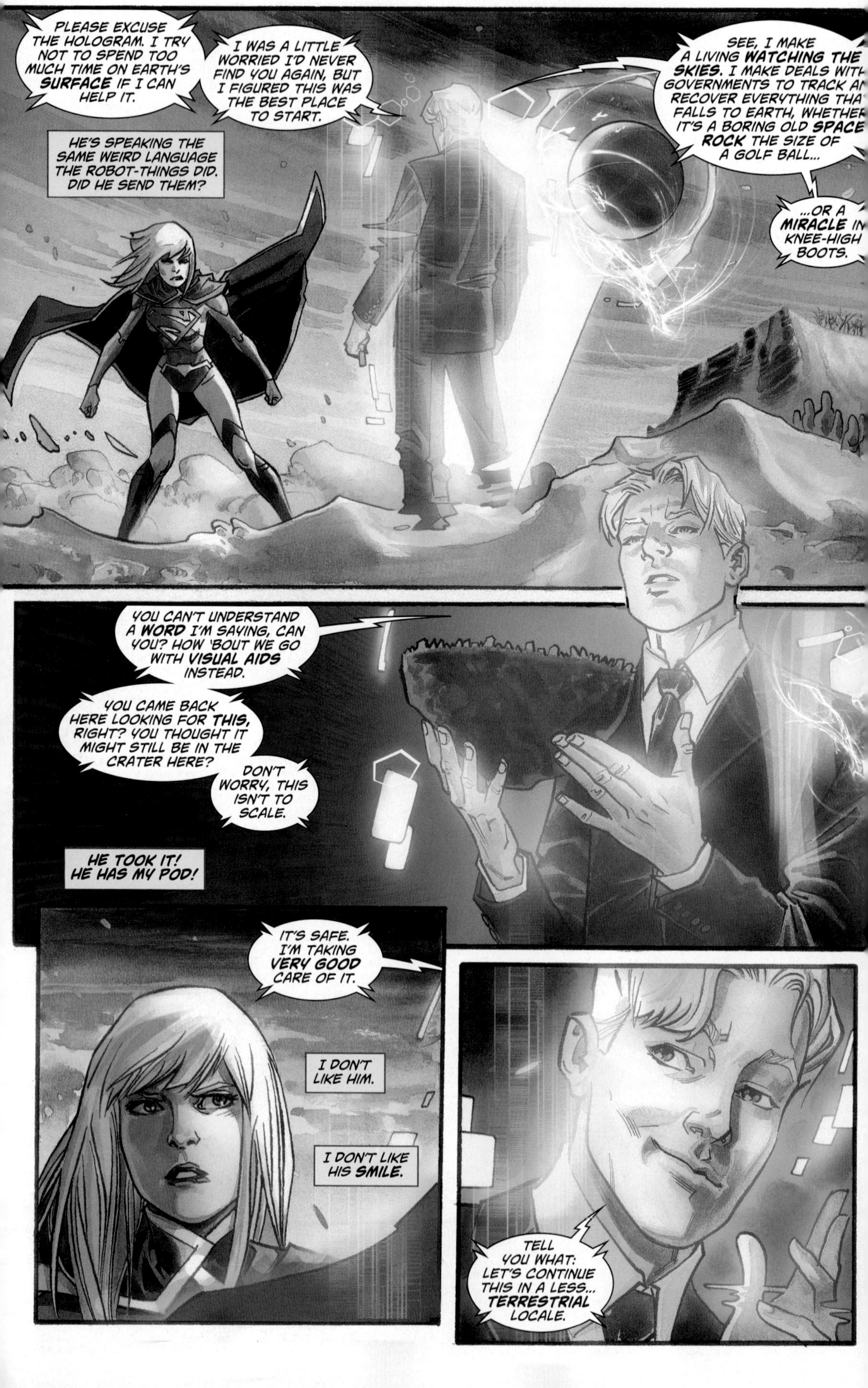
PLEASE EXCUSE THE HOLOGRAM. I TRY NOT TO SPEND TOO MUCH TIME ON EARTH'S SURFACE IF I CAN HELP IT.
I WAS A LITTLE WORRIED I'D NEVER FIND YOU AGAIN, BUT I FIGURED THIS WAS THE BEST PLACE TO START.
HE'S SPEAKING THE SAME WEIRD LANGUAGE THE ROBOT-THINGS DID. DID HE SEND THEM?
SEE, I MAKE A LIVING WATCHING THE SKIES. I MAKE DEALS WITH GOVERNMENTS TO TRACK AND RECOVER EVERYTHING THAT FALLS TO EARTH, WHETHER IT'S A BORING OLD SPACE ROCK THE SIZE OF A GOLF BALL...
...OR A MIRACLE IN KNEE-HIGH BOOTS.
YOU CAN'T UNDERSTAND A WORD I'M SAYING, CAN YOU? HOW 'BOUT WE GO WITH VISUAL AIDS INSTEAD.
YOU CAME BACK HERE LOOKING FOR THIS, RIGHT? YOU THOUGHT IT MIGHT STILL BE IN THE CRATER HERE?
DON'T WORRY, THIS ISN'T TO SCALE.
HE TOOK IT! HE HAS MY POD!
IT'S SAFE. I'M TAKING VERY GOOD CARE OF IT.
I DON'T LIKE HIM.
I DON'T LIKE HIS SMILE.
TELL YOU WHAT: LET'S CONTINUE THIS IN A LESS... TERRESTRIAL LOCALE.

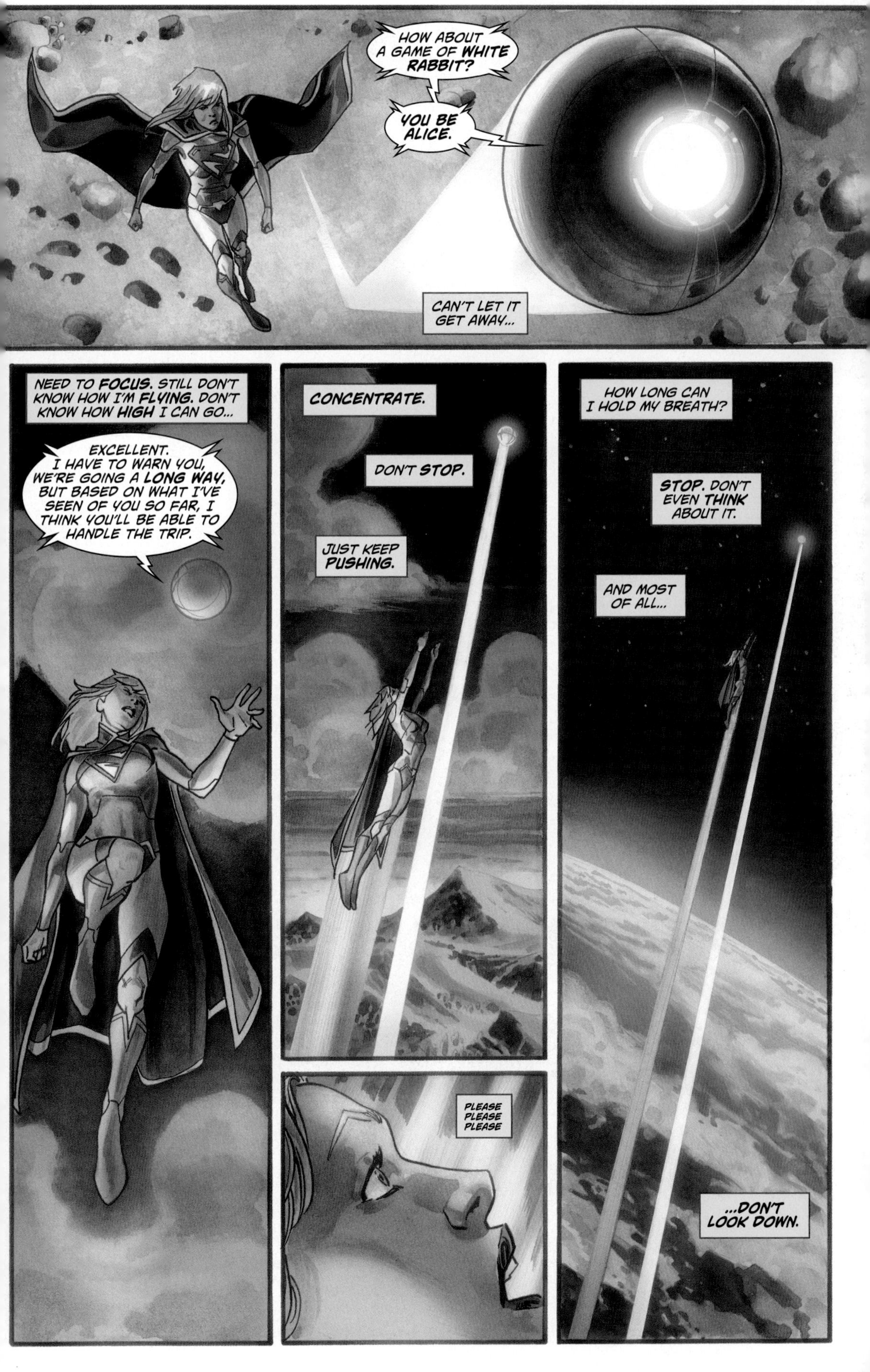
HOW ABOUT A GAME OF WHITE RABBIT?
YOU BE ALICE.
CAN'T LET IT GET AWAY...
NEED TO FOCUS. STILL DON'T KNOW HOW I'M FLYING. DON'T KNOW HOW HIGH I CAN GO...
EXCELLENT. I HAVE TO WARN YOU, WE'RE GOING A LONG WAY, BUT BASED ON WHAT I'VE SEEN OF YOU SO FAR, I THINK YOU'LL BE ABLE TO HANDLE THE TRIP.
CONCENTRATE.
DON'T STOP.
JUST KEEP PUSHING.
PLEASE PLEASE PLEASE
HOW LONG CAN I HOLD MY BREATH?
STOP. DON'T EVEN THINK ABOUT IT.
AND MOST OF ALL...
...DON'T LOOK DOWN.

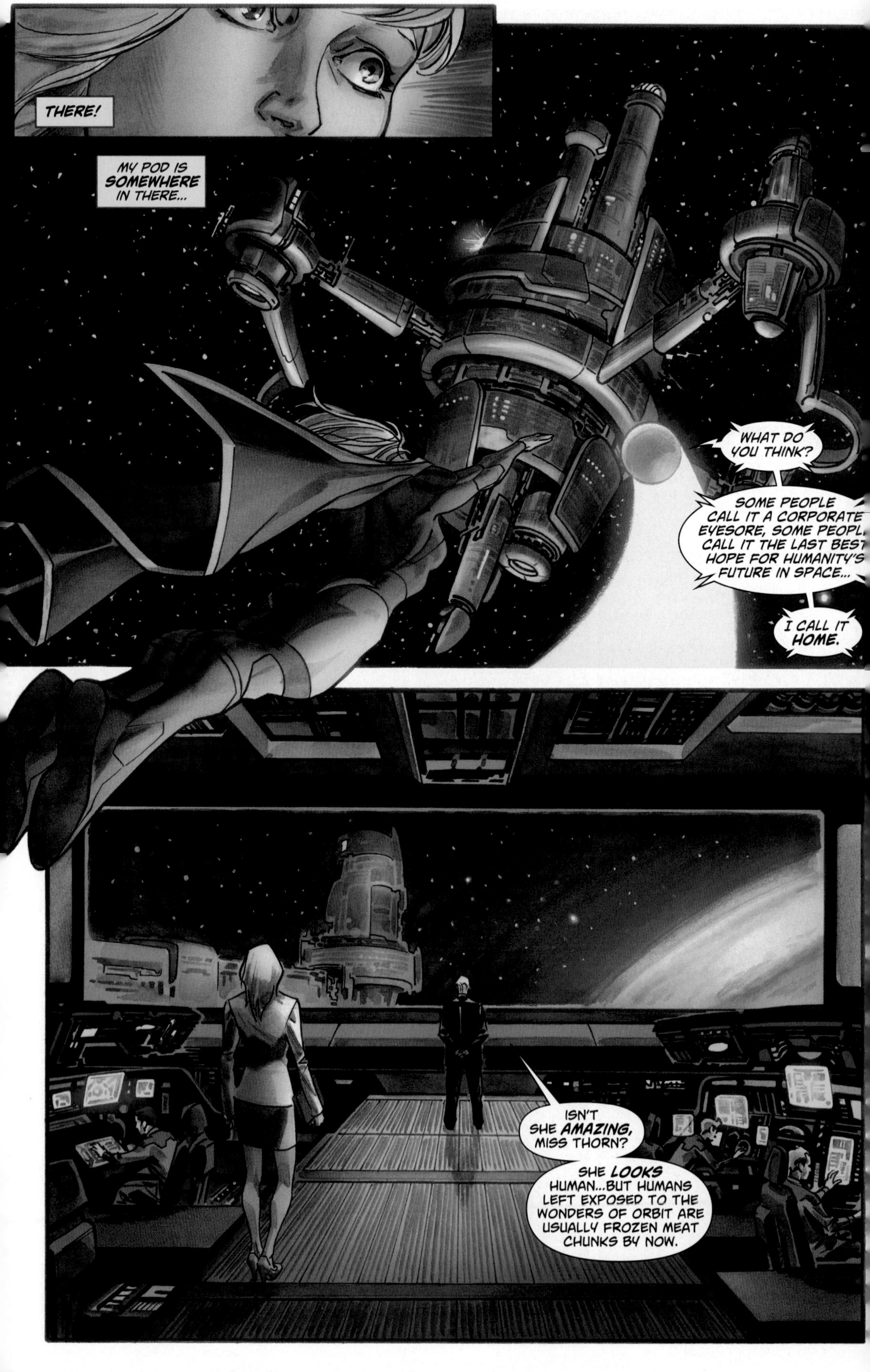
THERE!
MY POD IS SOMEWHERE IN THERE...
WHAT DO YOU THINK?
SOME PEOPLE CALL IT A CORPORATE EYESORE, SOME PEOPLE CALL IT THE LAST BEST HOPE FOR HUMANITY'S FUTURE IN SPACE...
I CALL IT HOME.
ISN'T SHE AMAZING, MISS THORN?
SHE LOOKS HUMAN...BUT HUMANS LEFT EXPOSED TO THE WONDERS OF ORBIT ARE USUALLY FROZEN MEAT CHUNKS BY NOW.

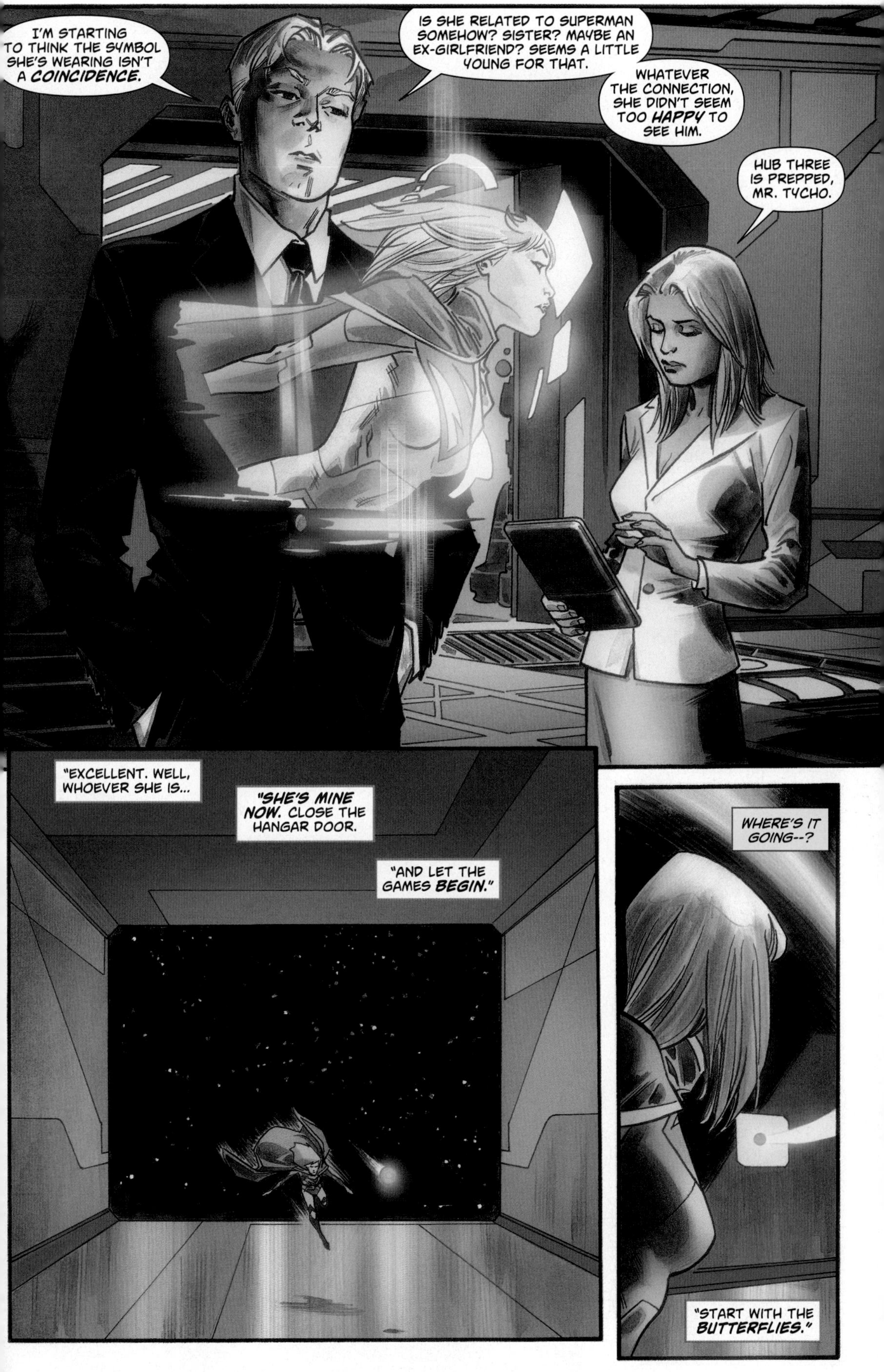

I'M STARTING TO THINK THE SYMBOL SHE'S WEARING ISN'T A *COINCIDENCE.*
IS SHE RELATED TO SUPERMAN SOMEHOW? SISTER? MAYBE AN EX-GIRLFRIEND? SEEMS A LITTLE YOUNG FOR THAT.
WHATEVER THE CONNECTION, SHE DIDN'T SEEM TOO *HAPPY* TO SEE HIM.
HUB THREE IS PREPPED, MR. TYCHO.
"EXCELLENT. WELL, WHOEVER SHE IS...
"SHE'S MINE NOW. CLOSE THE HANGAR DOOR.
"AND LET THE GAMES *BEGIN.*"
WHERE'S IT GOING--?
"START WITH THE *BUTTERFLIES.*"

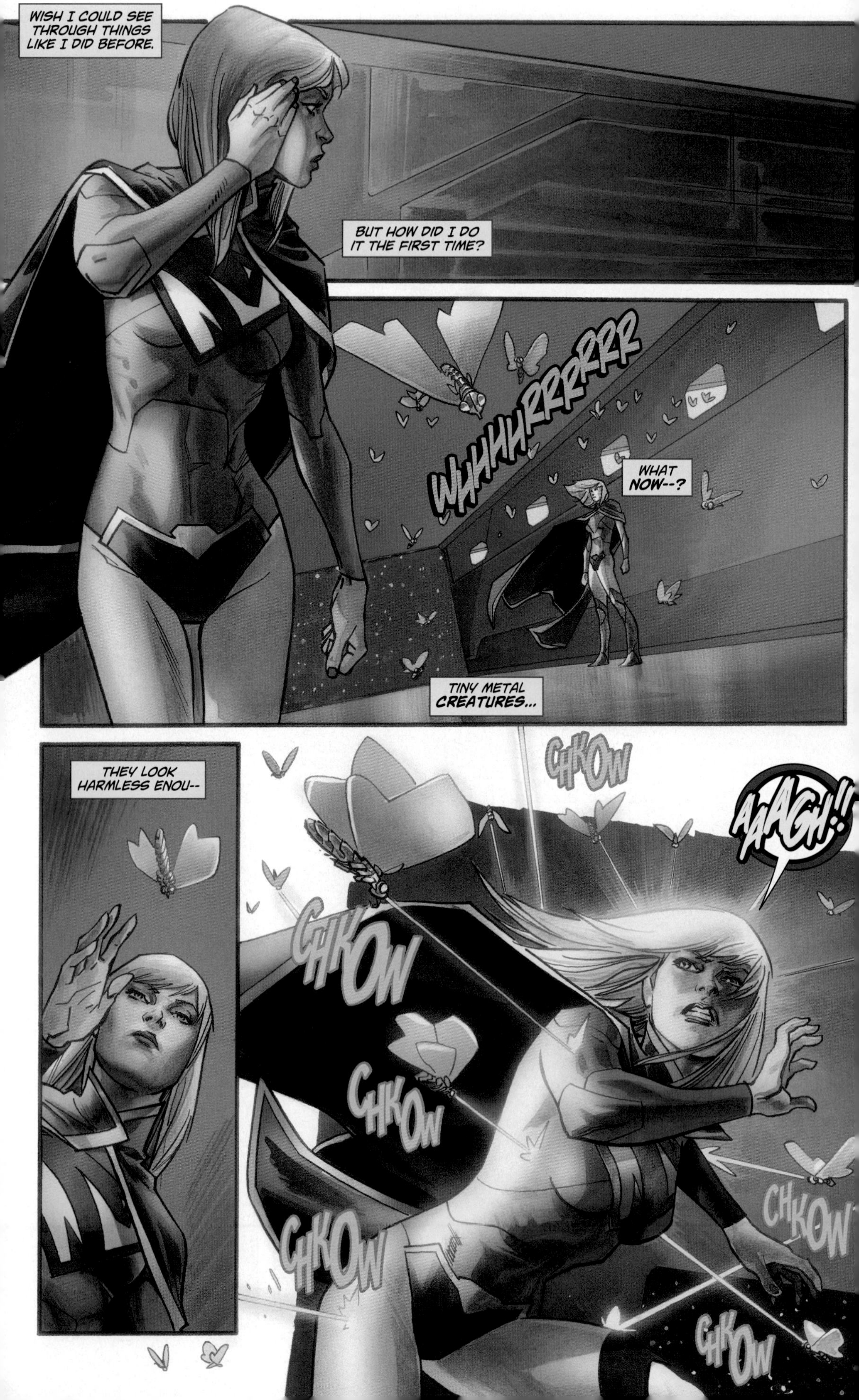

WISH I COULD SEE THROUGH THINGS LIKE I DID BEFORE.
BUT HOW DID I DO IT THE FIRST TIME?
WHHHHRRRRRR
WHAT NOW--?
TINY METAL CREATURES...
THEY LOOK HARMLESS ENOU--
CHKOW
AAAGH!!
CHKOW
CHKOW
CHKOW
CHKOW
CHKOW

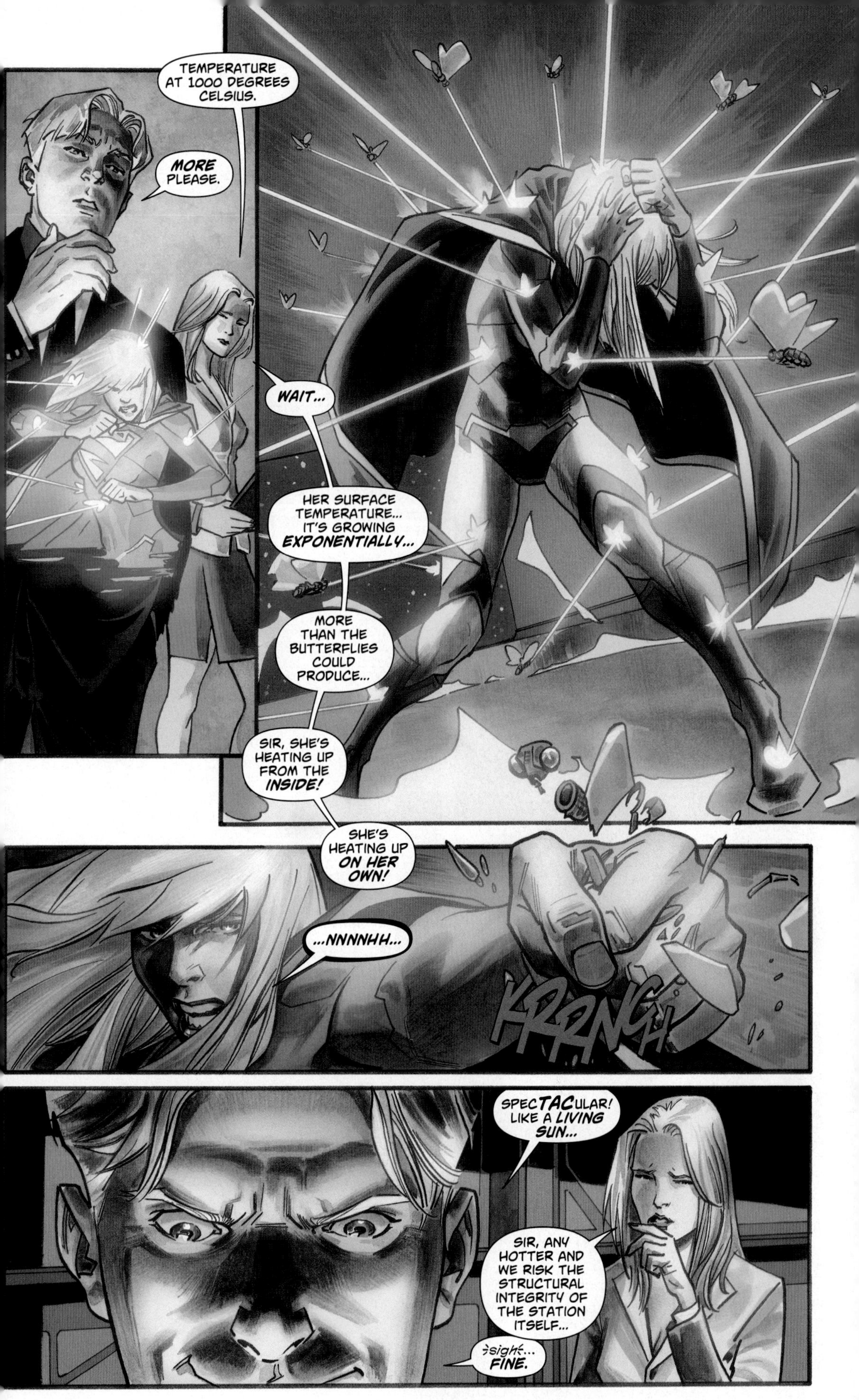
TEMPERATURE AT 1000 DEGREES CELSIUS.
MORE PLEASE.
WAIT...
HER SURFACE TEMPERATURE... IT'S GROWING EXPONENTIALLY...
MORE THAN THE BUTTERFLIES COULD PRODUCE...
SIR, SHE'S HEATING UP FROM THE INSIDE!
SHE'S HEATING UP ON HER OWN!
...NNNNHH...
KRRNCH
SPECTACULAR! LIKE A LIVING SUN...
SIR, ANY HOTTER AND WE RISK THE STRUCTURAL INTEGRITY OF THE STATION ITSELF...
sigh... FINE.

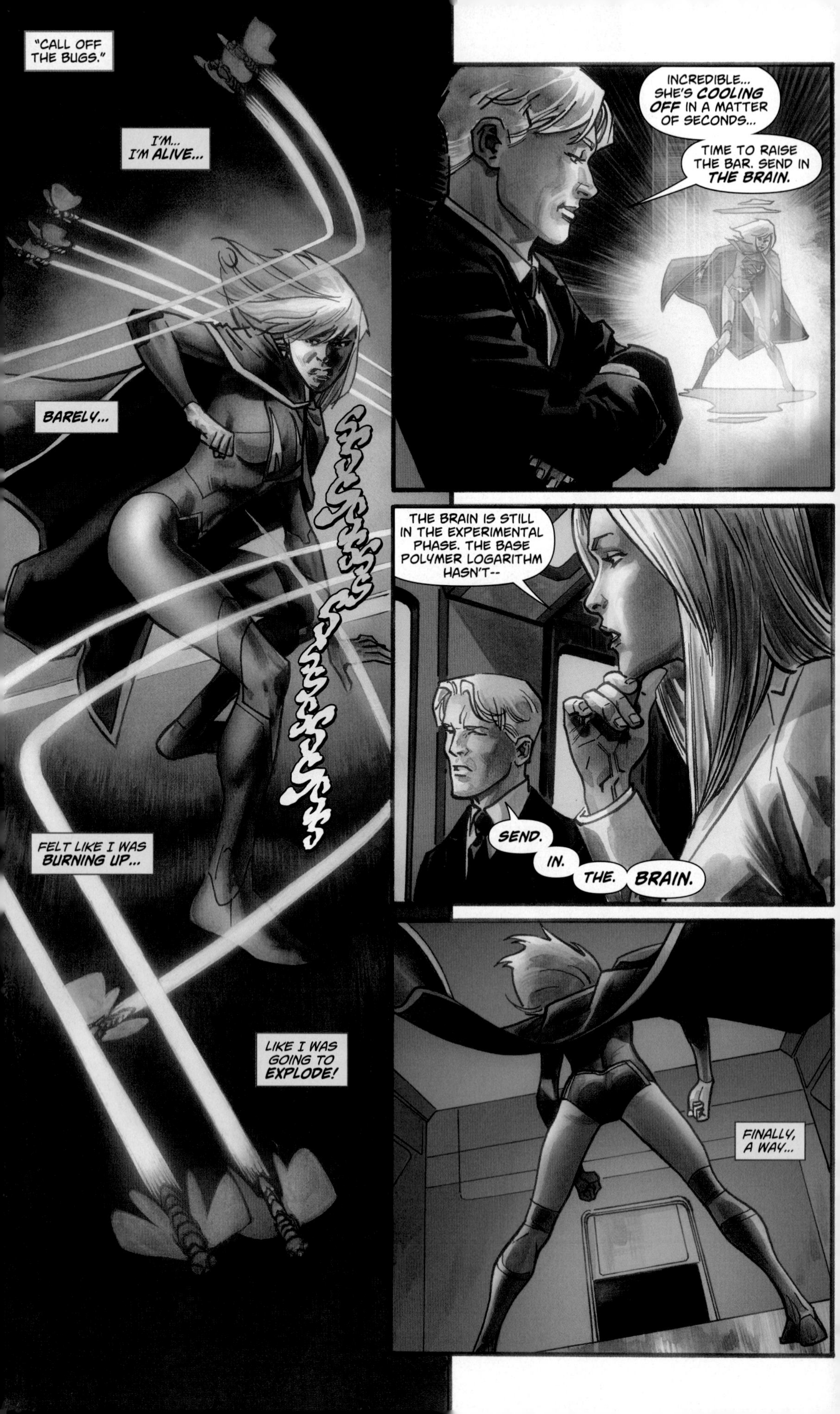
"CALL OFF THE BUGS."
I'M... I'M ALIVE...
BARELY...
FELT LIKE I WAS BURNING UP...
LIKE I WAS GOING TO EXPLODE!
INCREDIBLE... SHE'S COOLING OFF IN A MATTER OF SECONDS...
TIME TO RAISE THE BAR. SEND IN THE BRAIN.
THE BRAIN IS STILL IN THE EXPERIMENTAL PHASE. THE BASE POLYMER LOGARITHM HASN'T--
SEND.
IN.
THE.
BRAIN.
FINALLY, A WAY...

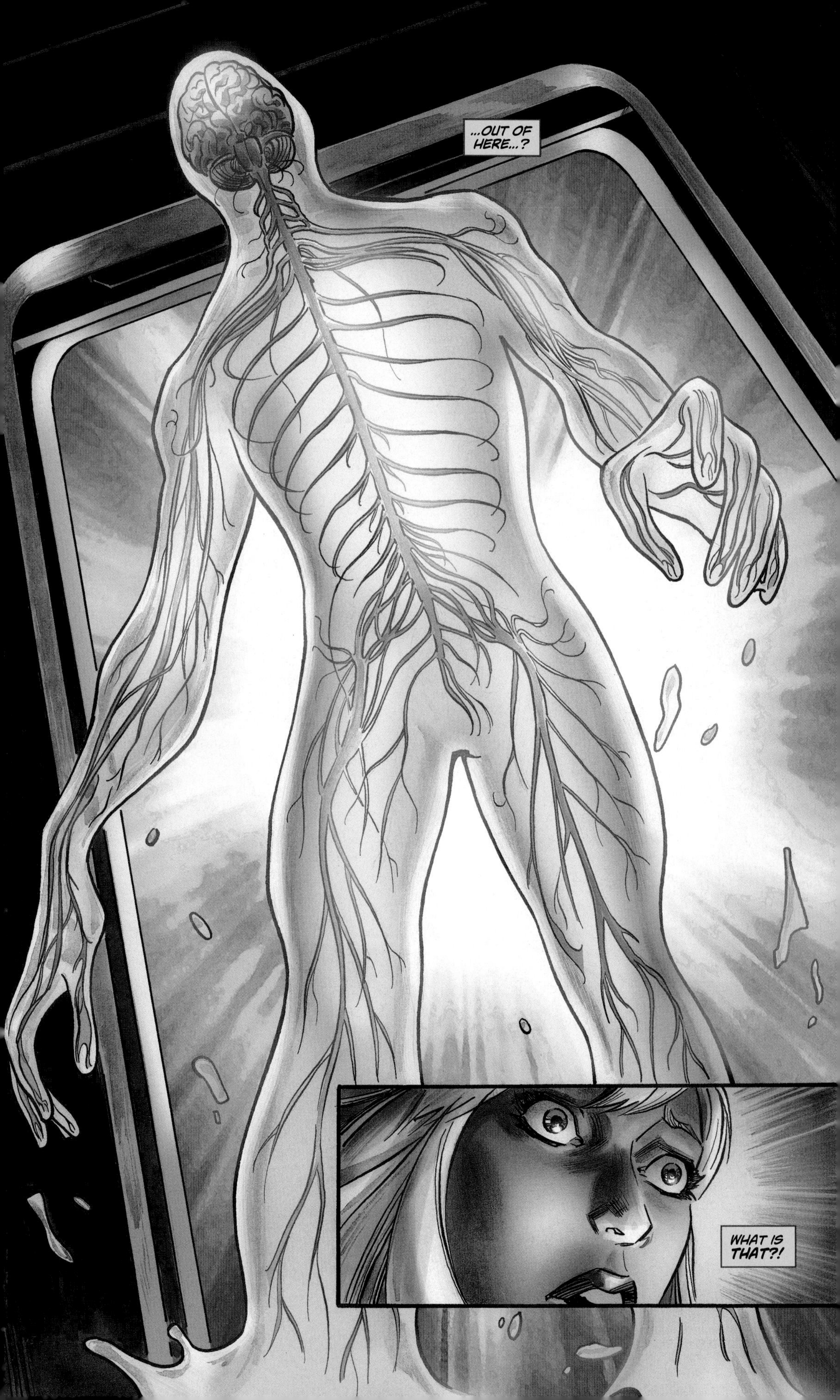
...OUT OF HERE...?
WHAT IS THAT?!

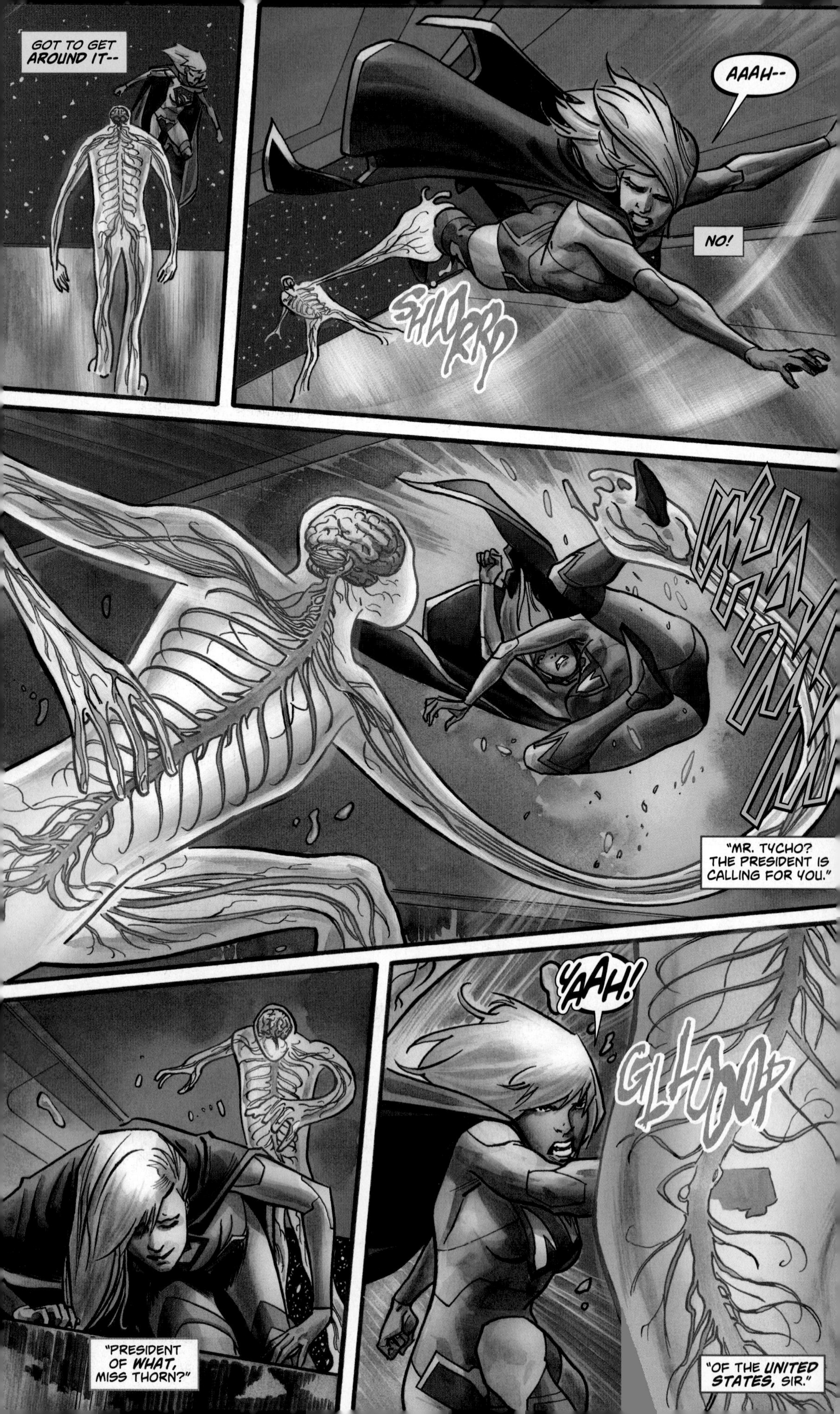
GOT TO GET AROUND IT--
AAAH--
NO!
SHLORRP
WUNNNNNN
"MR. TYCHO? THE PRESIDENT IS CALLING FOR YOU."
"PRESIDENT OF WHAT, MISS THORN?"
YAAH!
GLLOOP
"OF THE UNITED STATES, SIR."

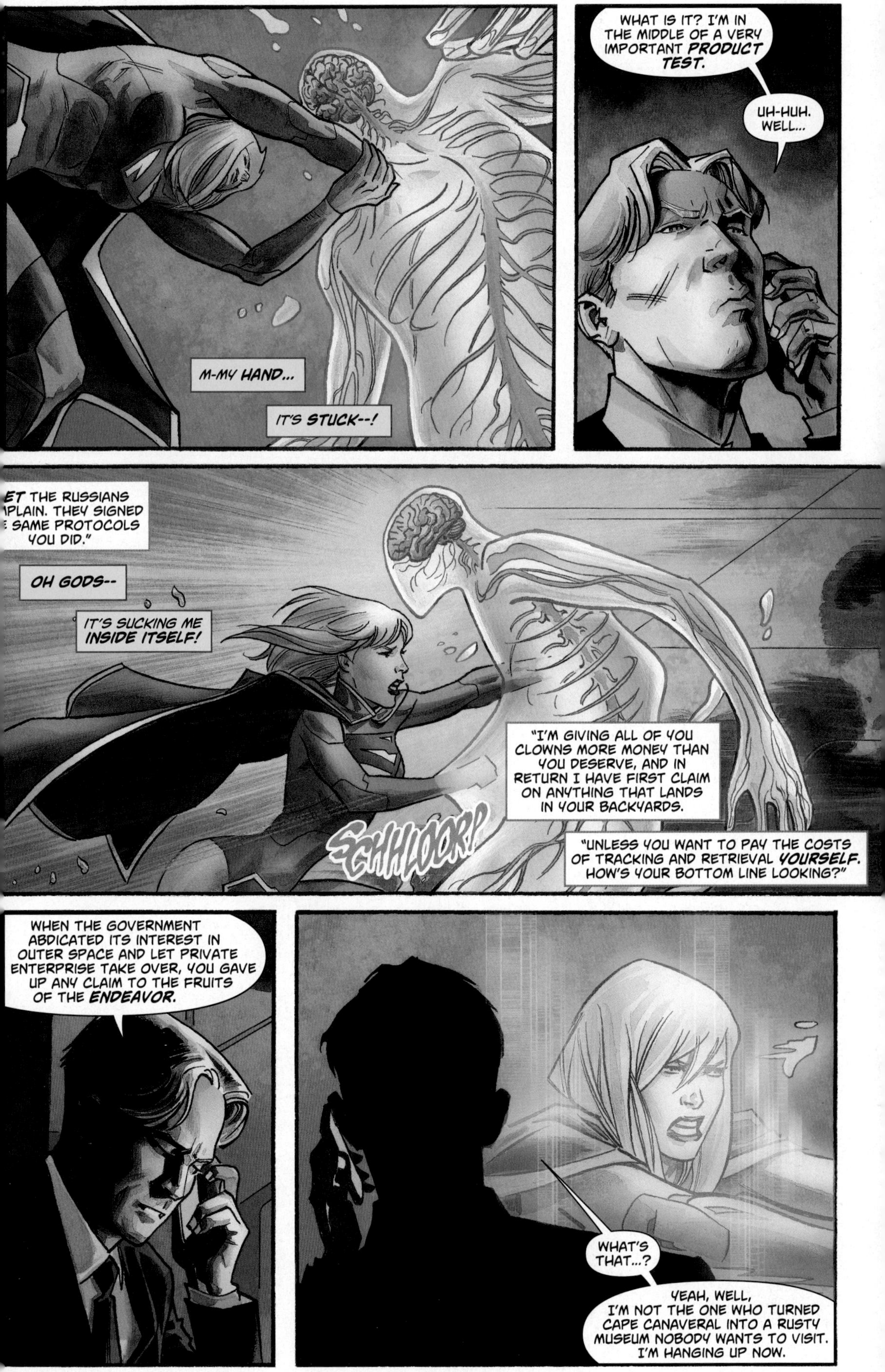
M-MY HAND...
IT'S STUCK--!
WHAT IS IT? I'M IN THE MIDDLE OF A VERY IMPORTANT PRODUCT TEST.
UH-HUH. WELL...
ET THE RUSSIANS IPLAIN. THEY SIGNED E SAME PROTOCOLS YOU DID."
OH GODS--
IT'S SUCKING ME INSIDE ITSELF!
"I'M GIVING ALL OF YOU CLOWNS MORE MONEY THAN YOU DESERVE, AND IN RETURN I HAVE FIRST CLAIM ON ANYTHING THAT LANDS IN YOUR BACKYARDS.
SCHHLOORP
"UNLESS YOU WANT TO PAY THE COSTS OF TRACKING AND RETRIEVAL YOURSELF. HOW'S YOUR BOTTOM LINE LOOKING?"
WHEN THE GOVERNMENT ABDICATED ITS INTEREST IN OUTER SPACE AND LET PRIVATE ENTERPRISE TAKE OVER, YOU GAVE UP ANY CLAIM TO THE FRUITS OF THE ENDEAVOR.
WHAT'S THAT...?
YEAH, WELL, I'M NOT THE ONE WHO TURNED CAPE CANAVERAL INTO A RUSTY MUSEUM NOBODY WANTS TO VISIT. I'M HANGING UP NOW.

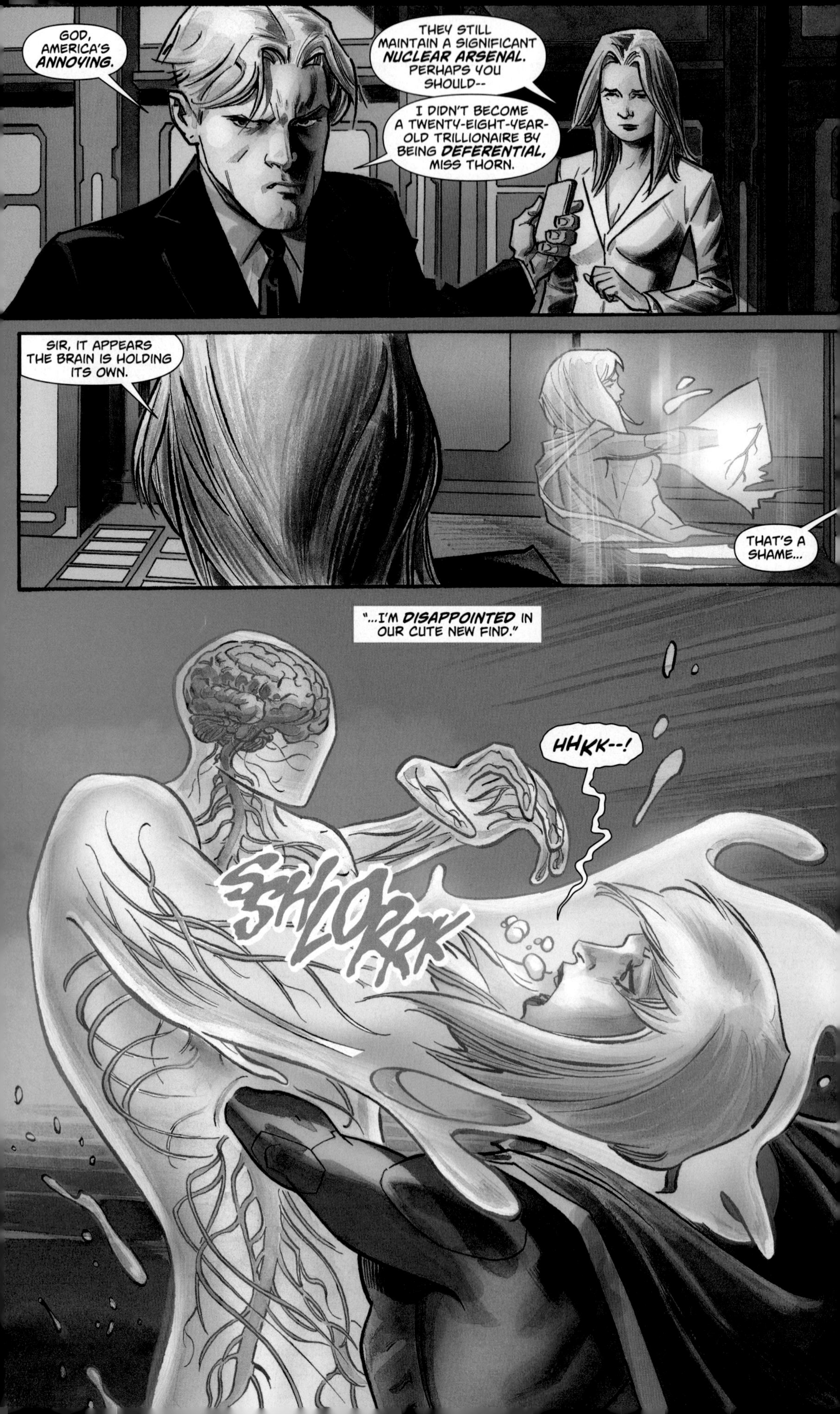
GOD, AMERICA'S ANNOYING.
THEY STILL MAINTAIN A SIGNIFICANT NUCLEAR ARSENAL. PERHAPS YOU SHOULD--
I DIDN'T BECOME A TWENTY-EIGHT-YEAR-OLD TRILLIONAIRE BY BEING DEFERENTIAL, MISS THORN.
SIR, IT APPEARS THE BRAIN IS HOLDING ITS OWN.
THAT'S A SHAME...
"...I'M DISAPPOINTED IN OUR CUTE NEW FIND."
HHKK--!
SSHLORRK

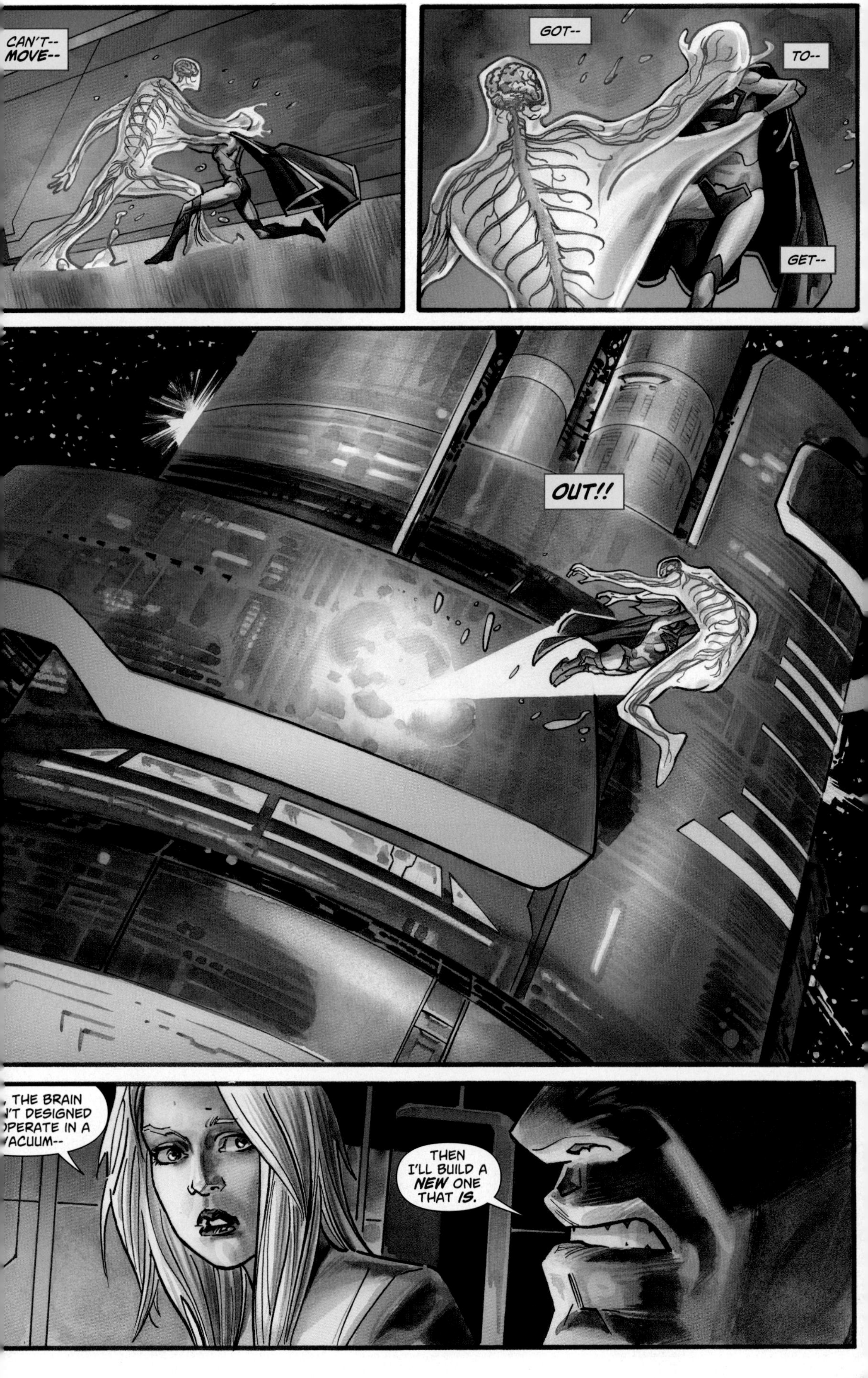
CAN'T--
MOVE--
GOT--
TO--
GET--
OUT!!
THE BRAIN
'T DESIGNED
OPERATE IN A
VACUUM--
THEN
I'LL BUILD A
NEW ONE
THAT IS.

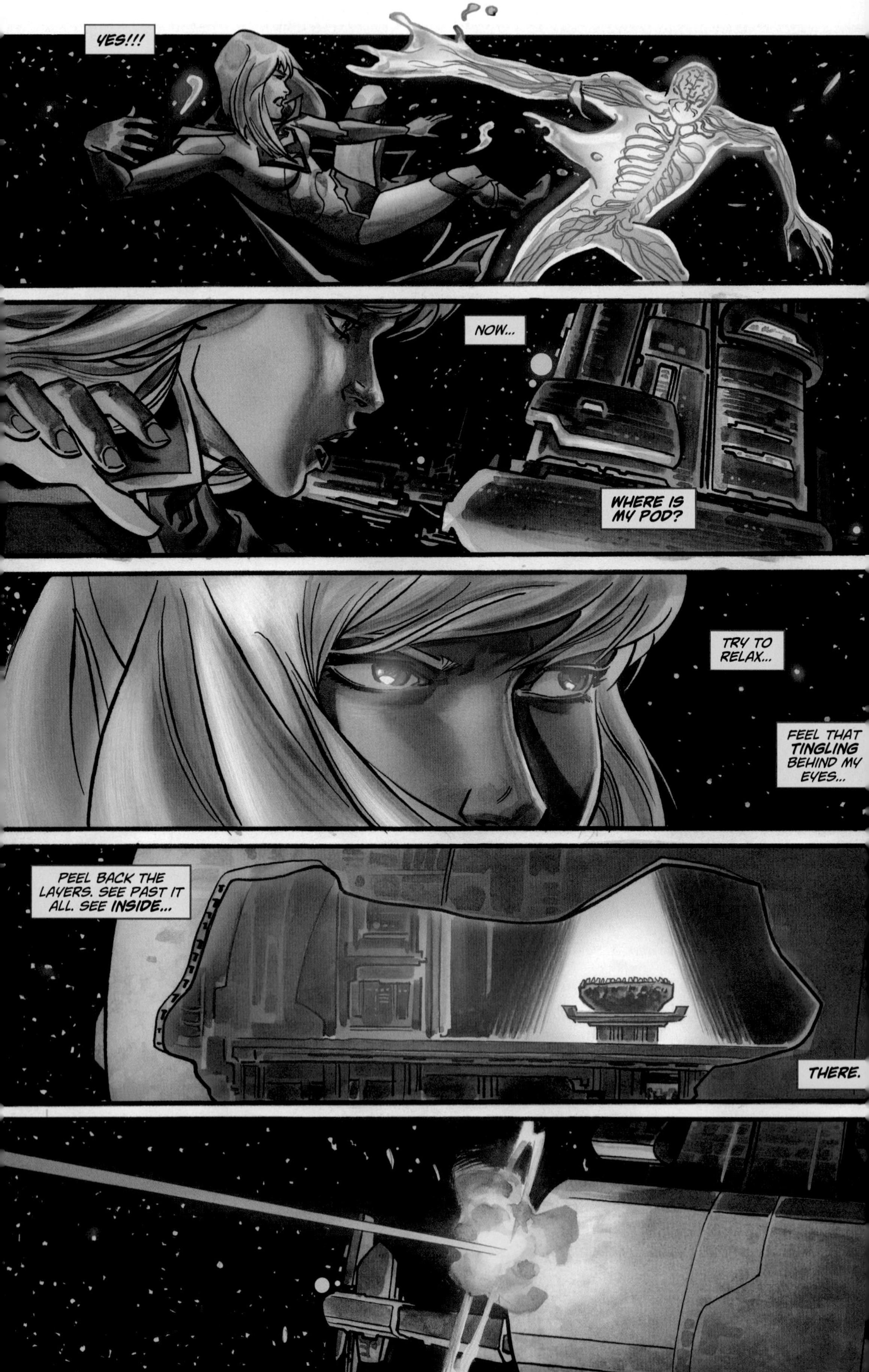
YES!!!
NOW...
WHERE IS MY POD?
TRY TO RELAX...
FEEL THAT TINGLING BEHIND MY EYES...
PEEL BACK THE LAYERS. SEE PAST IT ALL. SEE INSIDE...
THERE.

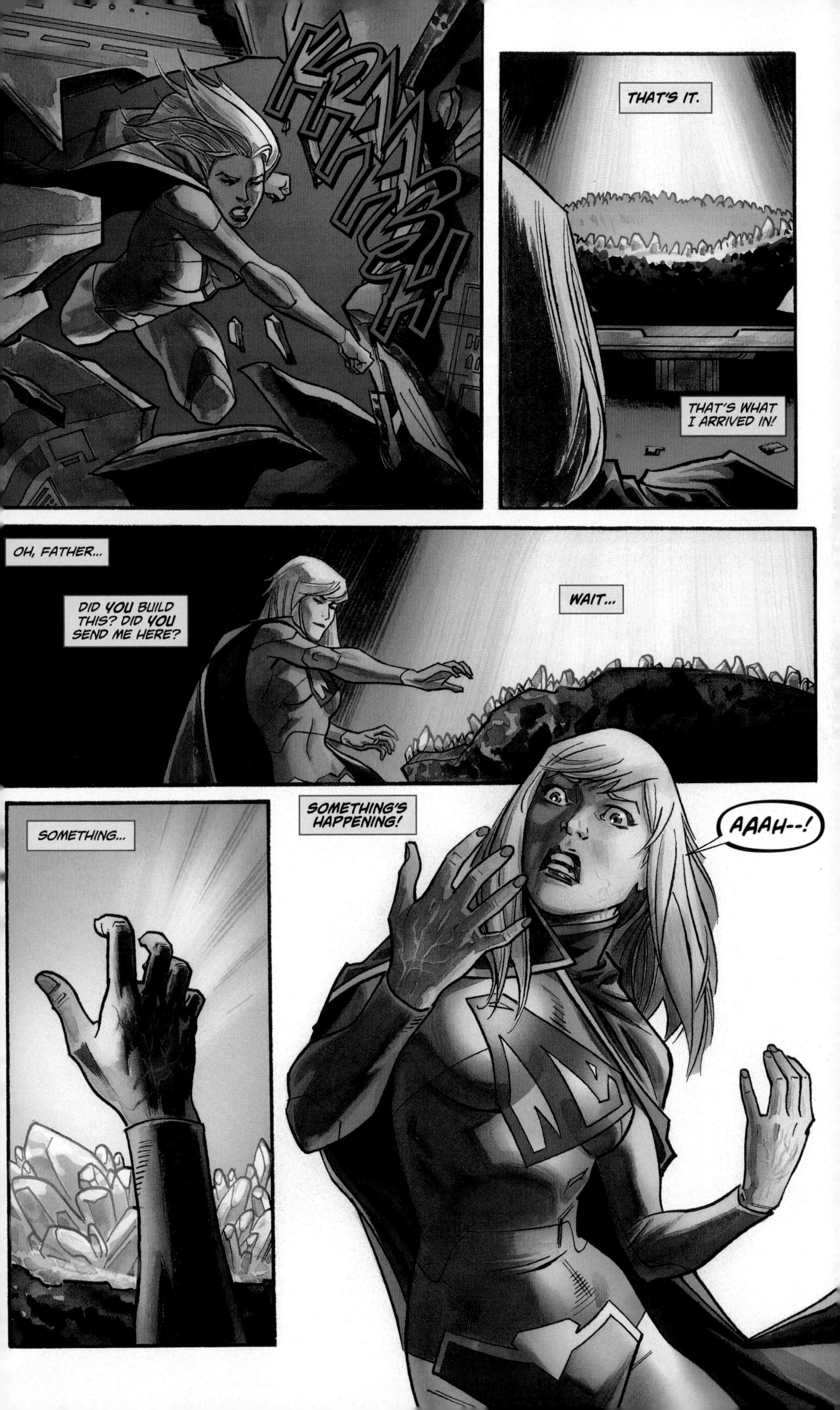

KRAKKSSH
THAT'S IT.
THAT'S WHAT I ARRIVED IN!
OH, FATHER...
DID YOU BUILD THIS? DID YOU SEND ME HERE?
WAIT...
SOMETHING...
SOMETHING'S HAPPENING!
AAAH--!

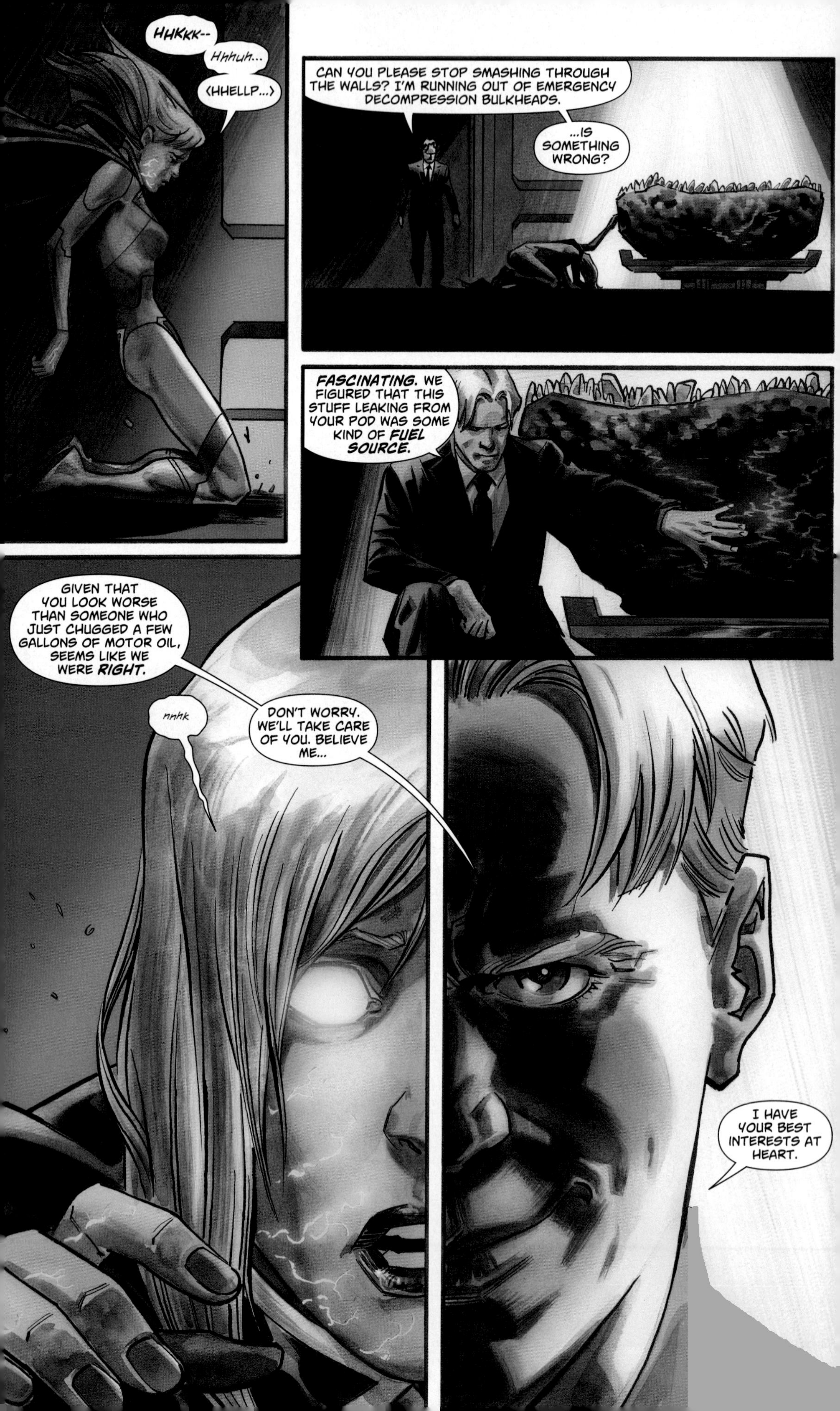
HHKKK--
Hhhuh...
(HHELLP...)
CAN YOU PLEASE STOP SMASHING THROUGH THE WALLS? I'M RUNNING OUT OF EMERGENCY DECOMPRESSION BULKHEADS.
...IS SOMETHING WRONG?
FASCINATING. WE FIGURED THAT THIS STUFF LEAKING FROM YOUR POD WAS SOME KIND OF FUEL SOURCE.
GIVEN THAT YOU LOOK WORSE THAN SOMEONE WHO JUST CHUGGED A FEW GALLONS OF MOTOR OIL, SEEMS LIKE WE WERE RIGHT.
nnhk
DON'T WORRY. WE'LL TAKE CARE OF YOU. BELIEVE ME...
I HAVE YOUR BEST INTERESTS AT HEART.

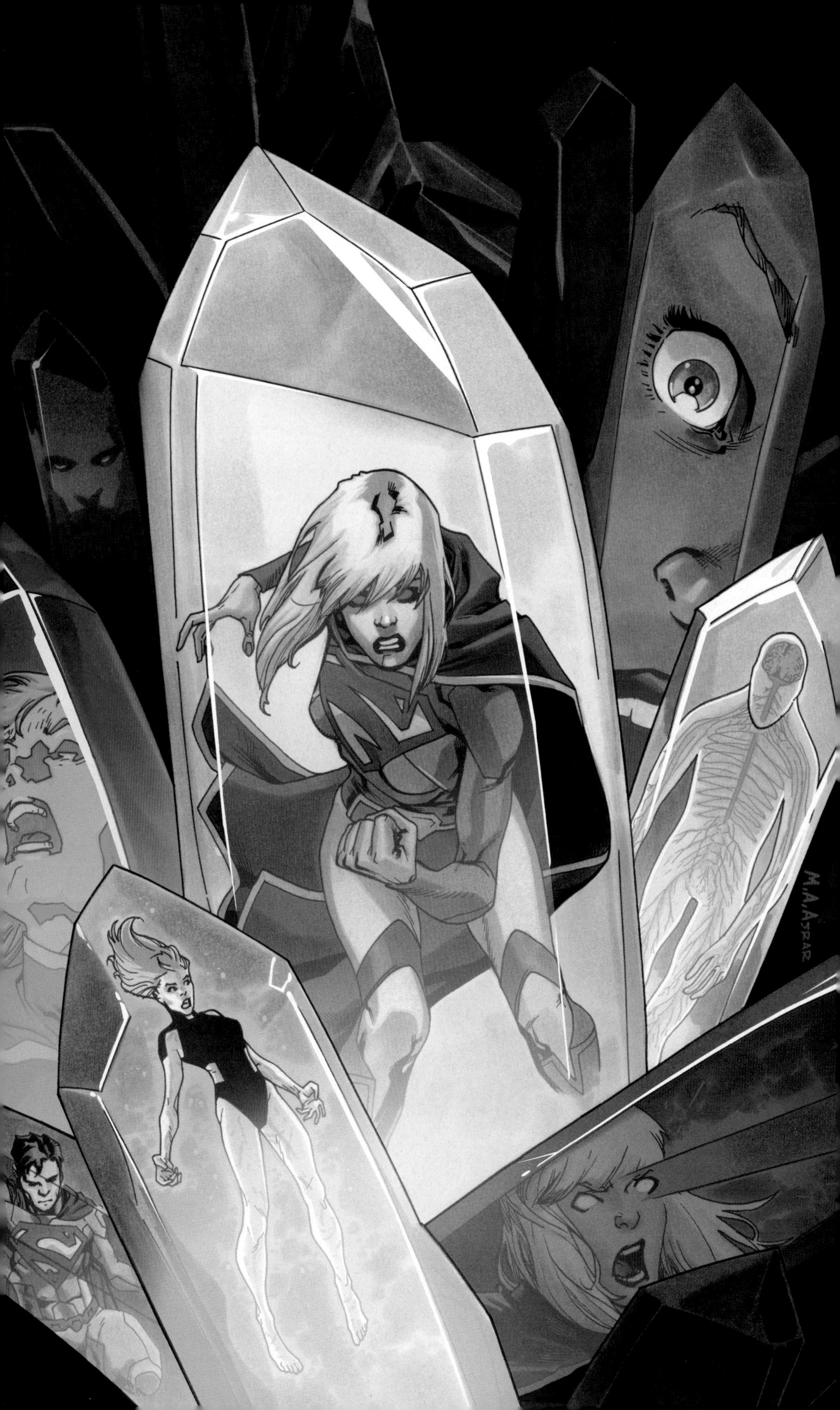

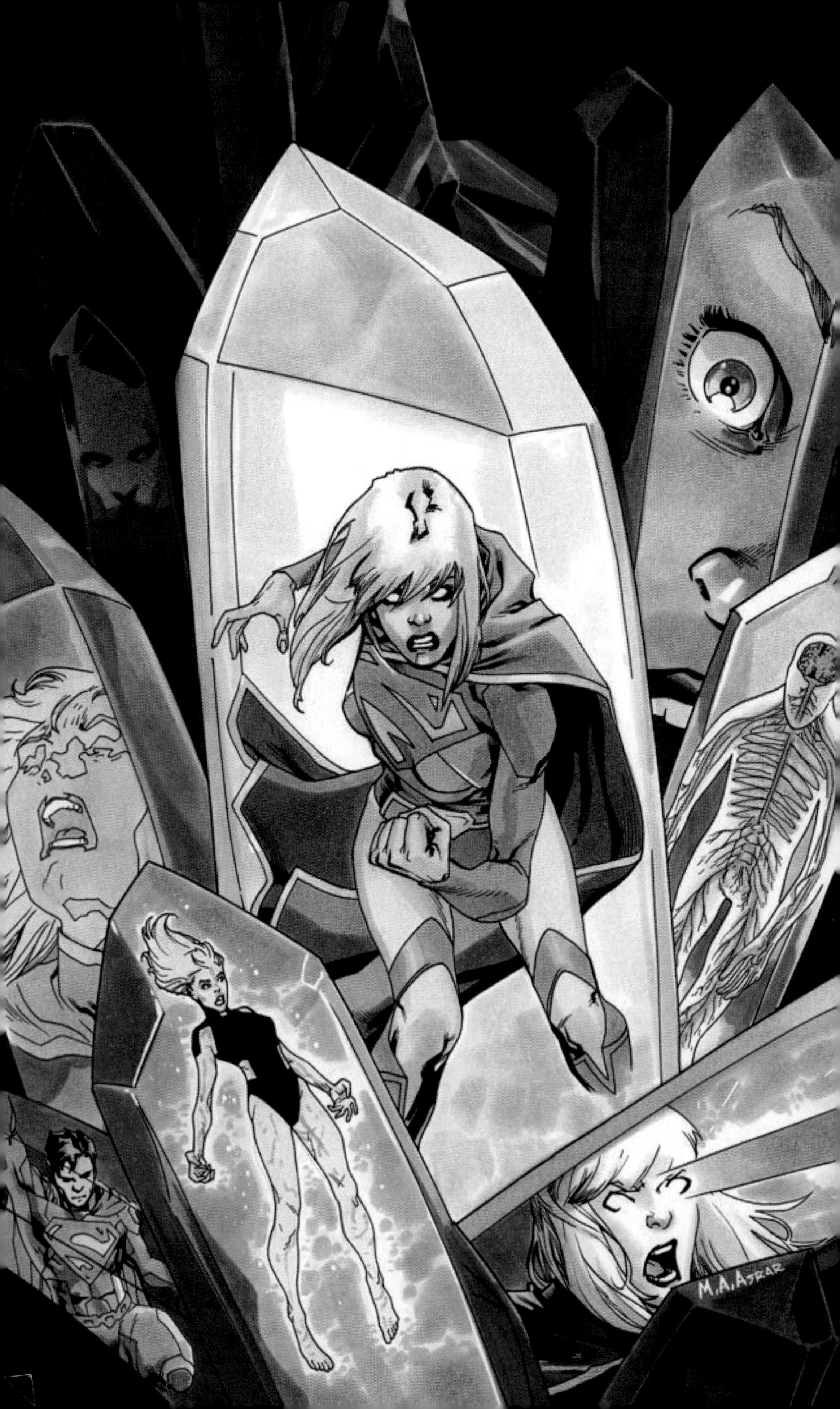
M.A.Asrar

SIR, WE ARE ALREADY **GIGAPASCALS** PAST THE ULTIMATE TENSILE STRENGTH OF ANY MATERIAL KNOWN TO SCIENCE.

C'MON, JUST **SAY** IT, MISS THORN...IT'S INDESTRUCTIBLE!

IT'S NOT CLOTHING. IT'S **ARMOR!**

NOW HOW DO I **REPLICATE** IT? IMAGINE THE POSSIBILITIES FOR EXPLORATION. NO PLANET, NO MOON, NO ENVIRONMENT WOULD BE TOO DANGEROUS IF YOU'RE WEARING A SUIT MADE OF THIS STUFF.

NOT TO MENTION THE SALES ON EARTH. BIKINIS AND BOXER SHORTS. DIAPERS AND DISHTOWELS.

"HOW'S THE REPAIR WORK GOING?"

"UNDER WAY. SIGNIFICANT DAMAGE TO HUB THREE, BUT THE STRUCTURAL INTEGRITY OF THE STATION ITSELF REMAINS SOUND."

"WHAT ABOUT **THE BRAIN?**"

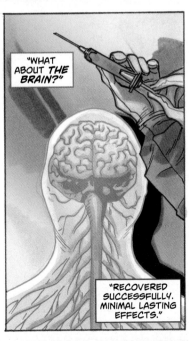

"RECOVERED SUCCESSFULLY. MINIMAL LASTING EFFECTS."

GOOD. I'D BE DISAPPOINTED IF IT COULDN'T HANDLE A **TEENAGE GIRL.**

THANKFULLY...

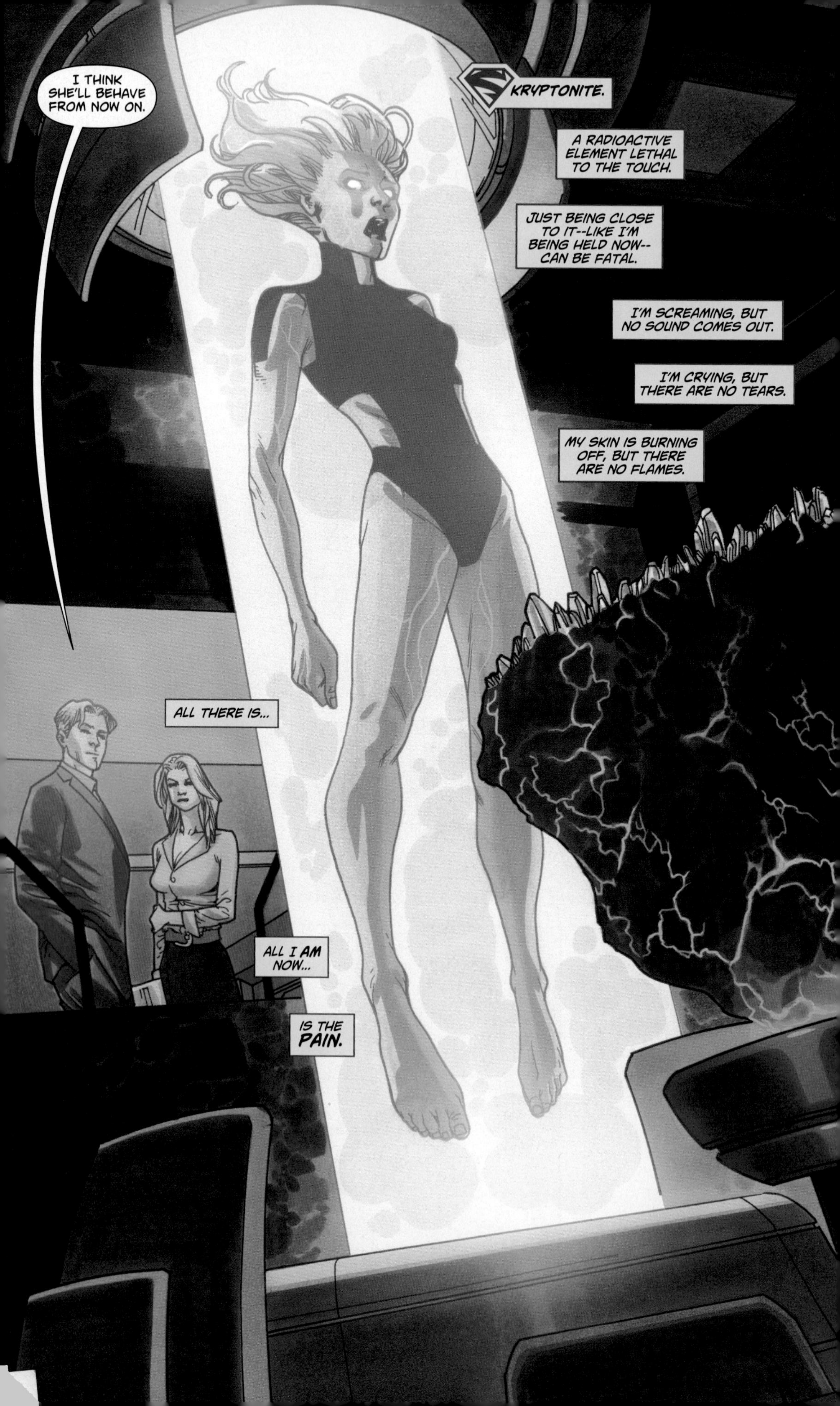

I THINK SHE'LL BEHAVE FROM NOW ON.
KRYPTONITE.
A RADIOACTIVE ELEMENT LETHAL TO THE TOUCH.
JUST BEING CLOSE TO IT--LIKE I'M BEING HELD NOW--CAN BE FATAL.
I'M SCREAMING, BUT NO SOUND COMES OUT.
I'M CRYING, BUT THERE ARE NO TEARS.
MY SKIN IS BURNING OFF, BUT THERE ARE NO FLAMES.
ALL THERE IS...
ALL I AM NOW...
IS THE PAIN.

WHAT NEXT FOR HER, SIR?

WE FIND OUT WHAT MAKES HER *TICK*.

...IT MIGHT GET *MESSY*.

JACOBS! I HEARD WHAT OUR CUTE LITTLE PRISONER DID TO YOUR *MECH* IN SIBERIA. YOU COMING TO GET SOME PAYBACK?

KRAKK

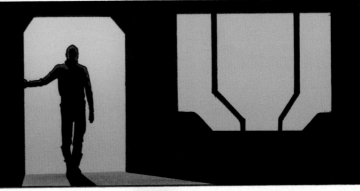

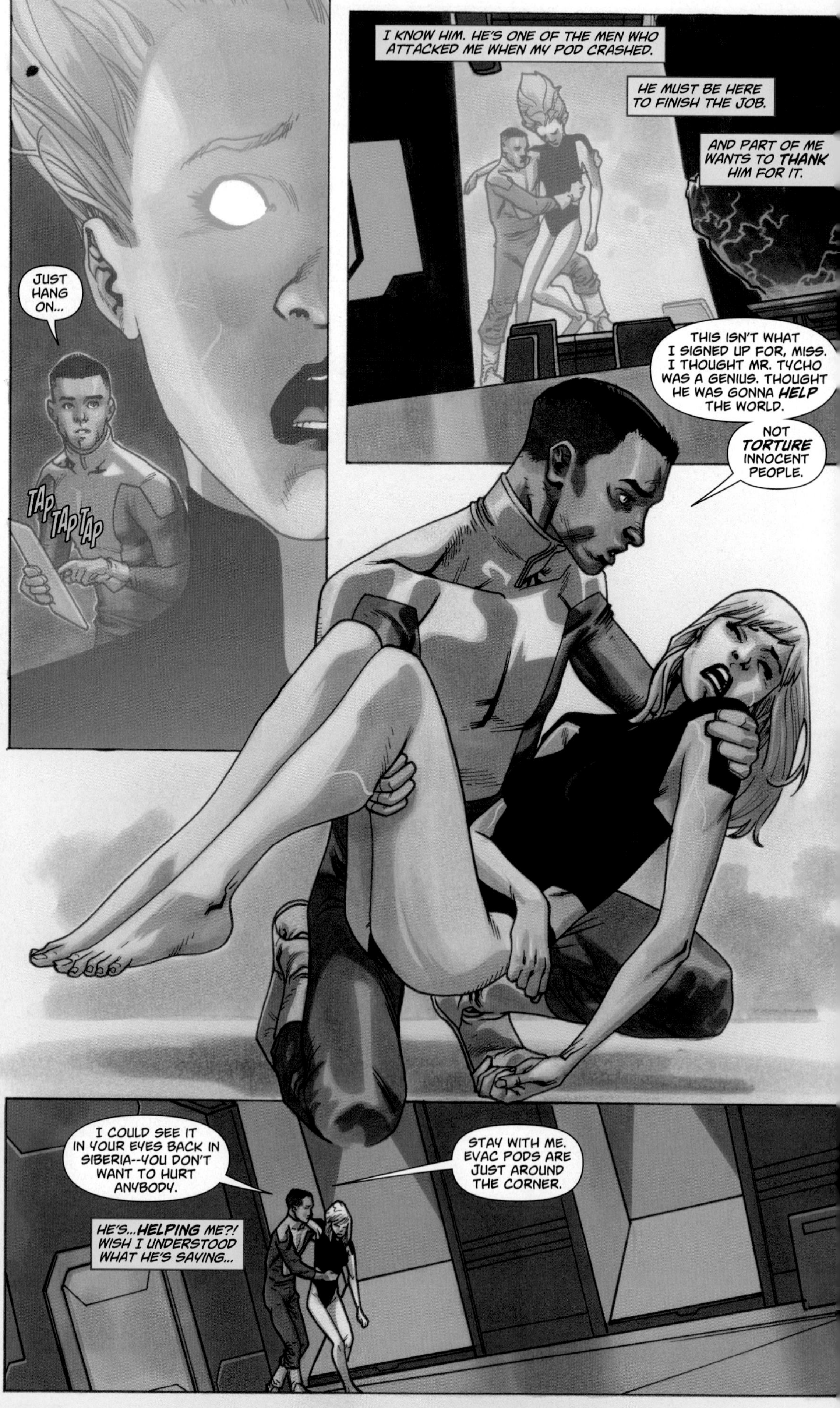

JUST HANG ON...
TAP TAP TAP
I KNOW HIM. HE'S ONE OF THE MEN WHO ATTACKED ME WHEN MY POD CRASHED.
HE MUST BE HERE TO FINISH THE JOB.
AND PART OF ME WANTS TO THANK HIM FOR IT.
THIS ISN'T WHAT I SIGNED UP FOR, MISS. I THOUGHT MR. TYCHO WAS A GENIUS. THOUGHT HE WAS GONNA HELP THE WORLD.
NOT TORTURE INNOCENT PEOPLE.
I COULD SEE IT IN YOUR EYES BACK IN SIBERIA--YOU DON'T WANT TO HURT ANYBODY.
STAY WITH ME. EVAC PODS ARE JUST AROUND THE CORNER.
HE'S...HELPING ME?! WISH I UNDERSTOOD WHAT HE'S SAYING...

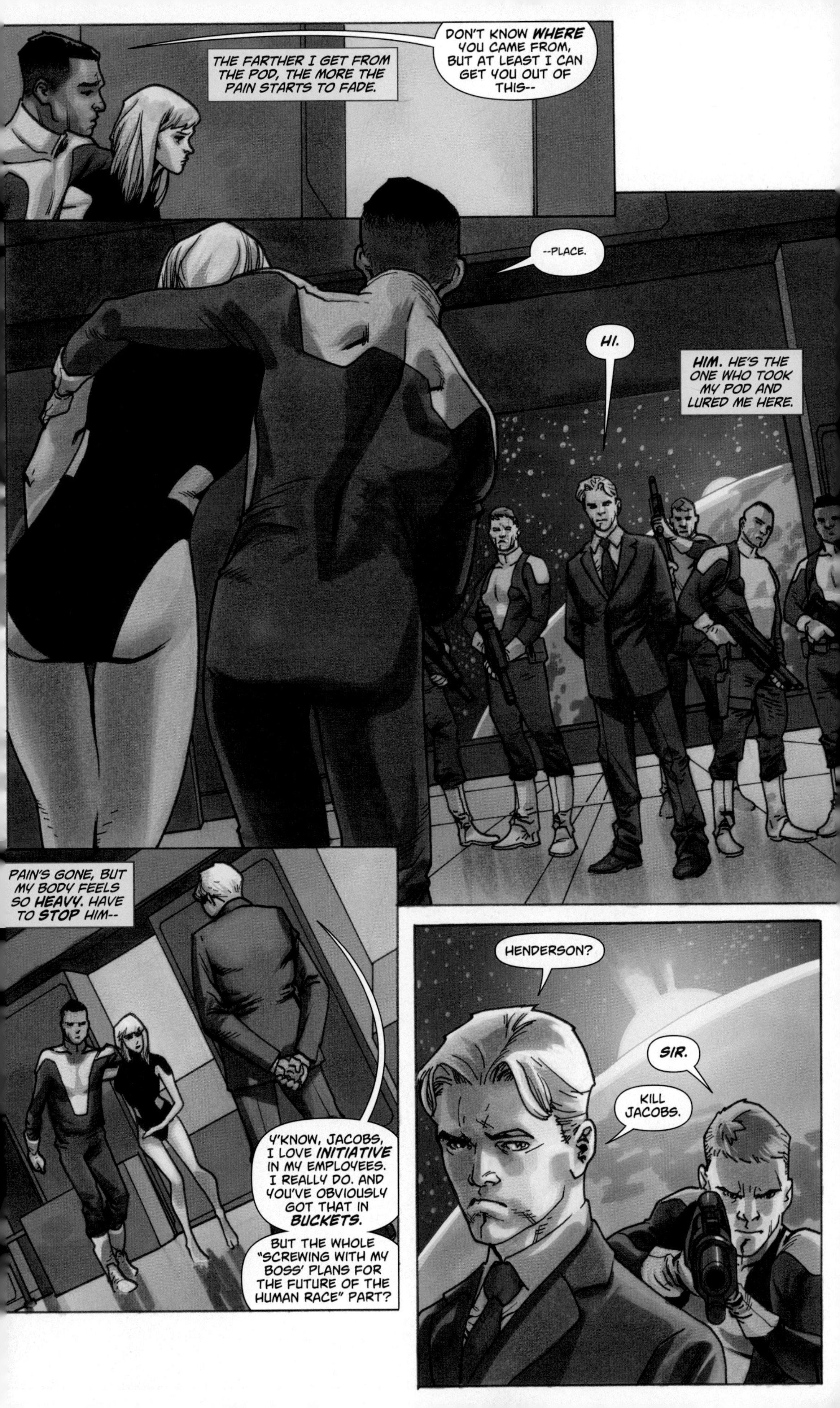
THE FARTHER I GET FROM THE POD, THE MORE THE PAIN STARTS TO FADE.
DON'T KNOW WHERE YOU CAME FROM, BUT AT LEAST I CAN GET YOU OUT OF THIS--
--PLACE.
HI.
HIM. HE'S THE ONE WHO TOOK MY POD AND LURED ME HERE.
PAIN'S GONE, BUT MY BODY FEELS SO HEAVY. HAVE TO STOP HIM--
Y'KNOW, JACOBS, I LOVE INITIATIVE IN MY EMPLOYEES. I REALLY DO. AND YOU'VE OBVIOUSLY GOT THAT IN BUCKETS.
BUT THE WHOLE "SCREWING WITH MY BOSS' PLANS FOR THE FUTURE OF THE HUMAN RACE" PART?
HENDERSON?
SIR.
KILL JACOBS.

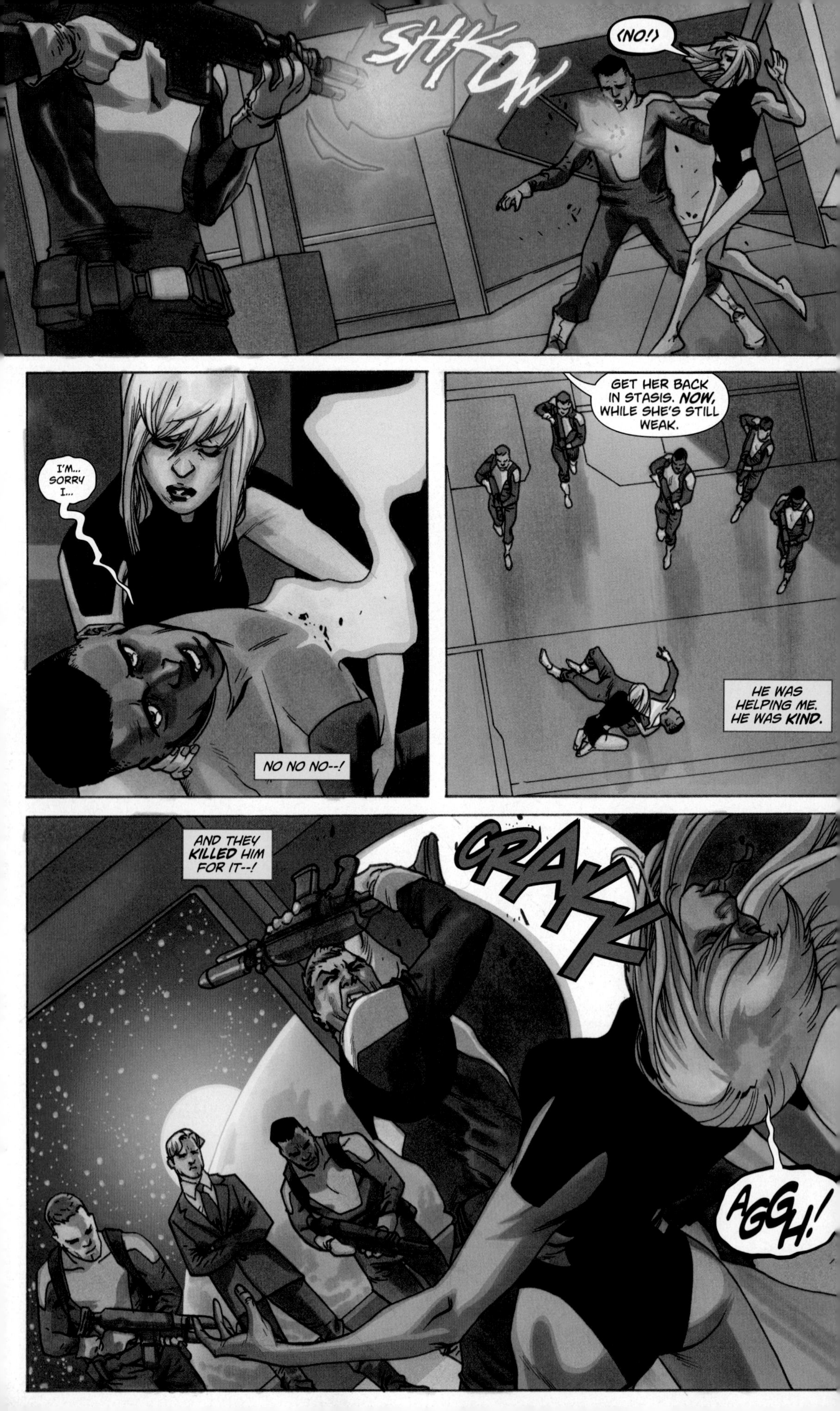
SHKOW
(NO!)
I'M... SORRY I...
NO NO NO--!
GET HER BACK IN STASIS. NOW, WHILE SHE'S STILL WEAK.
HE WAS HELPING ME. HE WAS KIND.
AND THEY KILLED HIM FOR IT--!
CRAKK
AGGH!

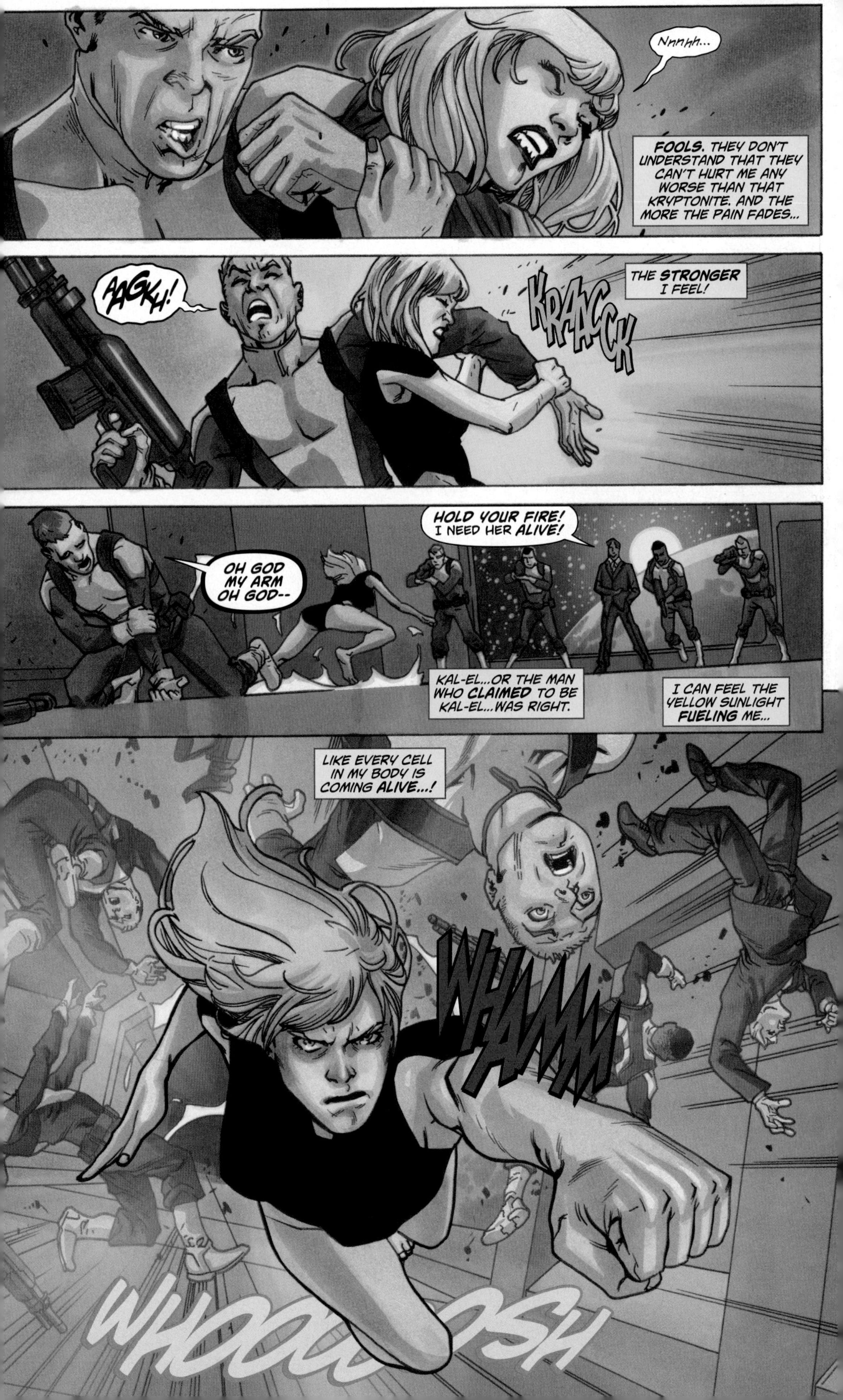
Nnnhh...
FOOLS. THEY DON'T UNDERSTAND THAT THEY CAN'T HURT ME ANY WORSE THAN THAT KRYPTONITE. AND THE MORE THE PAIN FADES...
AAGKH!
KRAACCK
THE STRONGER I FEEL!
HOLD YOUR FIRE! I NEED HER ALIVE!
OH GOD MY ARM OH GOD--
KAL-EL...OR THE MAN WHO CLAIMED TO BE KAL-EL...WAS RIGHT.
I CAN FEEL THE YELLOW SUNLIGHT FUELING ME...
LIKE EVERY CELL IN MY BODY IS COMING ALIVE...!
WHAMM
WHOOOOOSH

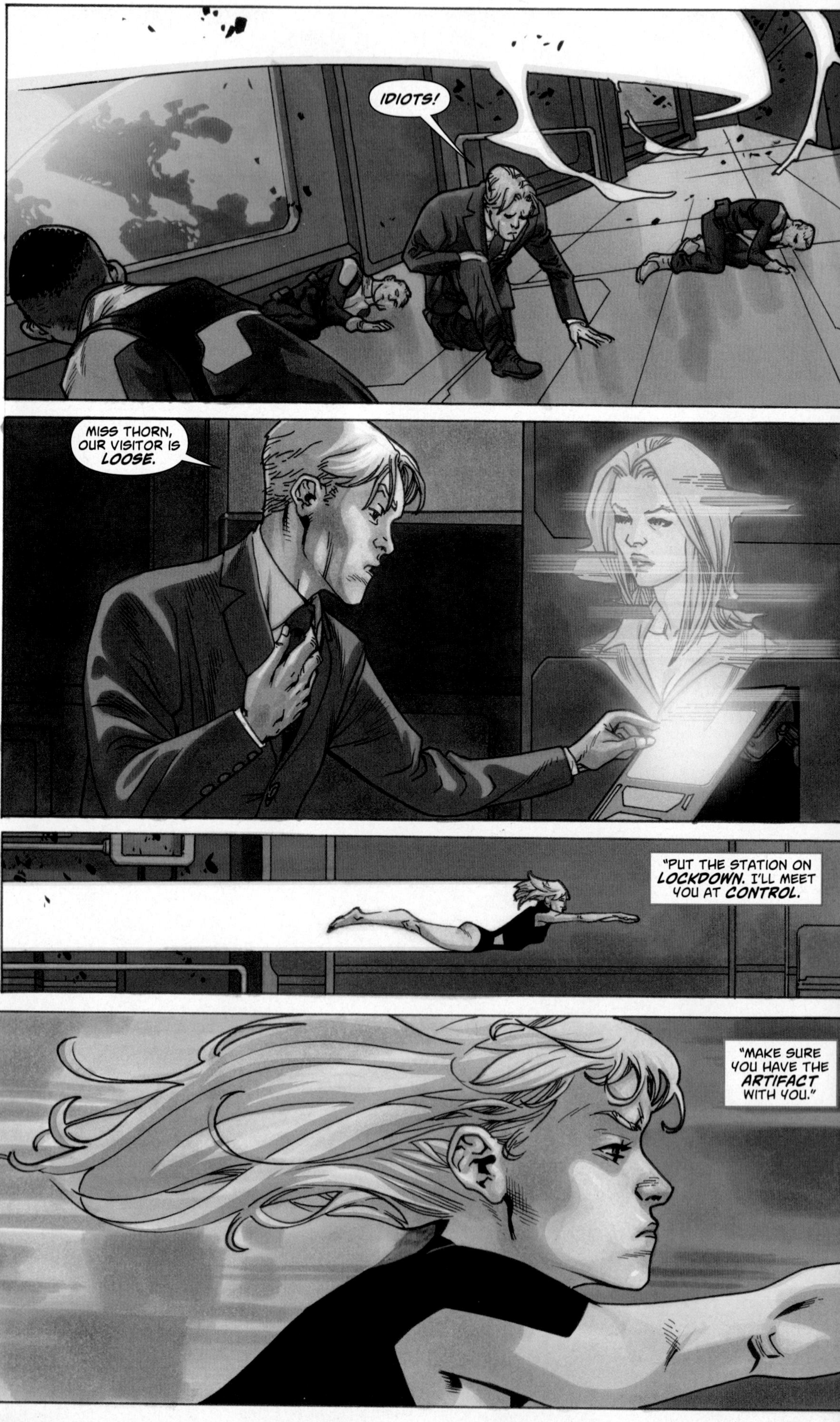
IDIOTS!
MISS THORN, OUR VISITOR IS LOOSE.
"PUT THE STATION ON LOCKDOWN. I'LL MEET YOU AT CONTROL.
"MAKE SURE YOU HAVE THE ARTIFACT WITH YOU."

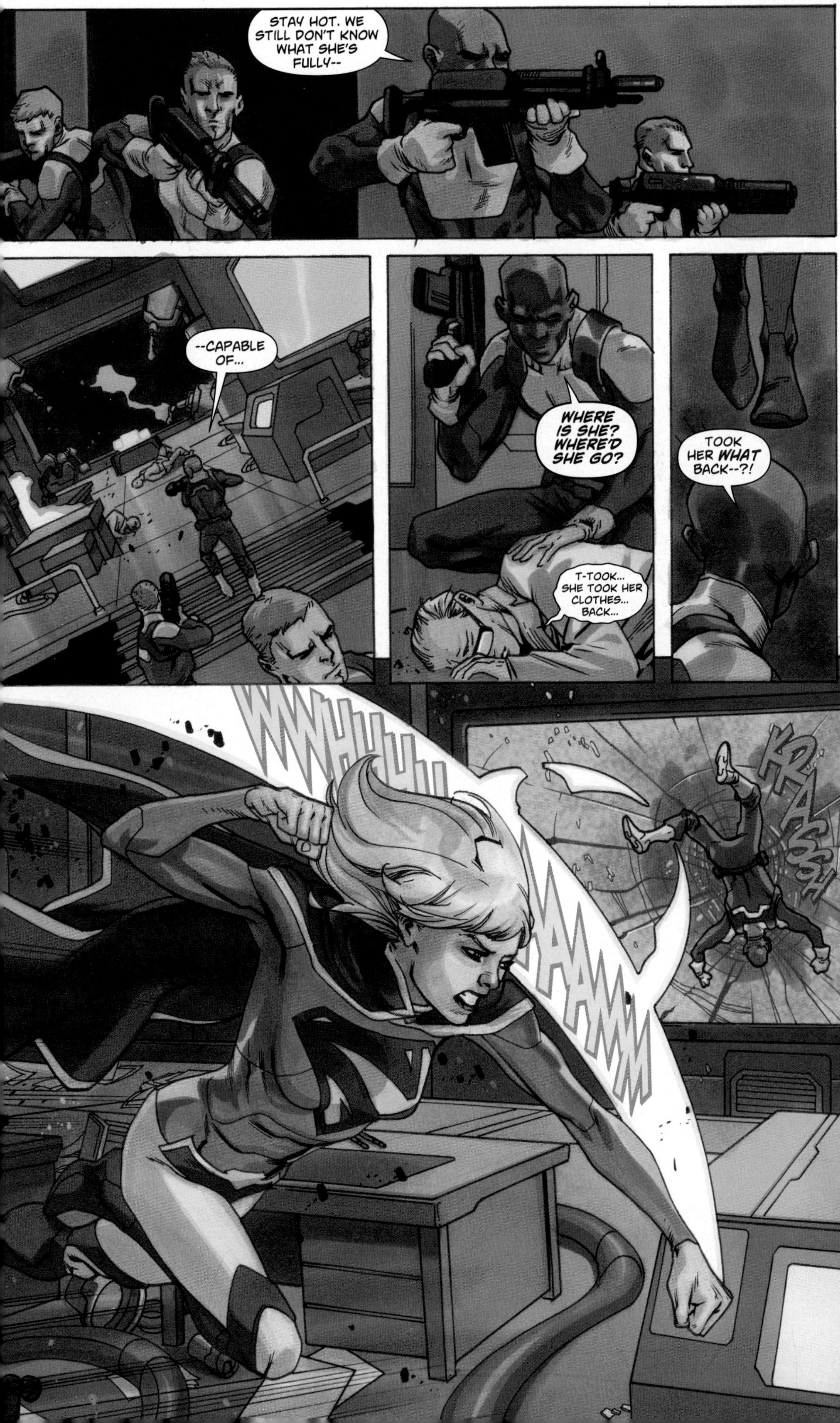
STAY HOT. WE STILL DON'T KNOW WHAT SHE'S FULLY--
--CAPABLE OF...
WHERE IS SHE? WHERE'D SHE GO?
T-TOOK... SHE TOOK HER CLOTHES... BACK...
TOOK HER WHAT BACK--?!
WWHUUU
KRASSH
BRAAMM

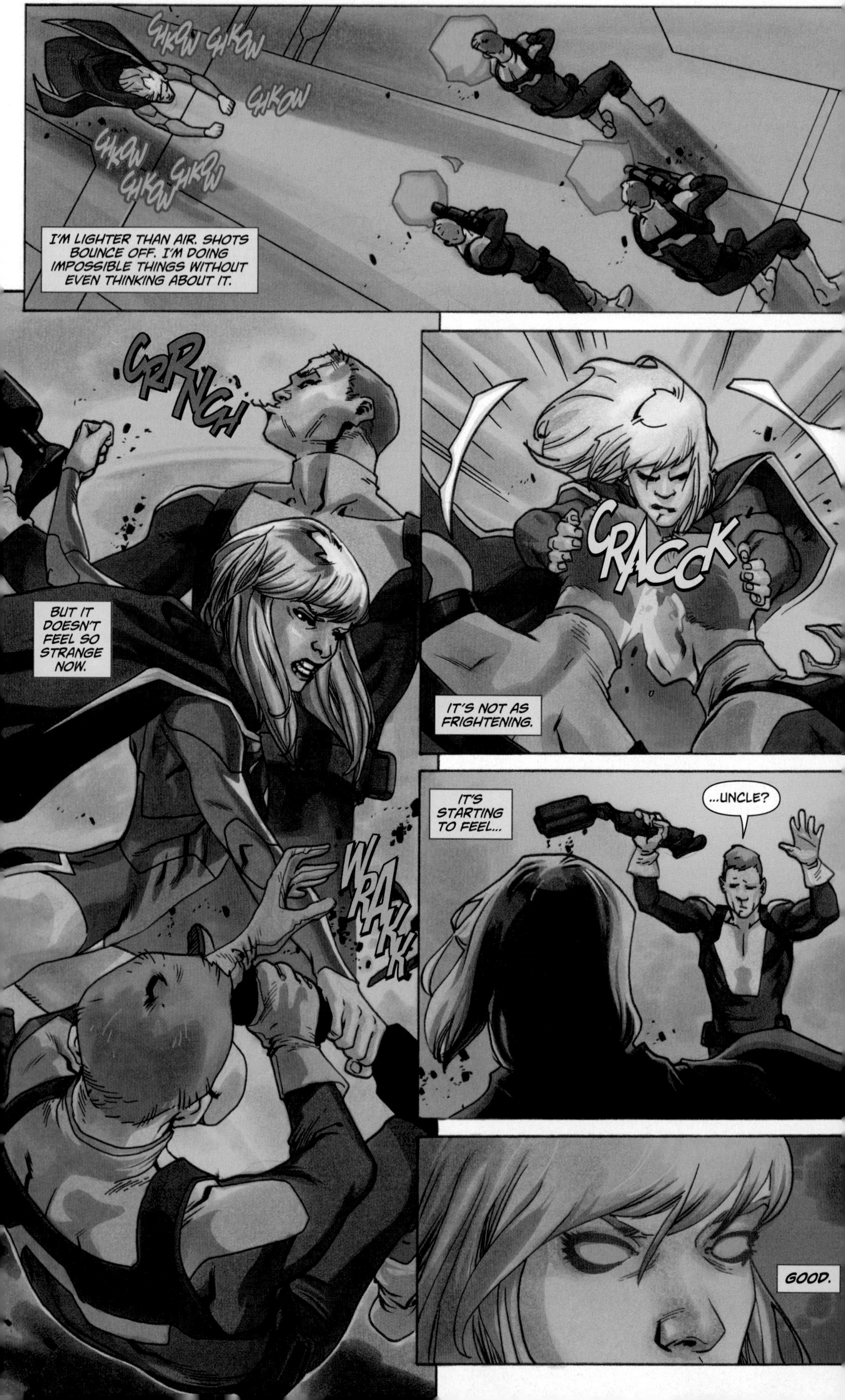
CHKOW CHKOW
CHKOW
CHKOW
CHKOW CHKOW
I'M LIGHTER THAN AIR. SHOTS BOUNCE OFF. I'M DOING IMPOSSIBLE THINGS WITHOUT EVEN THINKING ABOUT IT.
CRRNCH
BUT IT DOESN'T FEEL SO STRANGE NOW.
WRAKK
CRACCK
IT'S NOT AS FRIGHTENING.
IT'S STARTING TO FEEL...
...UNCLE?
GOOD.

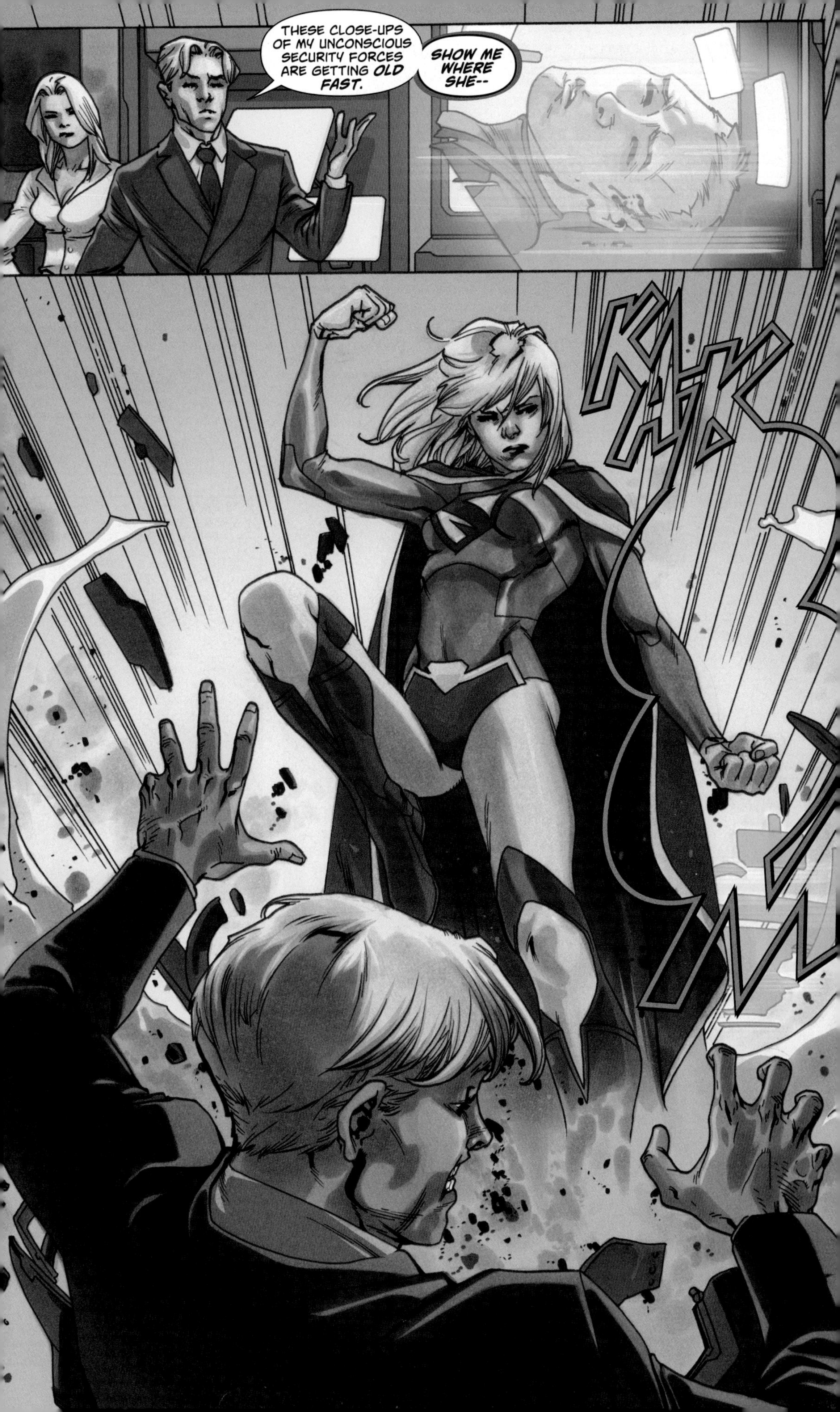
THESE CLOSE-UPS OF MY UNCONSCIOUS SECURITY FORCES ARE GETTING OLD FAST.
SHOW ME WHERE SHE--

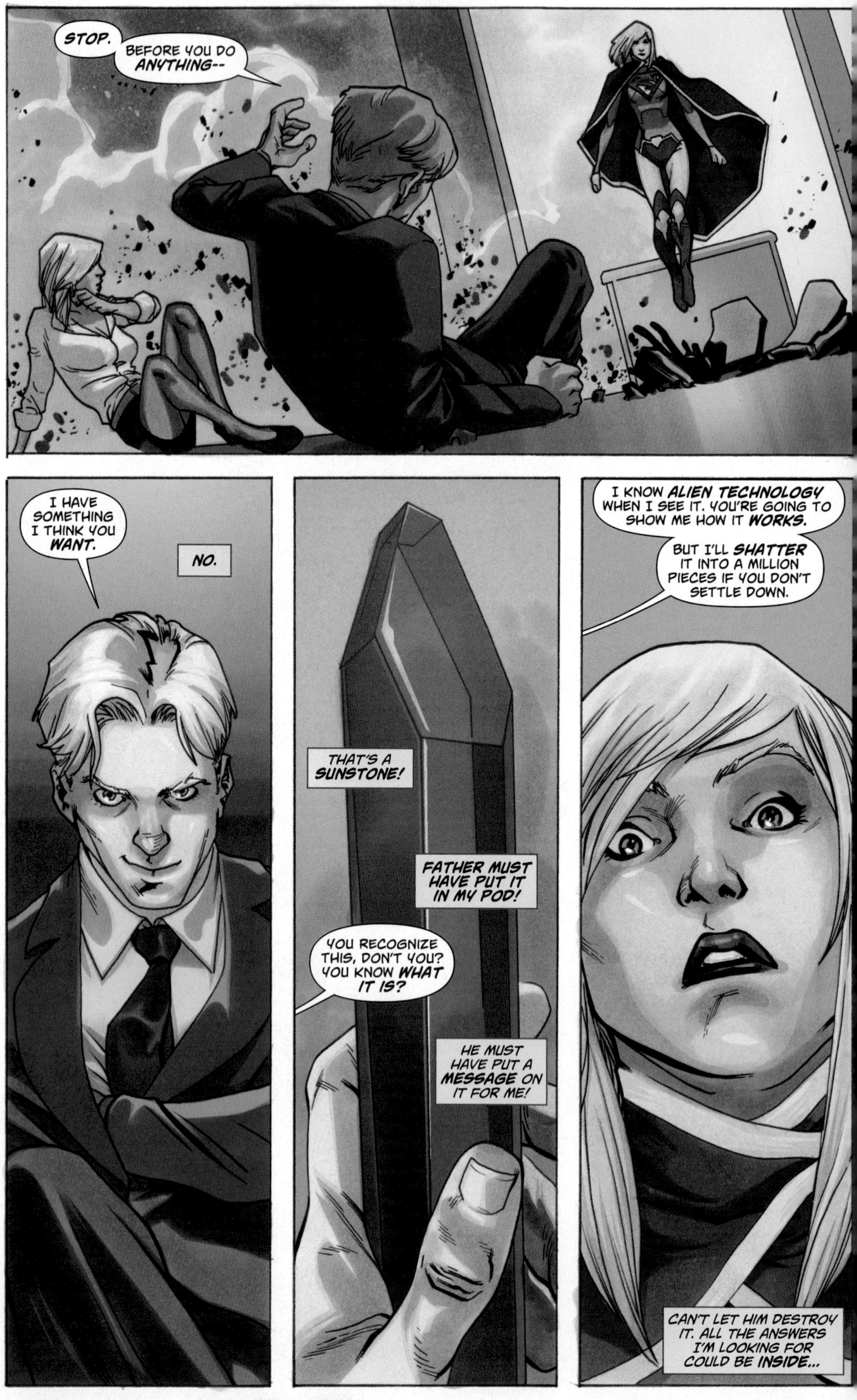
STOP.
BEFORE YOU DO ANYTHING--
I HAVE SOMETHING I THINK YOU WANT.
NO.
THAT'S A SUNSTONE!
FATHER MUST HAVE PUT IT IN MY POD!
YOU RECOGNIZE THIS, DON'T YOU? YOU KNOW WHAT IT IS?
HE MUST HAVE PUT A MESSAGE ON IT FOR ME!
I KNOW ALIEN TECHNOLOGY WHEN I SEE IT. YOU'RE GOING TO SHOW ME HOW IT WORKS.
BUT I'LL SHATTER IT INTO A MILLION PIECES IF YOU DON'T SETTLE DOWN.
CAN'T LET HIM DESTROY IT. ALL THE ANSWERS I'M LOOKING FOR COULD BE INSIDE...

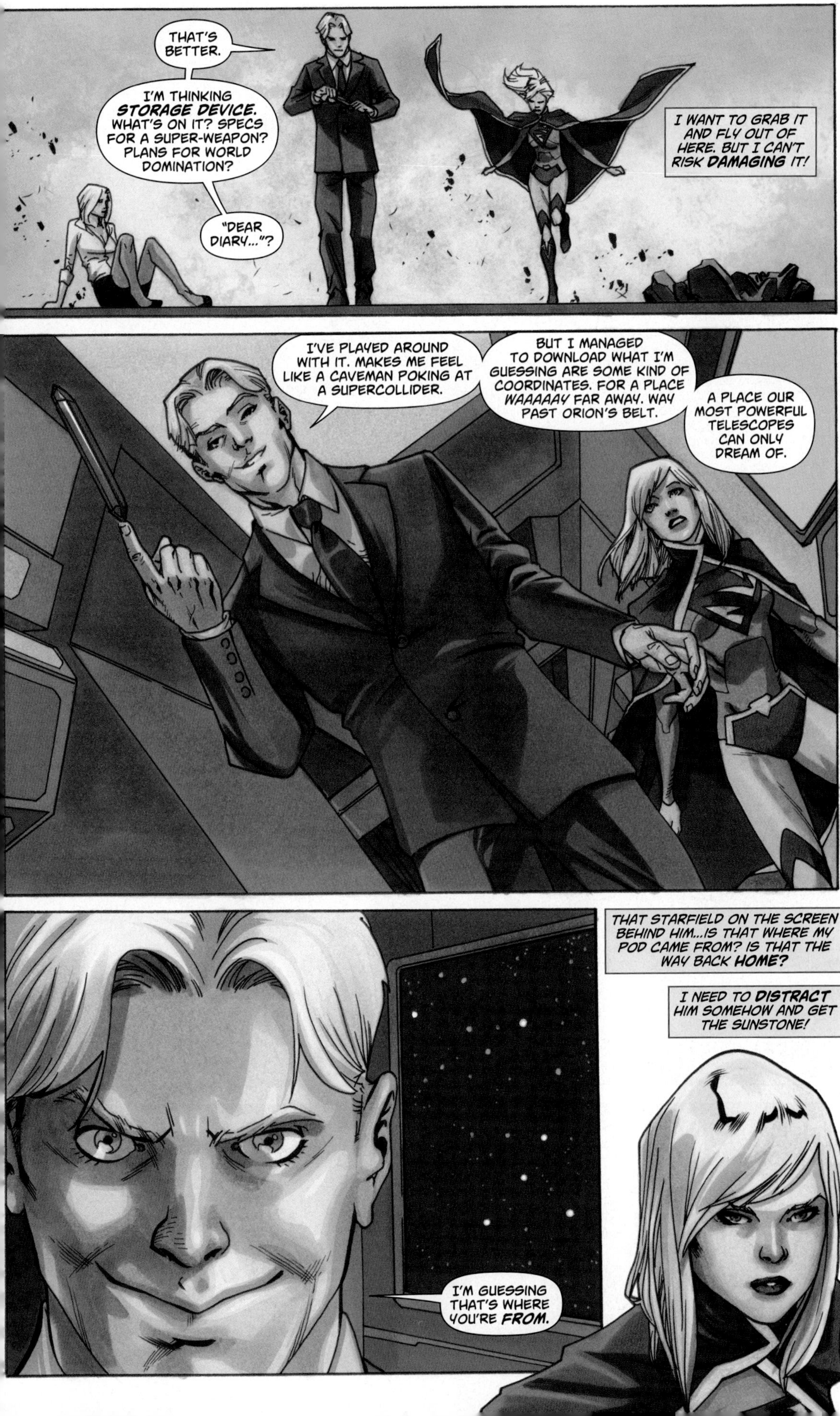
THAT'S BETTER.
I'M THINKING **STORAGE DEVICE.** WHAT'S ON IT? SPECS FOR A SUPER-WEAPON? PLANS FOR WORLD DOMINATION?
"DEAR DIARY..."?
*I WANT TO GRAB IT AND FLY OUT OF HERE. BUT I CAN'T RISK **DAMAGING** IT!*
I'VE PLAYED AROUND WITH IT. MAKES ME FEEL LIKE A CAVEMAN POKING AT A SUPERCOLLIDER.
BUT I MANAGED TO DOWNLOAD WHAT I'M GUESSING ARE SOME KIND OF COORDINATES. FOR A PLACE WAAAAAAY FAR AWAY. WAY PAST ORION'S BELT.
A PLACE OUR MOST POWERFUL TELESCOPES CAN ONLY DREAM OF.
*THAT STARFIELD ON THE SCREEN BEHIND HIM...IS THAT WHERE MY POD CAME FROM? IS THAT THE WAY BACK **HOME?***
*I NEED TO **DISTRACT** HIM SOMEHOW AND GET THE SUNSTONE!*
I'M GUESSING THAT'S WHERE YOU'RE **FROM.**

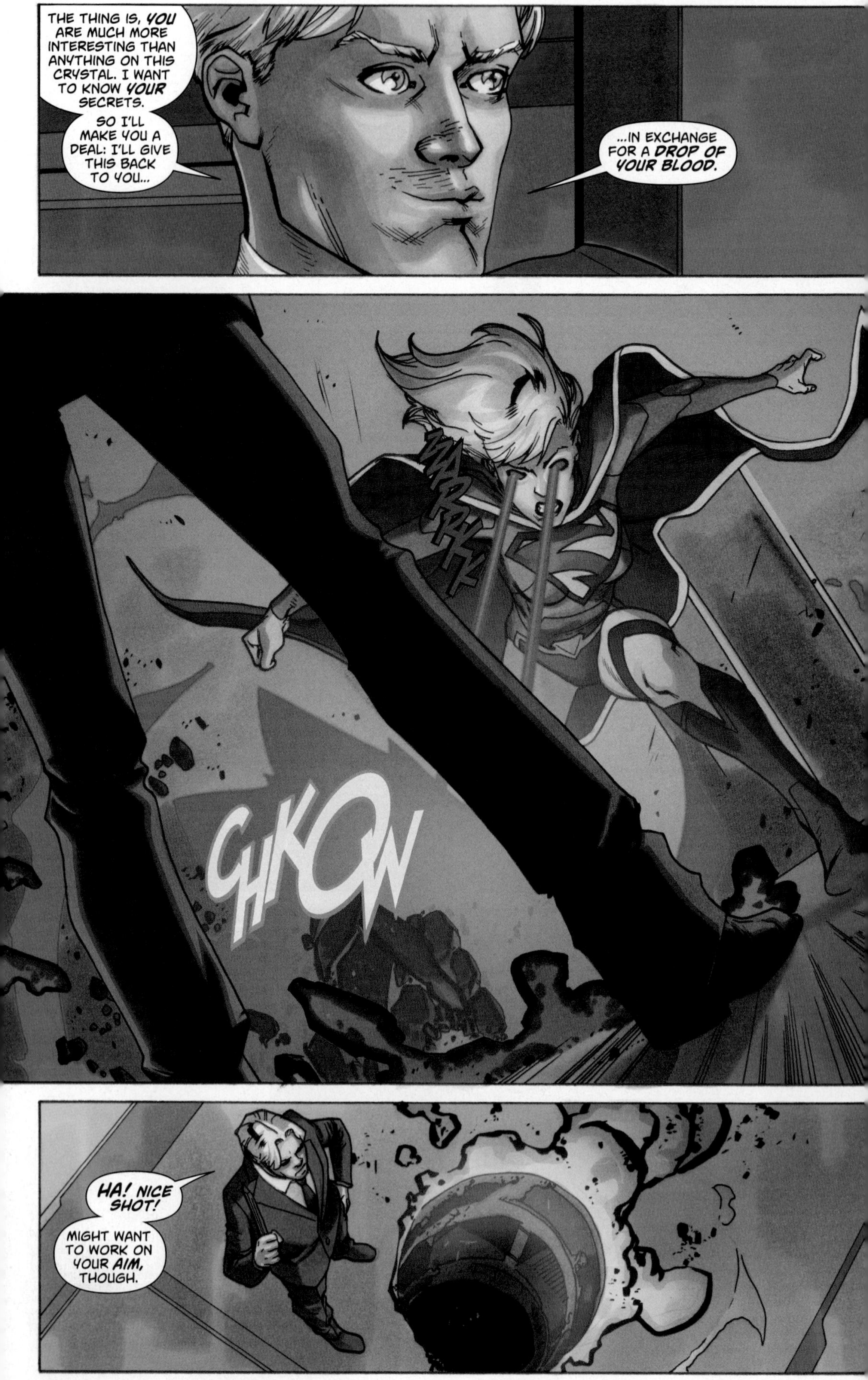
THE THING IS, *YOU* ARE MUCH MORE INTERESTING THAN ANYTHING ON THIS CRYSTAL. I WANT TO KNOW *YOUR* SECRETS.
SO I'LL MAKE YOU A DEAL: I'LL GIVE THIS BACK TO YOU...
...IN EXCHANGE FOR A *DROP OF YOUR BLOOD*.
CHKOW
HA! NICE SHOT!
MIGHT WANT TO WORK ON YOUR *AIM*, THOUGH.

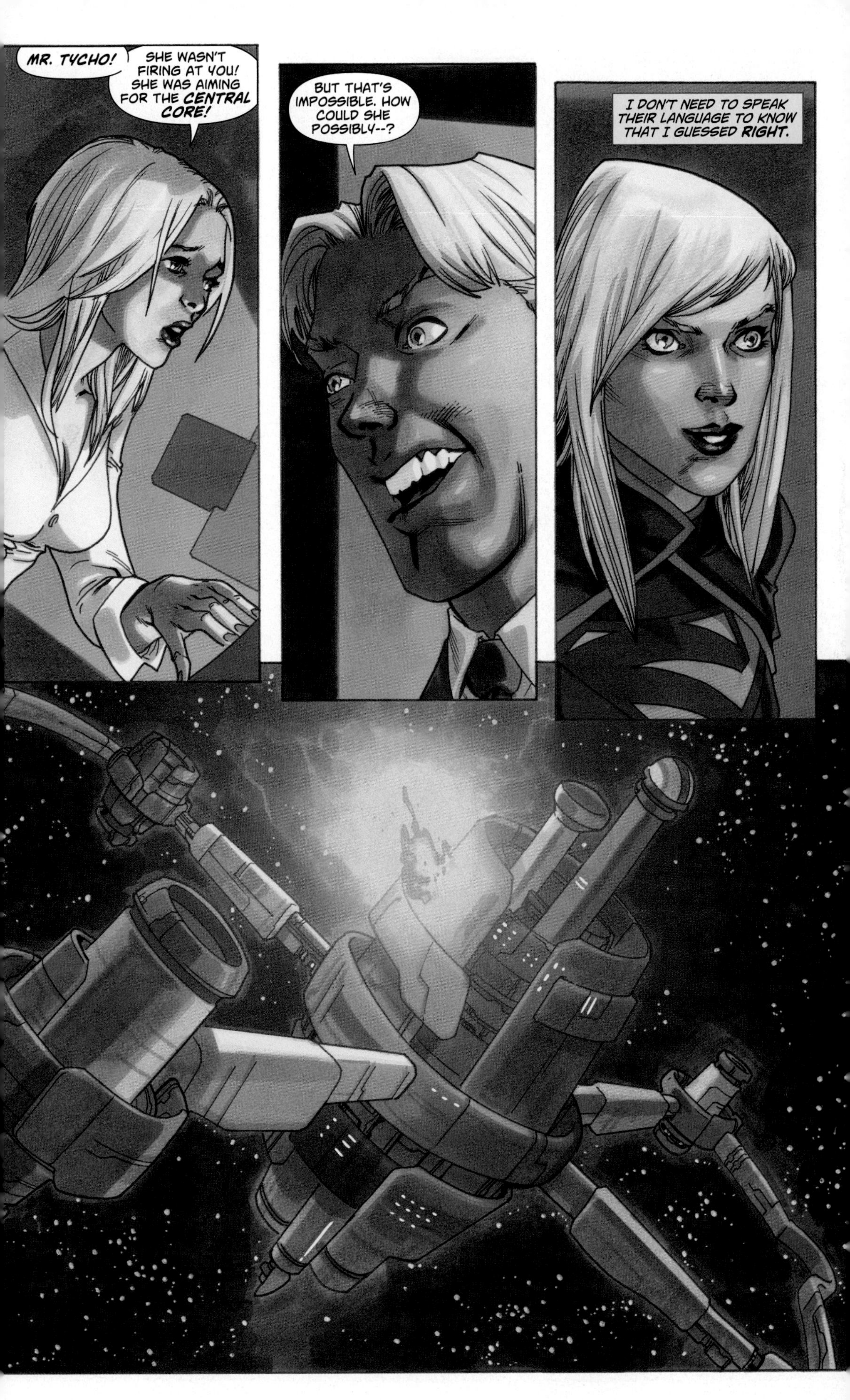
MR. TYCHO!
SHE WASN'T FIRING AT YOU! SHE WAS AIMING FOR THE CENTRAL CORE!
BUT THAT'S IMPOSSIBLE. HOW COULD SHE POSSIBLY--?
I DON'T NEED TO SPEAK THEIR LANGUAGE TO KNOW THAT I GUESSED RIGHT.

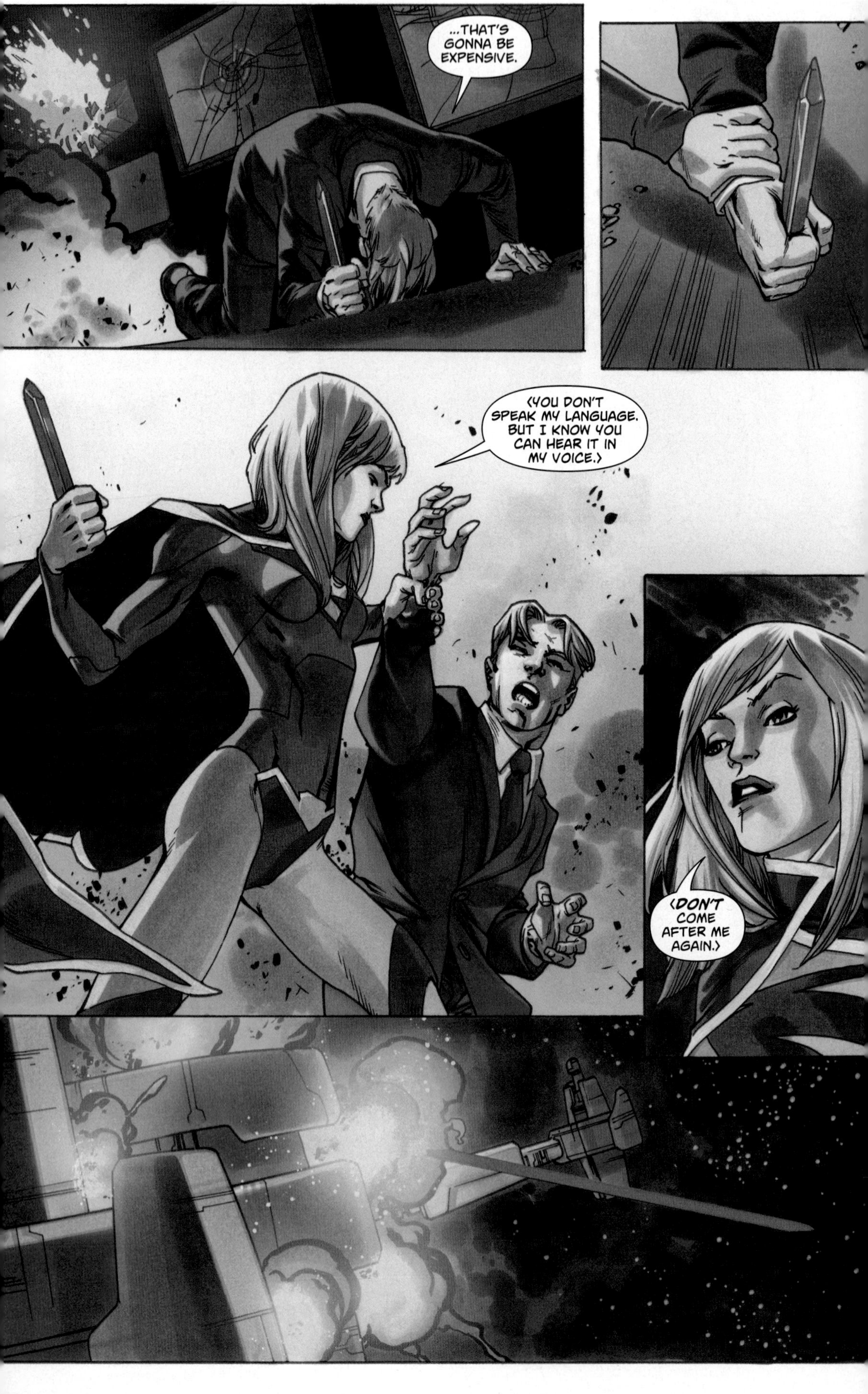
...THAT'S GONNA BE EXPENSIVE.
‹YOU DON'T SPEAK MY LANGUAGE. BUT I KNOW YOU CAN HEAR IT IN MY VOICE.›
‹DON'T COME AFTER ME AGAIN.›

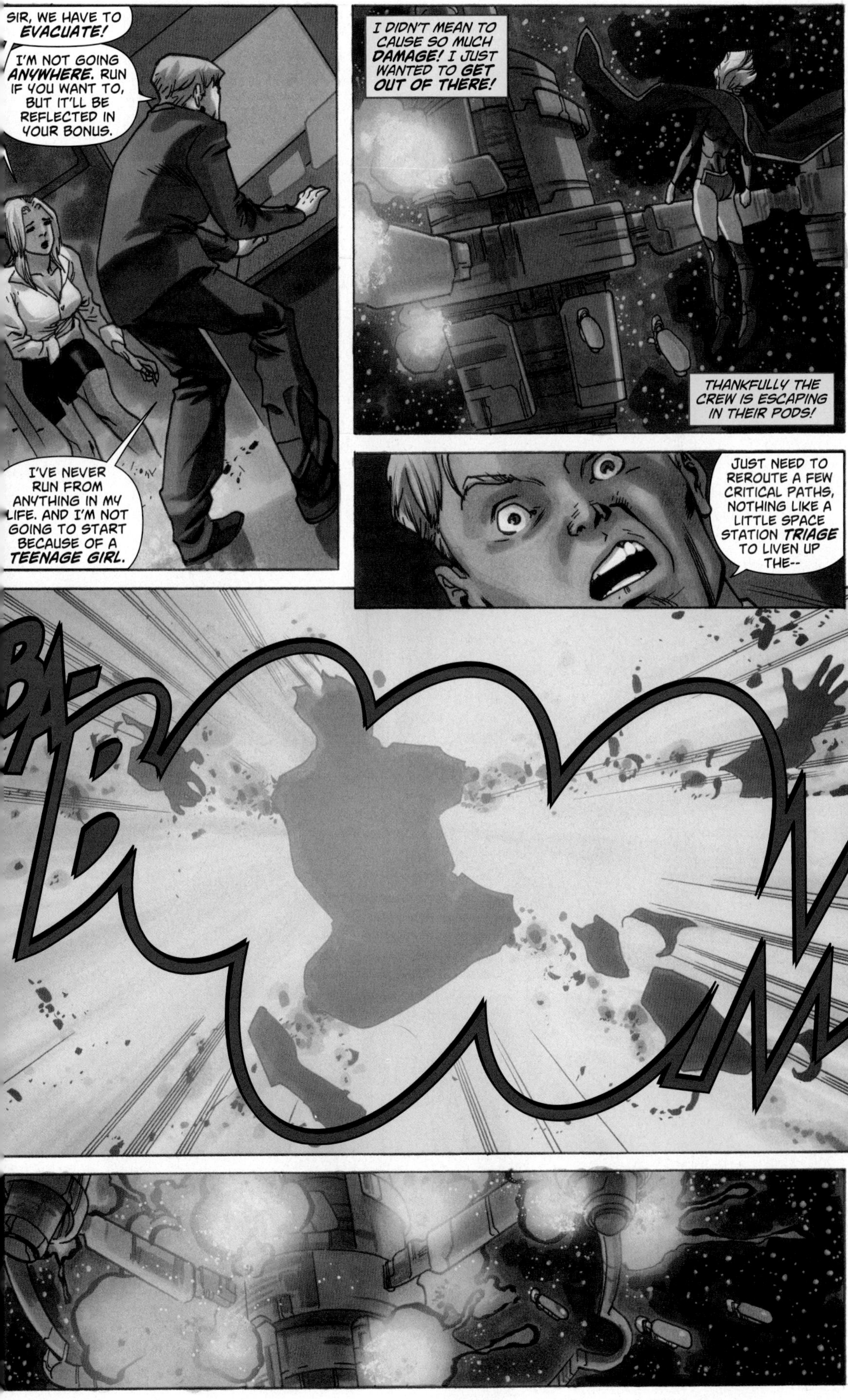
SIR, WE HAVE TO EVACUATE!
I'M NOT GOING ANYWHERE. RUN IF YOU WANT TO, BUT IT'LL BE REFLECTED IN YOUR BONUS.
I'VE NEVER RUN FROM ANYTHING IN MY LIFE. AND I'M NOT GOING TO START BECAUSE OF A TEENAGE GIRL.
I DIDN'T MEAN TO CAUSE SO MUCH DAMAGE! I JUST WANTED TO GET OUT OF THERE!
THANKFULLY THE CREW IS ESCAPING IN THEIR PODS!
JUST NEED TO REROUTE A FEW CRITICAL PATHS, NOTHING LIKE A LITTLE SPACE STATION TRIAGE TO LIVEN UP THE--
BA-BOOM

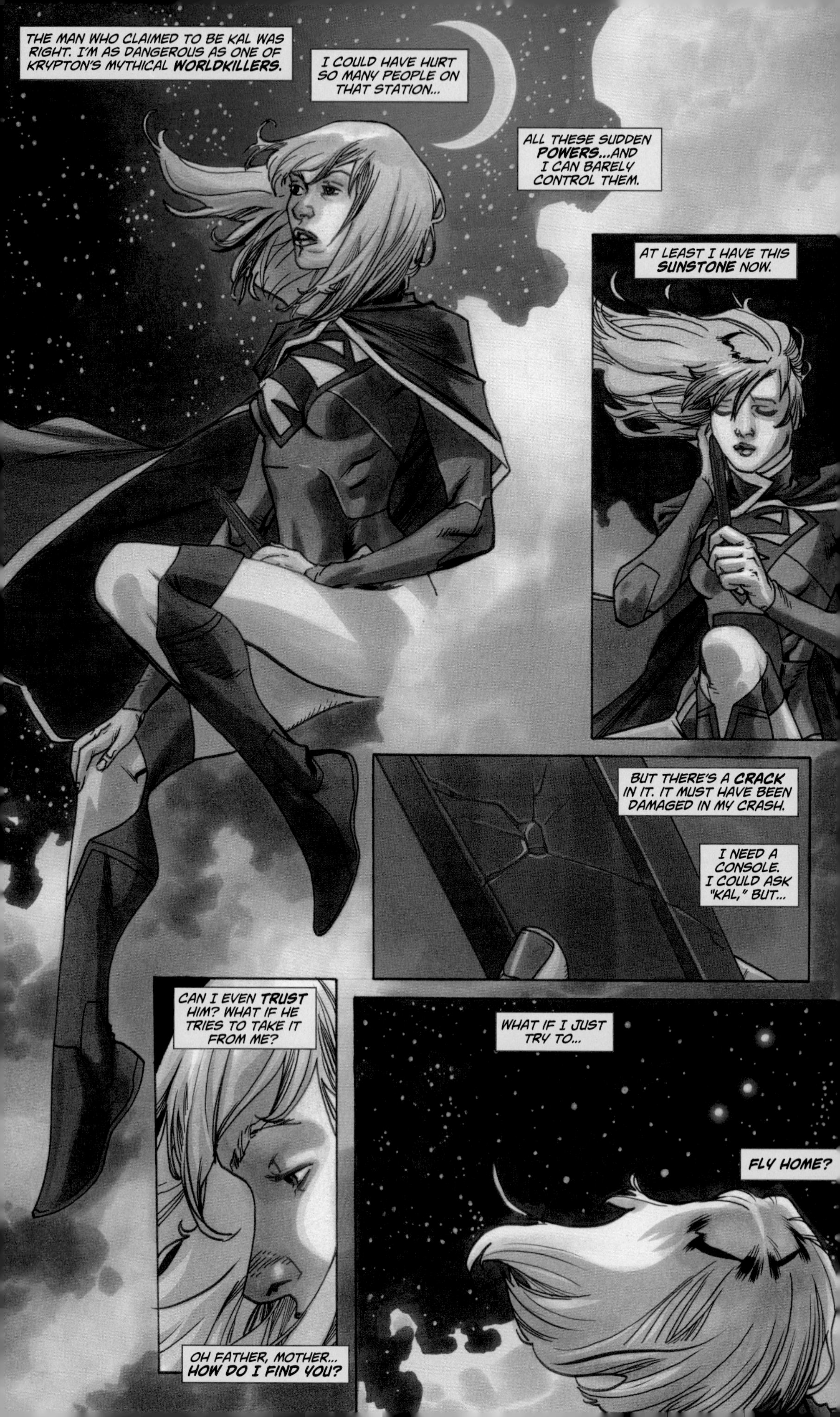
THE MAN WHO CLAIMED TO BE KAL WAS RIGHT. I'M AS DANGEROUS AS ONE OF KRYPTON'S MYTHICAL **WORLDKILLERS**.
I COULD HAVE HURT SO MANY PEOPLE ON THAT STATION...
ALL THESE SUDDEN **POWERS**...AND I CAN BARELY CONTROL THEM.
AT LEAST I HAVE THIS **SUNSTONE** NOW.
BUT THERE'S A **CRACK** IN IT. IT MUST HAVE BEEN DAMAGED IN MY CRASH.
I NEED A CONSOLE. I COULD ASK "KAL," BUT...
CAN I EVEN **TRUST** HIM? WHAT IF HE TRIES TO TAKE IT FROM ME?
OH FATHER, MOTHER... **HOW DO I FIND YOU?**
WHAT IF I JUST TRY TO...
FLY HOME?

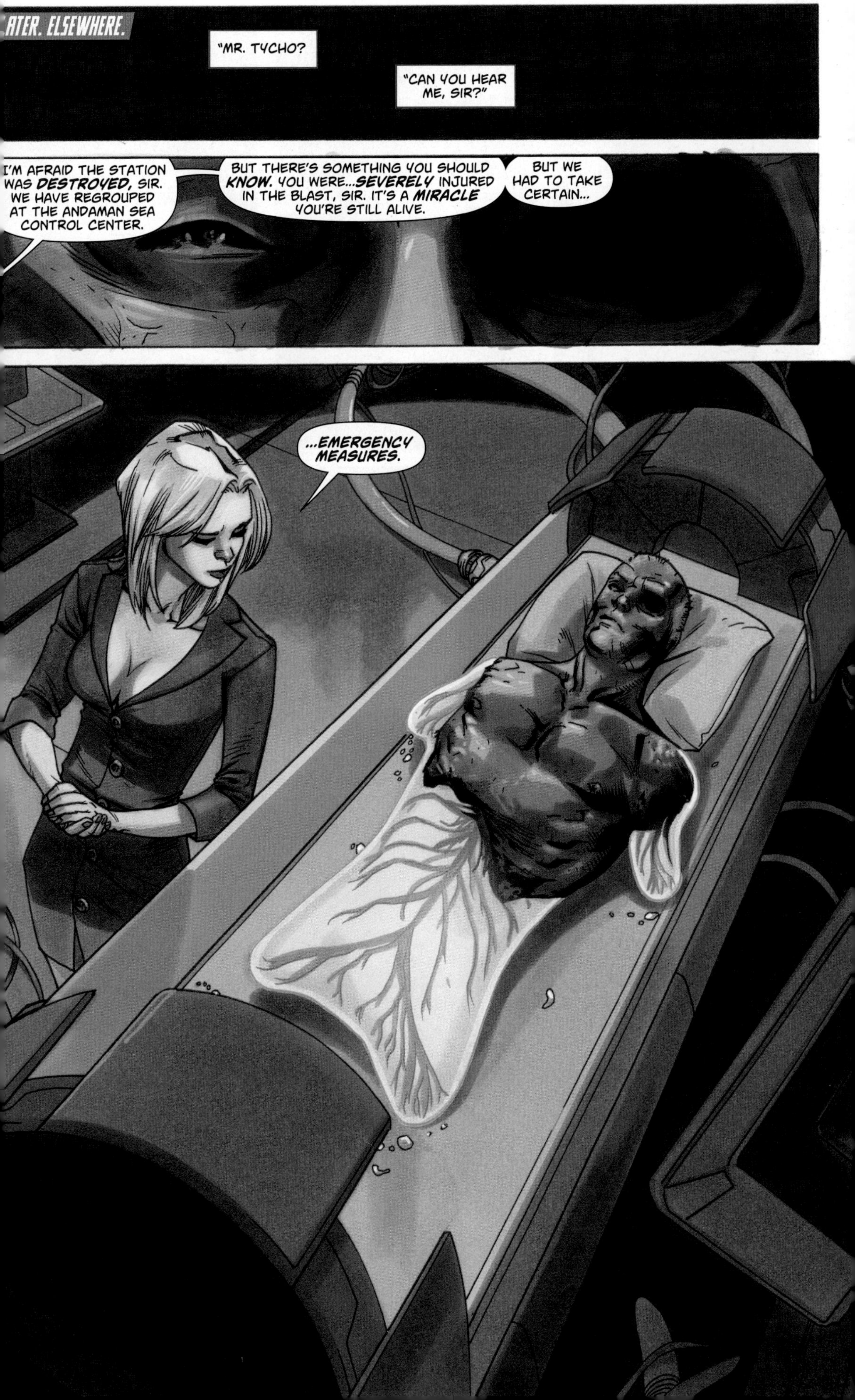
ATER. ELSEWHERE.
"MR. TYCHO?
"CAN YOU HEAR ME, SIR?"
I'M AFRAID THE STATION WAS DESTROYED, SIR. WE HAVE REGROUPED AT THE ANDAMAN SEA CONTROL CENTER.
BUT THERE'S SOMETHING YOU SHOULD KNOW. YOU WERE...SEVERELY INJURED IN THE BLAST, SIR. IT'S A MIRACLE YOU'RE STILL ALIVE.
BUT WE HAD TO TAKE CERTAIN...
...EMERGENCY MEASURES.

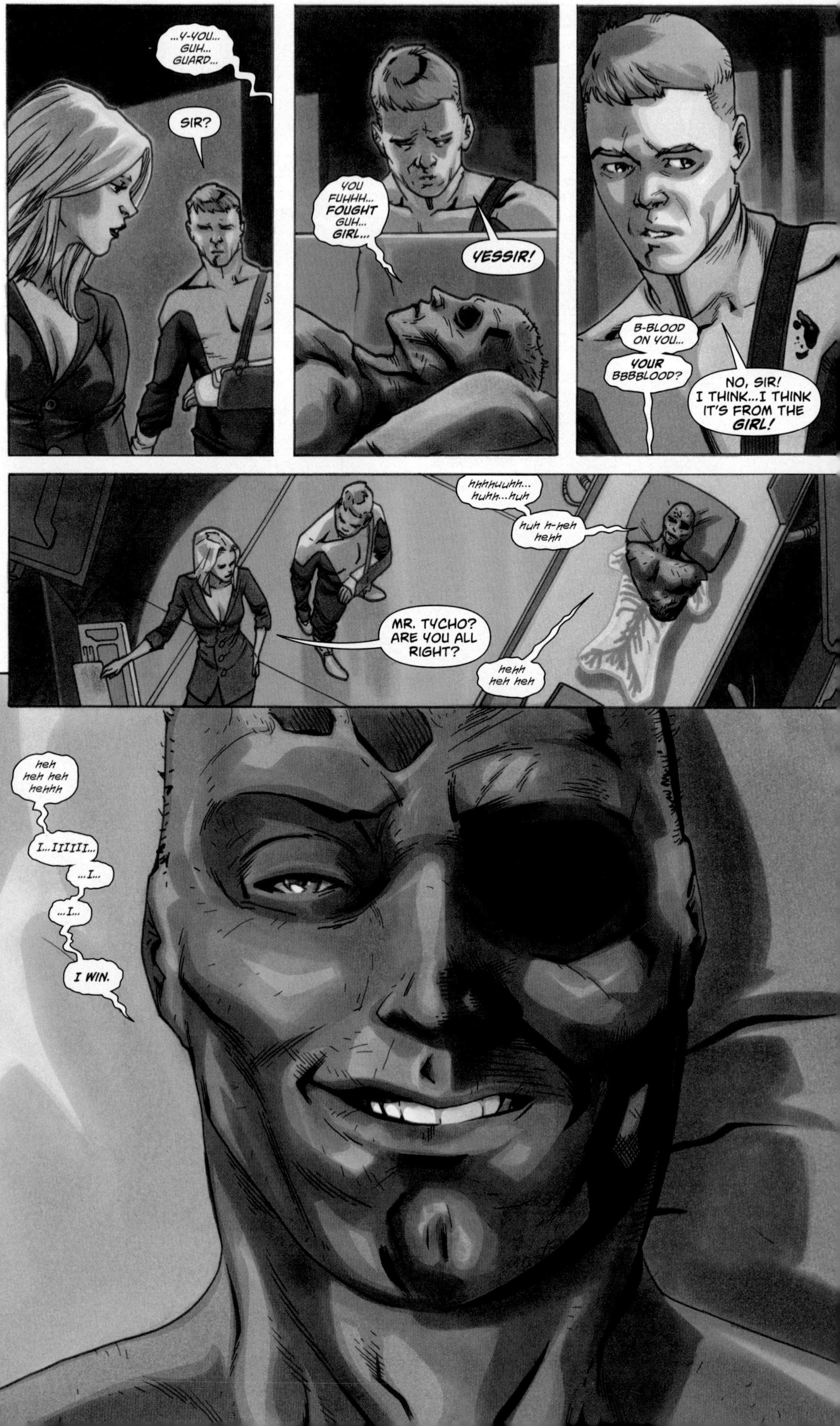
...Y-YOU... GUH... GUARD...
SIR?
YOU FUHHH... FOUGHT GUH... GIRL...
YESSIR!
B-BLOOD ON YOU...
YOUR BBBBLOOD?
NO, SIR! I THINK...I THINK IT'S FROM THE GIRL!
hhhhuuhh... huhh...huh
huh h-heh hehh
MR. TYCHO? ARE YOU ALL RIGHT?
hehh heh heh
heh heh heh hehhh
I...IIIIII...
...I...
...I...
I WIN.

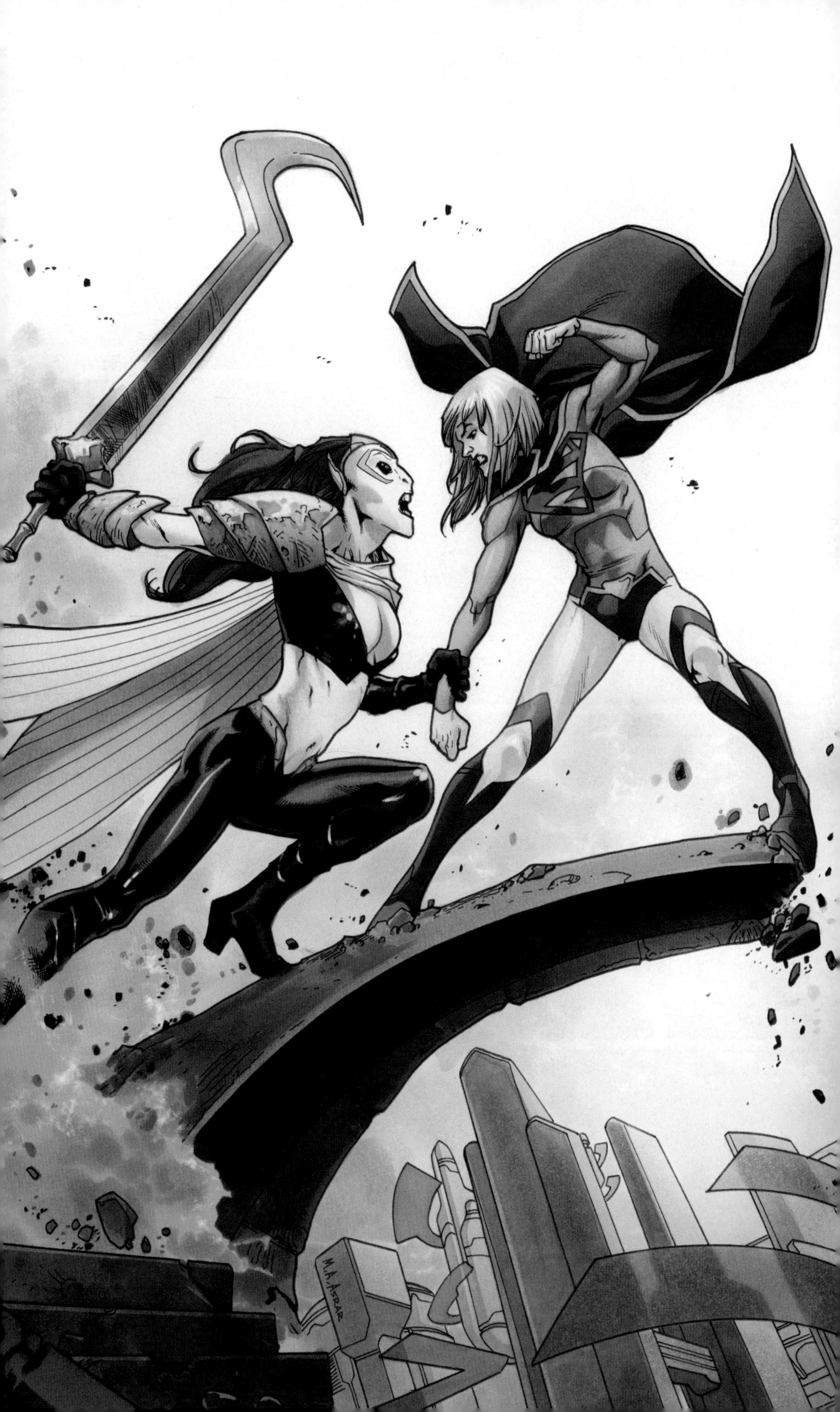
M.A. ASRAR

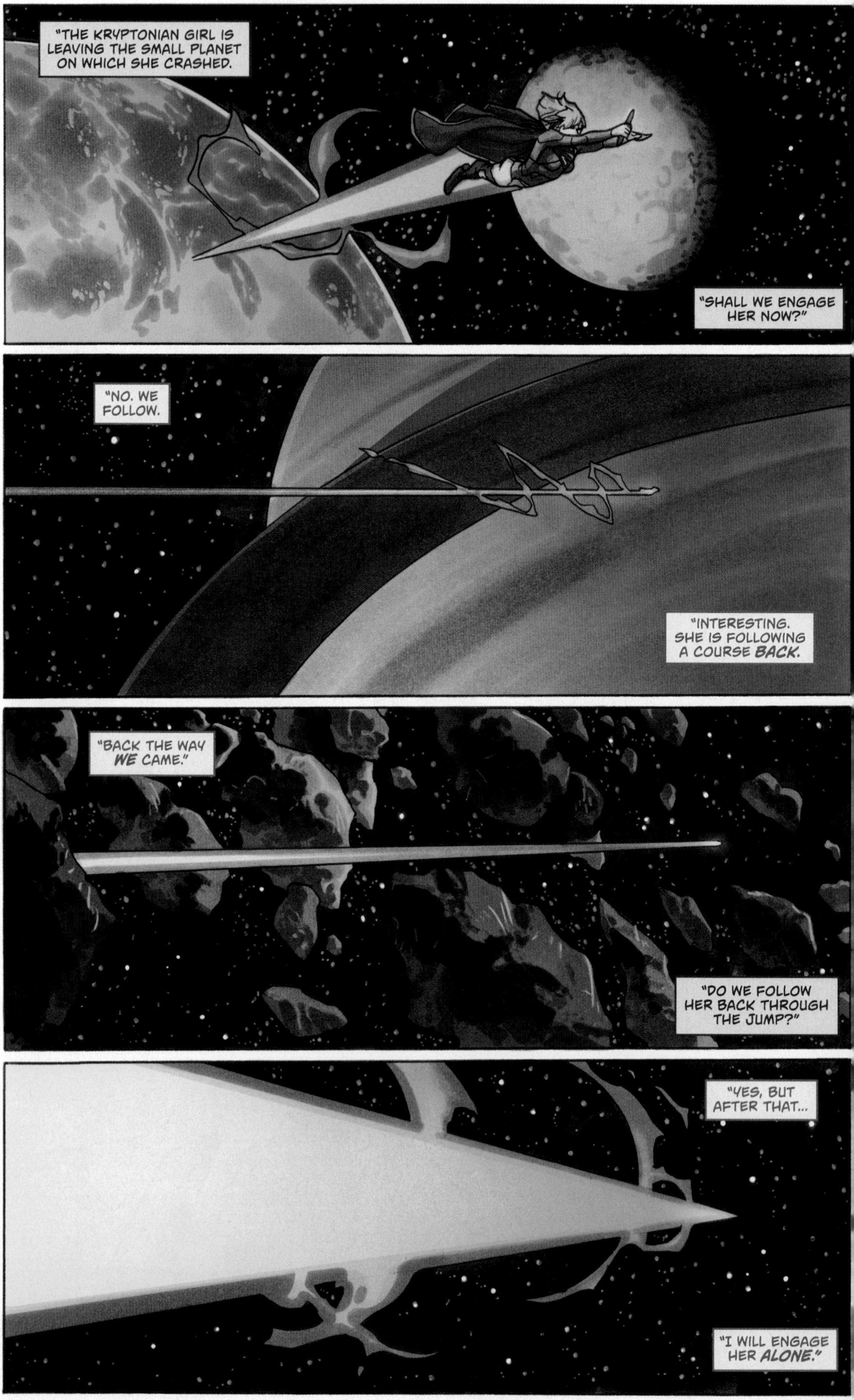
"THE KRYPTONIAN GIRL IS LEAVING THE SMALL PLANET ON WHICH SHE CRASHED.
"SHALL WE ENGAGE HER NOW?"
"NO. WE FOLLOW.
"INTERESTING. SHE IS FOLLOWING A COURSE BACK.
"BACK THE WAY WE CAME."
"DO WE FOLLOW HER BACK THROUGH THE JUMP?"
"YES, BUT AFTER THAT...
"I WILL ENGAGE HER ALONE."

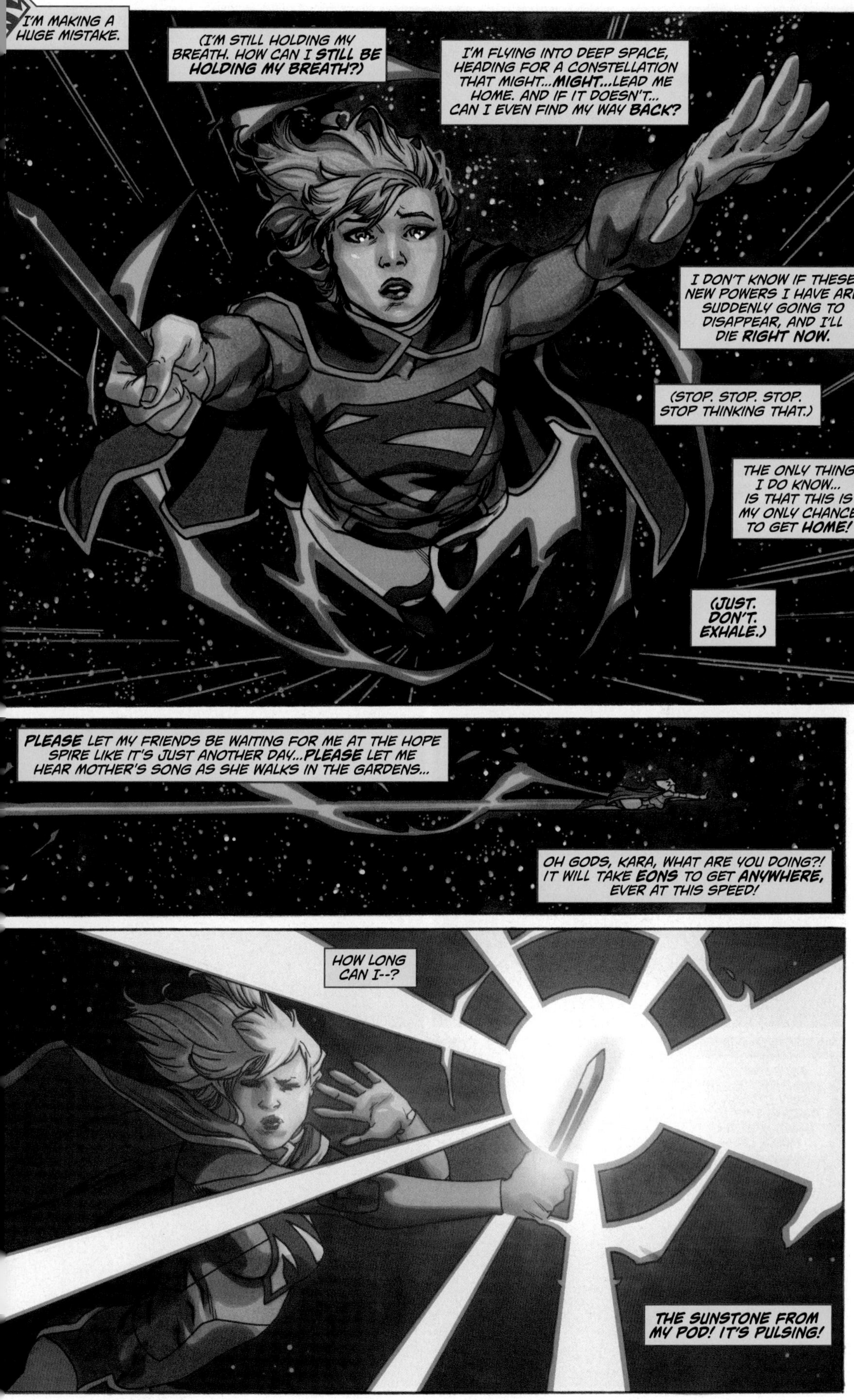
I'M MAKING A HUGE MISTAKE.
(I'M STILL HOLDING MY BREATH. HOW CAN I STILL BE HOLDING MY BREATH?)
I'M FLYING INTO DEEP SPACE, HEADING FOR A CONSTELLATION THAT MIGHT...MIGHT...LEAD ME HOME. AND IF IT DOESN'T... CAN I EVEN FIND MY WAY BACK?
I DON'T KNOW IF THESE NEW POWERS I HAVE ARE SUDDENLY GOING TO DISAPPEAR, AND I'LL DIE RIGHT NOW.
(STOP. STOP. STOP. STOP THINKING THAT.)
THE ONLY THING I DO KNOW... IS THAT THIS IS MY ONLY CHANCE TO GET HOME!
(JUST. DON'T. EXHALE.)
PLEASE LET MY FRIENDS BE WAITING FOR ME AT THE HOPE SPIRE LIKE IT'S JUST ANOTHER DAY...PLEASE LET ME HEAR MOTHER'S SONG AS SHE WALKS IN THE GARDENS...
OH GODS, KARA, WHAT ARE YOU DOING?! IT WILL TAKE EONS TO GET ANYWHERE, EVER AT THIS SPEED!
HOW LONG CAN I--?
THE SUNSTONE FROM MY POD! IT'S PULSING!

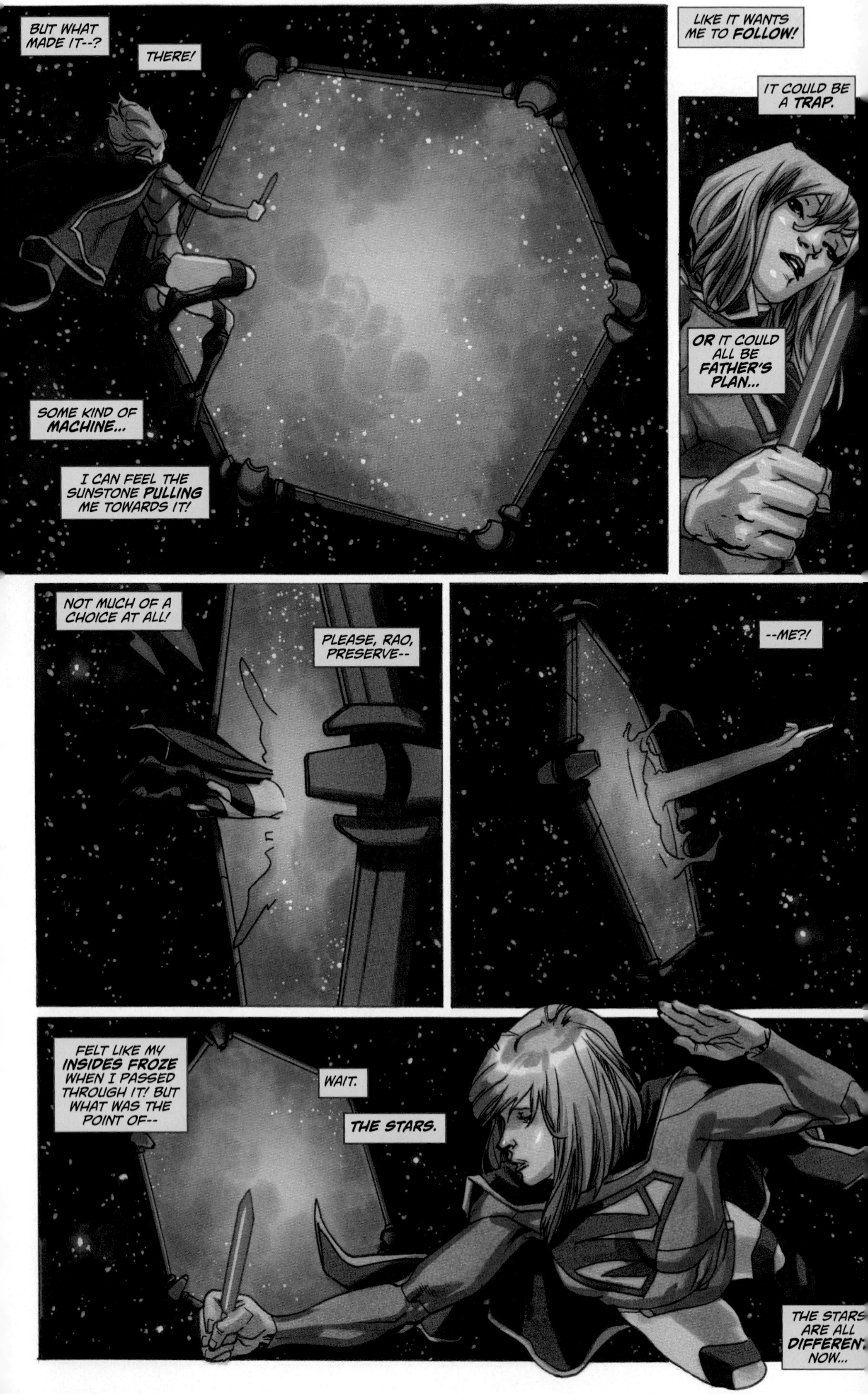
BUT WHAT MADE IT--?
THERE!
SOME KIND OF MACHINE...
I CAN FEEL THE SUNSTONE PULLING ME TOWARDS IT!
LIKE IT WANTS ME TO FOLLOW!
IT COULD BE A TRAP.
OR IT COULD ALL BE FATHER'S PLAN...
NOT MUCH OF A CHOICE AT ALL!
PLEASE, RAO, PRESERVE--
--ME?!
FELT LIKE MY INSIDES FROZE WHEN I PASSED THROUGH IT! BUT WHAT WAS THE POINT OF--
WAIT.
THE STARS.
THE STARS ARE ALL DIFFEREN NOW...

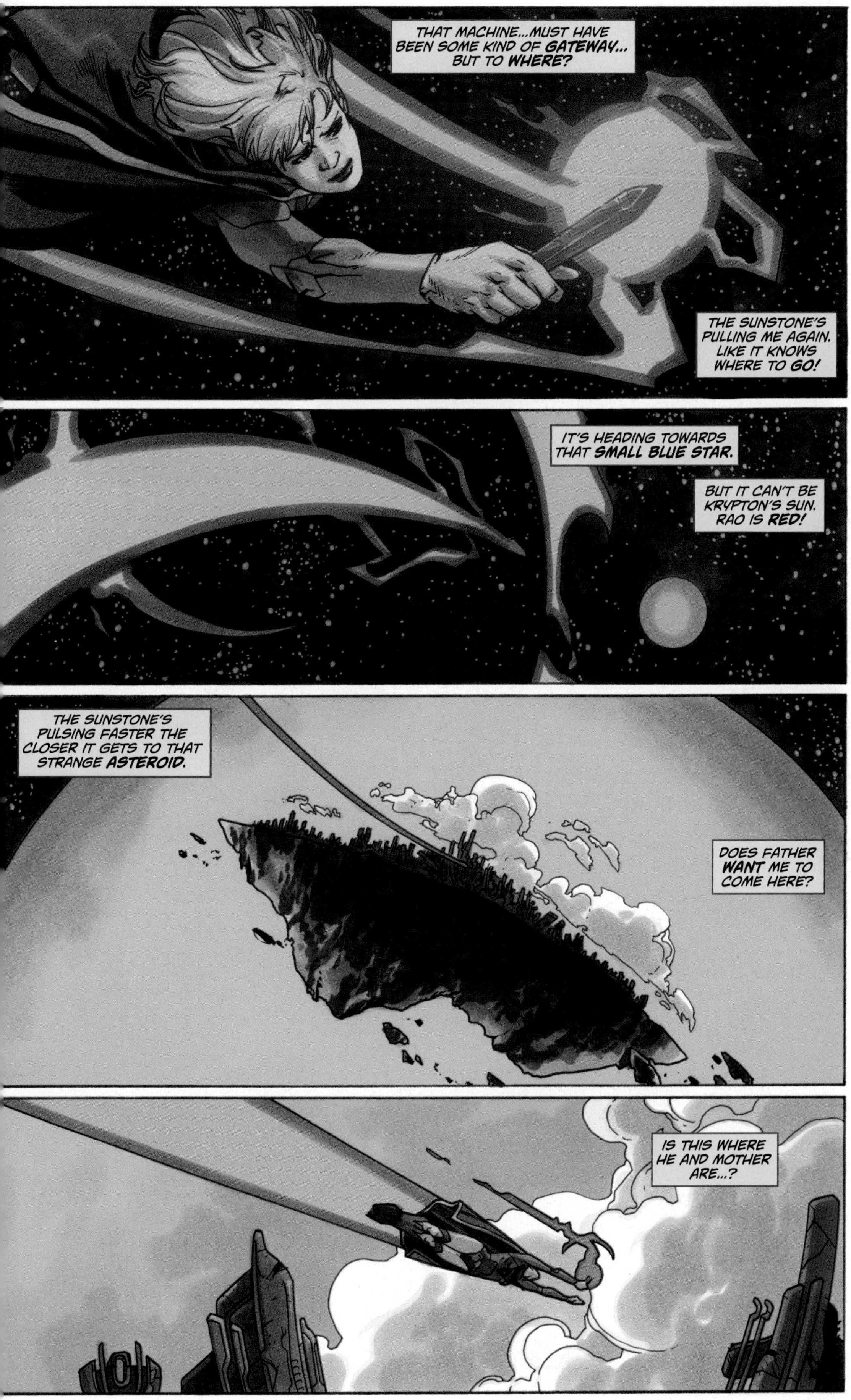
THAT MACHINE...MUST HAVE BEEN SOME KIND OF GATEWAY... BUT TO WHERE?
THE SUNSTONE'S PULLING ME AGAIN. LIKE IT KNOWS WHERE TO GO!
IT'S HEADING TOWARDS THAT SMALL BLUE STAR.
BUT IT CAN'T BE KRYPTON'S SUN. RAO IS RED!
THE SUNSTONE'S PULSING FASTER THE CLOSER IT GETS TO THAT STRANGE ASTEROID.
DOES FATHER WANT ME TO COME HERE?
IS THIS WHERE HE AND MOTHER ARE...?

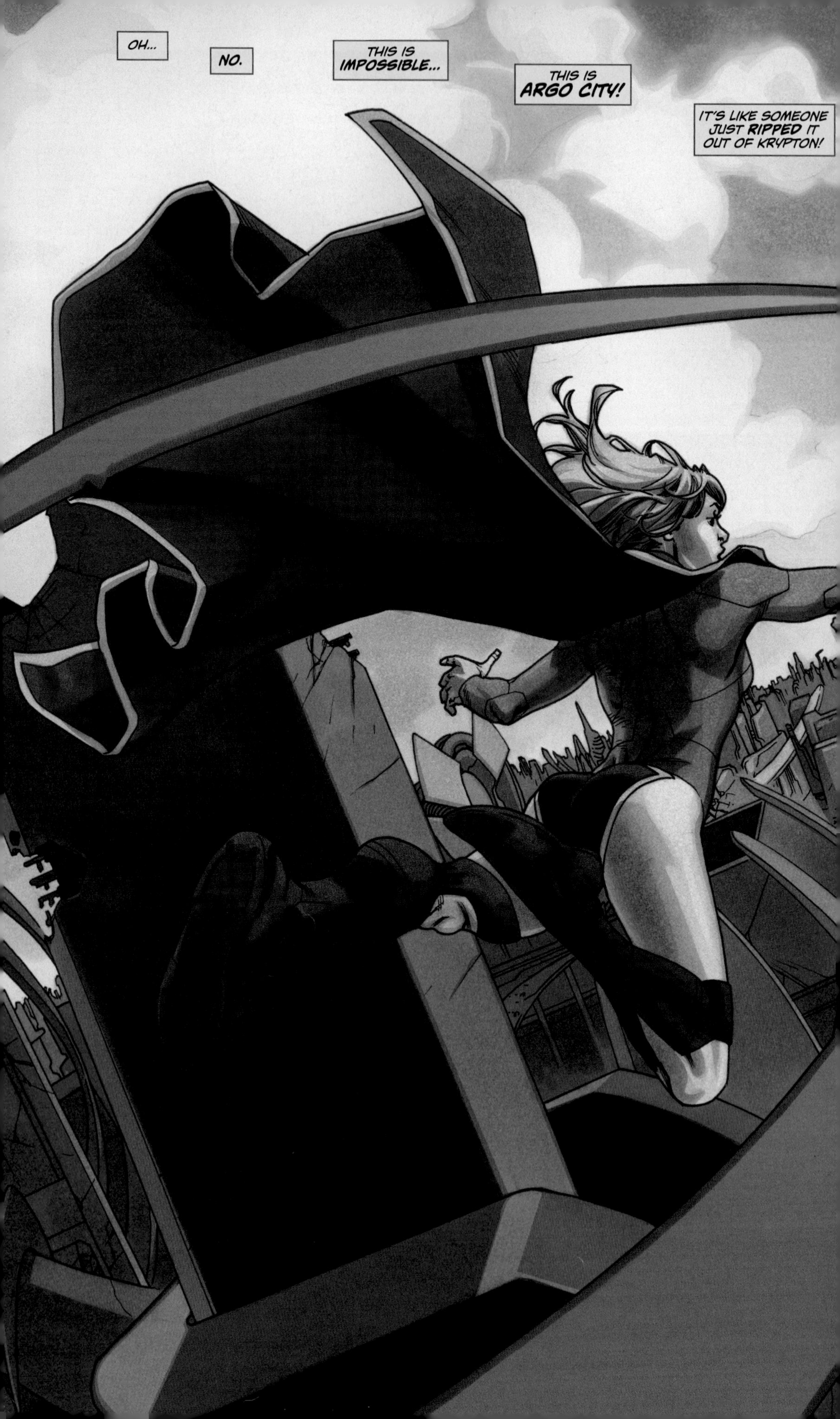
OH...
NO.
THIS IS IMPOSSIBLE...
THIS IS ARGO CITY!
IT'S LIKE SOMEONE JUST RIPPED IT OUT OF KRYPTON!

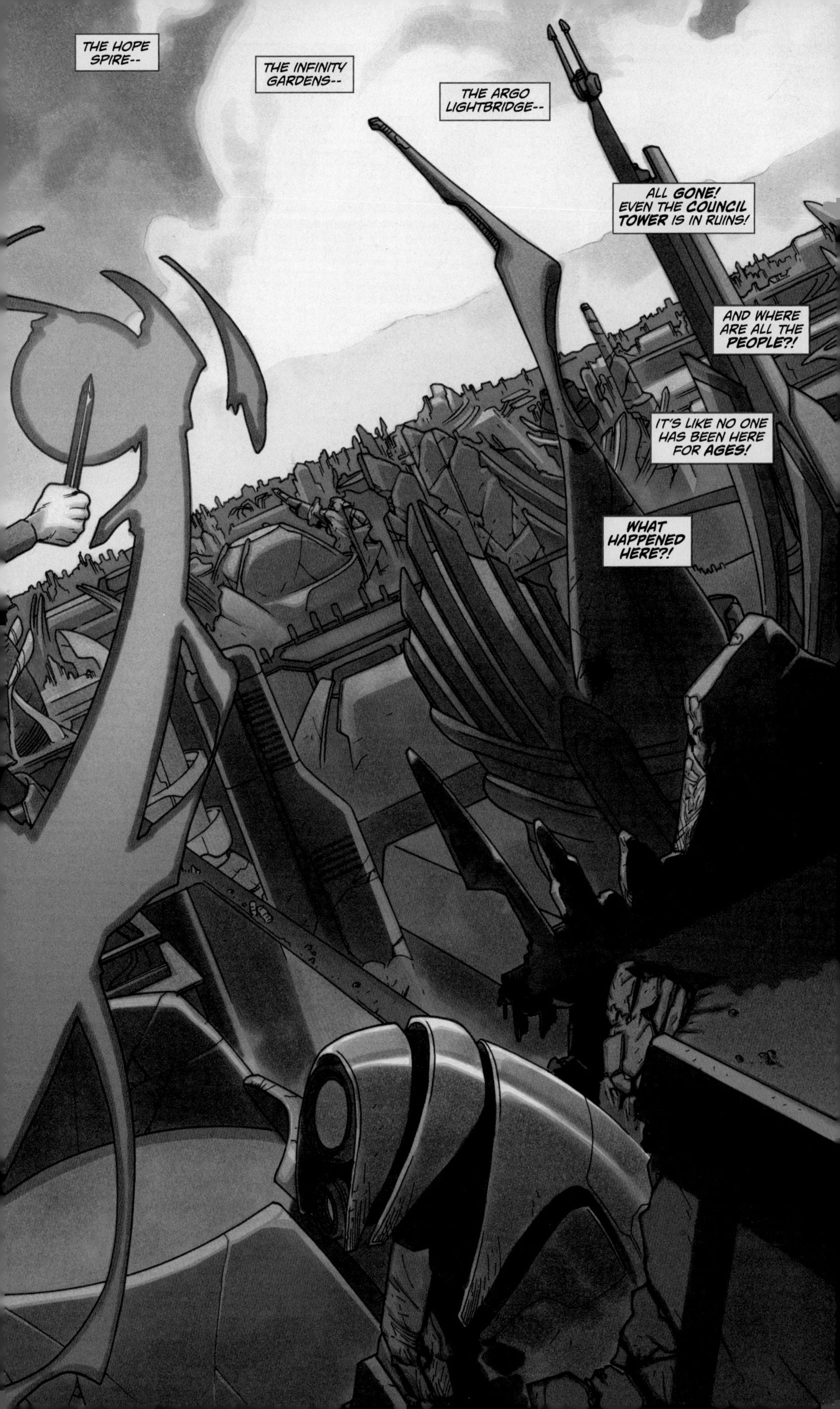
THE HOPE SPIRE--
THE INFINITY GARDENS--
THE ARGO LIGHTBRIDGE--
ALL GONE! EVEN THE COUNCIL TOWER IS IN RUINS!
AND WHERE ARE ALL THE PEOPLE?!
IT'S LIKE NO ONE HAS BEEN HERE FOR AGES!
WHAT HAPPENED HERE?!

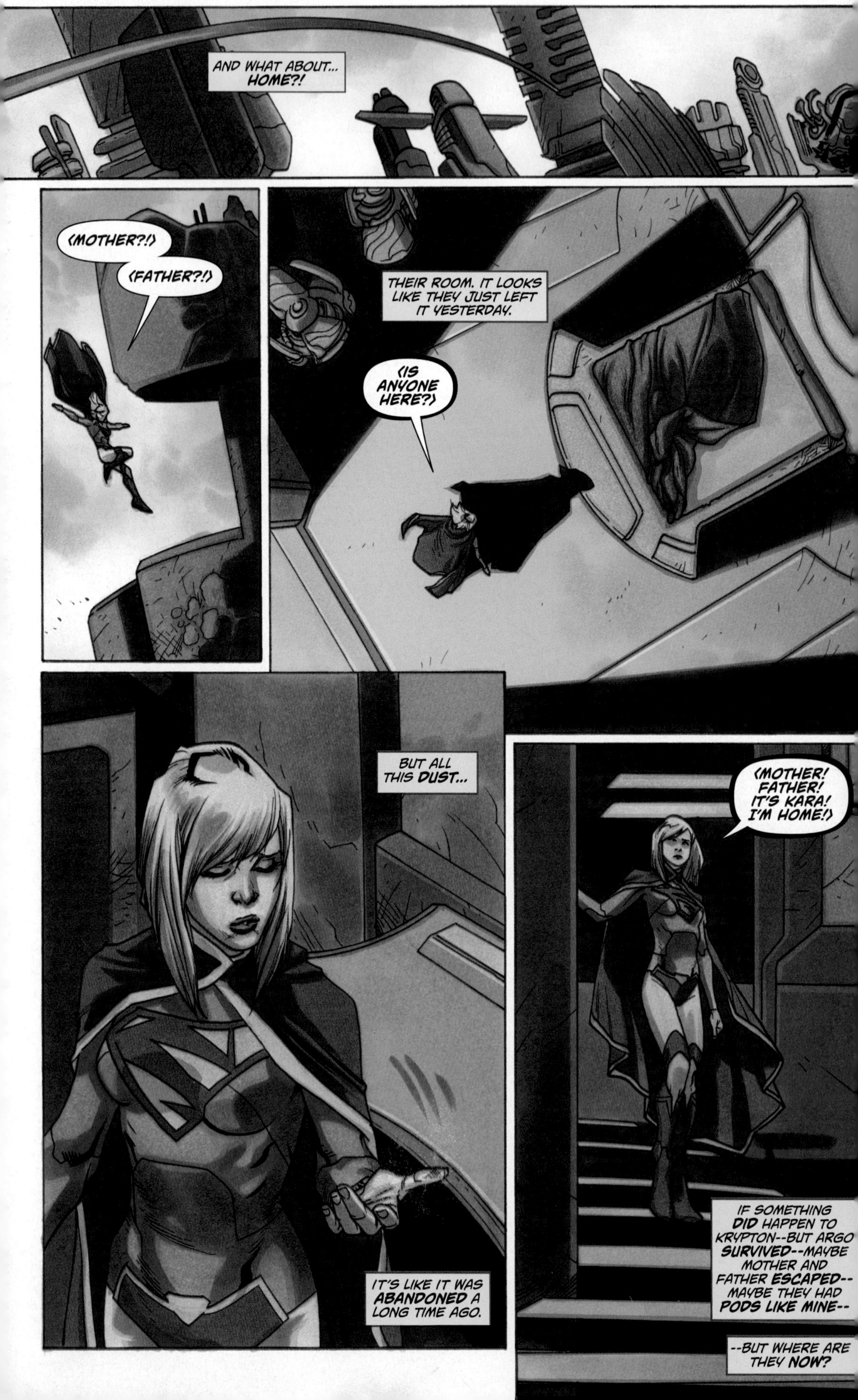
AND WHAT ABOUT... HOME?!
(MOTHER?!)
(FATHER?!)
THEIR ROOM. IT LOOKS LIKE THEY JUST LEFT IT YESTERDAY.
(IS ANYONE HERE?)
BUT ALL THIS DUST...
IT'S LIKE IT WAS ABANDONED A LONG TIME AGO.
(MOTHER! FATHER! IT'S KARA! I'M HOME!)
IF SOMETHING DID HAPPEN TO KRYPTON--BUT ARGO SURVIVED--MAYBE MOTHER AND FATHER ESCAPED--MAYBE THEY HAD PODS LIKE MINE--
--BUT WHERE ARE THEY NOW?

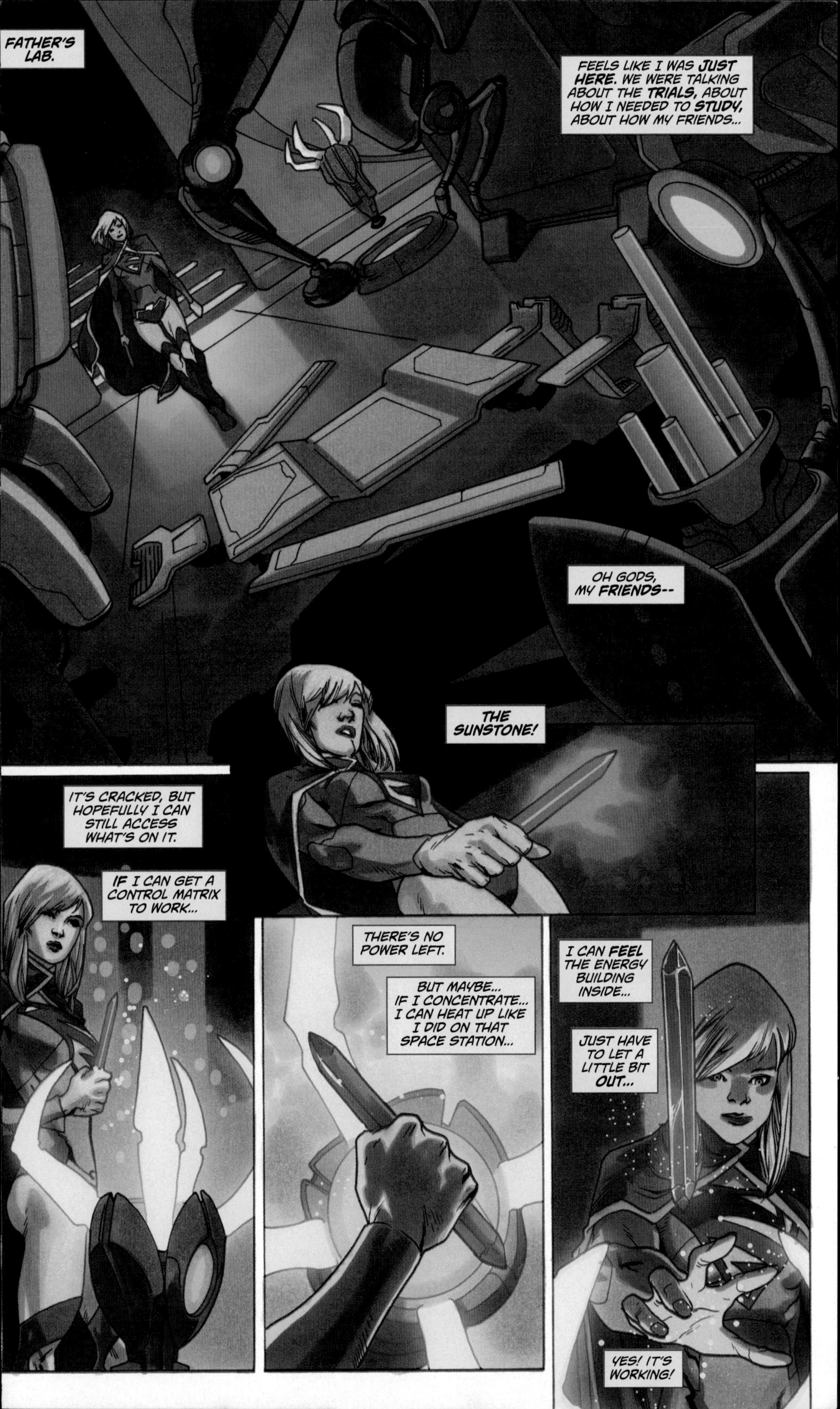
FATHER'S LAB.
FEELS LIKE I WAS JUST HERE. WE WERE TALKING ABOUT THE TRIALS, ABOUT HOW I NEEDED TO STUDY, ABOUT HOW MY FRIENDS...
OH GODS, MY FRIENDS--
THE SUNSTONE!
IT'S CRACKED, BUT HOPEFULLY I CAN STILL ACCESS WHAT'S ON IT.
IF I CAN GET A CONTROL MATRIX TO WORK...
THERE'S NO POWER LEFT.
BUT MAYBE... IF I CONCENTRATE... I CAN HEAT UP LIKE I DID ON THAT SPACE STATION...
I CAN FEEL THE ENERGY BUILDING INSIDE...
JUST HAVE TO LET A LITTLE BIT OUT...
YES! IT'S WORKING!

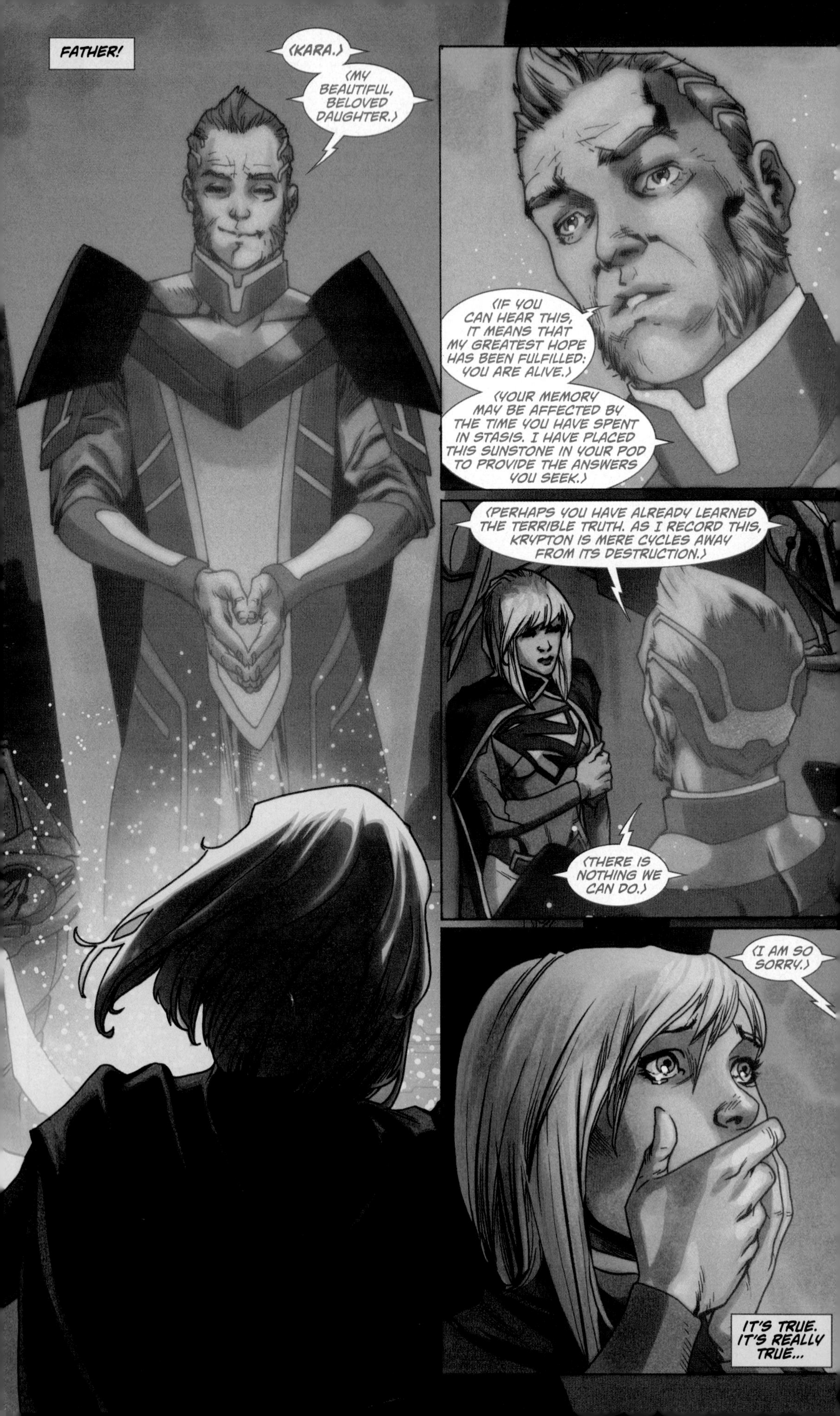
FATHER!
(KARA.)
(MY BEAUTIFUL, BELOVED DAUGHTER.)
(IF YOU CAN HEAR THIS, IT MEANS THAT MY GREATEST HOPE HAS BEEN FULFILLED: YOU ARE ALIVE.)
(YOUR MEMORY MAY BE AFFECTED BY THE TIME YOU HAVE SPENT IN STASIS. I HAVE PLACED THIS SUNSTONE IN YOUR POD TO PROVIDE THE ANSWERS YOU SEEK.)
(PERHAPS YOU HAVE ALREADY LEARNED THE TERRIBLE TRUTH. AS I RECORD THIS, KRYPTON IS MERE CYCLES AWAY FROM ITS DESTRUCTION.)
(THERE IS NOTHING WE CAN DO.)
(I AM SO SORRY.)
IT'S TRUE. IT'S REALLY TRUE...

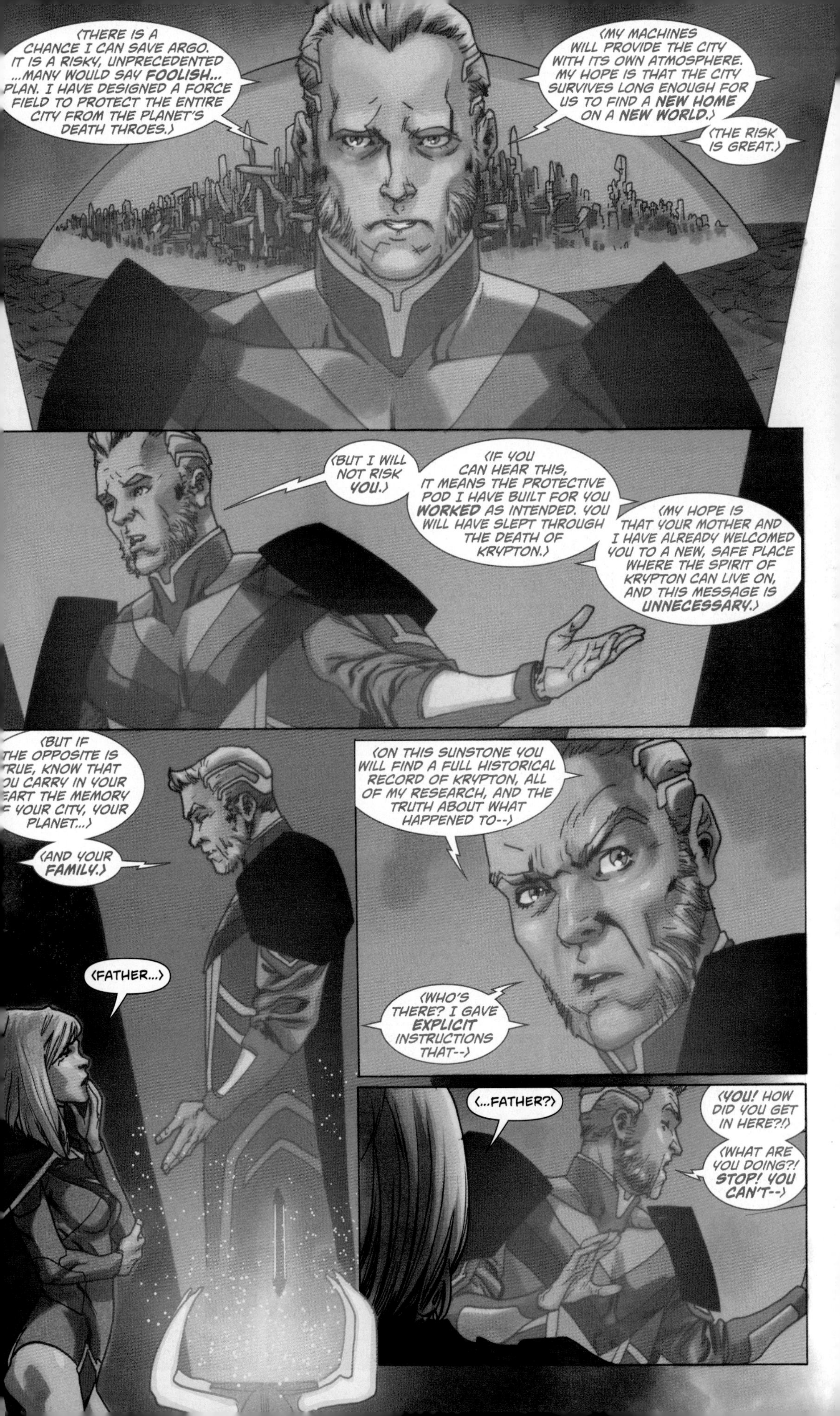
(THERE IS A CHANCE I CAN SAVE ARGO. IT IS A RISKY, UNPRECEDENTED ...MANY WOULD SAY FOOLISH... PLAN. I HAVE DESIGNED A FORCE FIELD TO PROTECT THE ENTIRE CITY FROM THE PLANET'S DEATH THROES.)
(MY MACHINES WILL PROVIDE THE CITY WITH ITS OWN ATMOSPHERE. MY HOPE IS THAT THE CITY SURVIVES LONG ENOUGH FOR US TO FIND A NEW HOME ON A NEW WORLD.)
(THE RISK IS GREAT.)
(BUT I WILL NOT RISK YOU.)
(IF YOU CAN HEAR THIS, IT MEANS THE PROTECTIVE POD I HAVE BUILT FOR YOU WORKED AS INTENDED. YOU WILL HAVE SLEPT THROUGH THE DEATH OF KRYPTON.)
(MY HOPE IS THAT YOUR MOTHER AND I HAVE ALREADY WELCOMED YOU TO A NEW, SAFE PLACE WHERE THE SPIRIT OF KRYPTON CAN LIVE ON, AND THIS MESSAGE IS UNNECESSARY.)
(BUT IF THE OPPOSITE IS TRUE, KNOW THAT YOU CARRY IN YOUR HEART THE MEMORY OF YOUR CITY, YOUR PLANET...)
(AND YOUR FAMILY.)
(FATHER...)
(ON THIS SUNSTONE YOU WILL FIND A FULL HISTORICAL RECORD OF KRYPTON, ALL OF MY RESEARCH, AND THE TRUTH ABOUT WHAT HAPPENED TO--)
(WHO'S THERE? I GAVE EXPLICIT INSTRUCTIONS THAT--)
(...FATHER?)
(YOU! HOW DID YOU GET IN HERE?!)
(WHAT ARE YOU DOING?! STOP! YOU CAN'T--)

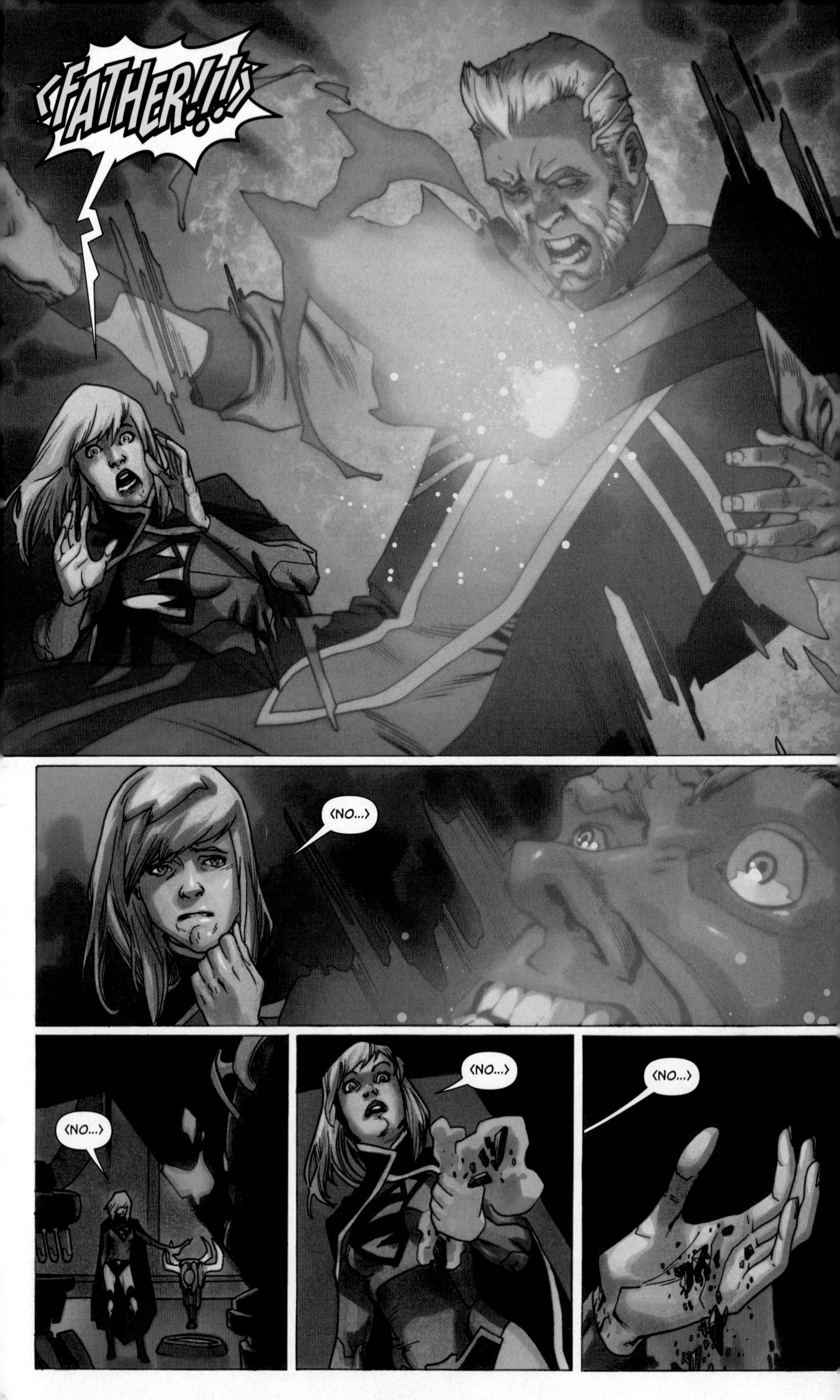
‹FATHER!!!›
‹NO...›
‹NO...›
‹NO...›
‹NO...›

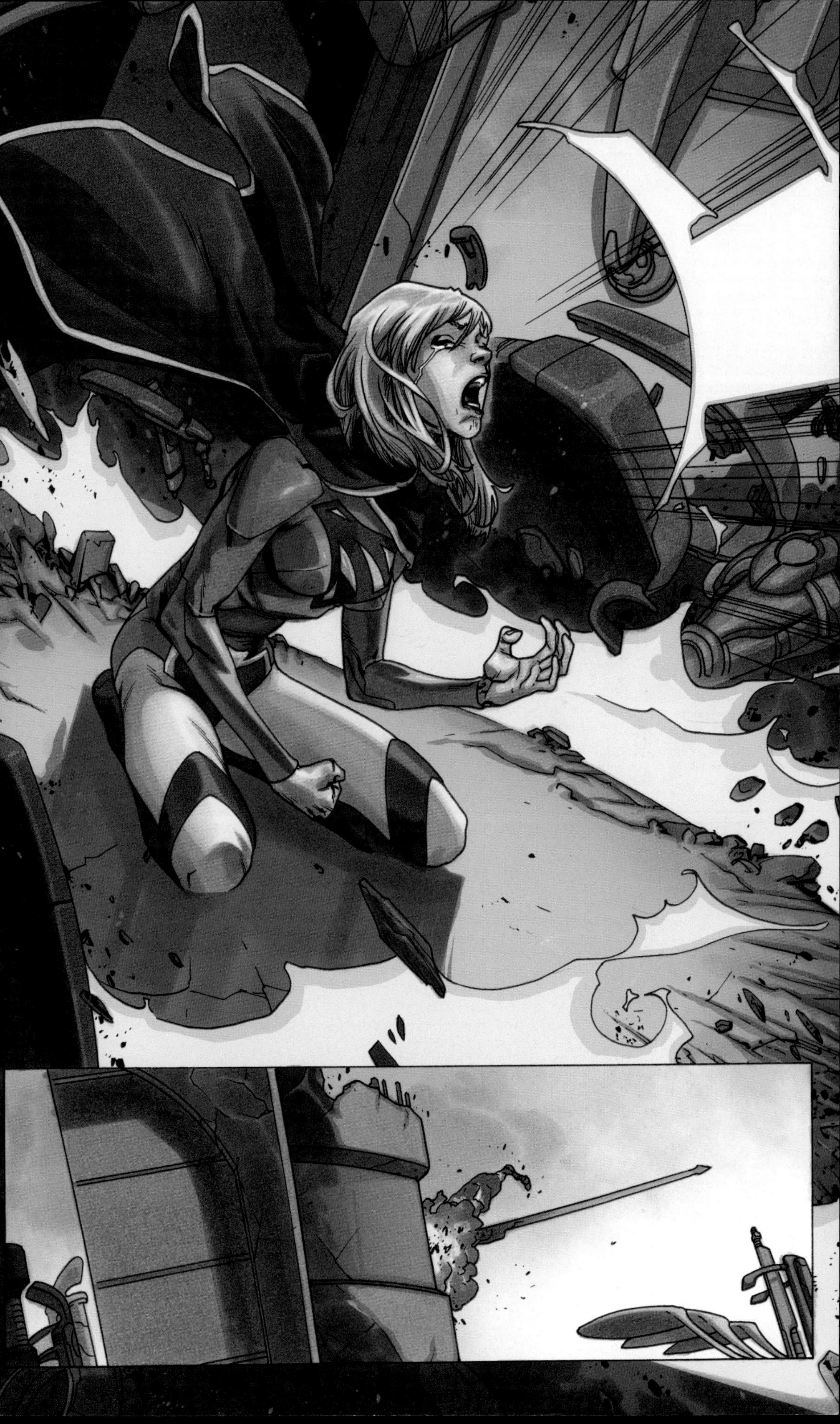

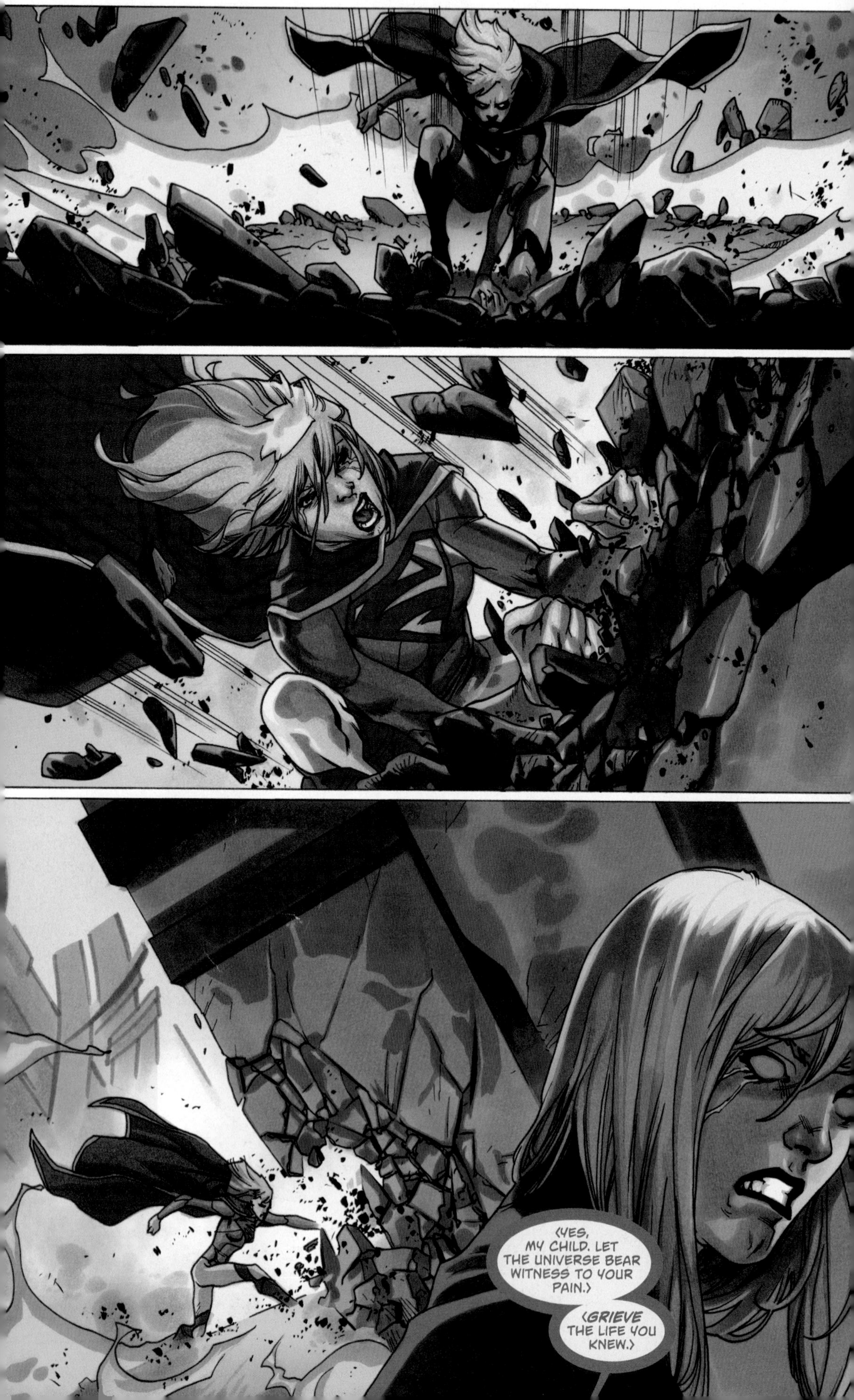
‹YES, MY CHILD. LET THE UNIVERSE BEAR WITNESS TO YOUR PAIN.›
‹GRIEVE THE LIFE YOU KNEW.›

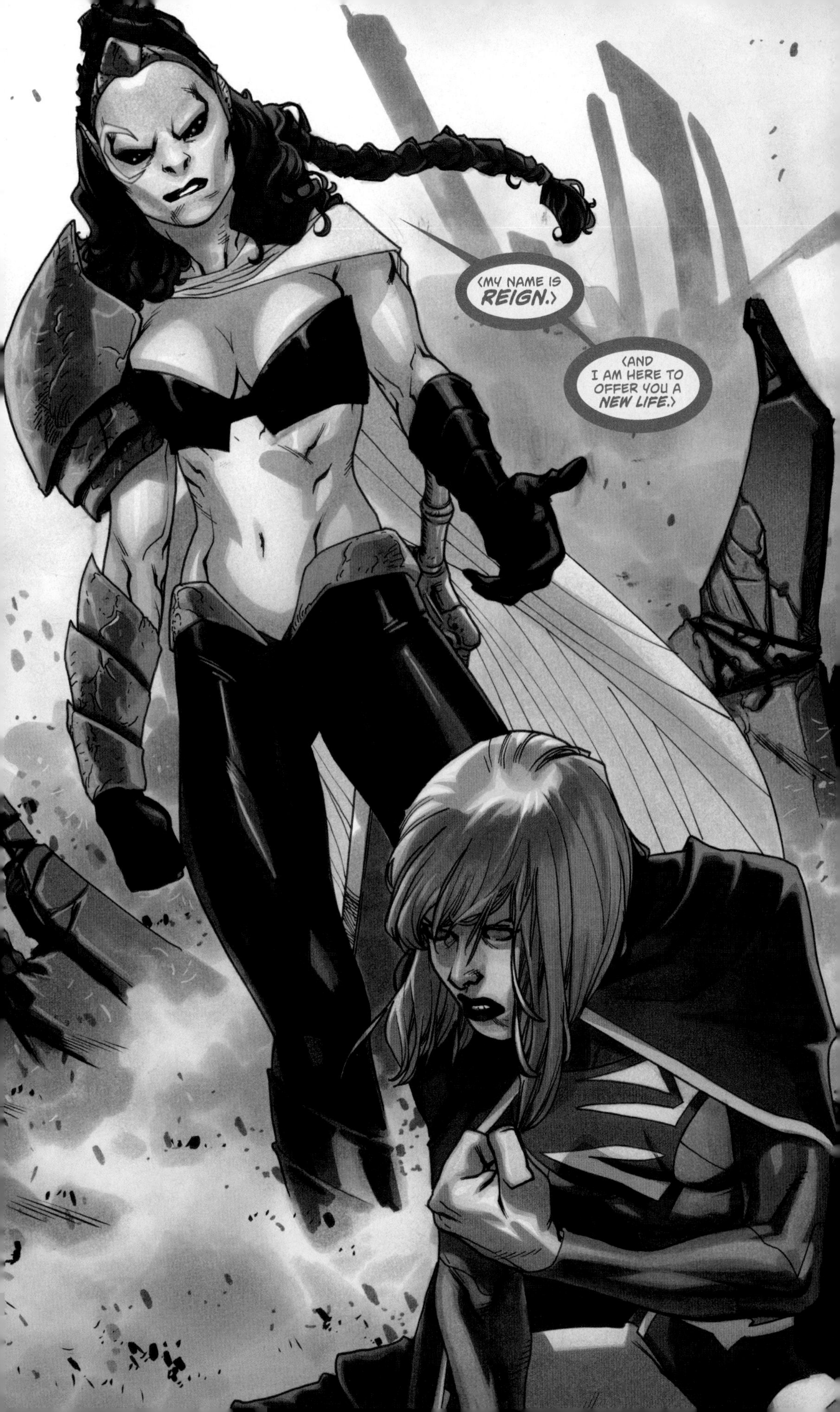
‹MY NAME IS REIGN.›
‹AND I AM HERE TO OFFER YOU A NEW LIFE.›

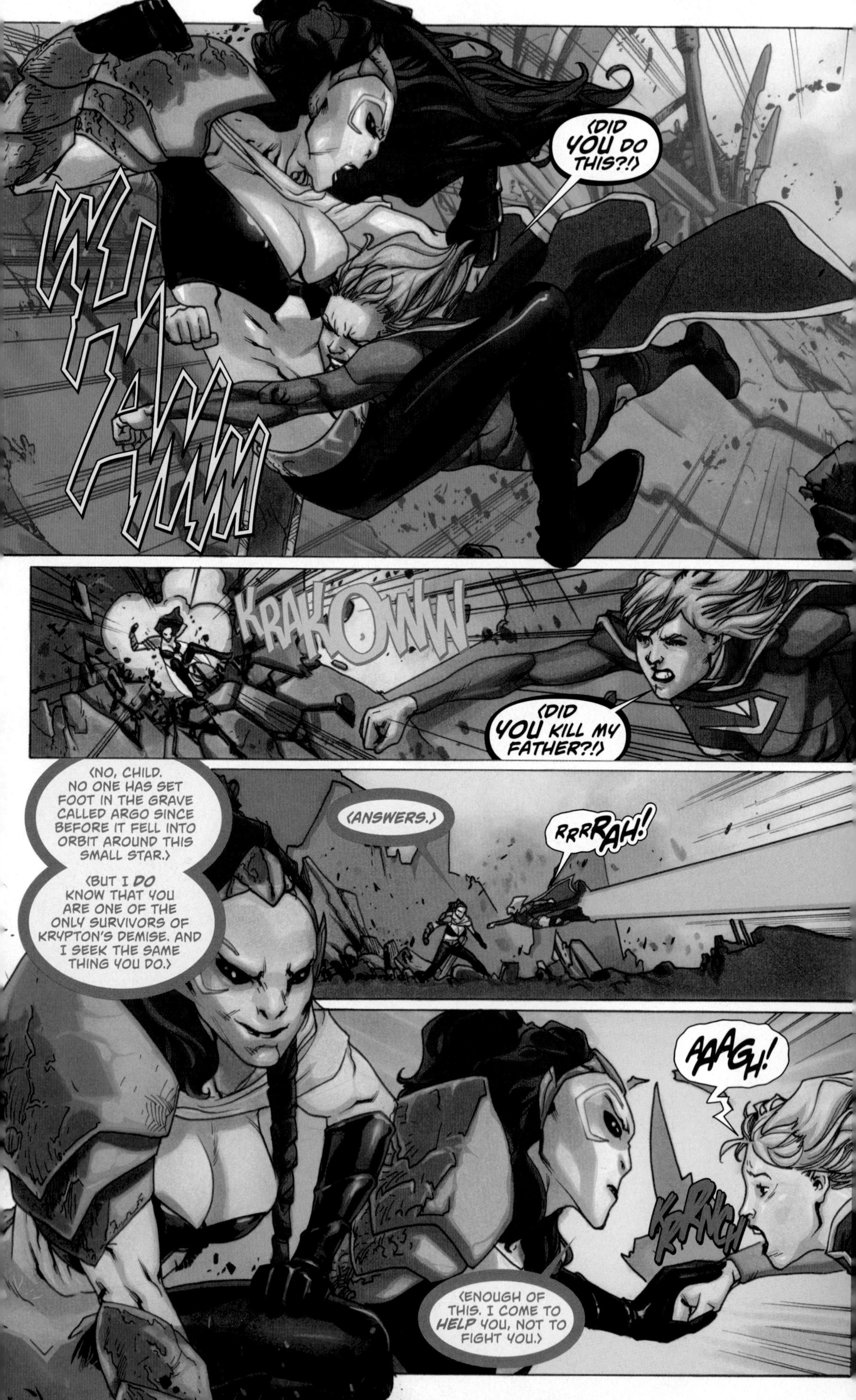
WHAMM
(DID YOU DO THIS?!)
KRAKOWW
(DID YOU KILL MY FATHER?!)
(NO, CHILD. NO ONE HAS SET FOOT IN THE GRAVE CALLED ARGO SINCE BEFORE IT FELL INTO ORBIT AROUND THIS SMALL STAR.)
(BUT I DO KNOW THAT YOU ARE ONE OF THE ONLY SURVIVORS OF KRYPTON'S DEMISE. AND I SEEK THE SAME THING YOU DO.)
(ANSWERS.)
RRRRAH!
AAAGH!
KRRNCH
(ENOUGH OF THIS. I COME TO HELP YOU, NOT TO FIGHT YOU.)

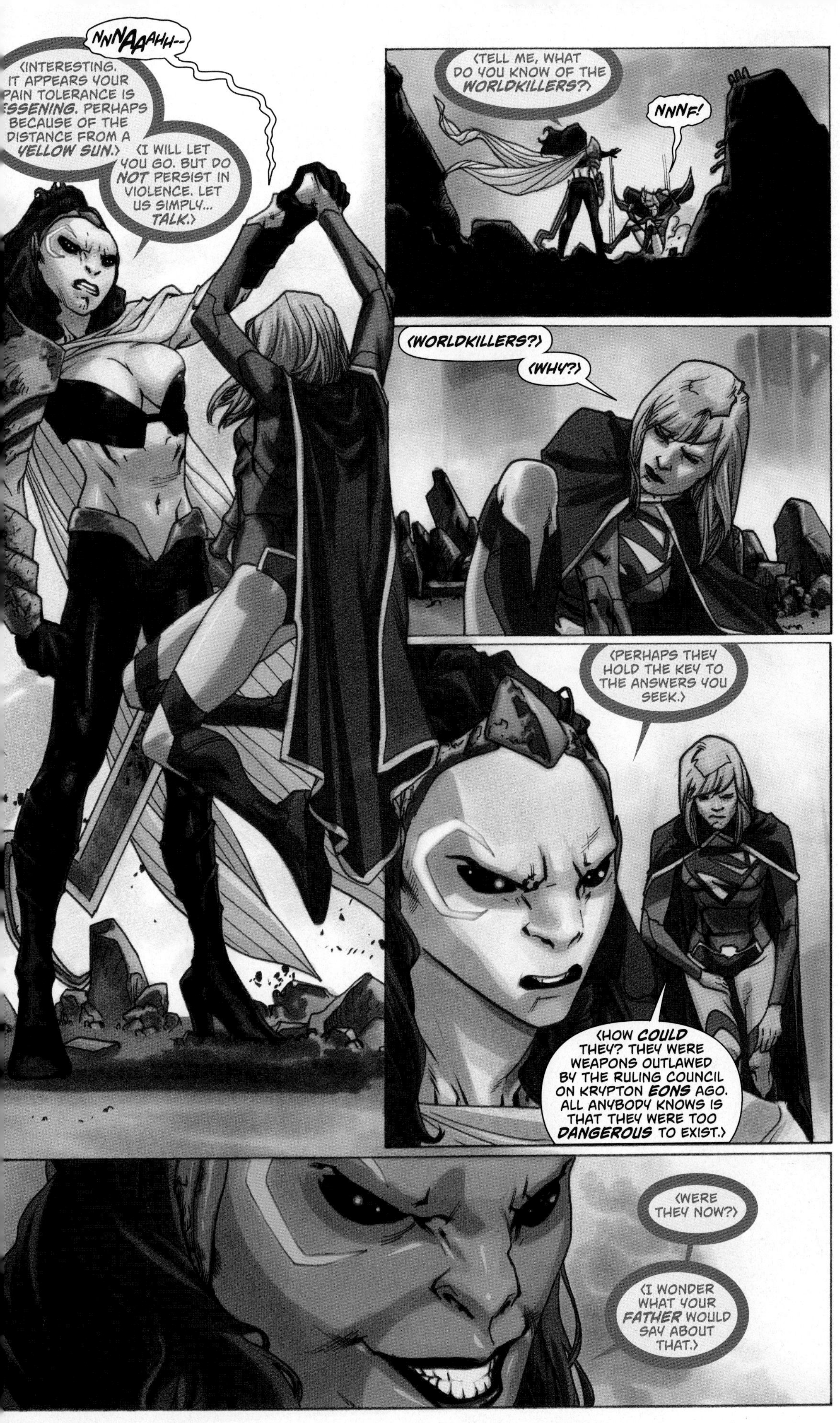
NNNAAAHH--
‹INTERESTING. IT APPEARS YOUR PAIN TOLERANCE IS LESSENING. PERHAPS BECAUSE OF THE DISTANCE FROM A YELLOW SUN.›
‹I WILL LET YOU GO. BUT DO NOT PERSIST IN VIOLENCE. LET US SIMPLY... TALK.›
‹TELL ME, WHAT DO YOU KNOW OF THE WORLDKILLERS?›
NNNF!
‹WORLDKILLERS?›
‹WHY?›
‹PERHAPS THEY HOLD THE KEY TO THE ANSWERS YOU SEEK.›
‹HOW COULD THEY? THEY WERE WEAPONS OUTLAWED BY THE RULING COUNCIL ON KRYPTON EONS AGO. ALL ANYBODY KNOWS IS THAT THEY WERE TOO DANGEROUS TO EXIST.›
‹WERE THEY NOW?›
‹I WONDER WHAT YOUR FATHER WOULD SAY ABOUT THAT.›

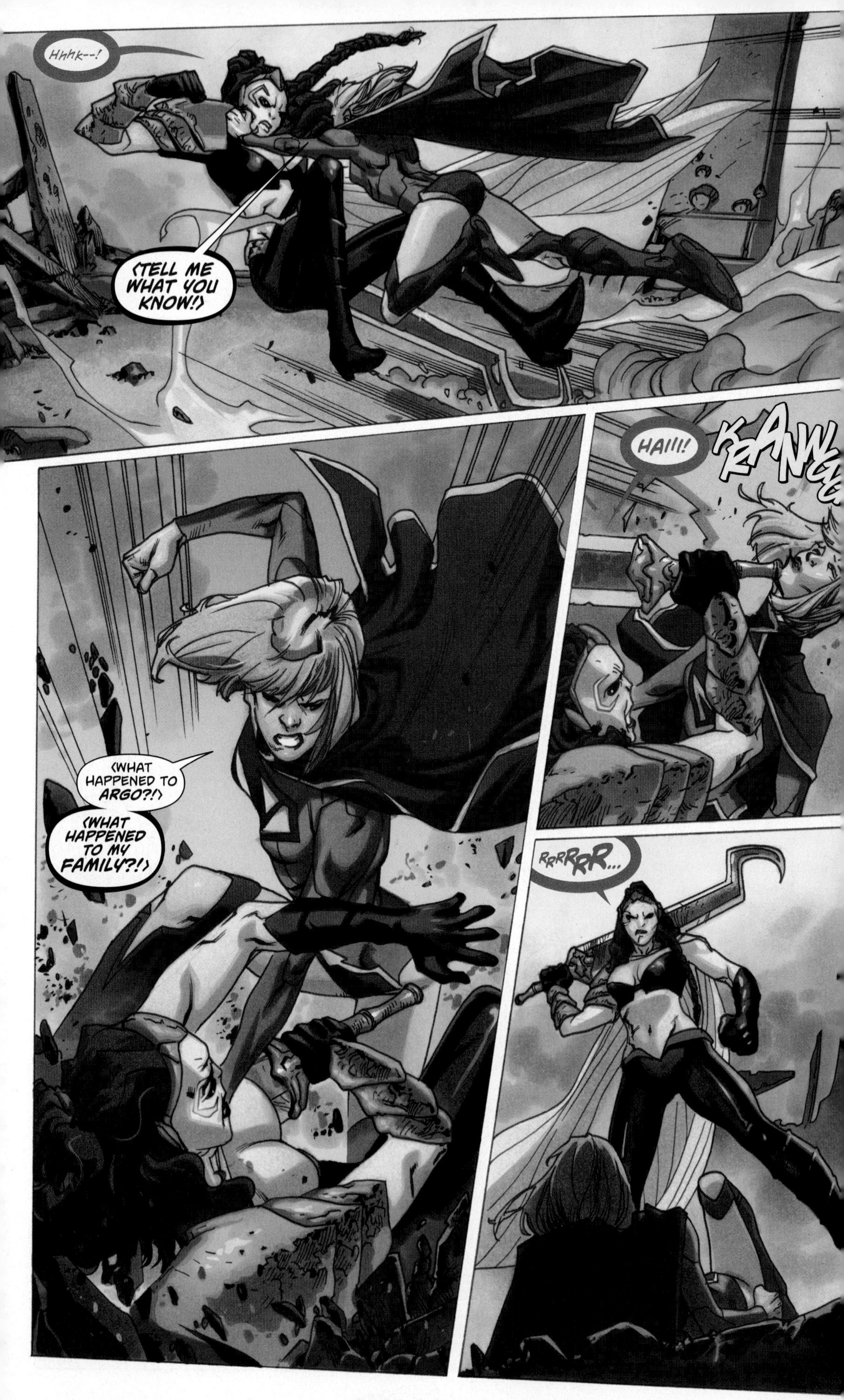
Hhhk--!
(TELL ME WHAT YOU KNOW!)
HAIII!
KRANNGG
(WHAT HAPPENED TO ARGO?!)
(WHAT HAPPENED TO MY FAMILY?!)
RRRRRR...

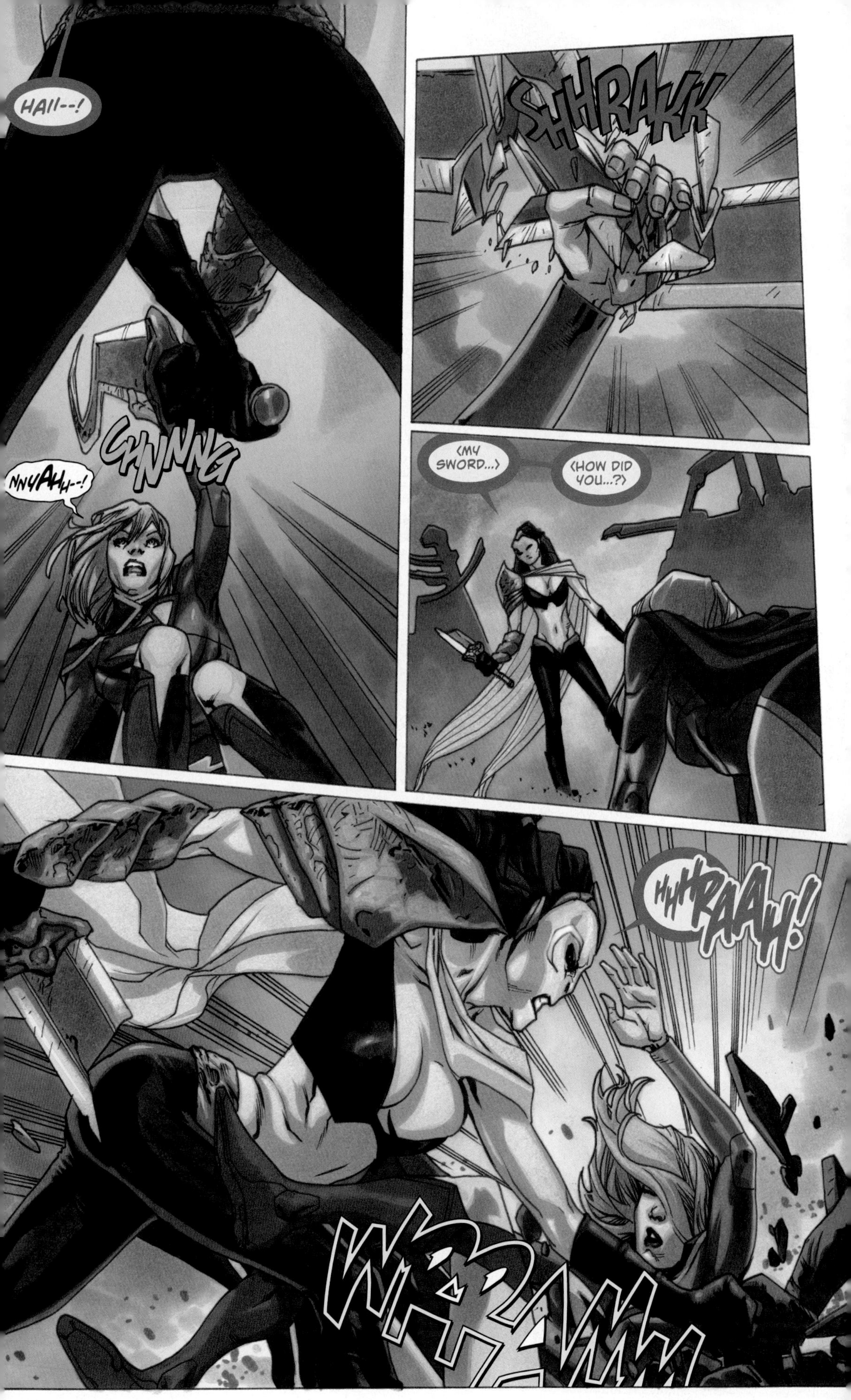
HAII--!
CHNNNG
NNYAHH--!
SHHRAKK
‹MY SWORD...›
‹HOW DID YOU...?›
HHHRAAAH!
WRRAMM

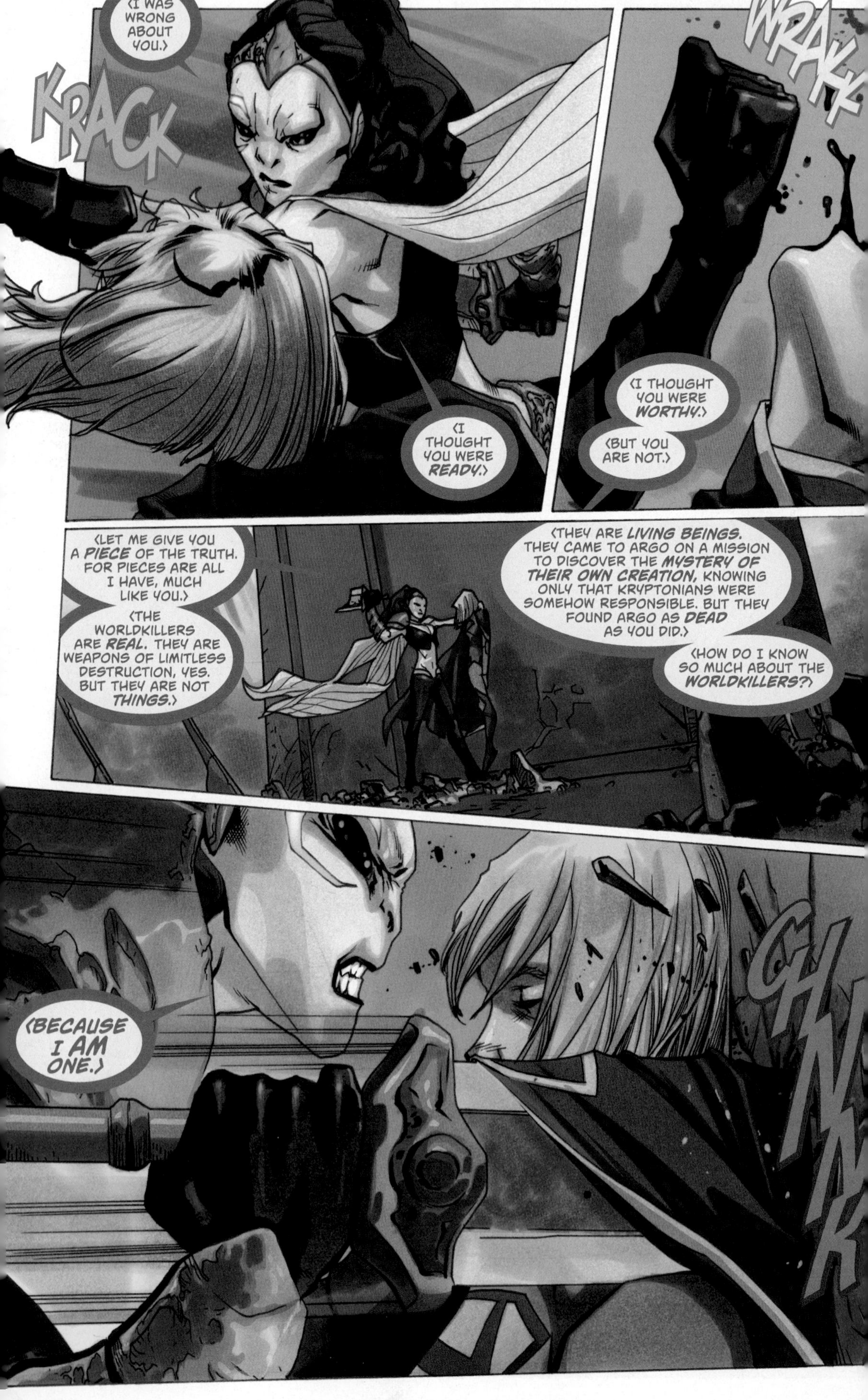
‹I WAS WRONG ABOUT YOU.›
KRACK
‹I THOUGHT YOU WERE *READY*.›
WRAKK
‹I THOUGHT YOU WERE *WORTHY*.›
‹BUT YOU ARE NOT.›
‹LET ME GIVE YOU A *PIECE* OF THE TRUTH. FOR PIECES ARE ALL I HAVE, MUCH LIKE YOU.›
‹THE WORLDKILLERS ARE *REAL*. THEY ARE WEAPONS OF LIMITLESS DESTRUCTION, YES. BUT THEY ARE NOT *THINGS*.›
‹THEY ARE *LIVING BEINGS*. THEY CAME TO ARGO ON A MISSION TO DISCOVER THE *MYSTERY OF THEIR OWN CREATION*, KNOWING ONLY THAT KRYPTONIANS WERE SOMEHOW RESPONSIBLE. BUT THEY FOUND ARGO AS *DEAD* AS YOU DID.›
‹HOW DO I KNOW SO MUCH ABOUT THE *WORLDKILLERS*?›
‹BECAUSE I *AM* ONE.›
CHNNAK

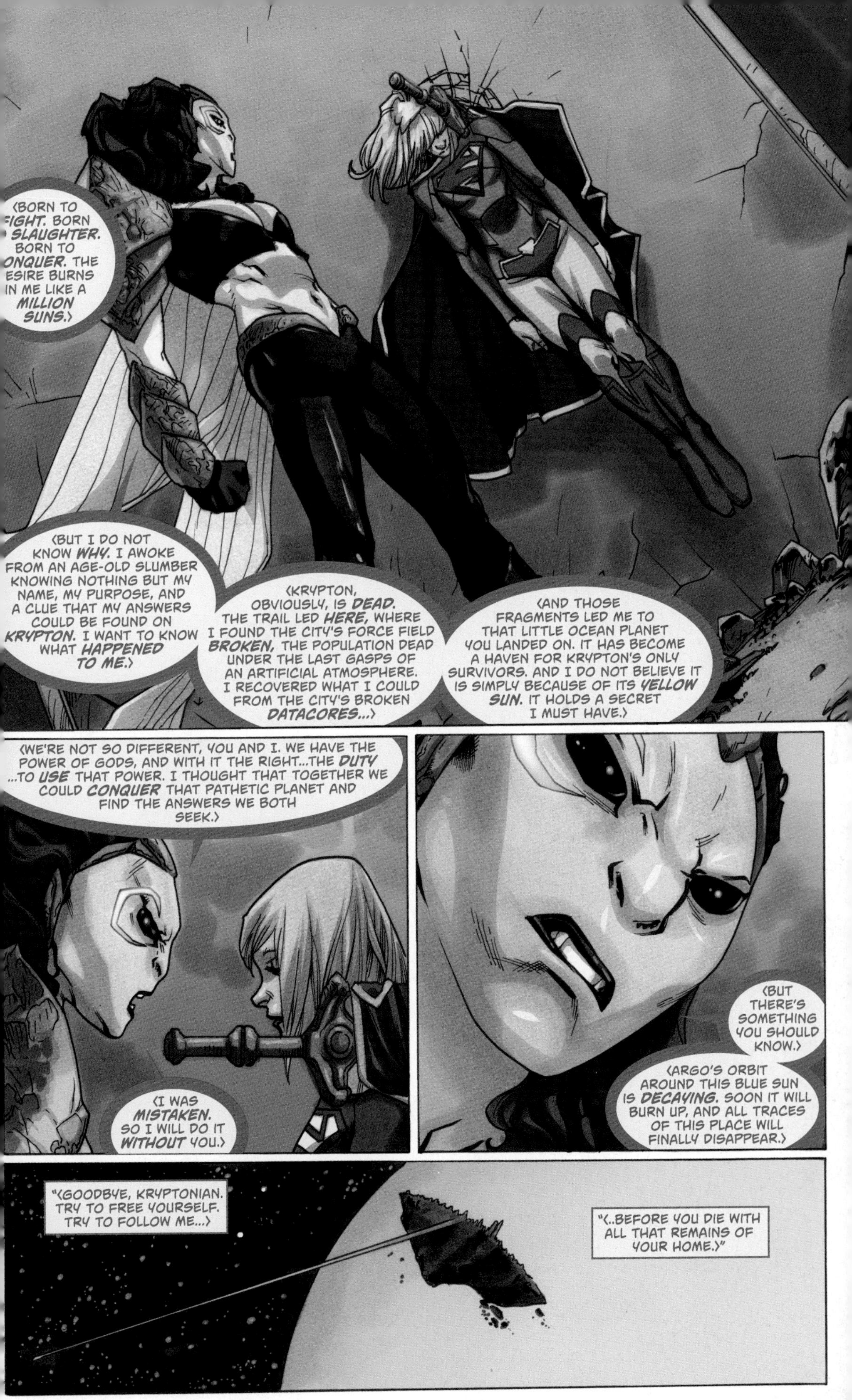

‹BORN TO FIGHT. BORN SLAUGHTER. BORN TO ONQUER. THE ESIRE BURNS IN ME LIKE A MILLION SUNS.›
‹BUT I DO NOT KNOW WHY. I AWOKE FROM AN AGE-OLD SLUMBER KNOWING NOTHING BUT MY NAME, MY PURPOSE, AND A CLUE THAT MY ANSWERS COULD BE FOUND ON KRYPTON. I WANT TO KNOW WHAT HAPPENED TO ME.›
‹KRYPTON, OBVIOUSLY, IS DEAD. THE TRAIL LED HERE, WHERE I FOUND THE CITY'S FORCE FIELD BROKEN, THE POPULATION DEAD UNDER THE LAST GASPS OF AN ARTIFICIAL ATMOSPHERE. I RECOVERED WHAT I COULD FROM THE CITY'S BROKEN DATACORES...›
‹AND THOSE FRAGMENTS LED ME TO THAT LITTLE OCEAN PLANET YOU LANDED ON. IT HAS BECOME A HAVEN FOR KRYPTON'S ONLY SURVIVORS. AND I DO NOT BELIEVE IT IS SIMPLY BECAUSE OF ITS YELLOW SUN. IT HOLDS A SECRET I MUST HAVE.›
‹WE'RE NOT SO DIFFERENT, YOU AND I. WE HAVE THE POWER OF GODS, AND WITH IT THE RIGHT...THE DUTY ...TO USE THAT POWER. I THOUGHT THAT TOGETHER WE COULD CONQUER THAT PATHETIC PLANET AND FIND THE ANSWERS WE BOTH SEEK.›
‹I WAS MISTAKEN. SO I WILL DO IT WITHOUT YOU.›
‹BUT THERE'S SOMETHING YOU SHOULD KNOW.›
‹ARGO'S ORBIT AROUND THIS BLUE SUN IS DECAYING. SOON IT WILL BURN UP, AND ALL TRACES OF THIS PLACE WILL FINALLY DISAPPEAR.›
"‹GOODBYE, KRYPTONIAN. TRY TO FREE YOURSELF. TRY TO FOLLOW ME...›
"‹..BEFORE YOU DIE WITH ALL THAT REMAINS OF YOUR HOME.›"

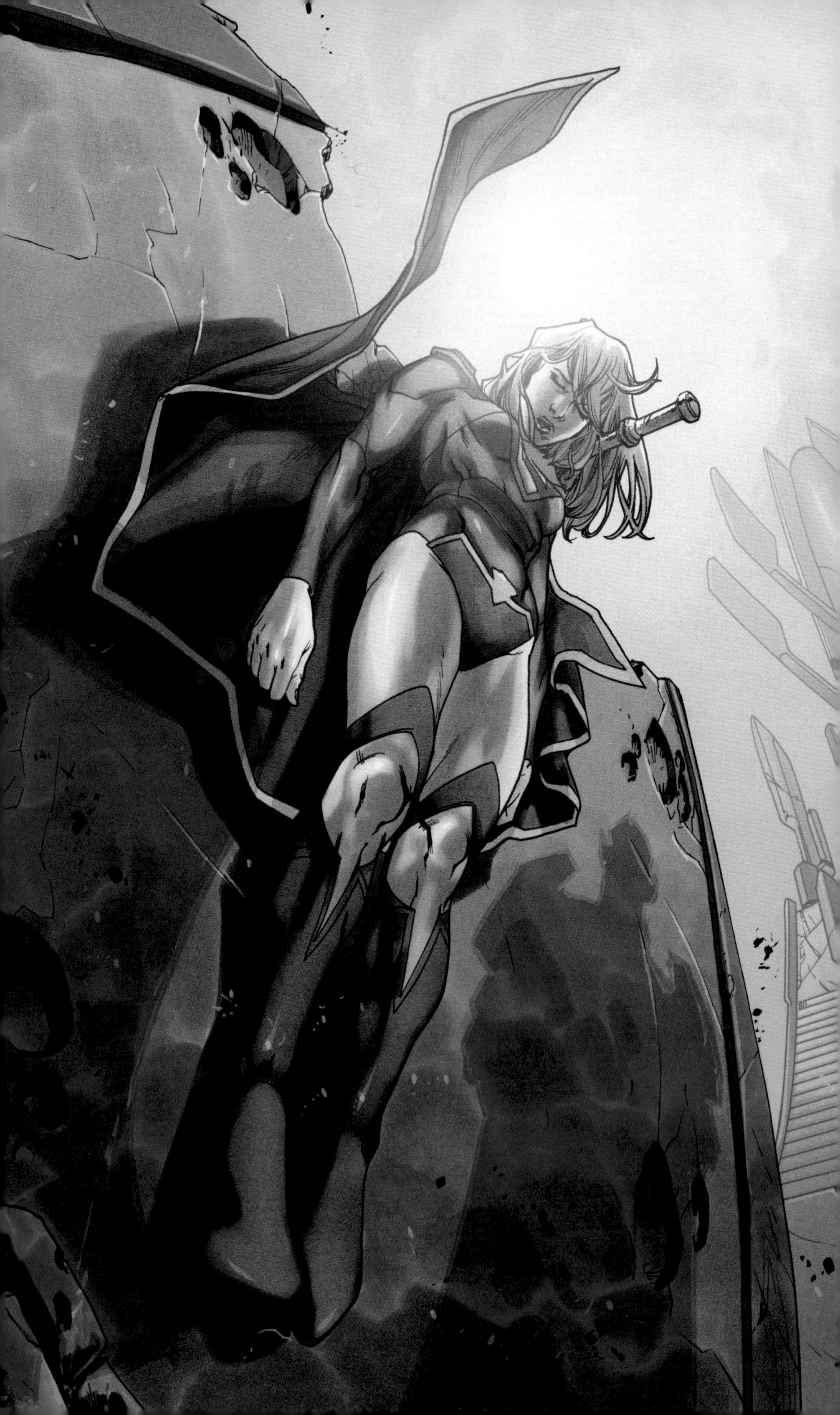

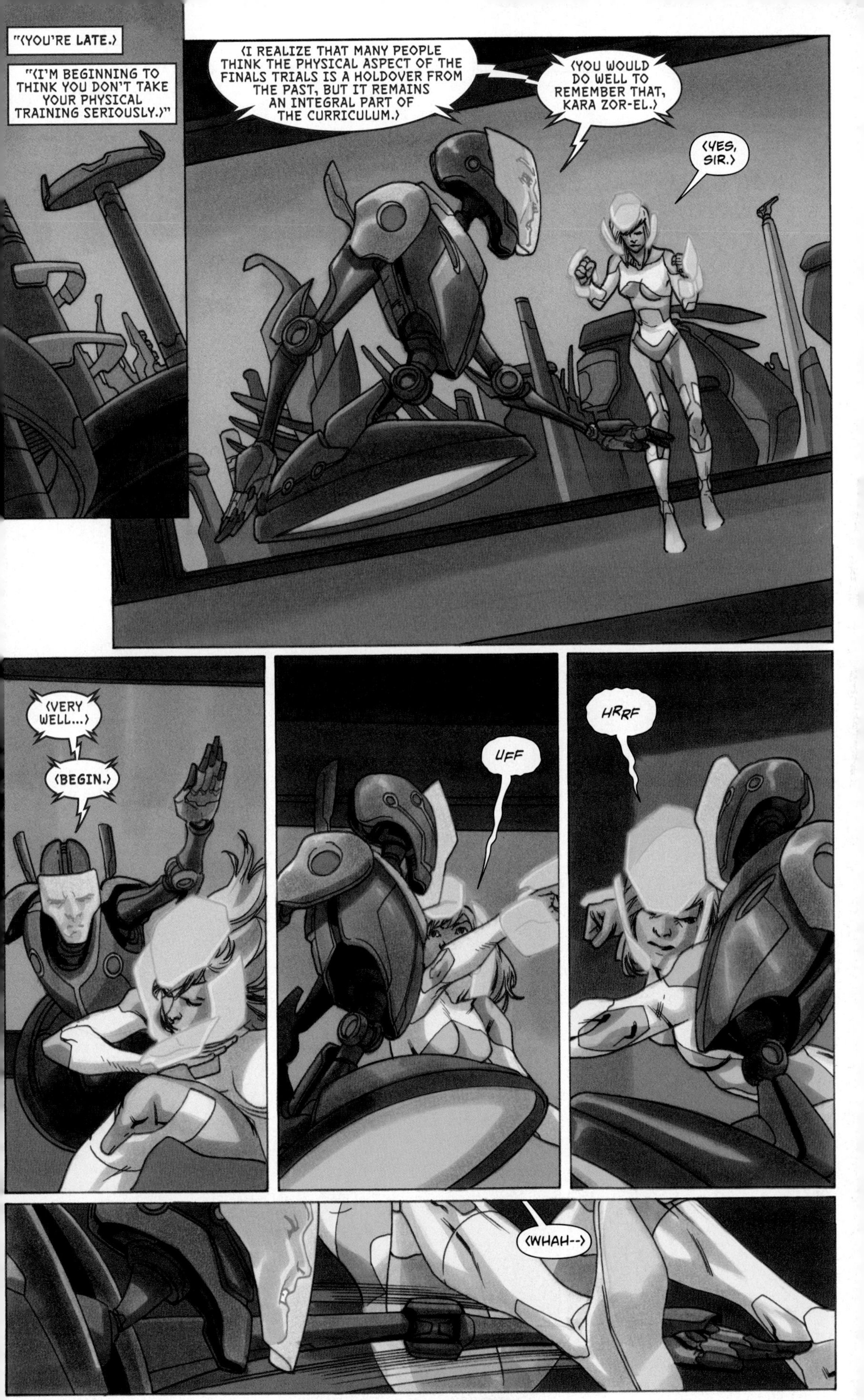
"‹YOU'RE LATE.›
"‹I'M BEGINNING TO THINK YOU DON'T TAKE YOUR PHYSICAL TRAINING SERIOUSLY.›"
‹I REALIZE THAT MANY PEOPLE THINK THE PHYSICAL ASPECT OF THE FINALS TRIALS IS A HOLDOVER FROM THE PAST, BUT IT REMAINS AN INTEGRAL PART OF THE CURRICULUM.›
‹YOU WOULD DO WELL TO REMEMBER THAT, KARA ZOR-EL.›
‹YES, SIR.›
‹VERY WELL...›
‹BEGIN.›
UFF
HRRF
‹WHAH--›

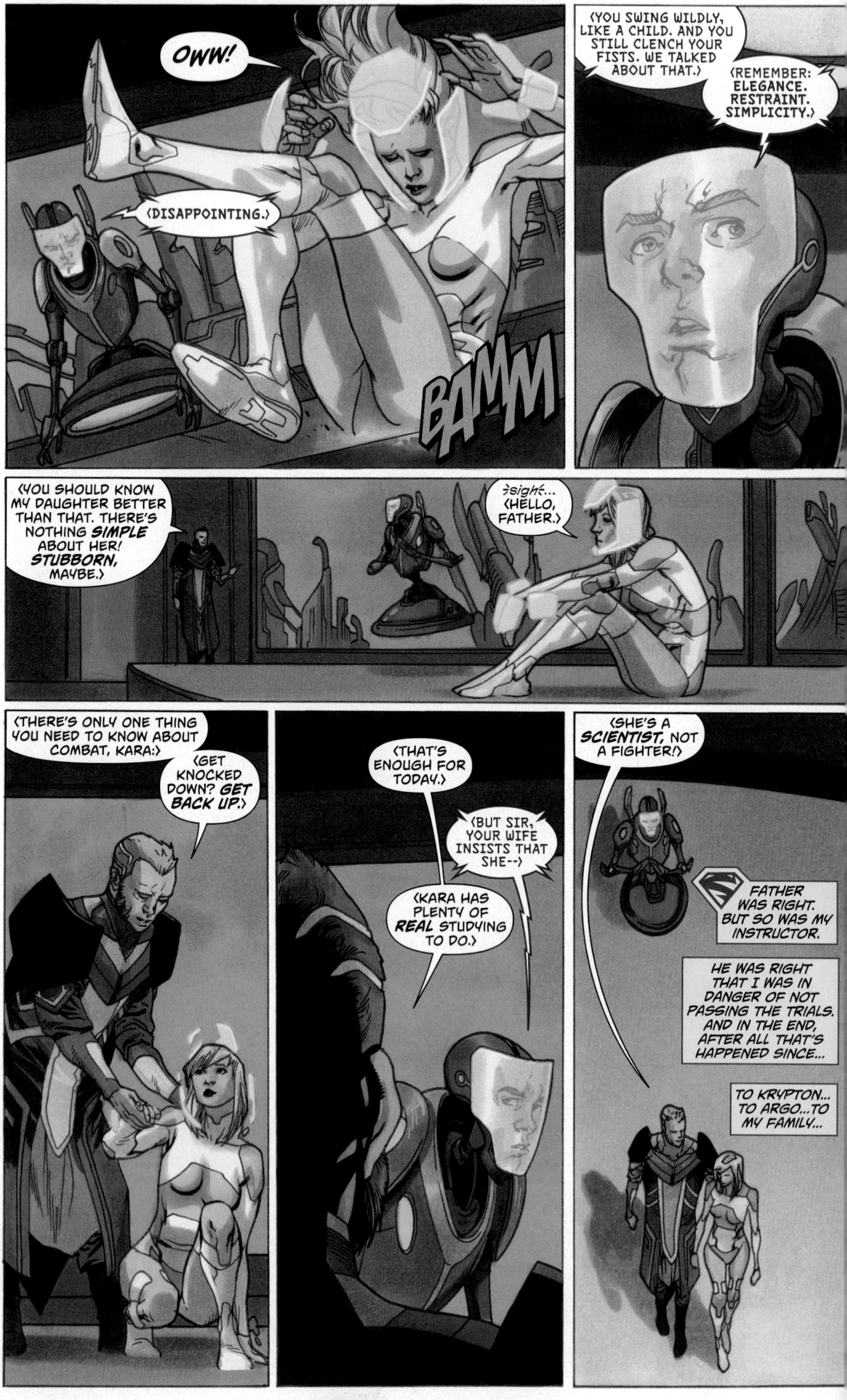
OWW!
⟨DISAPPOINTING.⟩
BAMM
⟨YOU SWING WILDLY, LIKE A CHILD. AND YOU STILL CLENCH YOUR FISTS. WE TALKED ABOUT THAT.⟩
⟨REMEMBER: ELEGANCE. RESTRAINT. SIMPLICITY.⟩
⟨YOU SHOULD KNOW MY DAUGHTER BETTER THAN THAT. THERE'S NOTHING SIMPLE ABOUT HER! STUBBORN, MAYBE.⟩
sigh... ⟨HELLO, FATHER.⟩
⟨THERE'S ONLY ONE THING YOU NEED TO KNOW ABOUT COMBAT, KARA:⟩
⟨GET KNOCKED DOWN? GET BACK UP.⟩
⟨THAT'S ENOUGH FOR TODAY.⟩
⟨BUT SIR, YOUR WIFE INSISTS THAT SHE--⟩
⟨KARA HAS PLENTY OF REAL STUDYING TO DO.⟩
⟨SHE'S A SCIENTIST, NOT A FIGHTER!⟩
FATHER WAS RIGHT. BUT SO WAS MY INSTRUCTOR.
HE WAS RIGHT THAT I WAS IN DANGER OF NOT PASSING THE TRIALS. AND IN THE END, AFTER ALL THAT'S HAPPENED SINCE...
TO KRYPTON... TO ARGO...TO MY FAMILY...

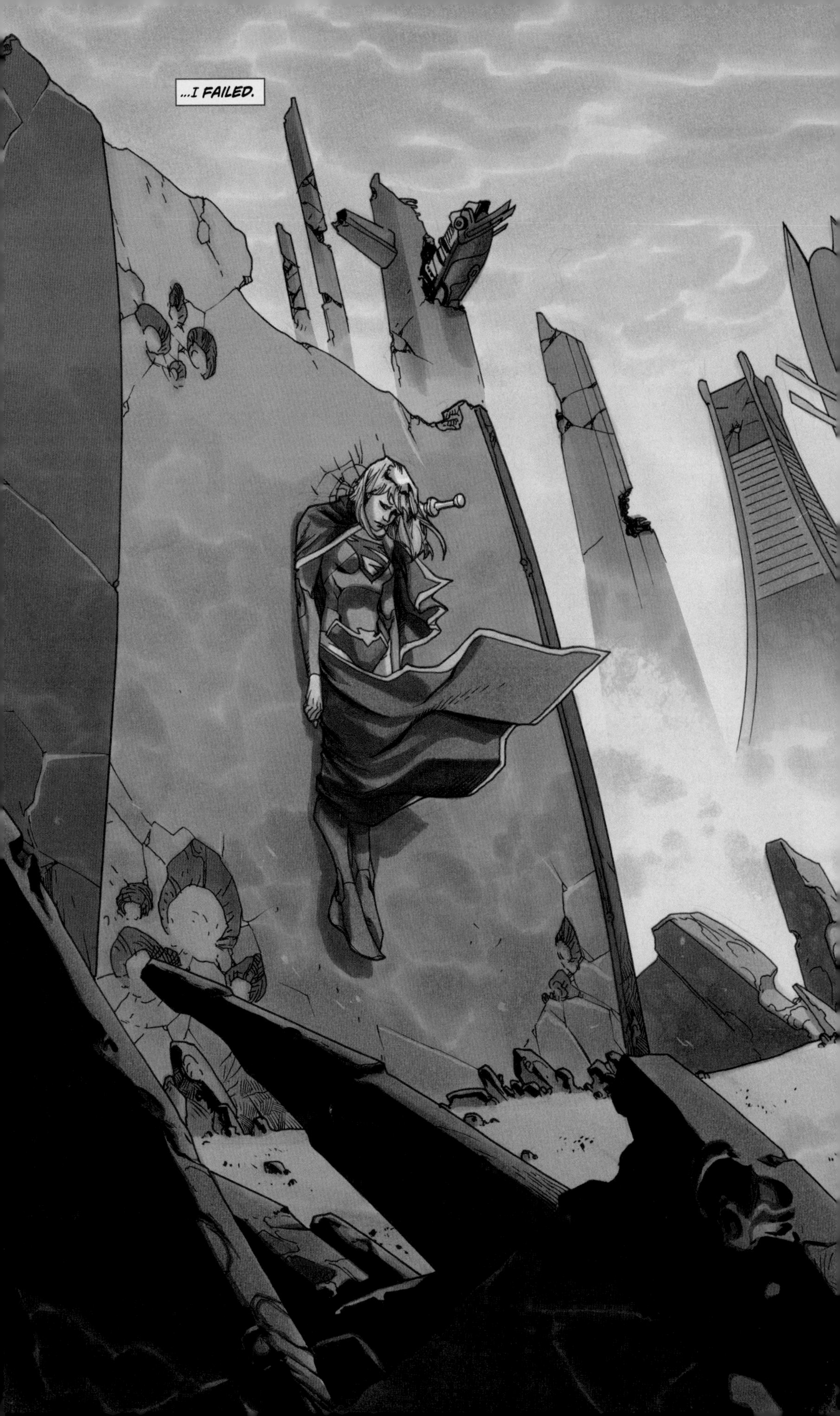
...I FAILED.

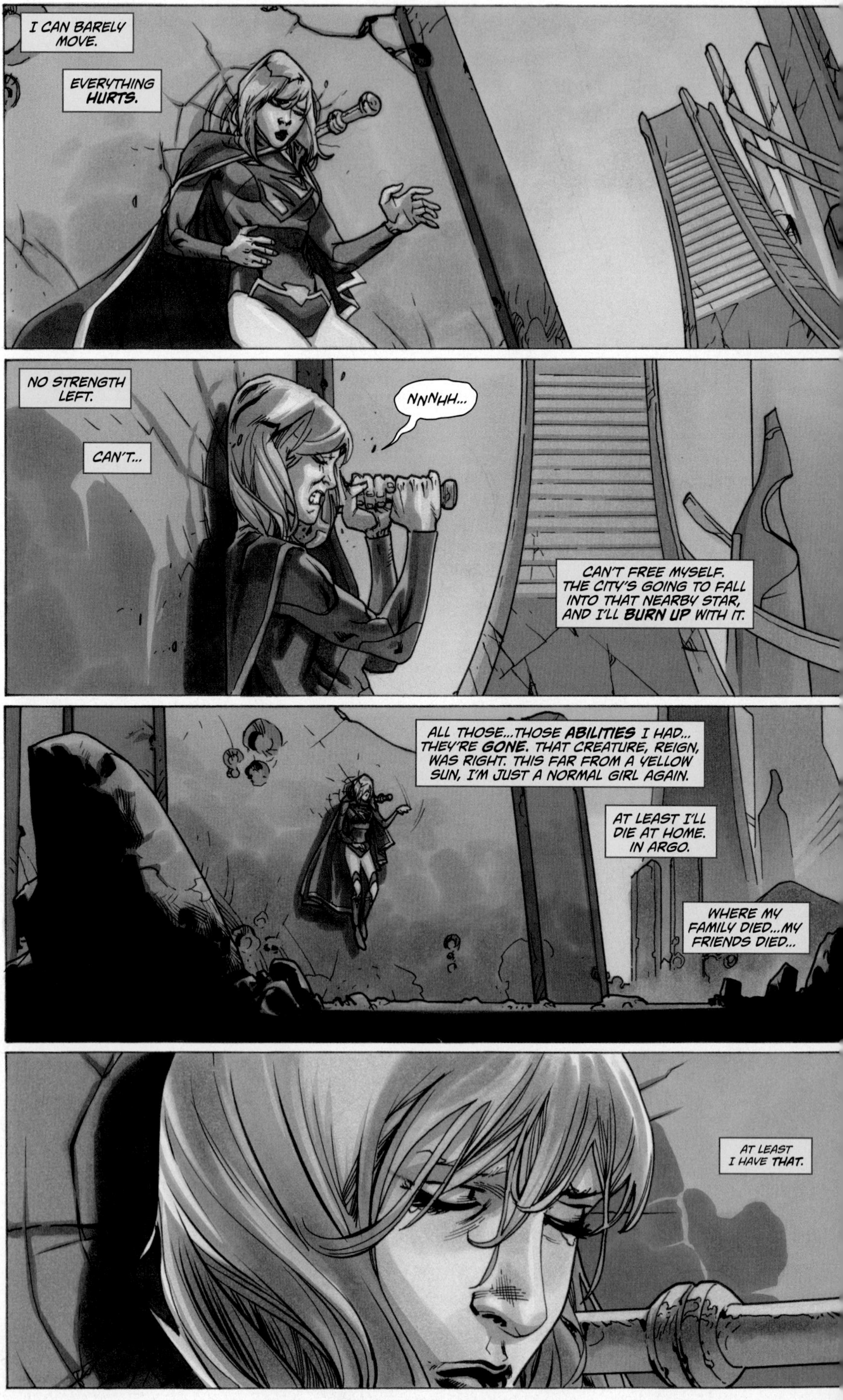
I CAN BARELY MOVE.
EVERYTHING **HURTS.**
NO STRENGTH LEFT.
NNNHH...
CAN'T...
CAN'T FREE MYSELF. THE CITY'S GOING TO FALL INTO THAT NEARBY STAR, AND I'LL **BURN UP** WITH IT.
ALL THOSE...THOSE **ABILITIES** I HAD... THEY'RE **GONE**. THAT CREATURE, REIGN, WAS RIGHT. THIS FAR FROM A YELLOW SUN, I'M JUST A NORMAL GIRL AGAIN.
AT LEAST I'LL DIE AT HOME. IN ARGO.
WHERE MY FAMILY DIED...MY FRIENDS DIED...
AT LEAST I HAVE **THAT.**

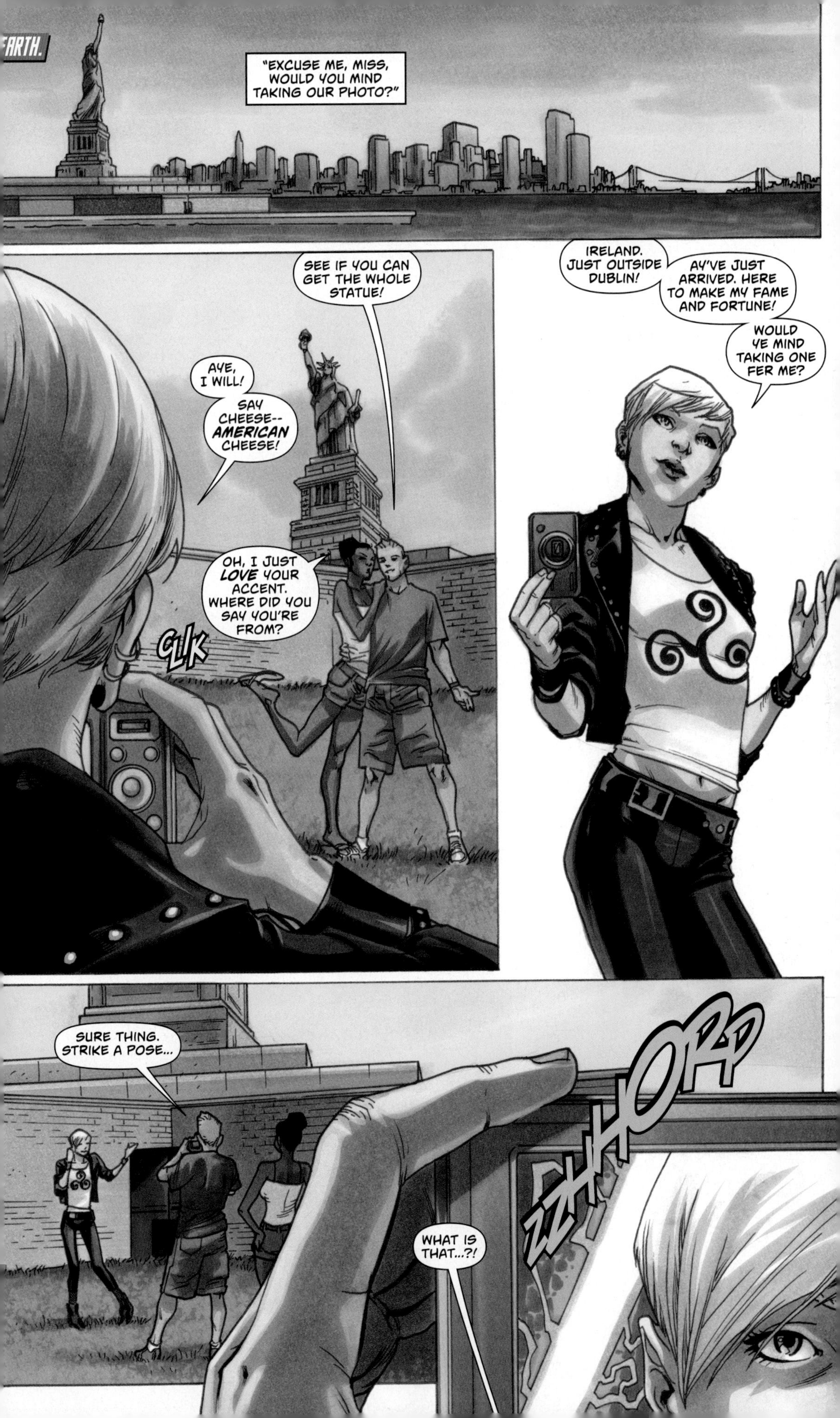
EARTH.
"EXCUSE ME, MISS, WOULD YOU MIND TAKING OUR PHOTO?"
SEE IF YOU CAN GET THE WHOLE STATUE!
AYE, I WILL!
SAY CHEESE-- **AMERICAN** CHEESE!
CLIK
OH, I JUST **LOVE** YOUR ACCENT. WHERE DID YOU SAY YOU'RE FROM?
IRELAND. JUST OUTSIDE DUBLIN!
AY'VE JUST ARRIVED. HERE TO MAKE MY FAME AND FORTUNE!
WOULD YE MIND TAKING ONE FER ME?
SURE THING. STRIKE A POSE...
ZZHHORD
WHAT IS THAT...?!

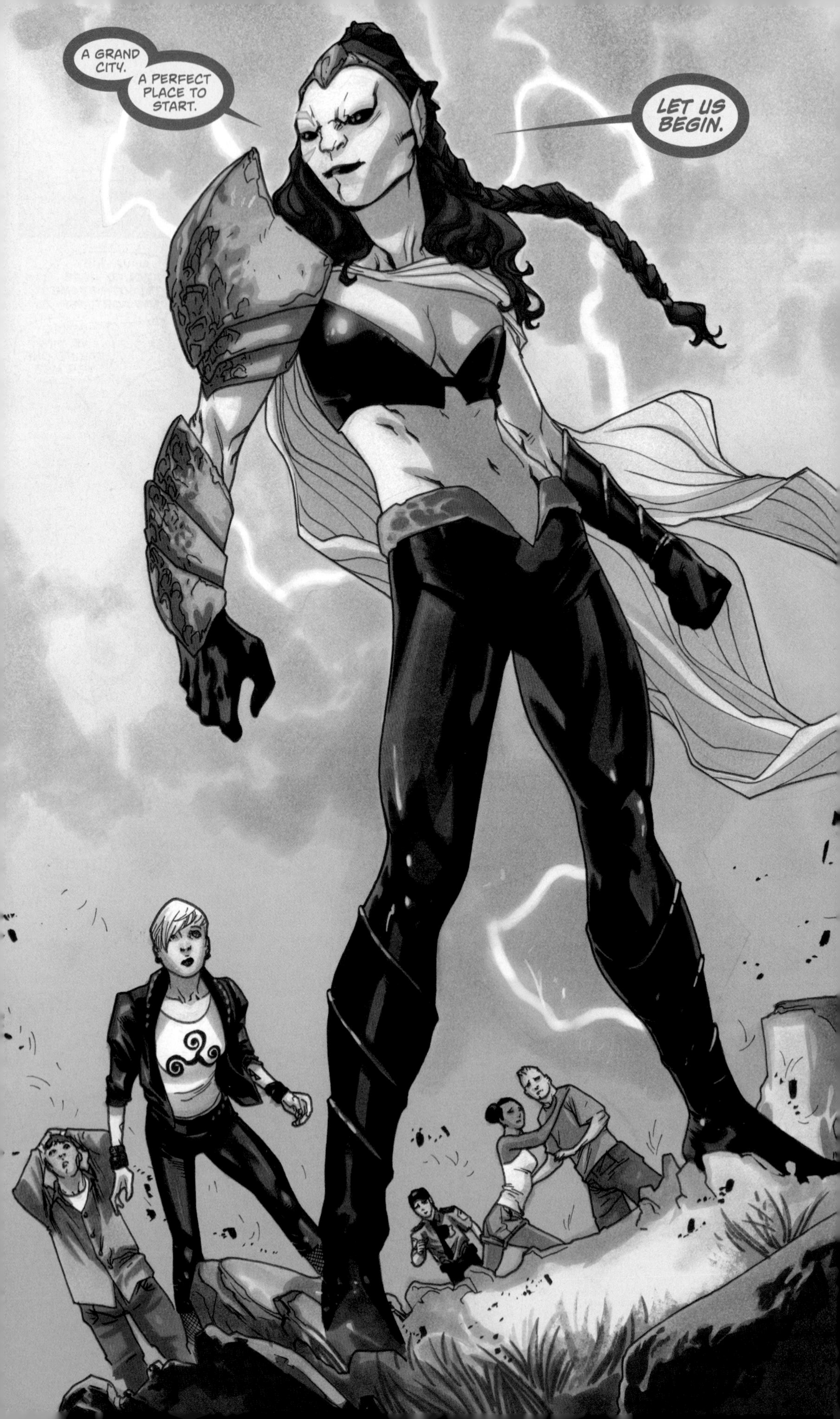
A GRAND CITY.
A PERFECT PLACE TO START.
LET US BEGIN.

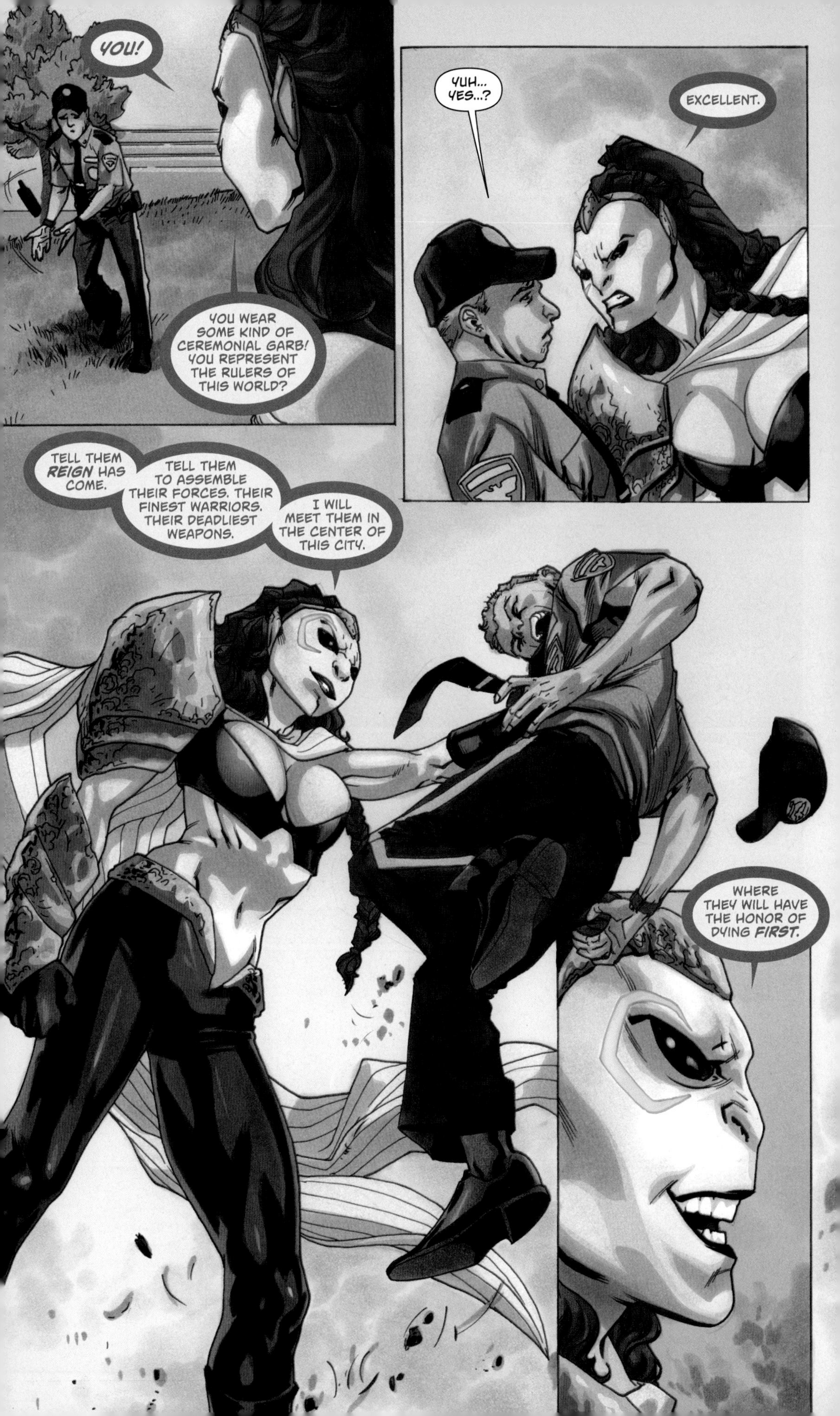
YOU!
YOU WEAR SOME KIND OF CEREMONIAL GARB! YOU REPRESENT THE RULERS OF THIS WORLD?
YUH... YES...?
EXCELLENT.
TELL THEM *REIGN* HAS COME.
TELL THEM TO ASSEMBLE THEIR FORCES. THEIR FINEST WARRIORS. THEIR DEADLIEST WEAPONS.
I WILL MEET THEM IN THE CENTER OF THIS CITY.
WHERE THEY WILL HAVE THE HONOR OF DYING ***FIRST.***

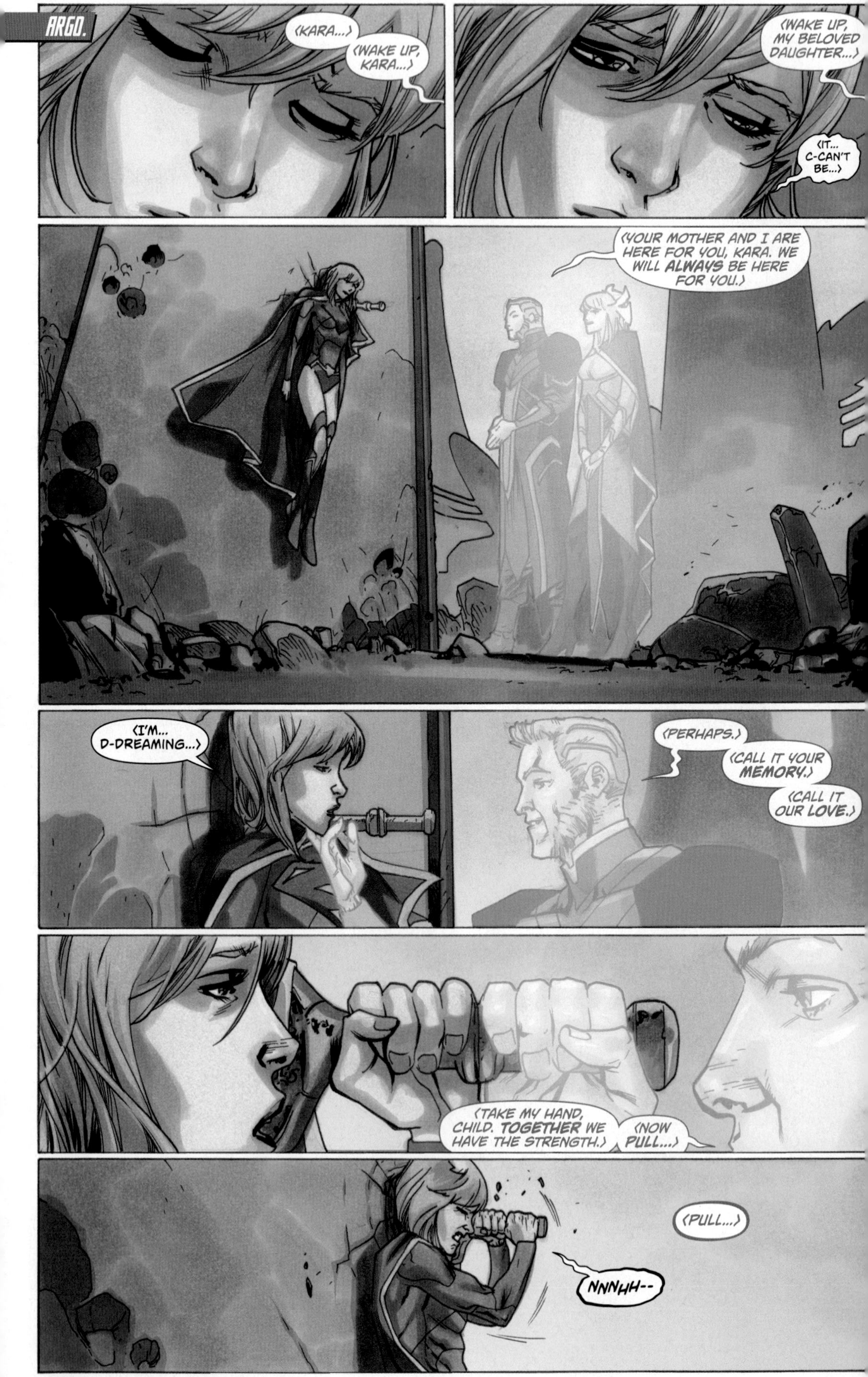
ARGO.
‹KARA...›
‹WAKE UP, KARA...›
‹WAKE UP, MY BELOVED DAUGHTER...›
‹IT... C-CAN'T BE...›
‹YOUR MOTHER AND I ARE HERE FOR YOU, KARA. WE WILL ALWAYS BE HERE FOR YOU.›
‹I'M... D-DREAMING...›
‹PERHAPS.›
‹CALL IT YOUR MEMORY.›
‹CALL IT OUR LOVE.›
‹TAKE MY HAND, CHILD. TOGETHER WE HAVE THE STRENGTH.›
‹NOW PULL...›
‹PULL...›
NNNHH--

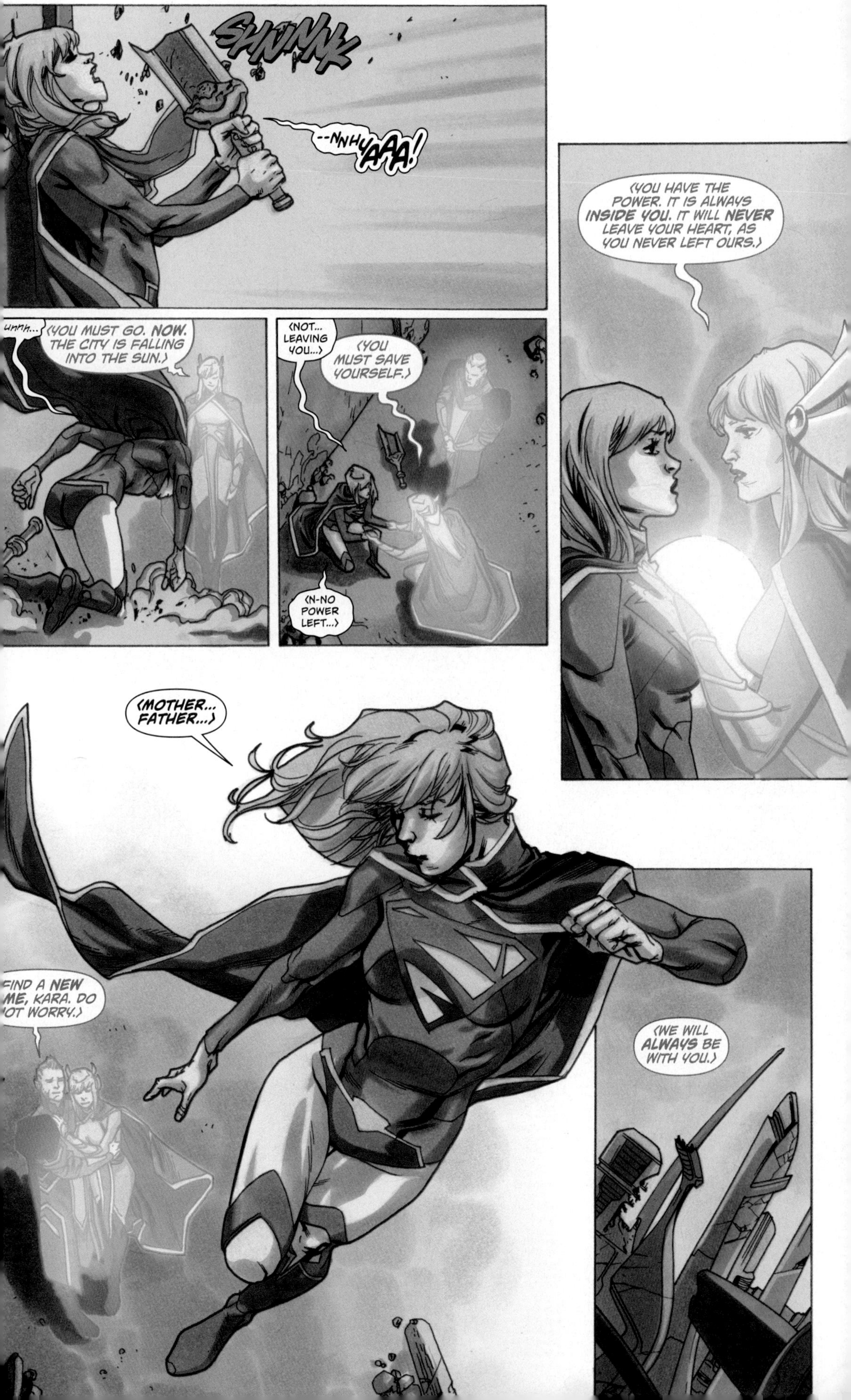
SHUNNK
--NNHYAAA!
(YOU HAVE THE POWER. IT IS ALWAYS INSIDE YOU. IT WILL NEVER LEAVE YOUR HEART, AS YOU NEVER LEFT OURS.)
unnh...
(YOU MUST GO. NOW. THE CITY IS FALLING INTO THE SUN.)
(NOT... LEAVING YOU...)
(YOU MUST SAVE YOURSELF.)
(N-NO POWER LEFT...)
(MOTHER... FATHER...)
FIND A NEW ME, KARA. DO OT WORRY.)
(WE WILL ALWAYS BE WITH YOU.)

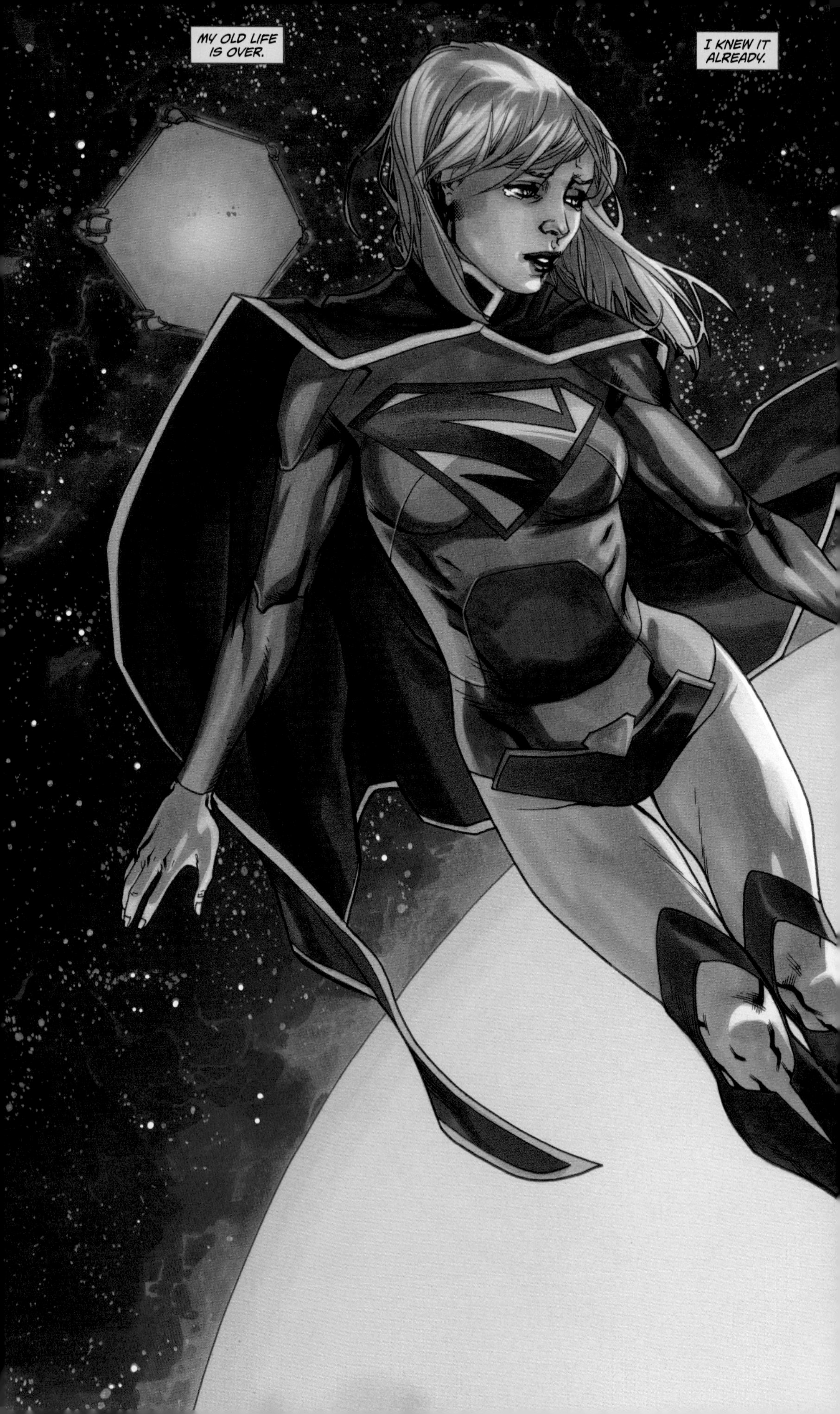
MY OLD LIFE IS OVER.
I KNEW IT ALREADY.

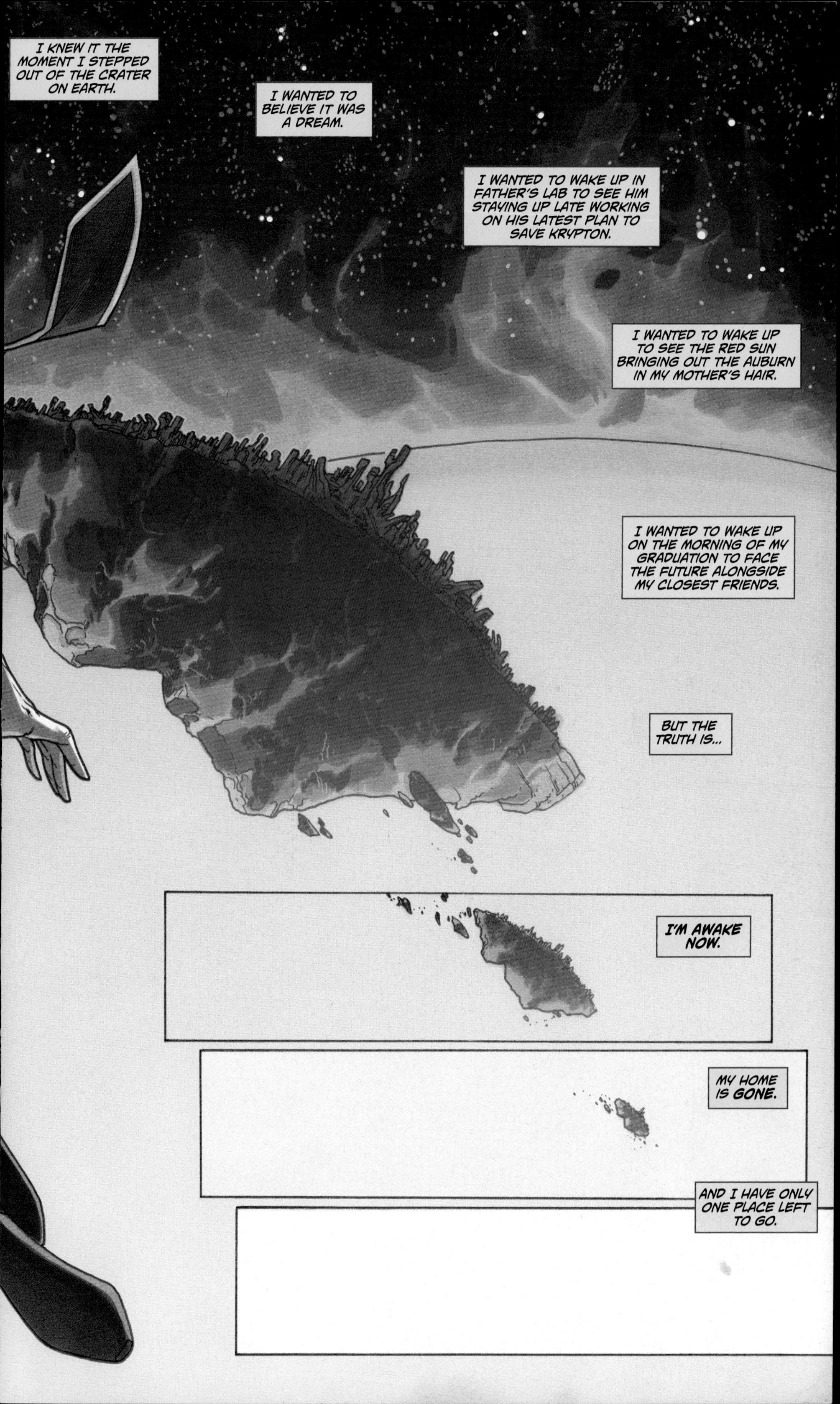
I KNEW IT THE MOMENT I STEPPED OUT OF THE CRATER ON EARTH.
I WANTED TO BELIEVE IT WAS A DREAM.
I WANTED TO WAKE UP IN FATHER'S LAB TO SEE HIM STAYING UP LATE WORKING ON HIS LATEST PLAN TO SAVE KRYPTON.
I WANTED TO WAKE UP TO SEE THE RED SUN BRINGING OUT THE AUBURN IN MY MOTHER'S HAIR.
I WANTED TO WAKE UP ON THE MORNING OF MY GRADUATION TO FACE THE FUTURE ALONGSIDE MY CLOSEST FRIENDS.
BUT THE TRUTH IS...
I'M AWAKE NOW.
MY HOME IS GONE.
AND I HAVE ONLY ONE PLACE LEFT TO GO.

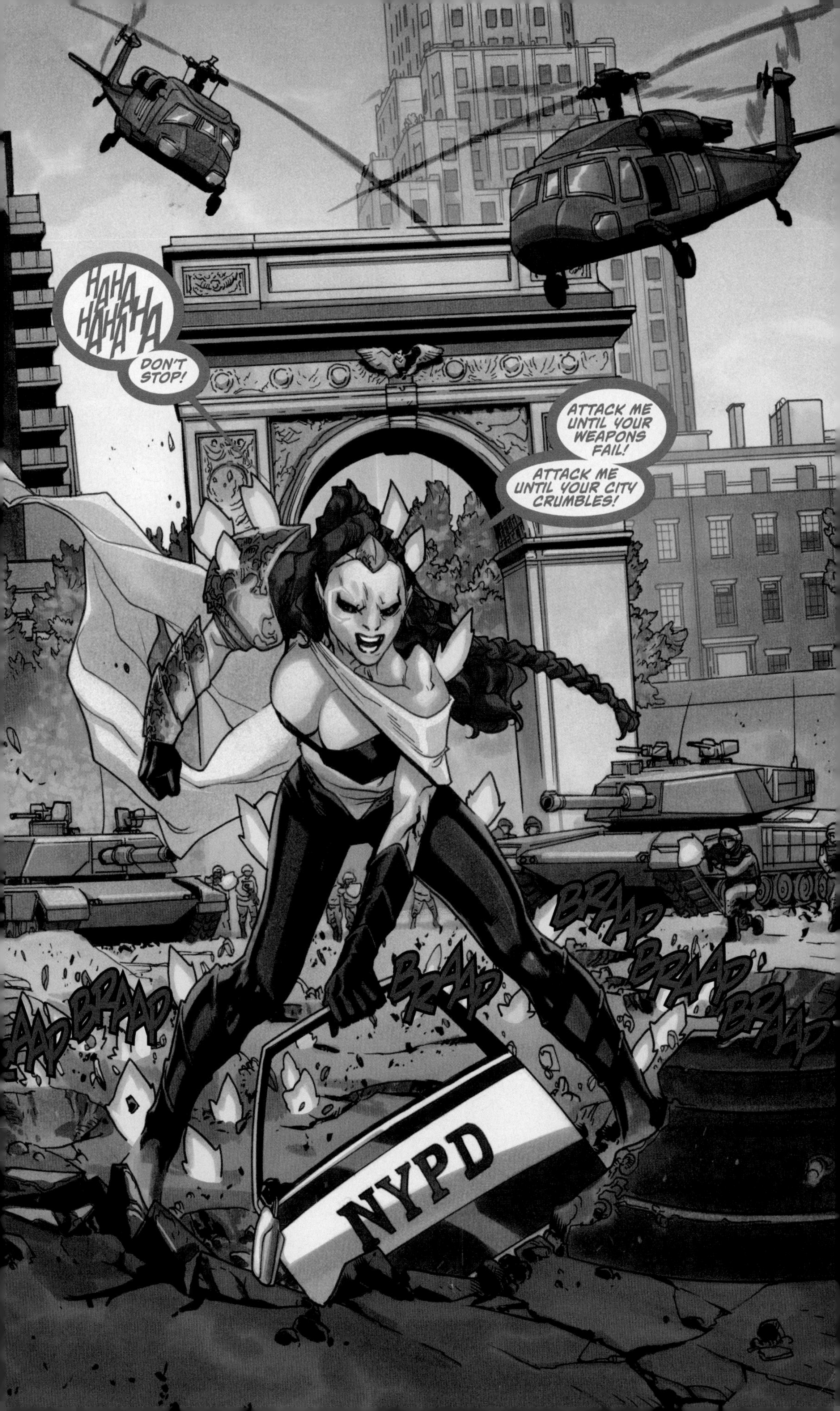

HAHAHAHAHAHA
DON'T STOP!
ATTACK ME UNTIL YOUR WEAPONS FAIL!
ATTACK ME UNTIL YOUR CITY CRUMBLES!
AAP BRAAP
BRAAP
BRAAP
BRAAP
BRAAP
NYPD

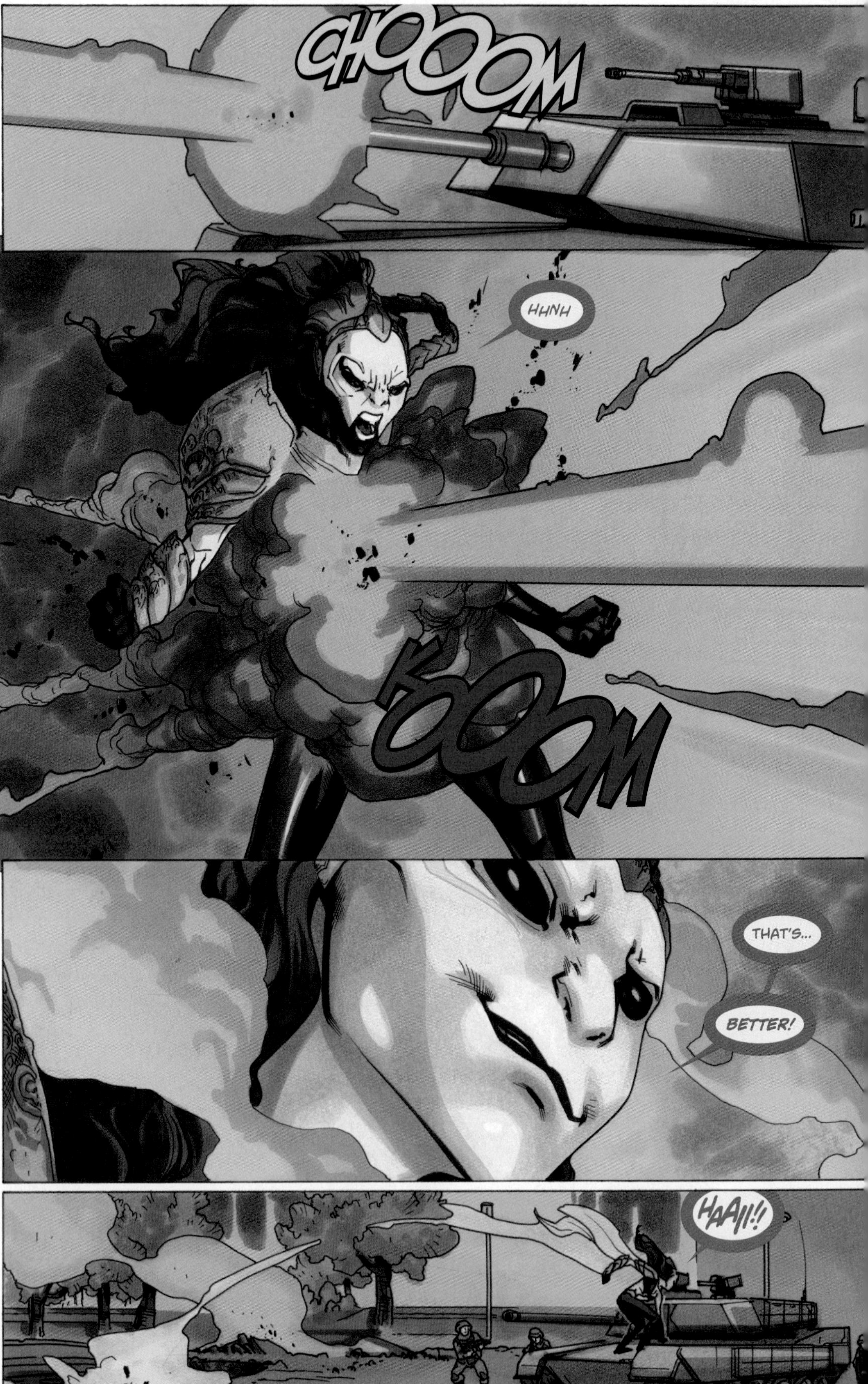
CHOOOOM
HHNH
KOOOM
THAT'S...
BETTER!
HAAII!!

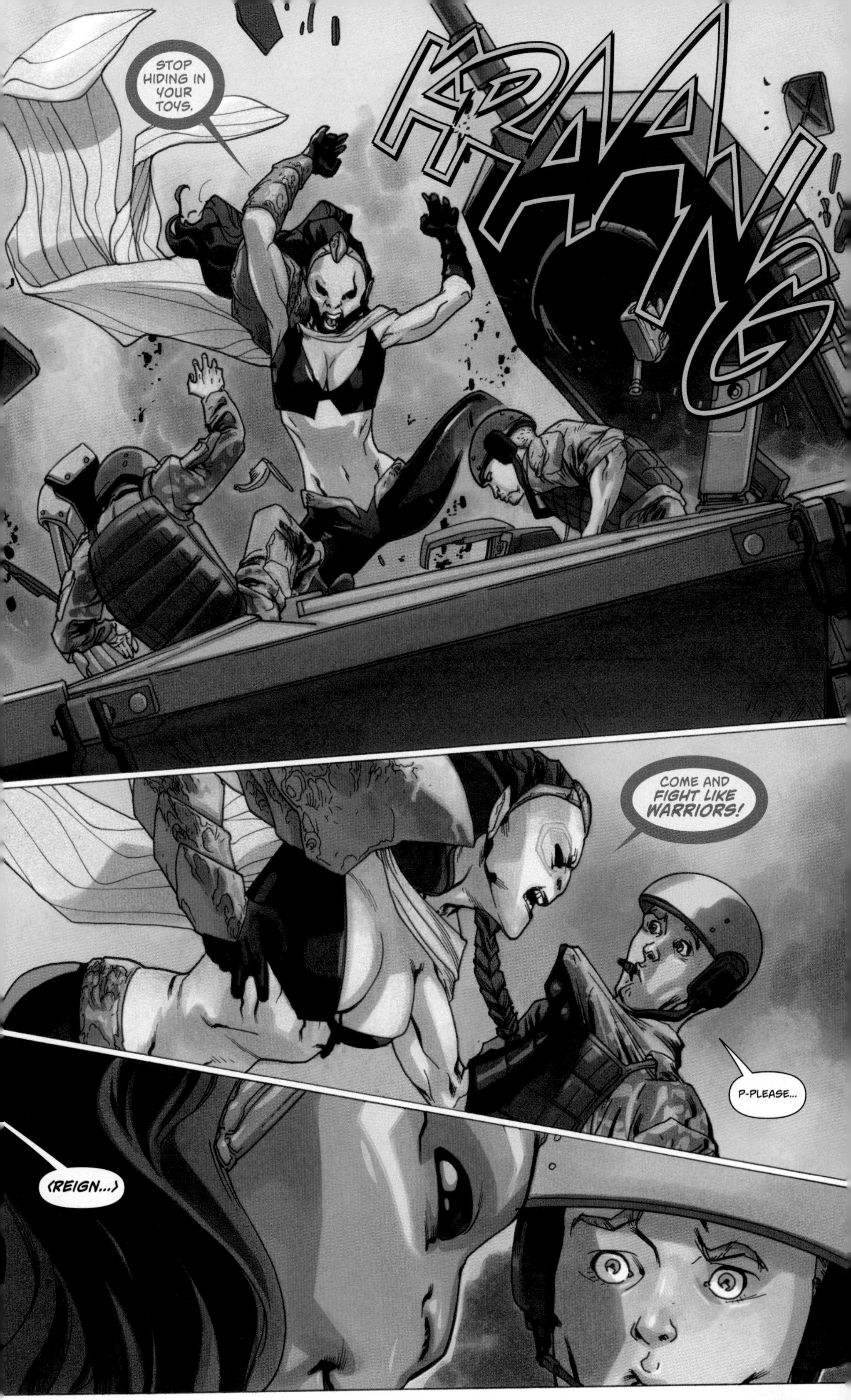

STOP HIDING IN YOUR TOYS.
KRAAANG
COME AND FIGHT LIKE WARRIORS!
P-PLEASE...
‹REIGN...›

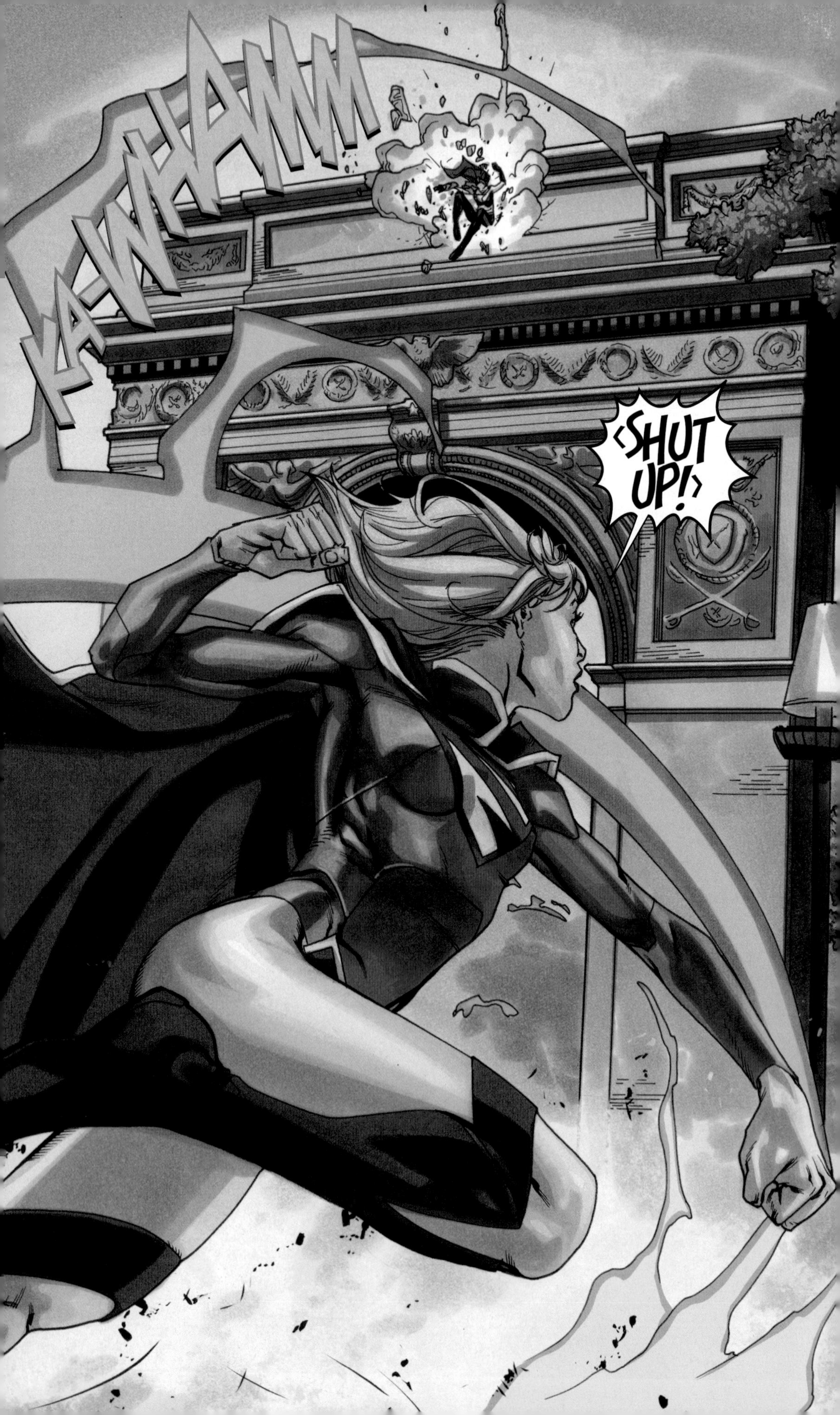
KA-WHAMM
‹SHUT UP!›

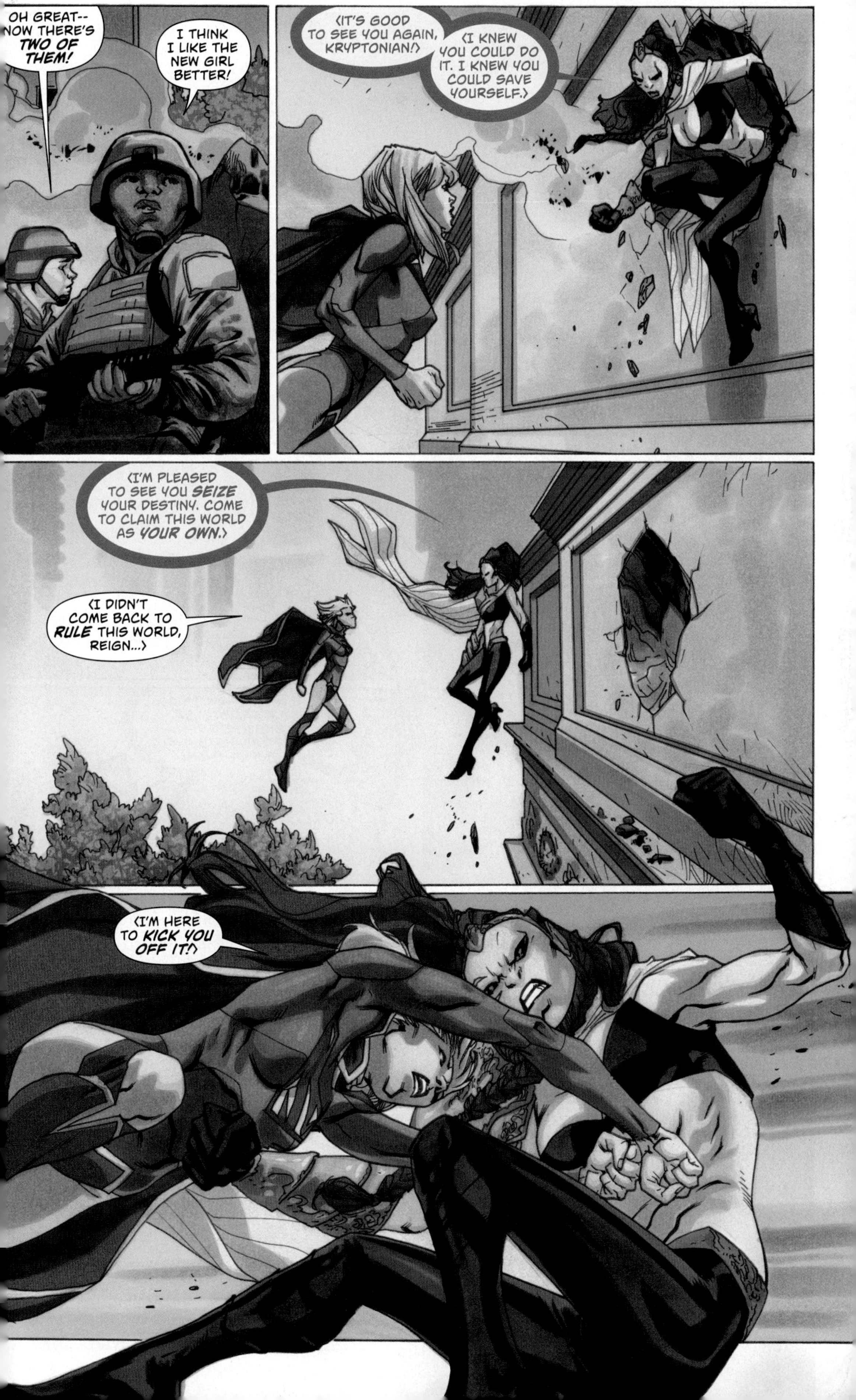

OH GREAT-- NOW THERE'S TWO OF THEM!
I THINK I LIKE THE NEW GIRL BETTER!
‹IT'S GOOD TO SEE YOU AGAIN, KRYPTONIAN!›
‹I KNEW YOU COULD DO IT. I KNEW YOU COULD SAVE YOURSELF.›
‹I'M PLEASED TO SEE YOU SEIZE YOUR DESTINY. COME TO CLAIM THIS WORLD AS YOUR OWN.›
‹I DIDN'T COME BACK TO RULE THIS WORLD, REIGN...›
‹I'M HERE TO KICK YOU OFF IT!›

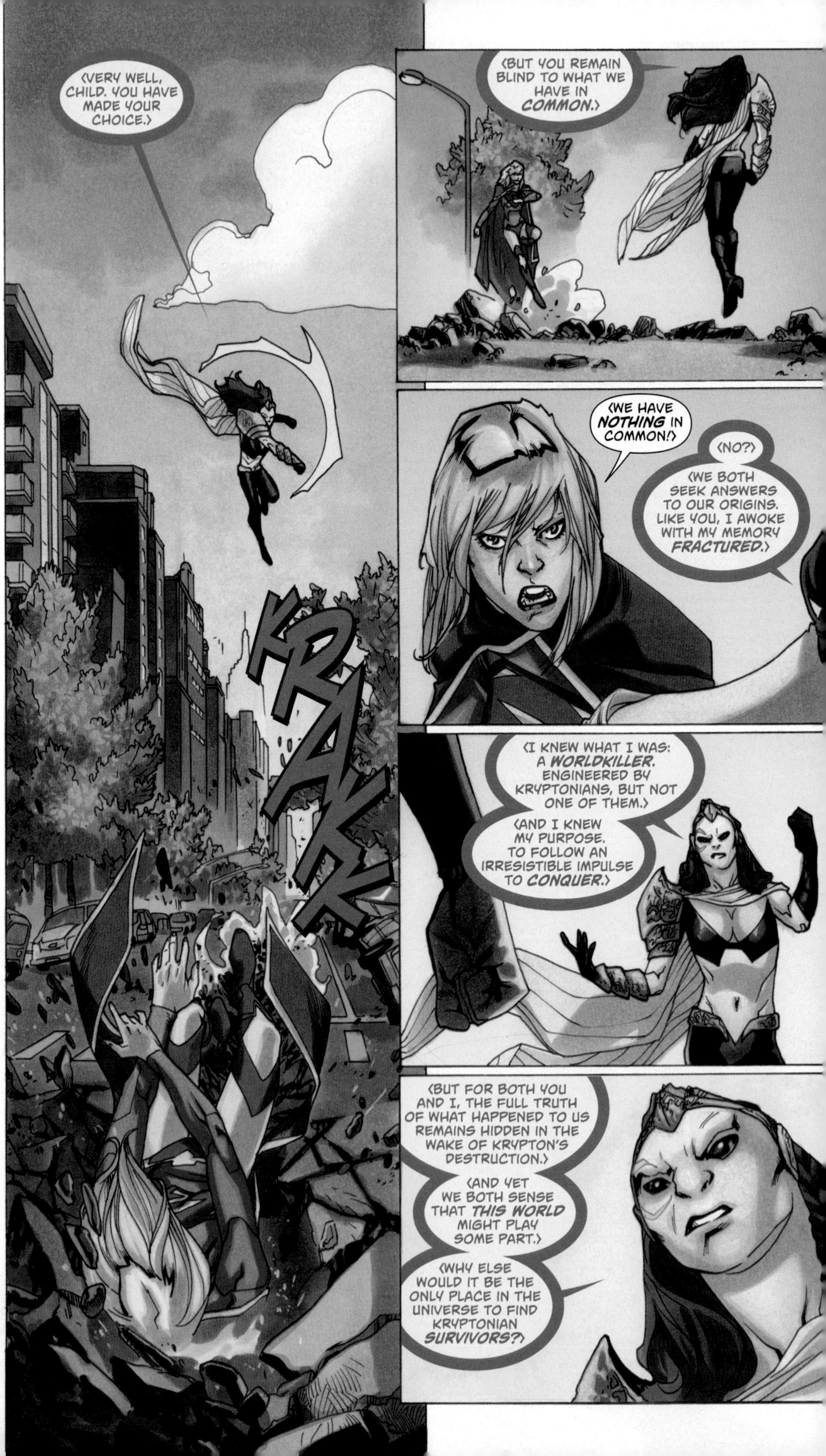

‹VERY WELL, CHILD. YOU HAVE MADE YOUR CHOICE.›
KRAKK
‹BUT YOU REMAIN BLIND TO WHAT WE HAVE IN COMMON.›
‹WE HAVE NOTHING IN COMMON!›
‹NO?›
‹WE BOTH SEEK ANSWERS TO OUR ORIGINS. LIKE YOU, I AWOKE WITH MY MEMORY FRACTURED.›
‹I KNEW WHAT I WAS: A WORLDKILLER. ENGINEERED BY KRYPTONIANS, BUT NOT ONE OF THEM.›
‹AND I KNEW MY PURPOSE. TO FOLLOW AN IRRESISTIBLE IMPULSE TO CONQUER.›
‹BUT FOR BOTH YOU AND I, THE FULL TRUTH OF WHAT HAPPENED TO US REMAINS HIDDEN IN THE WAKE OF KRYPTON'S DESTRUCTION.›
‹AND YET WE BOTH SENSE THAT THIS WORLD MIGHT PLAY SOME PART.›
‹WHY ELSE WOULD IT BE THE ONLY PLACE IN THE UNIVERSE TO FIND KRYPTONIAN SURVIVORS?›

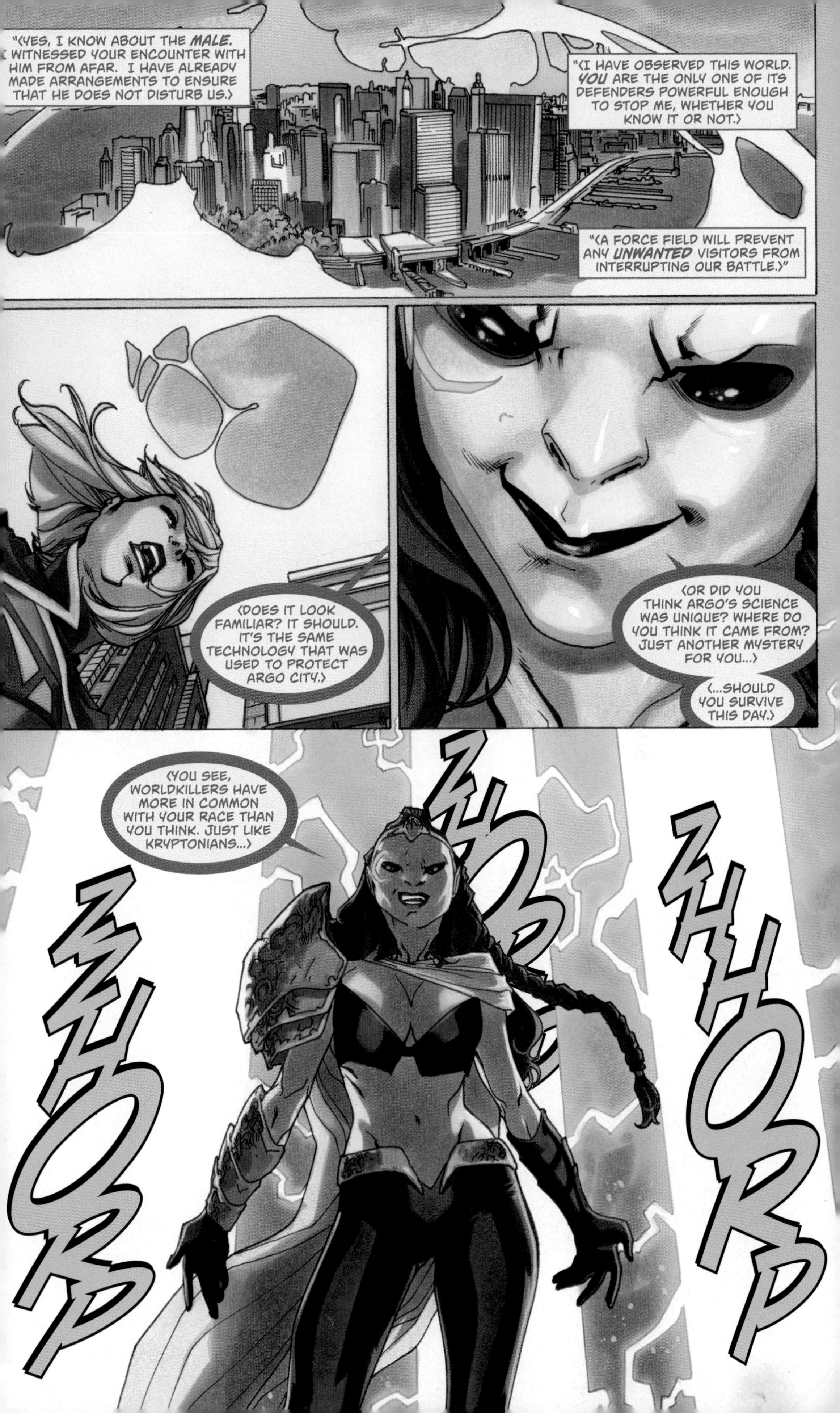
"〈YES, I KNOW ABOUT THE MALE. I WITNESSED YOUR ENCOUNTER WITH HIM FROM AFAR. I HAVE ALREADY MADE ARRANGEMENTS TO ENSURE THAT HE DOES NOT DISTURB US.〉
"〈I HAVE OBSERVED THIS WORLD. YOU ARE THE ONLY ONE OF ITS DEFENDERS POWERFUL ENOUGH TO STOP ME, WHETHER YOU KNOW IT OR NOT.〉
"〈A FORCE FIELD WILL PREVENT ANY UNWANTED VISITORS FROM INTERRUPTING OUR BATTLE.〉"
〈DOES IT LOOK FAMILIAR? IT SHOULD. IT'S THE SAME TECHNOLOGY THAT WAS USED TO PROTECT ARGO CITY.〉
〈OR DID YOU THINK ARGO'S SCIENCE WAS UNIQUE? WHERE DO YOU THINK IT CAME FROM? JUST ANOTHER MYSTERY FOR YOU...〉
〈...SHOULD YOU SURVIVE THIS DAY.〉
〈YOU SEE, WORLDKILLERS HAVE MORE IN COMMON WITH YOUR RACE THAN YOU THINK. JUST LIKE KRYPTONIANS...〉
ZZHORP
ZZHORP
ZHORP

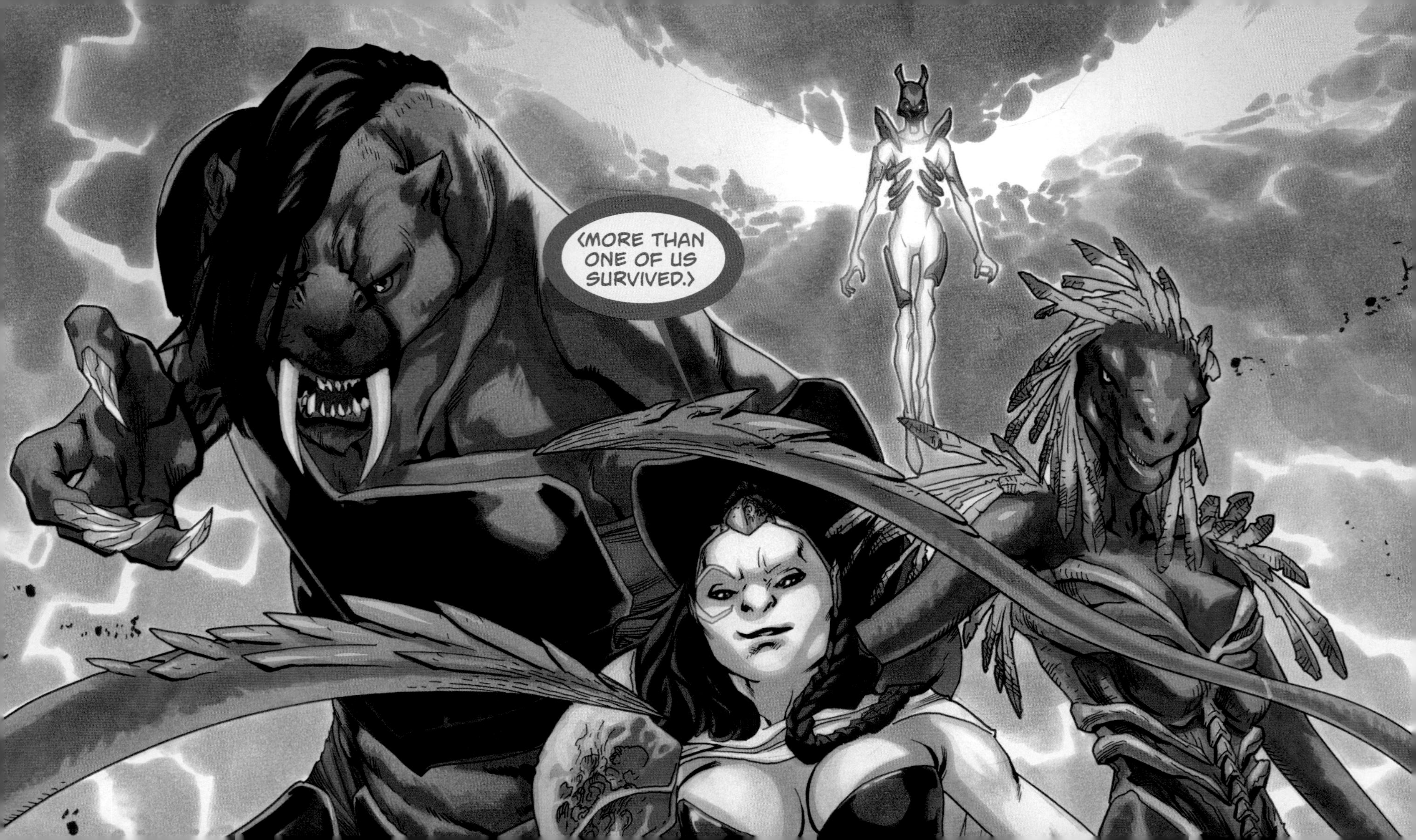
‹MORE THAN ONE OF US SURVIVED.›

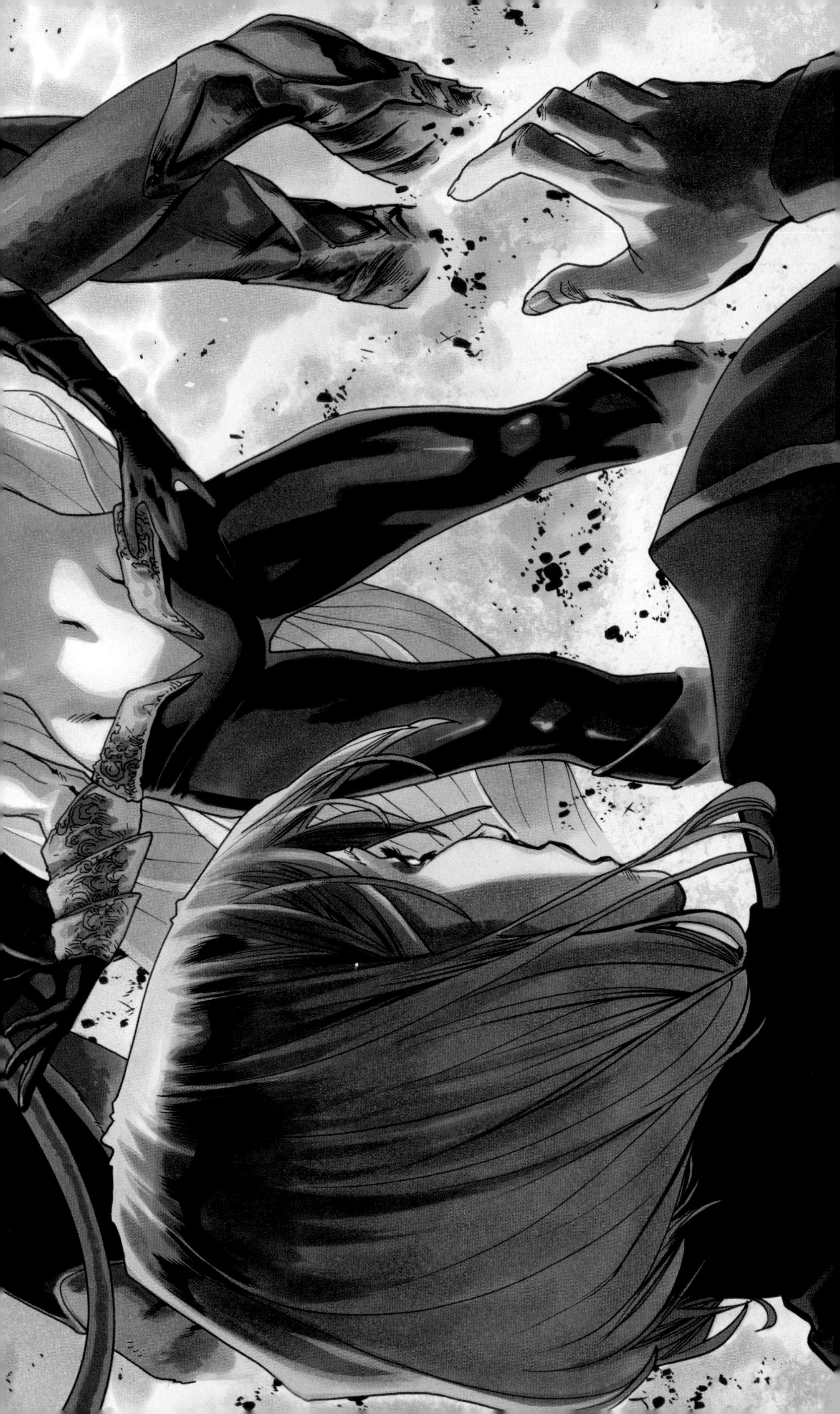

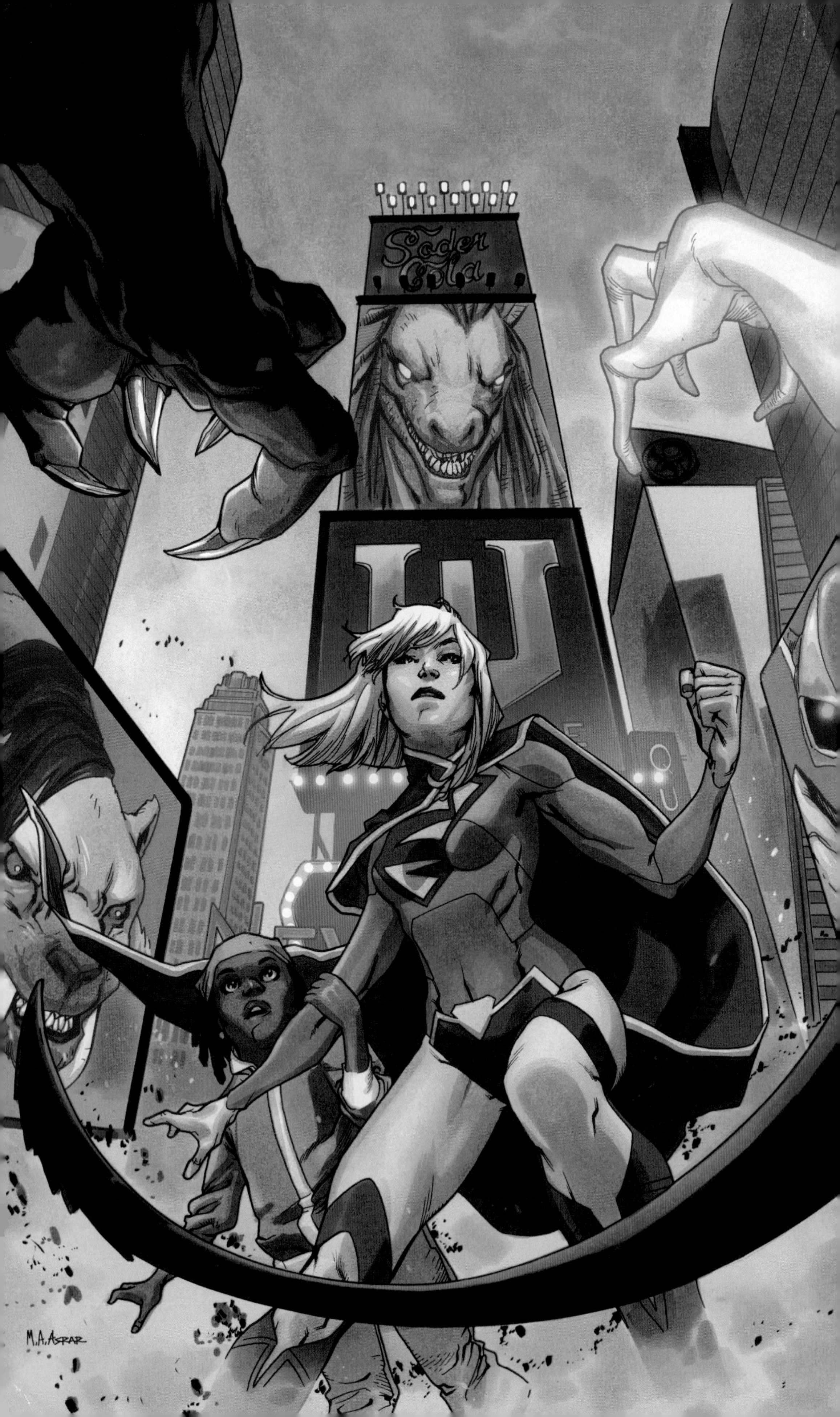
Soder Cola
M.A.Asrar

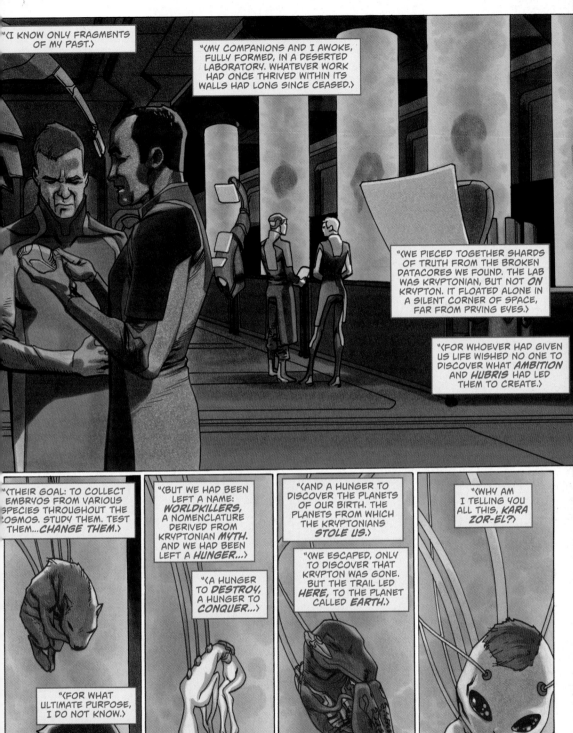

"⟨I KNOW ONLY FRAGMENTS OF MY PAST.⟩

"⟨MY COMPANIONS AND I AWOKE, FULLY FORMED, IN A DESERTED LABORATORY. WHATEVER WORK HAD ONCE THRIVED WITHIN ITS WALLS HAD LONG SINCE CEASED.⟩

"⟨WE PIECED TOGETHER SHARDS OF TRUTH FROM THE BROKEN DATACORES WE FOUND. THE LAB WAS KRYPTONIAN, BUT NOT *ON* KRYPTON. IT FLOATED ALONE IN A SILENT CORNER OF SPACE, FAR FROM PRYING EYES.⟩

"⟨FOR WHOEVER HAD GIVEN US LIFE WISHED NO ONE TO DISCOVER WHAT *AMBITION* AND *HUBRIS* HAD LED THEM TO CREATE.⟩

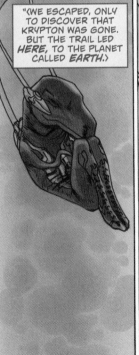

"⟨THEIR GOAL: TO COLLECT EMBRYOS FROM VARIOUS SPECIES THROUGHOUT THE COSMOS. STUDY THEM. TEST THEM...*CHANGE THEM.*⟩

"⟨FOR WHAT ULTIMATE PURPOSE, I DO NOT KNOW.⟩

"⟨BUT WE HAD BEEN LEFT A NAME: *WORLDKILLERS,* A NOMENCLATURE DERIVED FROM KRYPTONIAN *MYTH.* AND WE HAD BEEN LEFT A *HUNGER...*⟩

"⟨A HUNGER TO *DESTROY,* A HUNGER TO *CONQUER...*⟩

"⟨AND A HUNGER TO DISCOVER THE PLANETS OF OUR BIRTH. THE PLANETS FROM WHICH THE KRYPTONIANS *STOLE US.*⟩

"⟨WE ESCAPED, ONLY TO DISCOVER THAT KRYPTON WAS GONE. BUT THE TRAIL LED *HERE,* TO THE PLANET CALLED *EARTH.*⟩

"⟨WHY AM I TELLING YOU ALL THIS, *KARA ZOR-EL?*⟩

"⟨BECAUSE I WANT YOU TO *KNOW...*⟩"

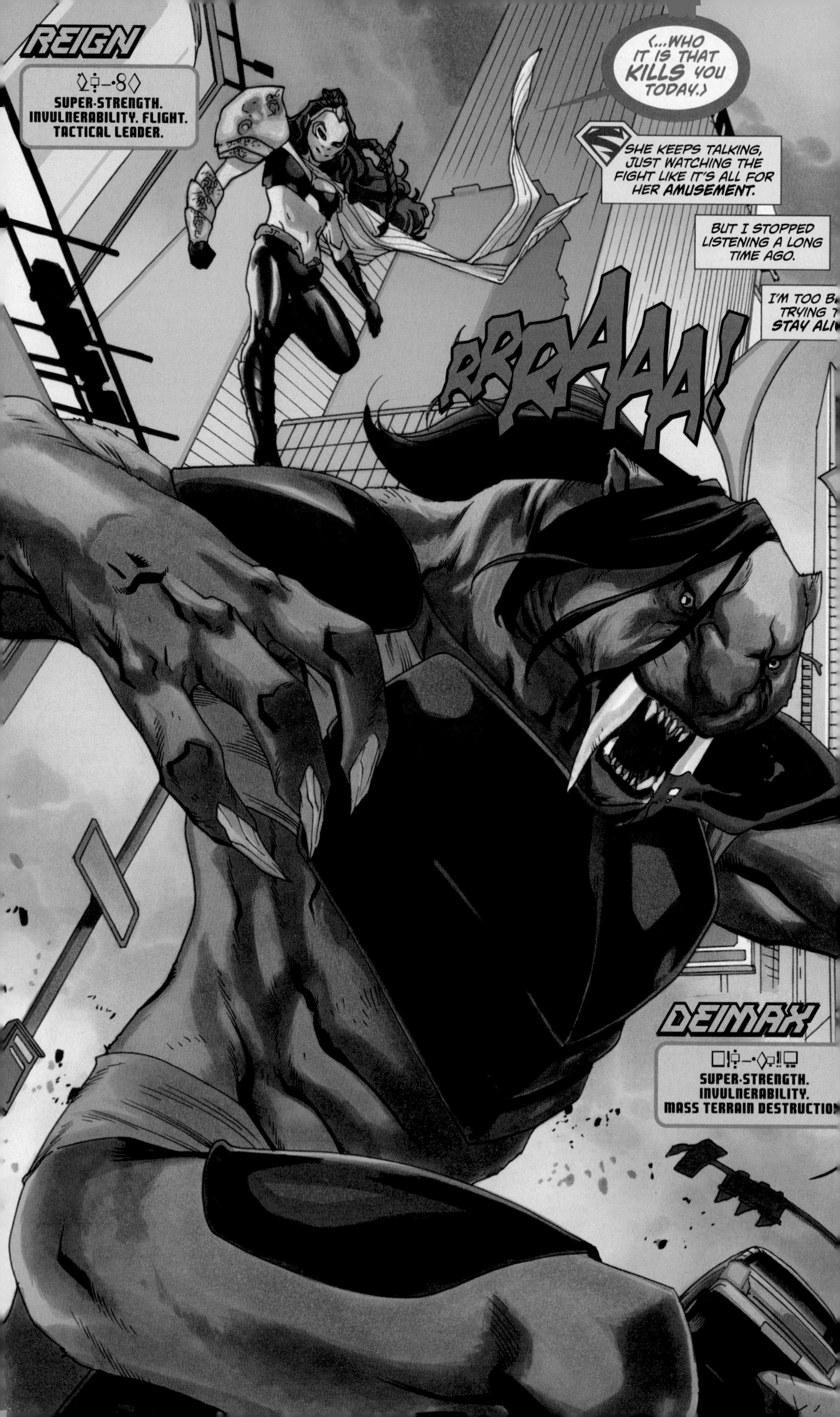
REIGN
SUPER-STRENGTH. INVULNERABILITY. FLIGHT. TACTICAL LEADER.
‹...WHO IT IS THAT KILLS YOU TODAY.›
SHE KEEPS TALKING, JUST WATCHING THE FIGHT LIKE IT'S ALL FOR HER AMUSEMENT.
BUT I STOPPED LISTENING A LONG TIME AGO.
I'M TOO B TRYING T STAY ALI
RRRAAAA!
DEIMAX
SUPER-STRENGTH. INVULNERABILITY. MASS TERRAIN DESTRUCTIO

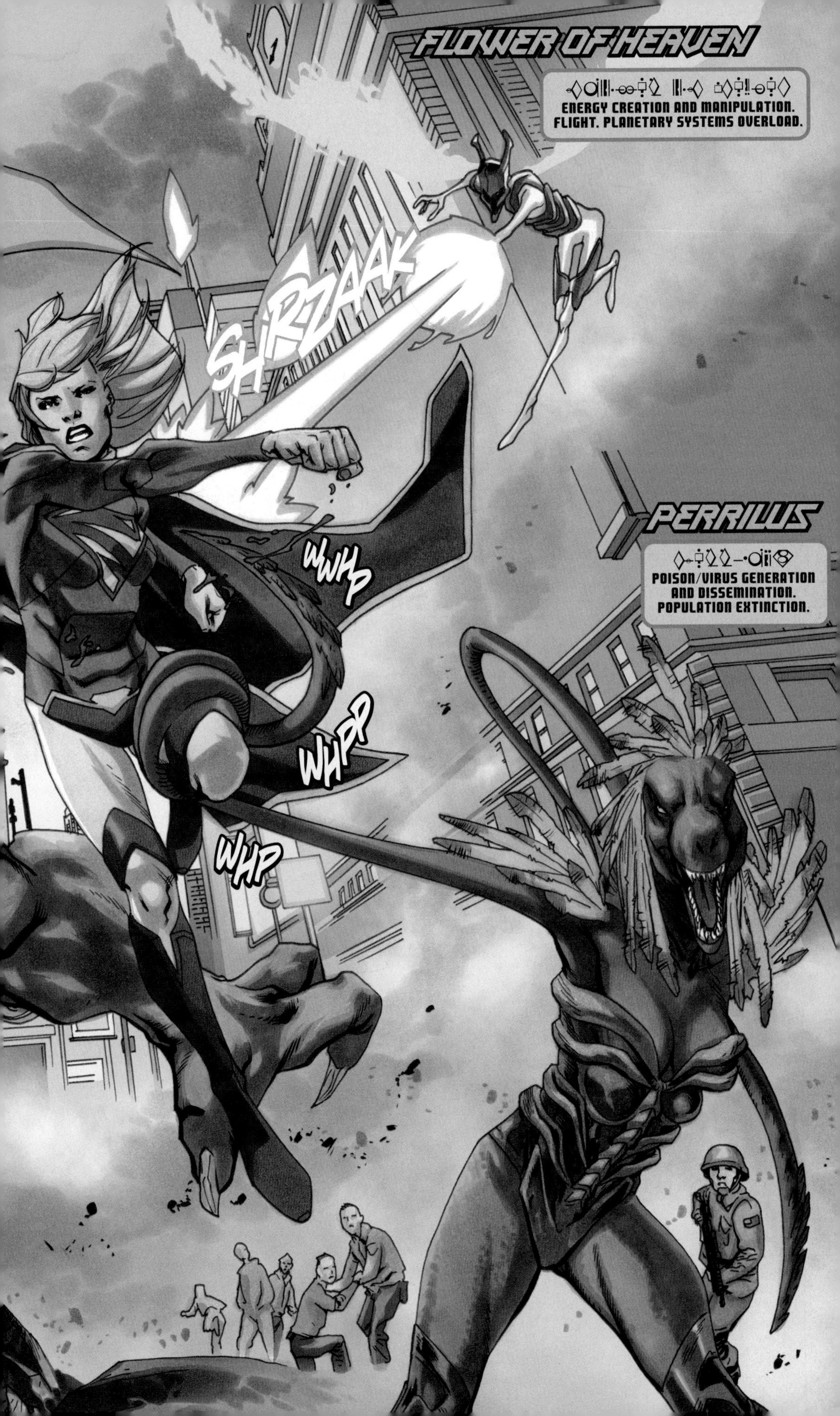
FLOWER OF HEAVEN
ENERGY CREATION AND MANIPULATION. FLIGHT. PLANETARY SYSTEMS OVERLOAD.
SHRZAAK
PERRILUS
POISON/VIRUS GENERATION AND DISSEMINATION. POPULATION EXTINCTION.
WWHP
WHPP
WHP

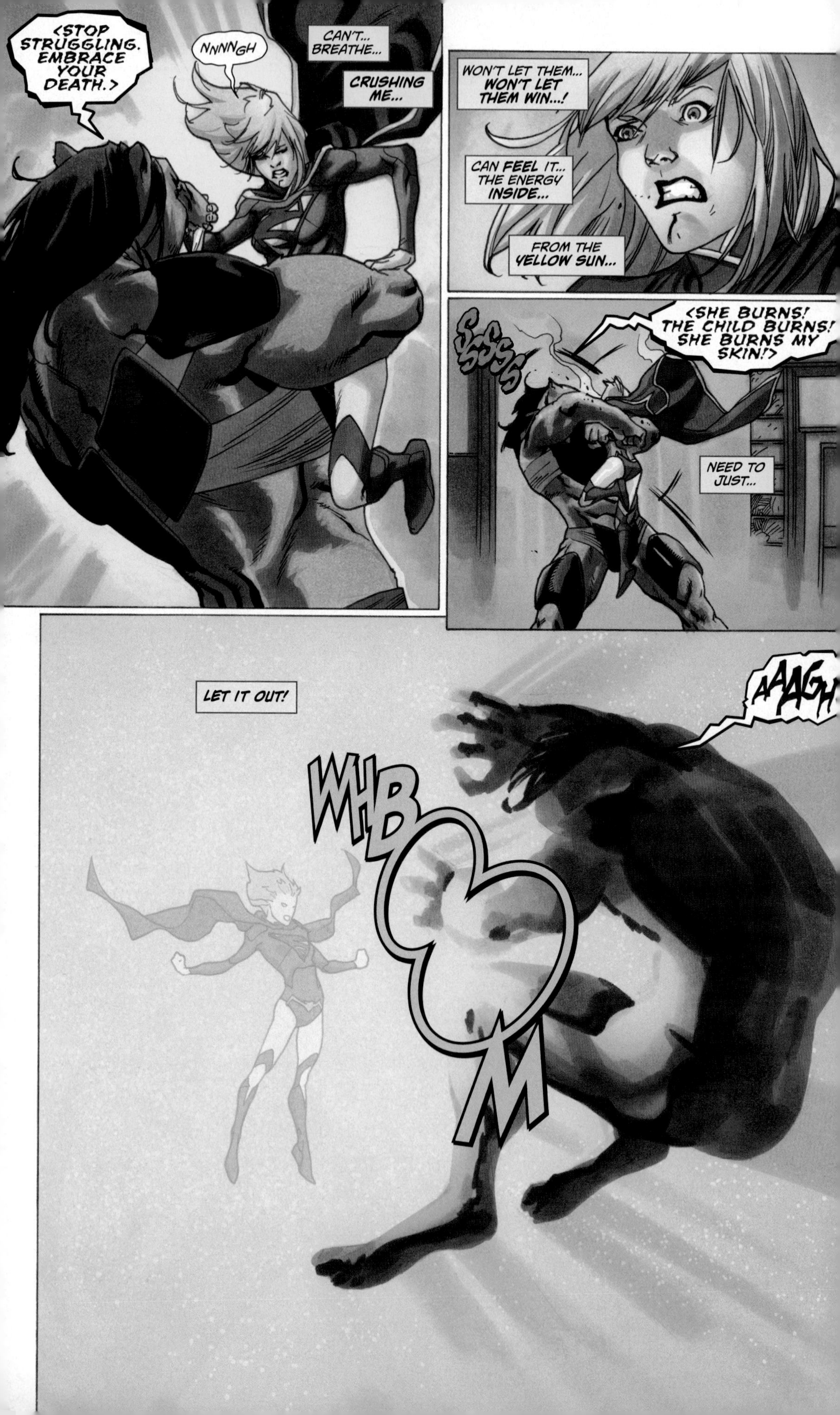

<STOP STRUGGLING. EMBRACE YOUR DEATH.>
NNNNGH
CAN'T... BREATHE...
CRUSHING ME...
WON'T LET THEM... WON'T LET THEM WIN...!
CAN FEEL IT... THE ENERGY INSIDE...
FROM THE YELLOW SUN...
SSSSS
<SHE BURNS! THE CHILD BURNS! SHE BURNS MY SKIN!>
NEED TO JUST...
LET IT OUT!
AAAGH
WHBOOM

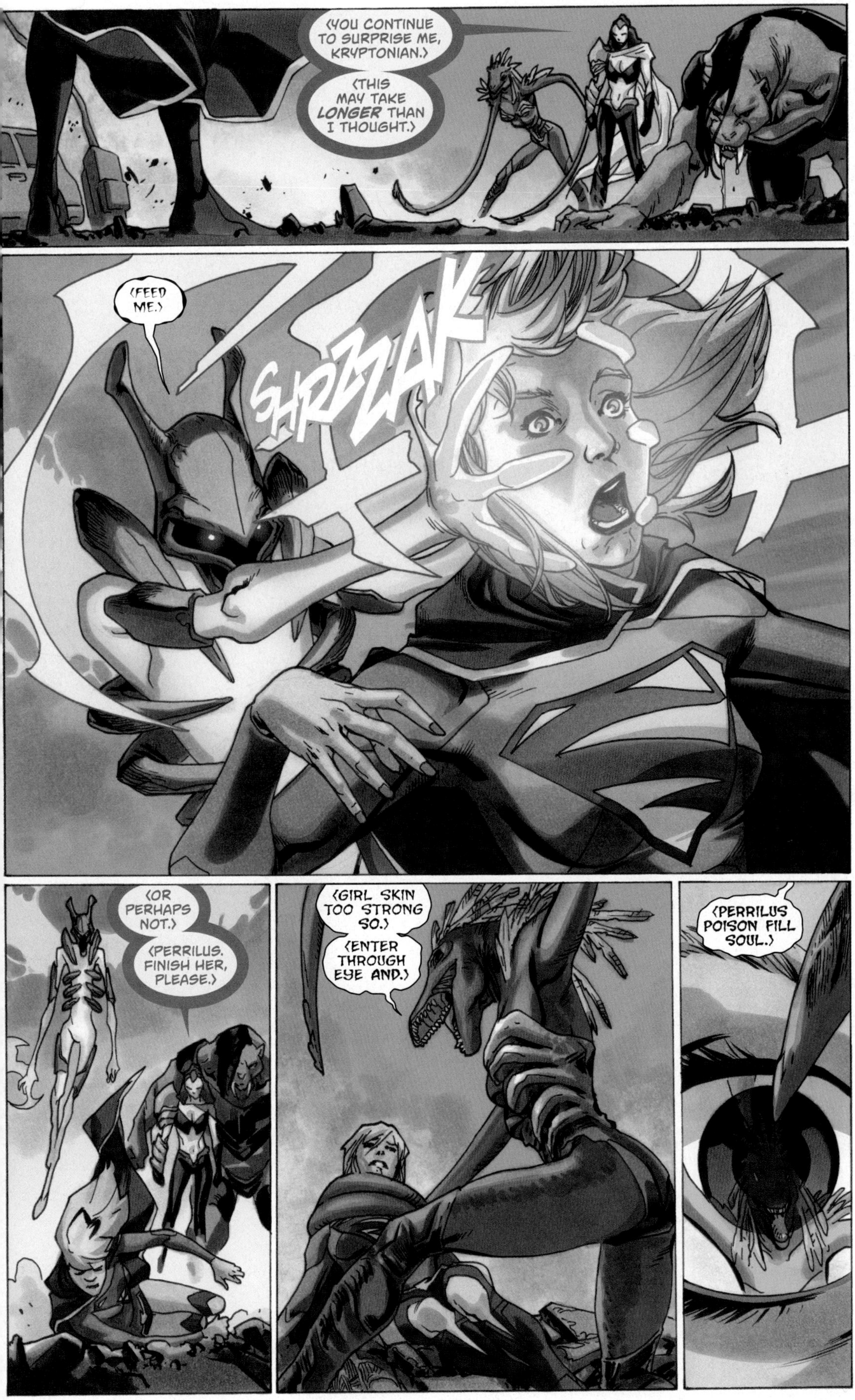

〈YOU CONTINUE TO SURPRISE ME, KRYPTONIAN.〉
〈THIS MAY TAKE LONGER THAN I THOUGHT.〉
〈FEED ME.〉
SHRZZZAK
〈OR PERHAPS NOT.〉
〈PERRILUS. FINISH HER, PLEASE.〉
〈GIRL SKIN TOO STRONG SO.〉
〈ENTER THROUGH EYE AND.〉
〈PERRILUS POISON FILL SOUL.〉

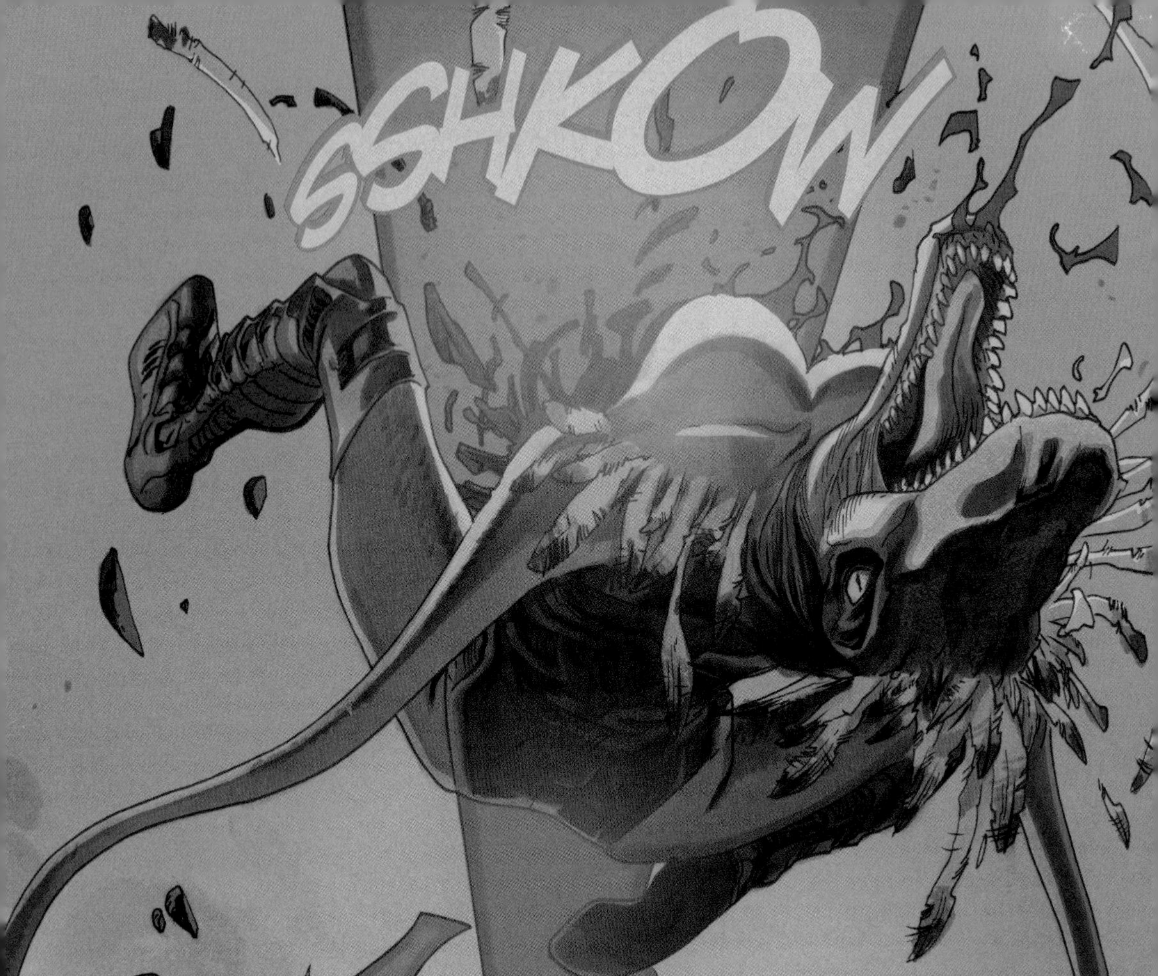
SSHKOW

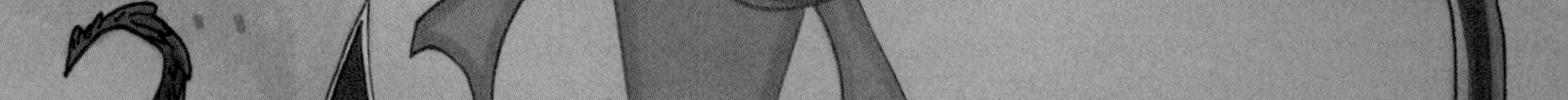
SSSS
HIK... HIKK...
‹BREATHTAKING.›
‹DO YOU EVEN COMPREHEND HOW POWERFUL YOU ARE?›
I HAVE TO GET AWAY FROM THEM.
TOO MANY

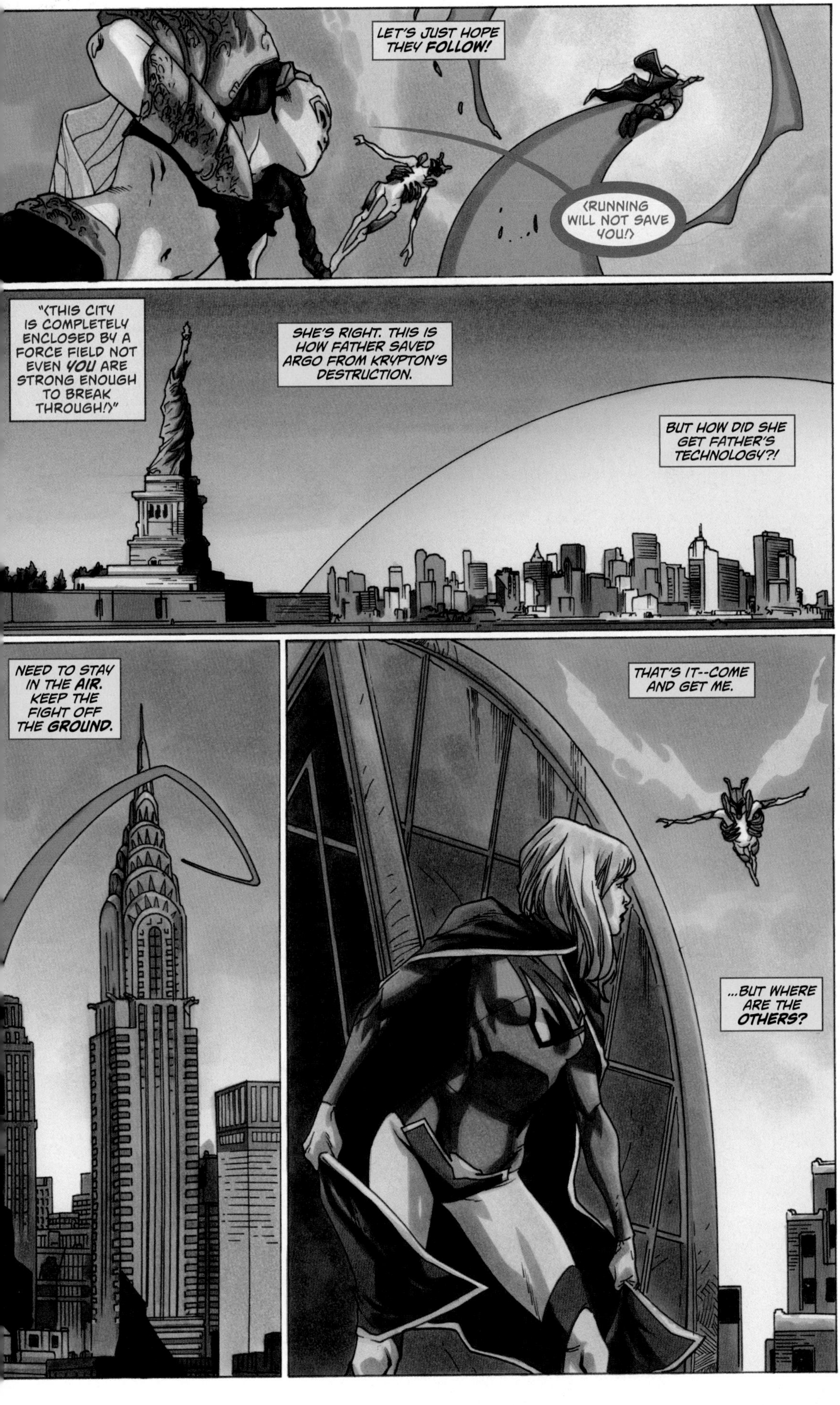
LET'S JUST HOPE THEY FOLLOW!
‹RUNNING WILL NOT SAVE YOU!›
"‹THIS CITY IS COMPLETELY ENCLOSED BY A FORCE FIELD NOT EVEN YOU ARE STRONG ENOUGH TO BREAK THROUGH!›"
SHE'S RIGHT. THIS IS HOW FATHER SAVED ARGO FROM KRYPTON'S DESTRUCTION.
BUT HOW DID SHE GET FATHER'S TECHNOLOGY?!
NEED TO STAY IN THE AIR. KEEP THE FIGHT OFF THE GROUND.
THAT'S IT--COME AND GET ME.
...BUT WHERE ARE THE OTHERS?

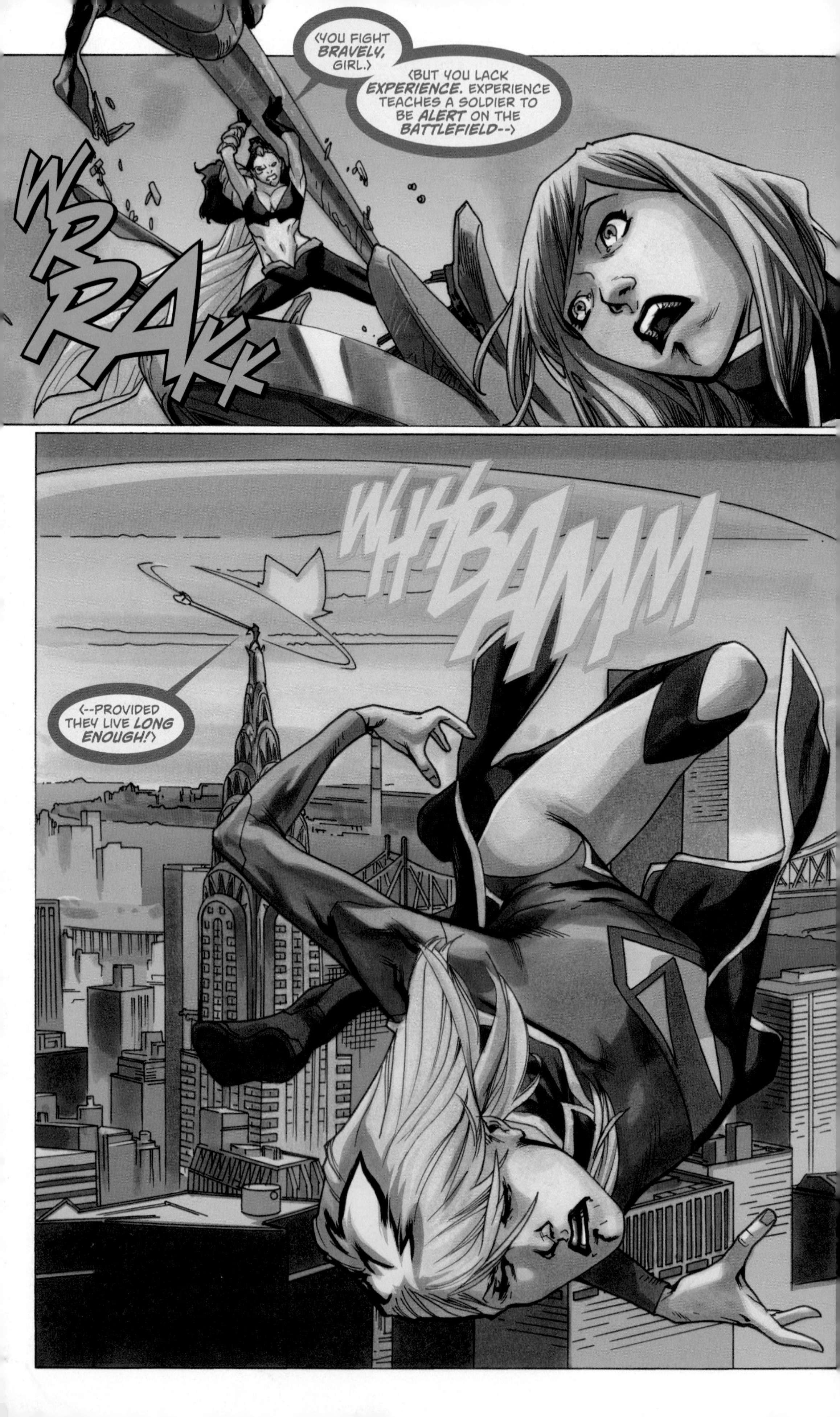
‹YOU FIGHT BRAVELY, GIRL.›
‹BUT YOU LACK EXPERIENCE. EXPERIENCE TEACHES A SOLDIER TO BE ALERT ON THE BATTLEFIELD--›
WRAKK
WHHBAMM
‹--PROVIDED THEY LIVE LONG ENOUGH!›

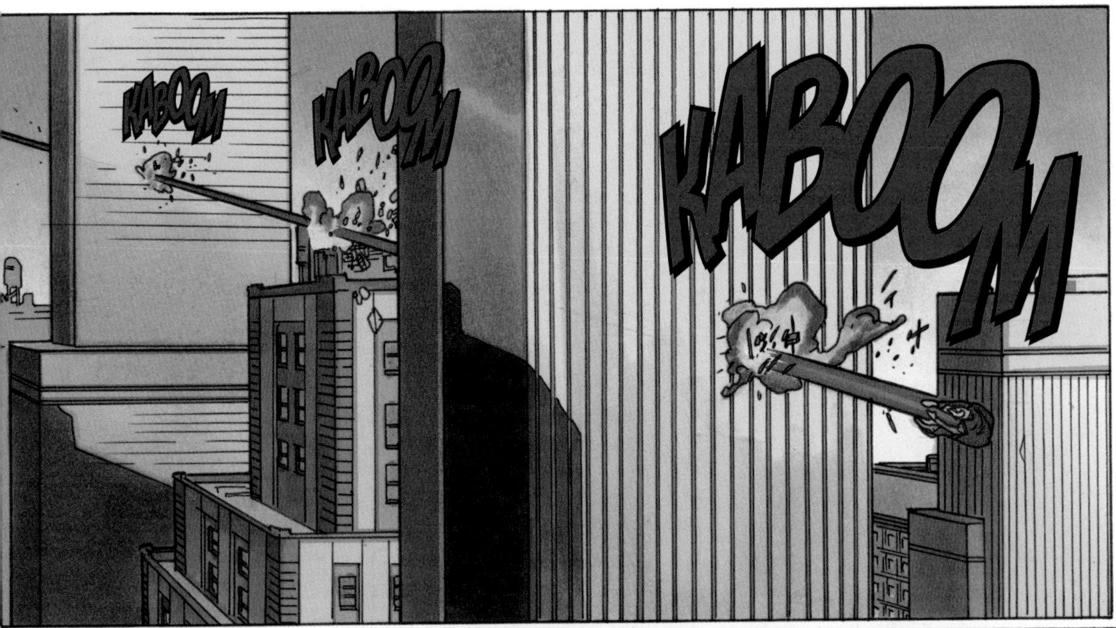
KABOOM
KABOOM
KABOOM

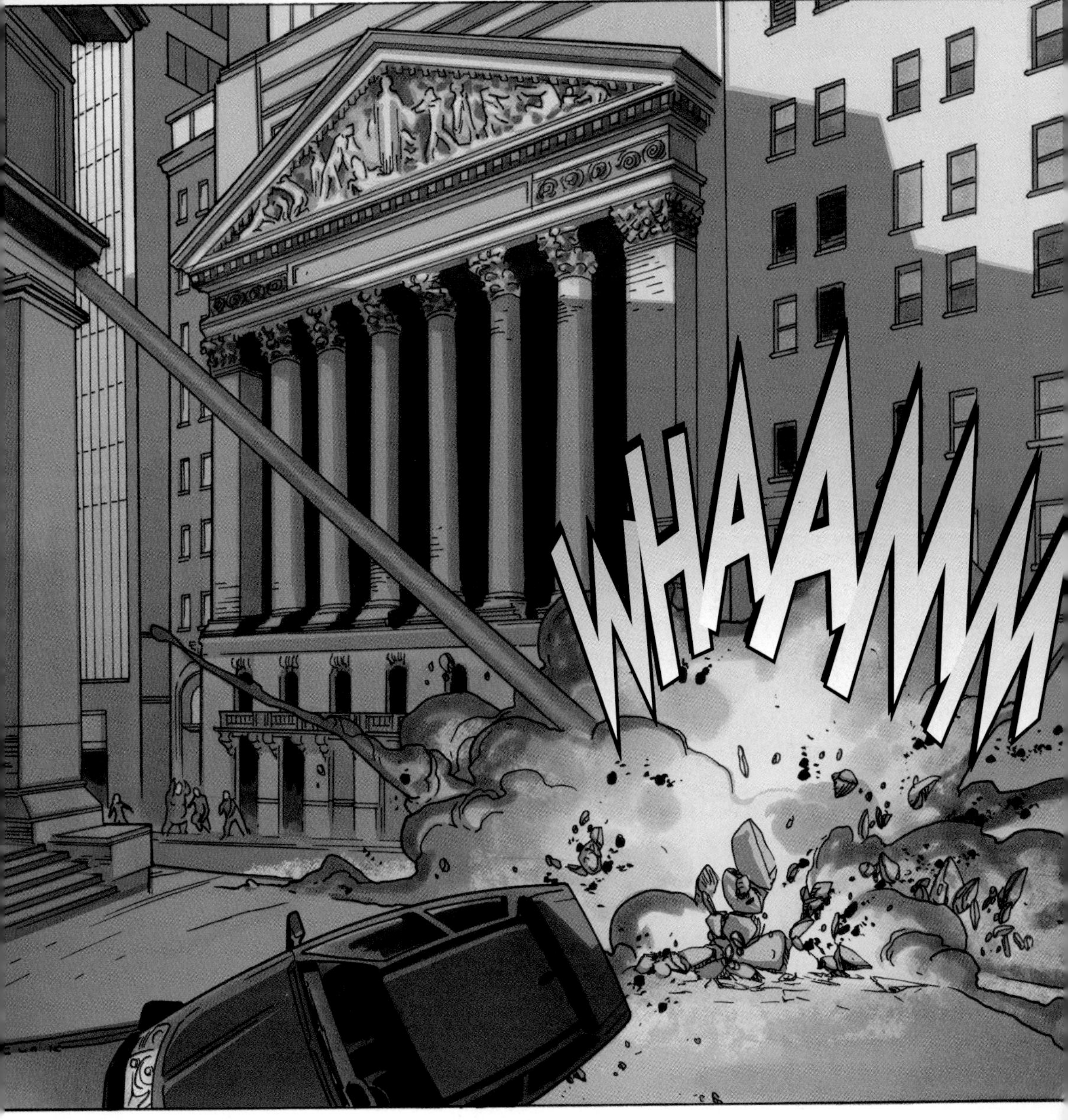
WHAAMM

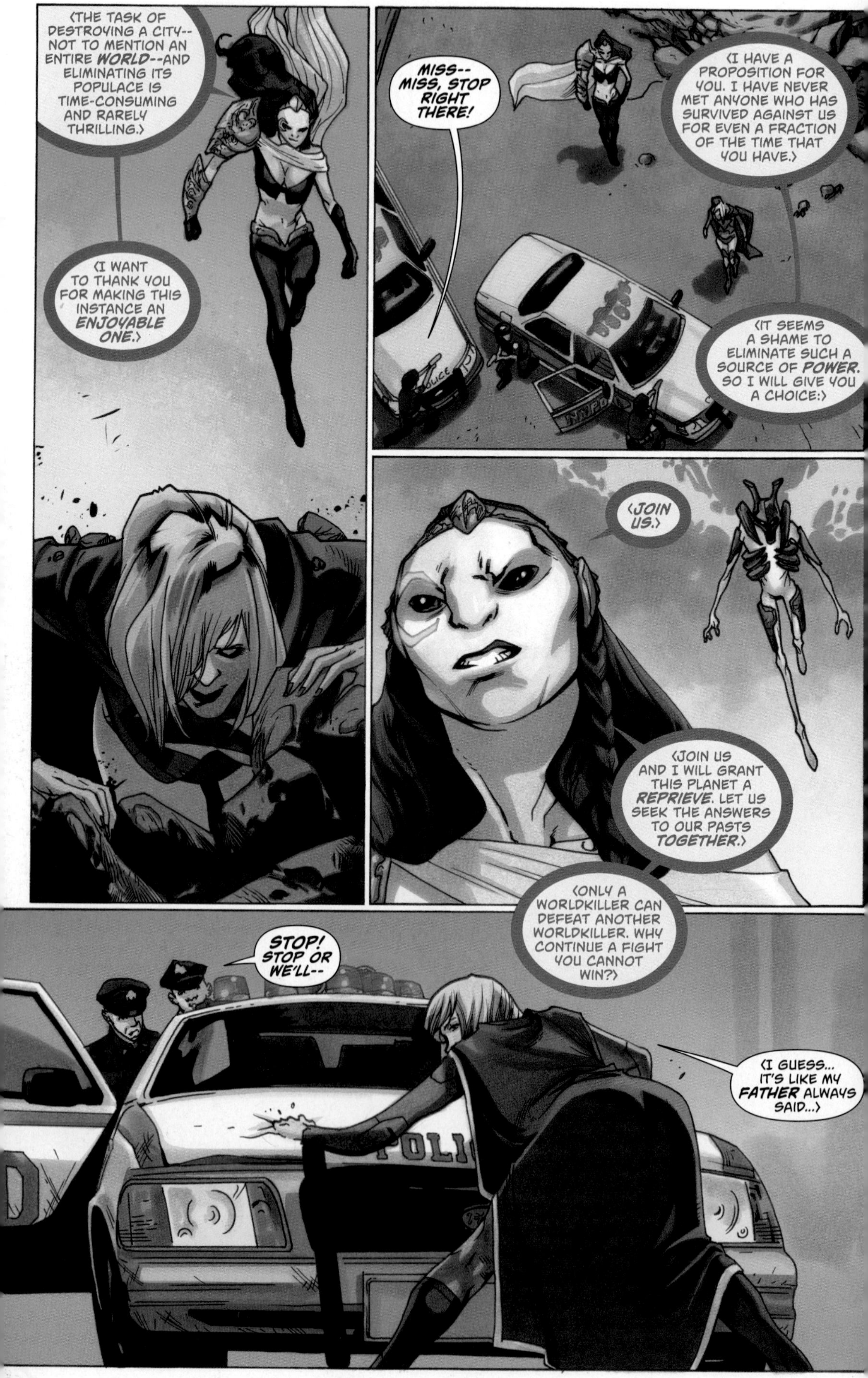

‹THE TASK OF DESTROYING A CITY-- NOT TO MENTION AN ENTIRE WORLD--AND ELIMINATING ITS POPULACE IS TIME-CONSUMING AND RARELY THRILLING.›
‹I WANT TO THANK YOU FOR MAKING THIS INSTANCE AN ENJOYABLE ONE.›
MISS-- MISS, STOP RIGHT THERE!
‹I HAVE A PROPOSITION FOR YOU. I HAVE NEVER MET ANYONE WHO HAS SURVIVED AGAINST US FOR EVEN A FRACTION OF THE TIME THAT YOU HAVE.›
‹IT SEEMS A SHAME TO ELIMINATE SUCH A SOURCE OF POWER. SO I WILL GIVE YOU A CHOICE:›
‹JOIN US.›
‹JOIN US AND I WILL GRANT THIS PLANET A REPRIEVE. LET US SEEK THE ANSWERS TO OUR PASTS TOGETHER.›
‹ONLY A WORLDKILLER CAN DEFEAT ANOTHER WORLDKILLER. WHY CONTINUE A FIGHT YOU CANNOT WIN?›
STOP! STOP OR WE'LL--
‹I GUESS... IT'S LIKE MY FATHER ALWAYS SAID...›

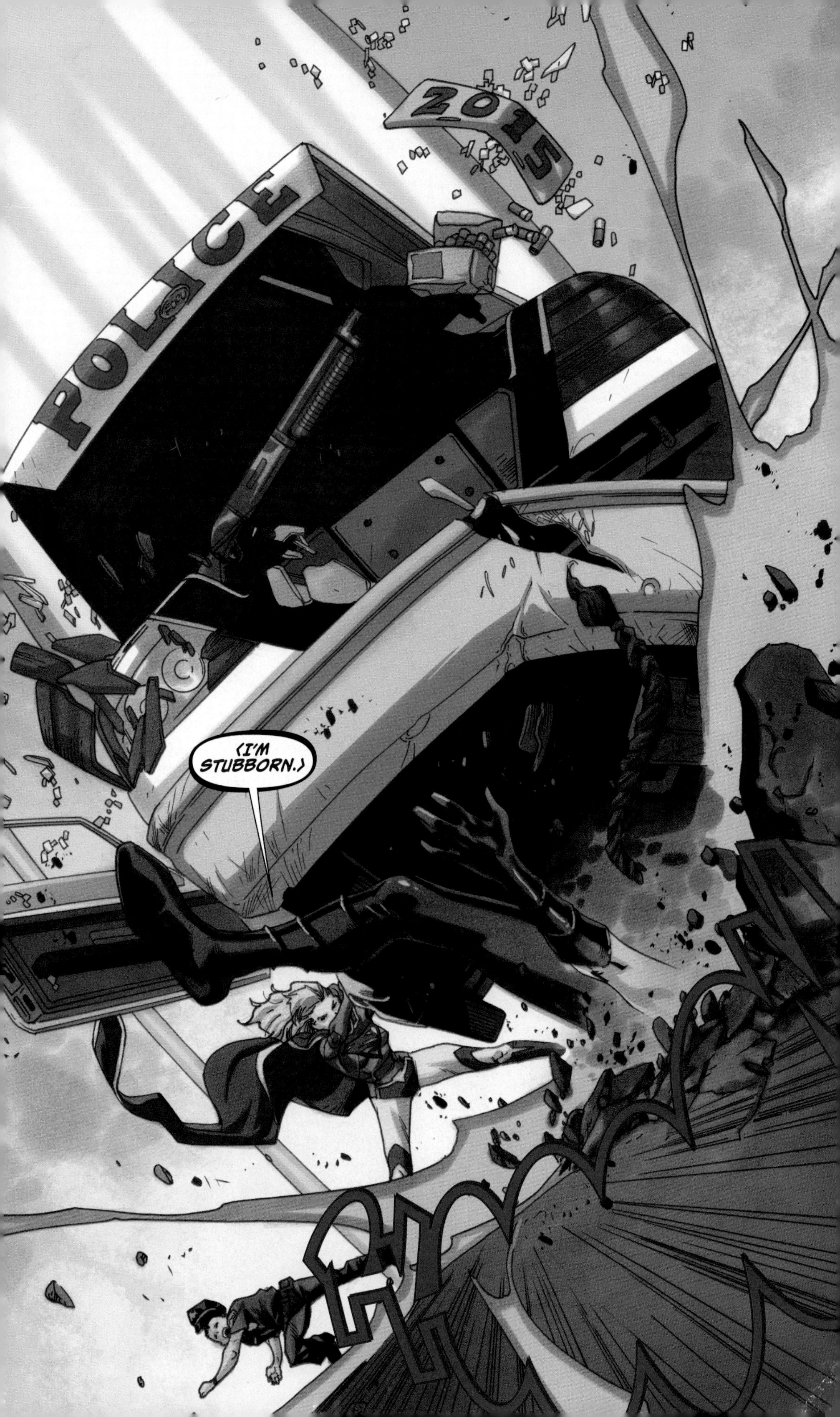
POLICE
2015
<I'M STUBBORN.>

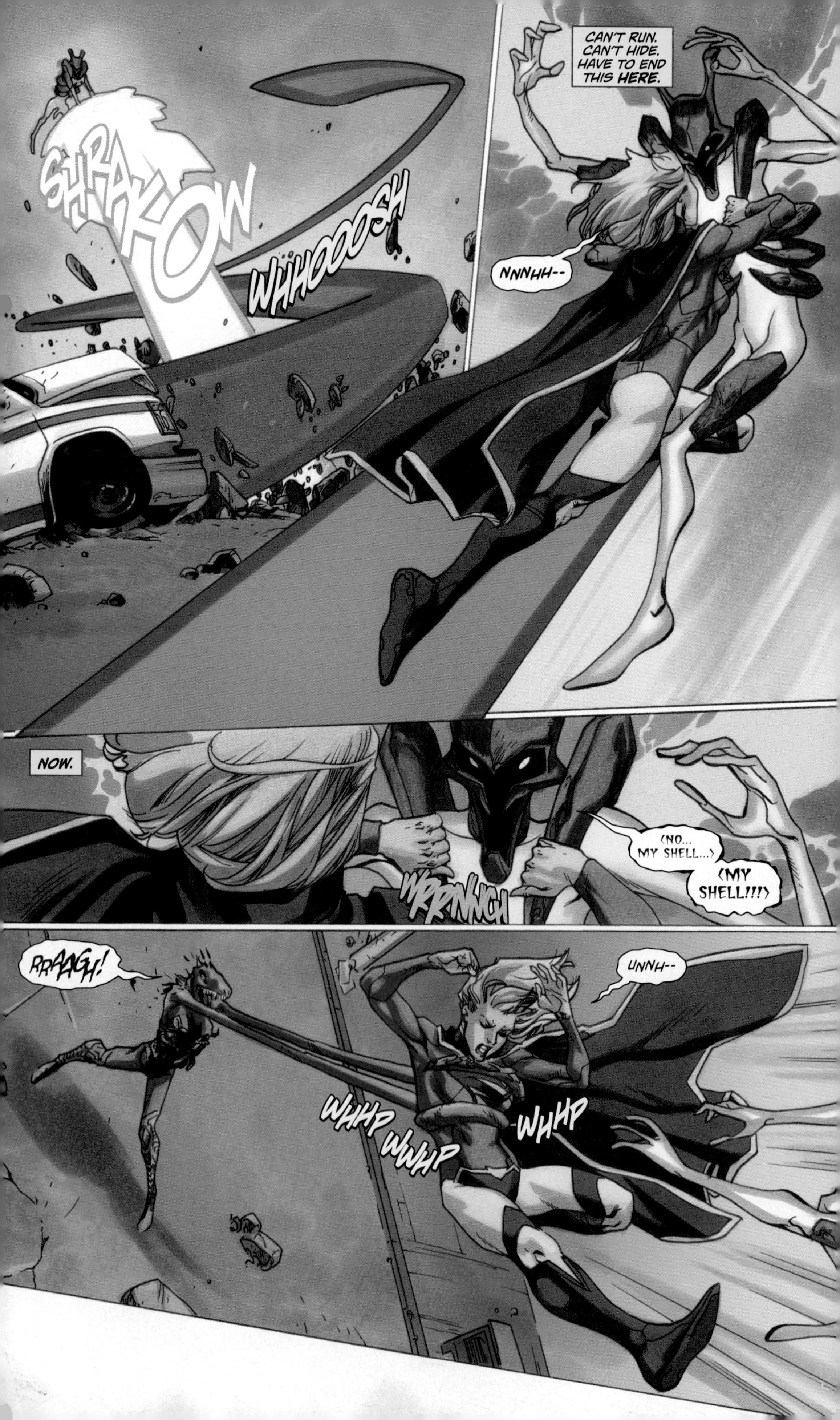
SHRAKOW
WHHOOOSH
CAN'T RUN. CAN'T HIDE. HAVE TO END THIS HERE.
NNNHH--
NOW.
‹NO... MY SHELL...›
‹MY SHELL!!!›
WRRNNGH
RRAAGH!
UNNH--
WHHP
WHHP
WHHP

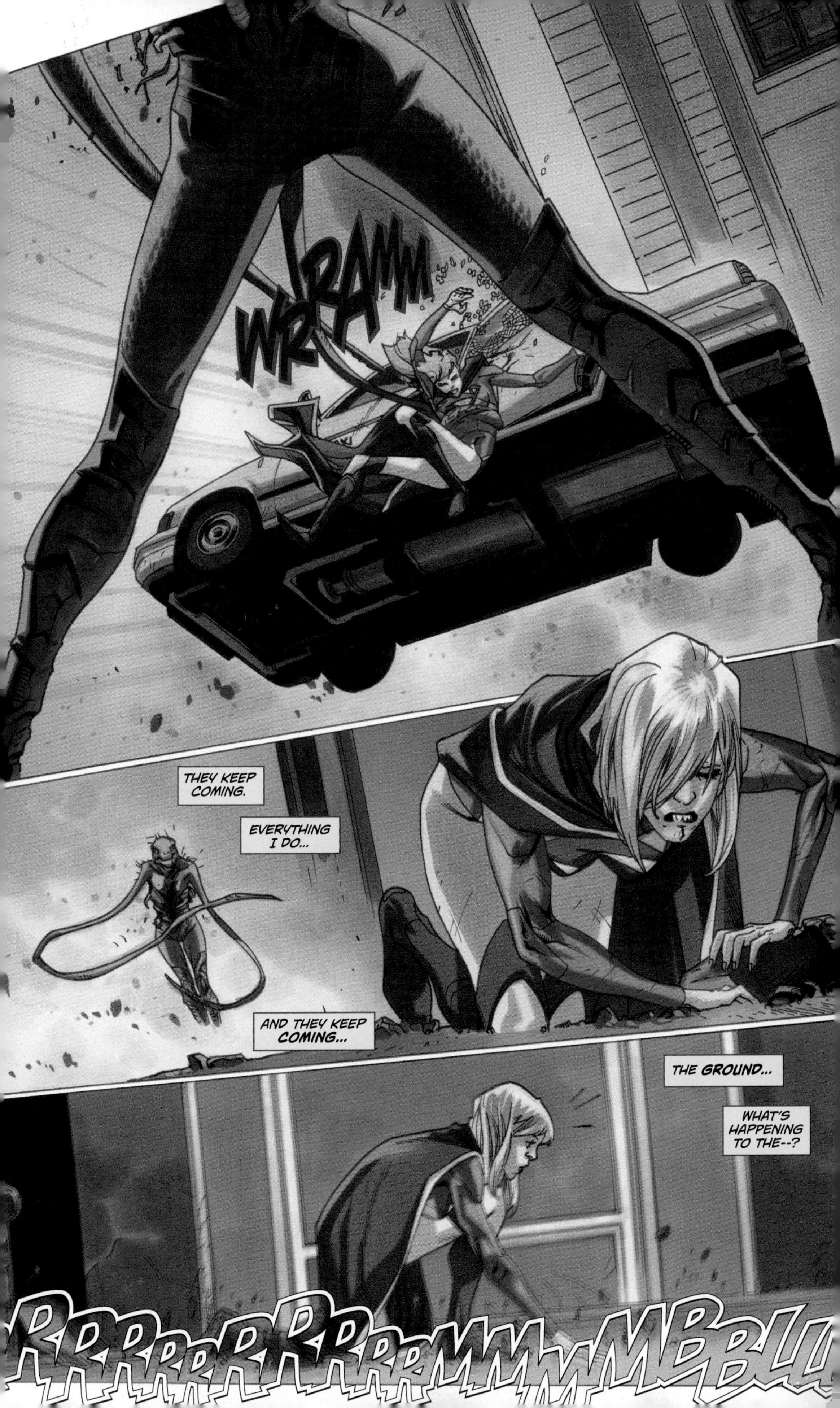
WRAMM
THEY KEEP COMING.
EVERYTHING I DO...
AND THEY KEEP COMING...
THE GROUND...
WHAT'S HAPPENING TO THE--?
RRRRRRRRRRRRMMMMMBBLL

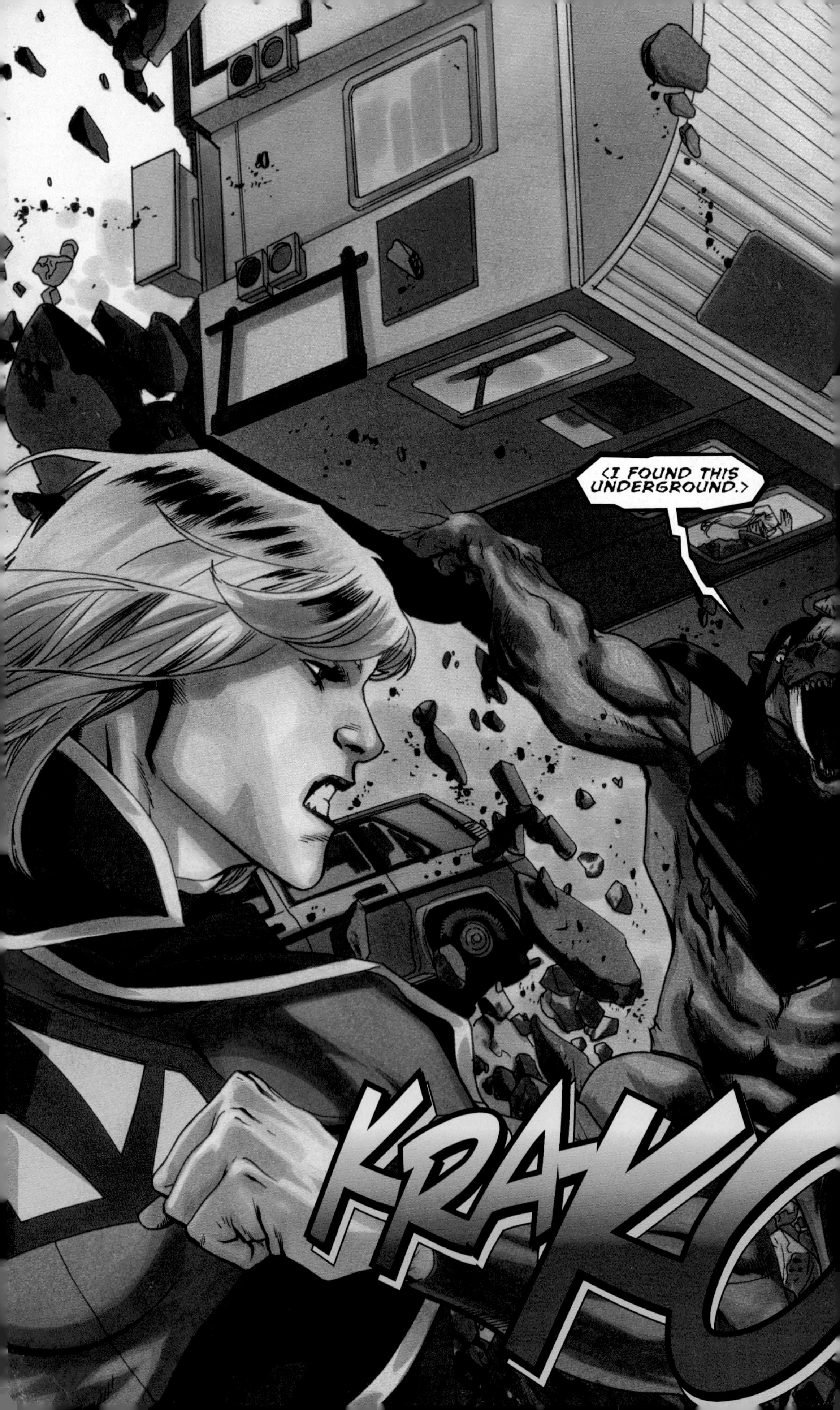

<I FOUND THIS UNDERGROUND.>
KRAK

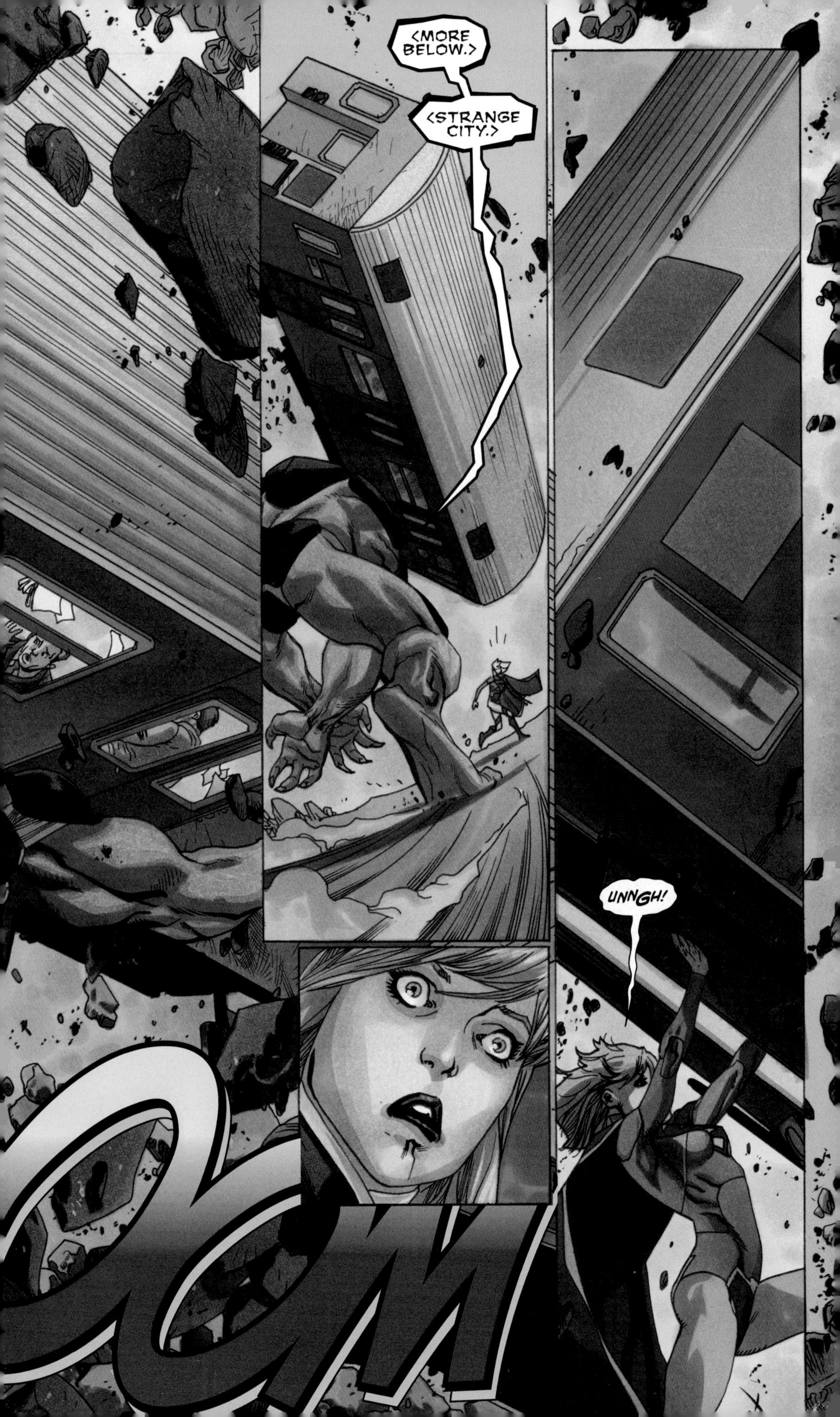
<MORE BELOW.>
<STRANGE CITY.>
UNNGH!

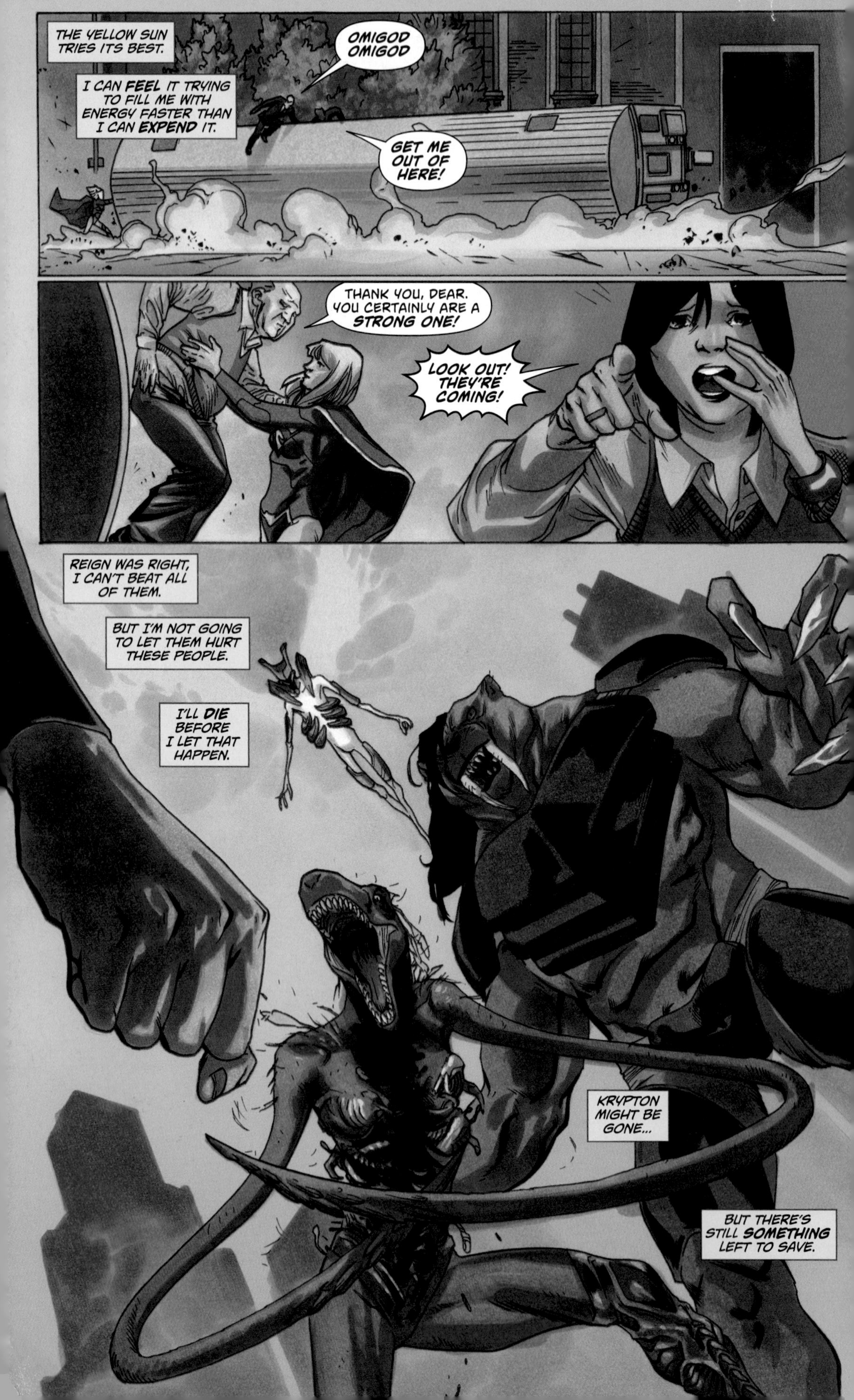
THE YELLOW SUN TRIES ITS BEST.
OMIGOD OMIGOD
I CAN FEEL IT TRYING TO FILL ME WITH ENERGY FASTER THAN I CAN EXPEND IT.
GET ME OUT OF HERE!
THANK YOU, DEAR. YOU CERTAINLY ARE A STRONG ONE!
LOOK OUT! THEY'RE COMING!
REIGN WAS RIGHT, I CAN'T BEAT ALL OF THEM.
BUT I'M NOT GOING TO LET THEM HURT THESE PEOPLE.
I'LL DIE BEFORE I LET THAT HAPPEN.
KRYPTON MIGHT BE GONE...
BUT THERE'S STILL SOMETHING LEFT TO SAVE.

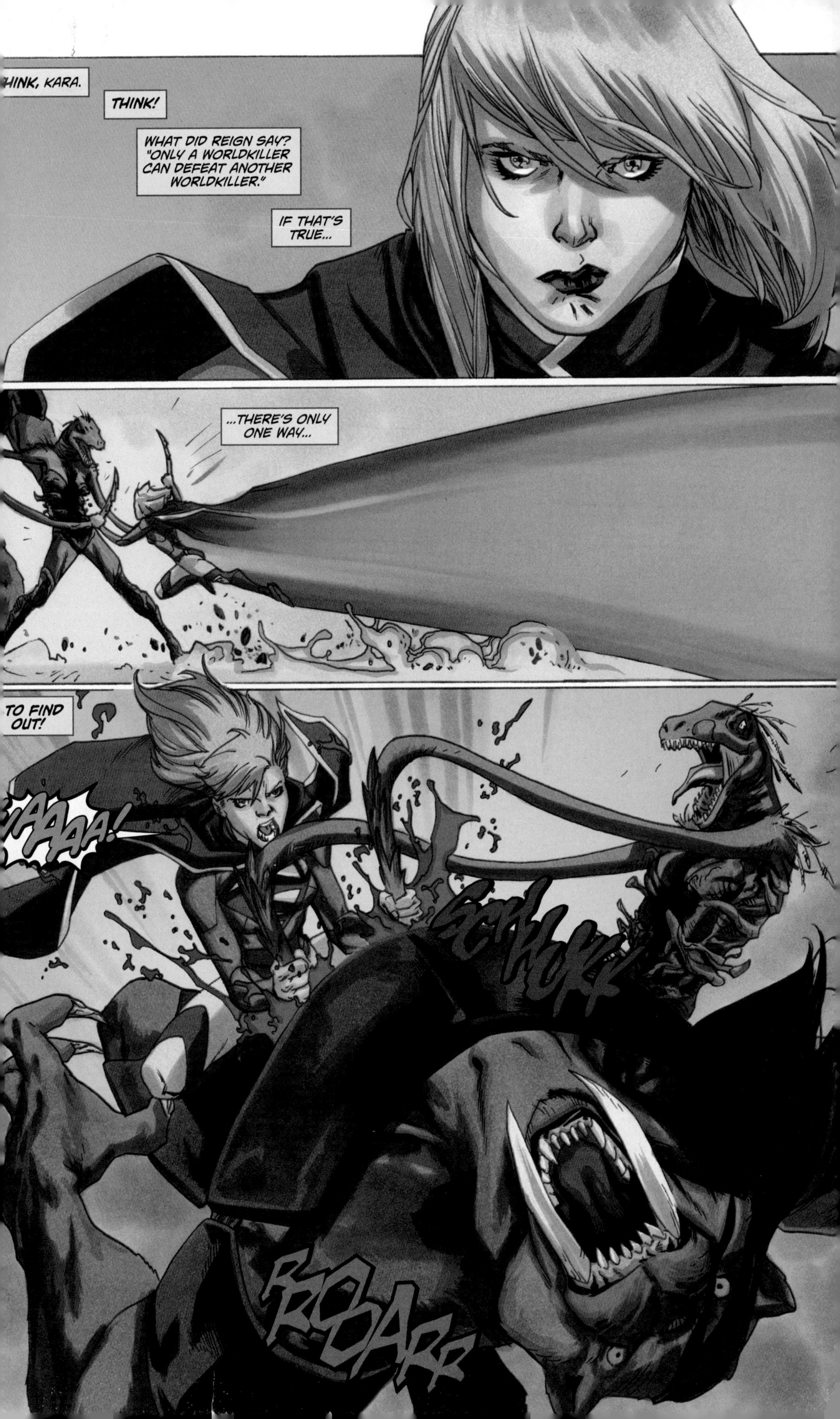

HINK, KARA.
THINK!
WHAT DID REIGN SAY? "ONLY A WORLDKILLER CAN DEFEAT ANOTHER WORLDKILLER."
IF THAT'S TRUE...
...THERE'S ONLY ONE WAY...
TO FIND OUT!
AAAA!
SCHLUKK
R-ROARR

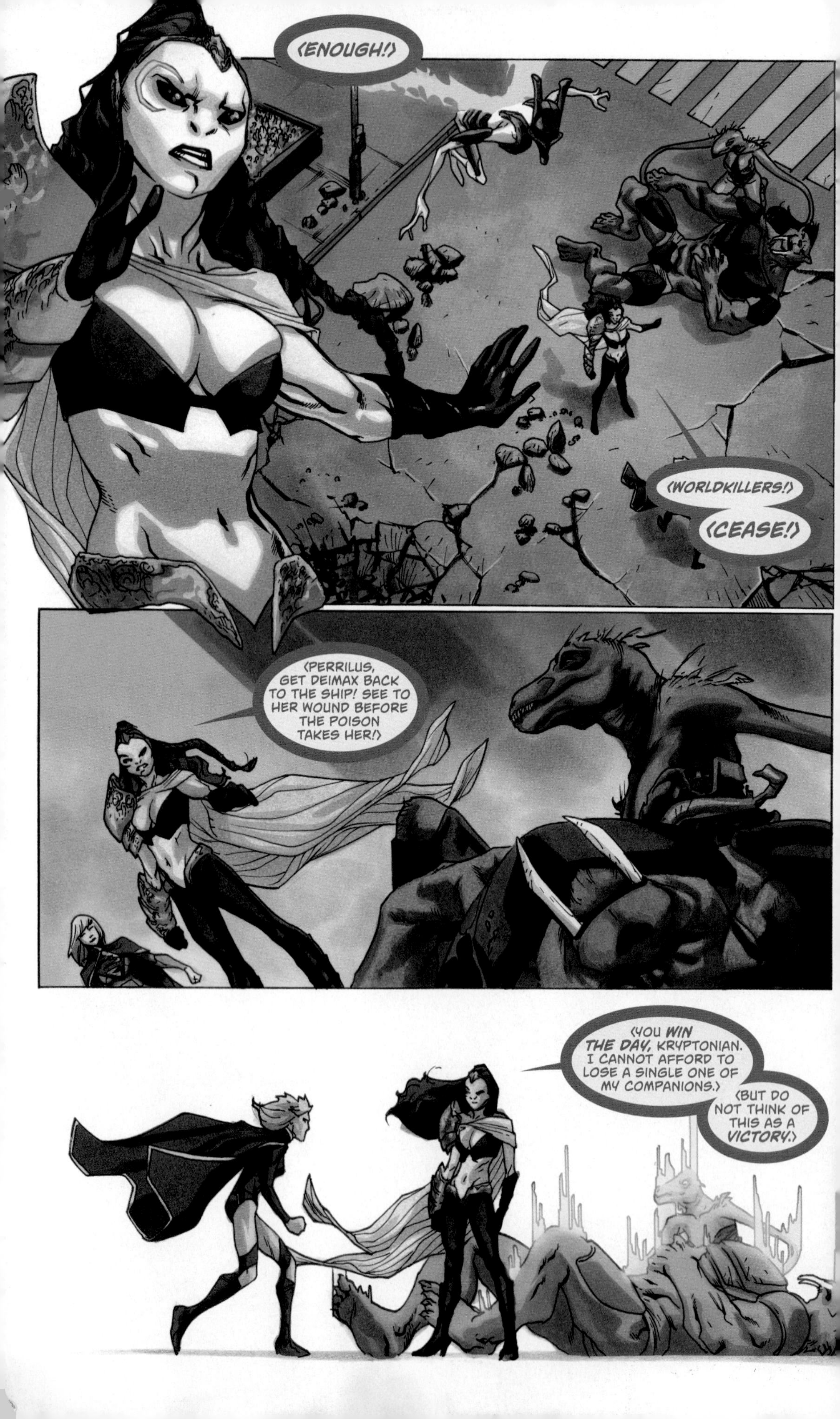

⟨ENOUGH!⟩
⟨WORLDKILLERS!⟩
⟨CEASE!⟩
⟨PERRILUS, GET DEIMAX BACK TO THE SHIP! SEE TO HER WOUND BEFORE THE POISON TAKES HER!⟩
⟨YOU WIN THE DAY, KRYPTONIAN. I CANNOT AFFORD TO LOSE A SINGLE ONE OF MY COMPANIONS.⟩
⟨BUT DO NOT THINK OF THIS AS A VICTORY.⟩

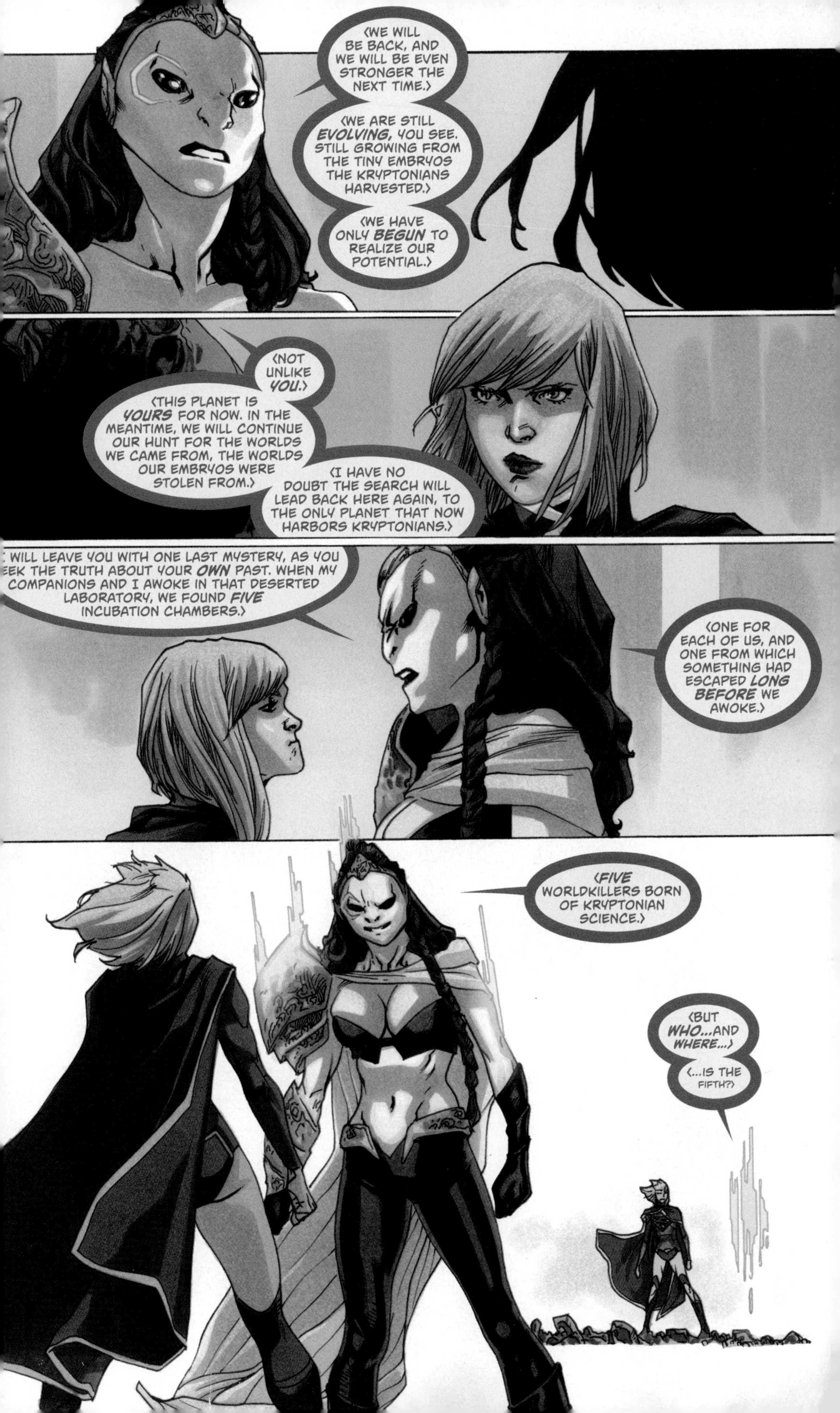

⟨WE WILL BE BACK, AND WE WILL BE EVEN STRONGER THE NEXT TIME.⟩
⟨WE ARE STILL EVOLVING, YOU SEE. STILL GROWING FROM THE TINY EMBRYOS THE KRYPTONIANS HARVESTED.⟩
⟨WE HAVE ONLY BEGUN TO REALIZE OUR POTENTIAL.⟩
⟨NOT UNLIKE YOU.⟩
⟨THIS PLANET IS YOURS FOR NOW. IN THE MEANTIME, WE WILL CONTINUE OUR HUNT FOR THE WORLDS WE CAME FROM, THE WORLDS OUR EMBRYOS WERE STOLEN FROM.⟩
⟨I HAVE NO DOUBT THE SEARCH WILL LEAD BACK HERE AGAIN, TO THE ONLY PLANET THAT NOW HARBORS KRYPTONIANS.⟩
WILL LEAVE YOU WITH ONE LAST MYSTERY, AS YOU EEK THE TRUTH ABOUT YOUR OWN PAST. WHEN MY COMPANIONS AND I AWOKE IN THAT DESERTED LABORATORY, WE FOUND FIVE INCUBATION CHAMBERS.⟩
⟨ONE FOR EACH OF US, AND ONE FROM WHICH SOMETHING HAD ESCAPED LONG BEFORE WE AWOKE.⟩
⟨FIVE WORLDKILLERS BORN OF KRYPTONIAN SCIENCE.⟩
⟨BUT WHO...AND WHERE...⟩
⟨...IS THE FIFTH?⟩

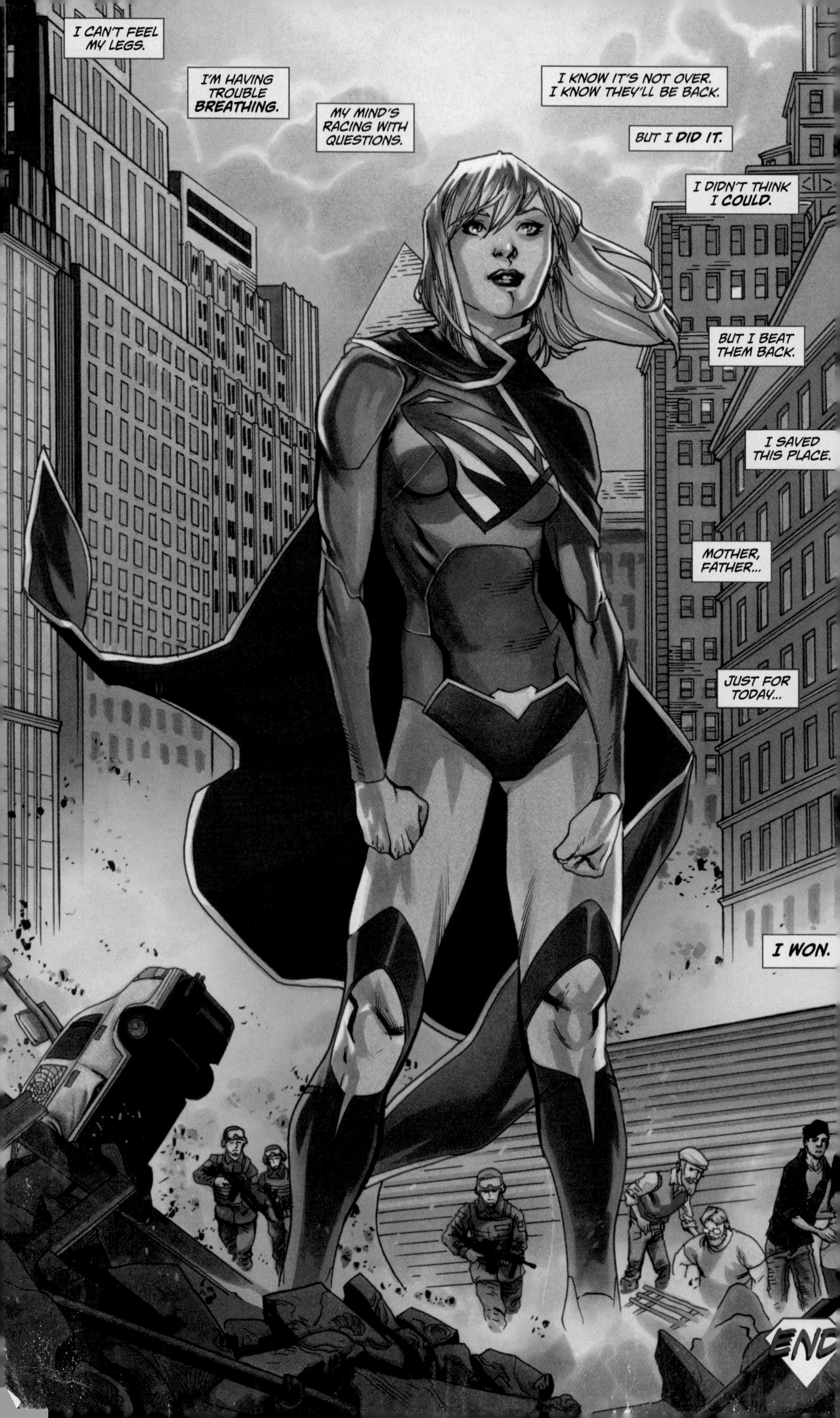
I CAN'T FEEL MY LEGS.
I'M HAVING TROUBLE BREATHING.
MY MIND'S RACING WITH QUESTIONS.
I KNOW IT'S NOT OVER. I KNOW THEY'LL BE BACK.
BUT I DID IT.
I DIDN'T THINK I COULD.
BUT I BEAT THEM BACK.
I SAVED THIS PLACE.
MOTHER, FATHER...
JUST FOR TODAY...
I WON.
END

upergirl costume designs by Jim Lee.

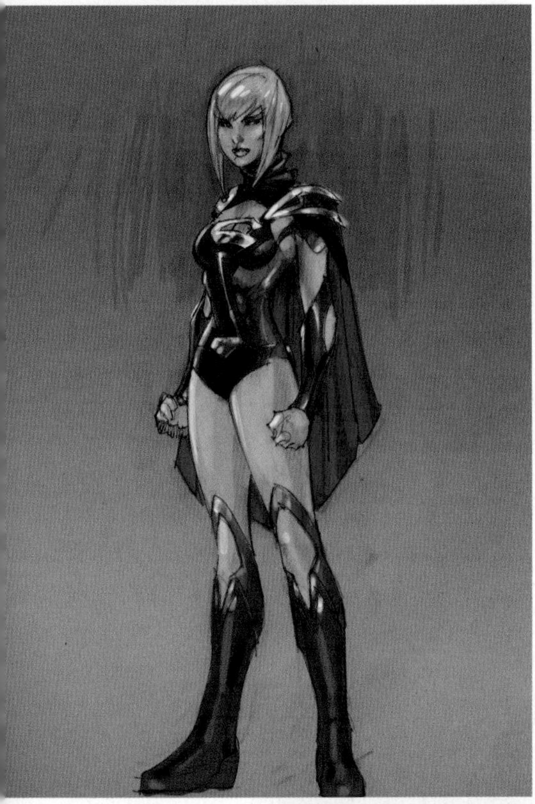

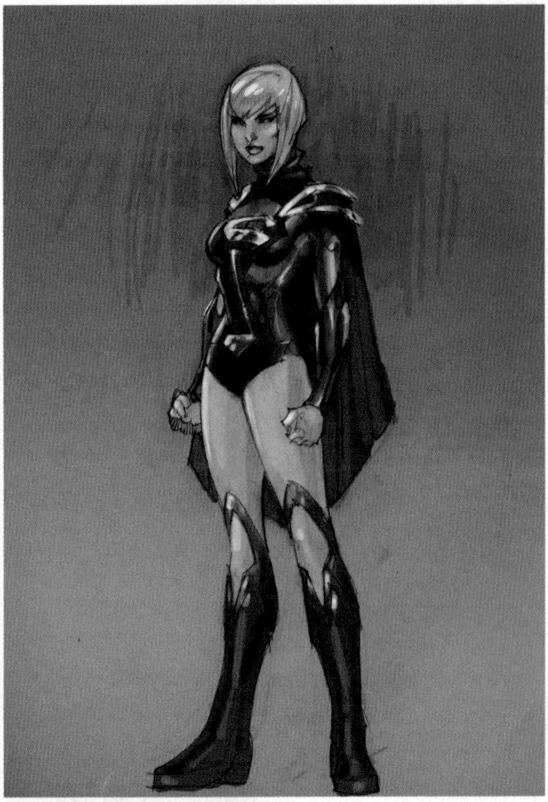

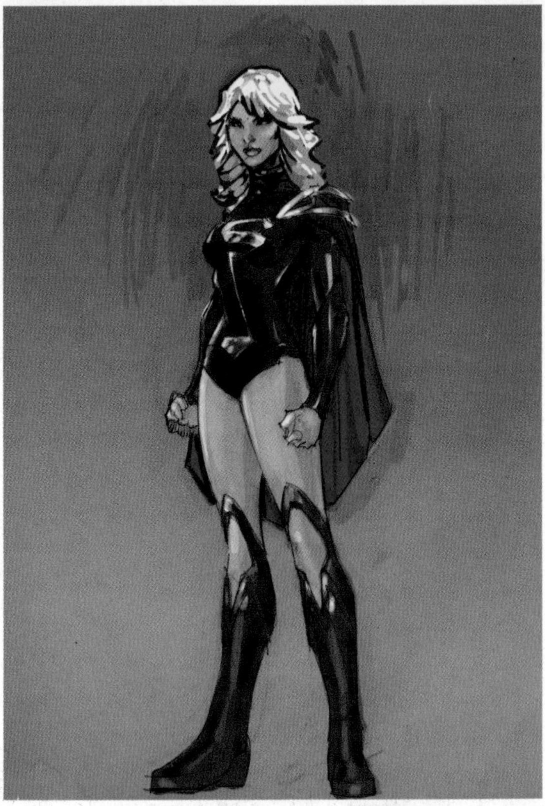

Supergirl costume designs by Mahmud Asrar.

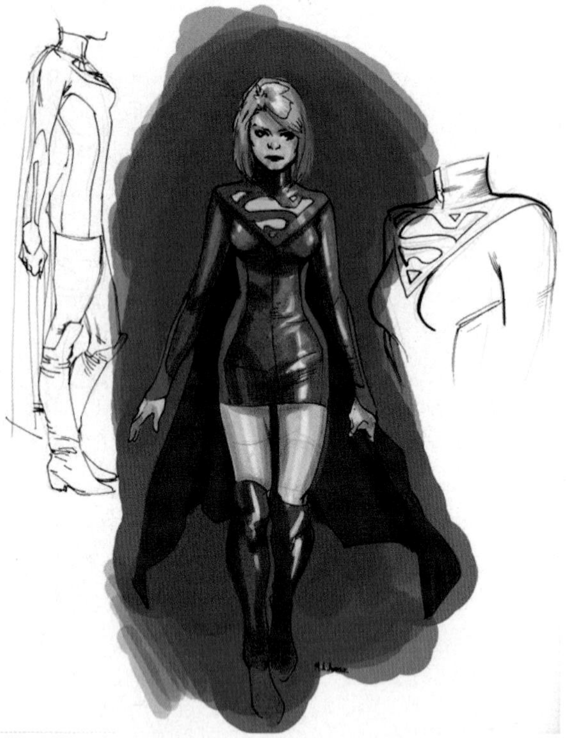

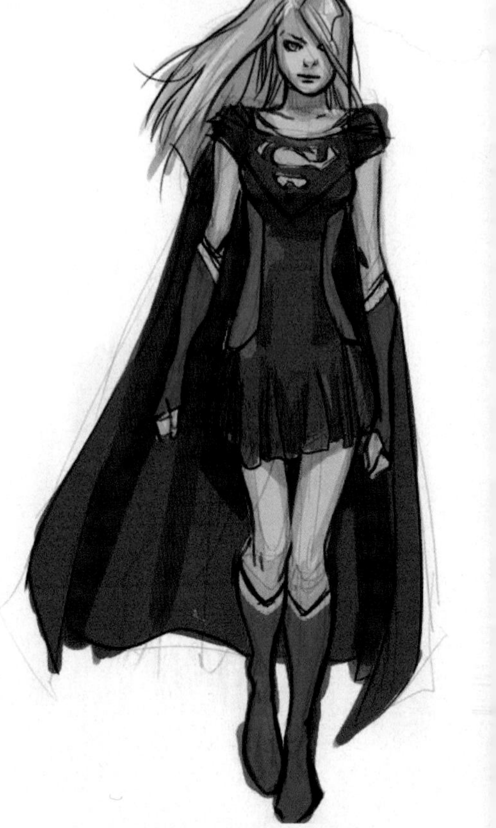

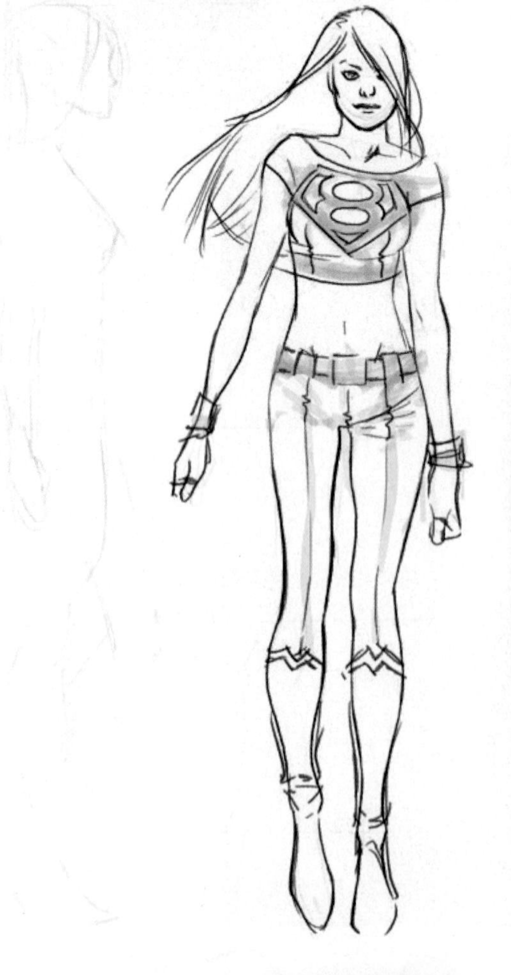

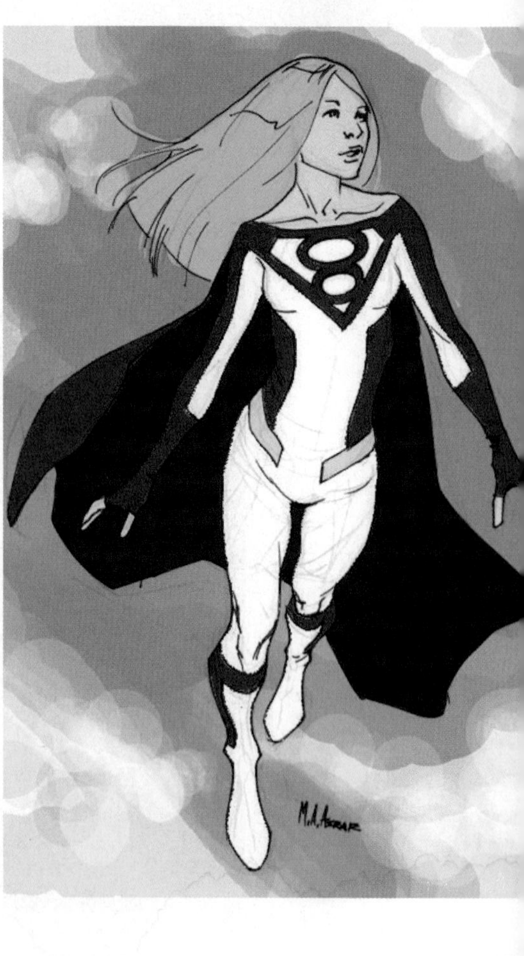

Worldkiller character designs by Mahmud Asrar.

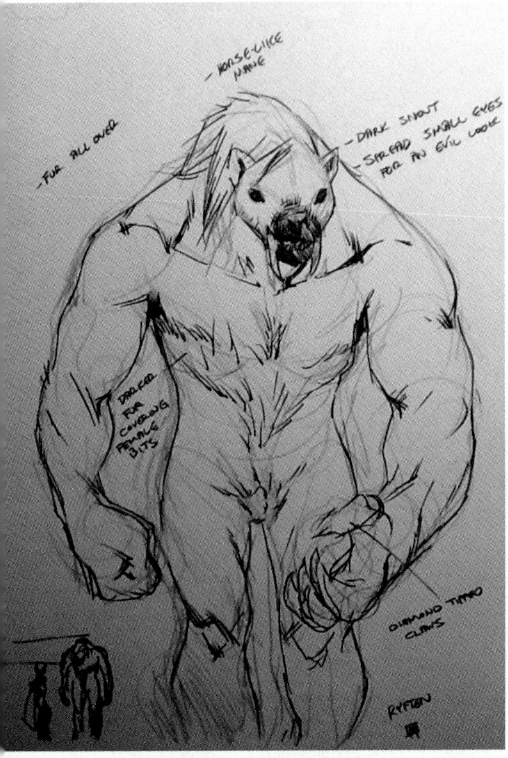
-HORSE-LIKE MANE
-DARK SNOUT
-SPREAD SMALL EYES FOR AN EVIL LOOK
-FUR ALL OVER
DARKER FUR COVERING FEMALE BITS
DIAMOND TIPPED CLAWS
RYFTEN

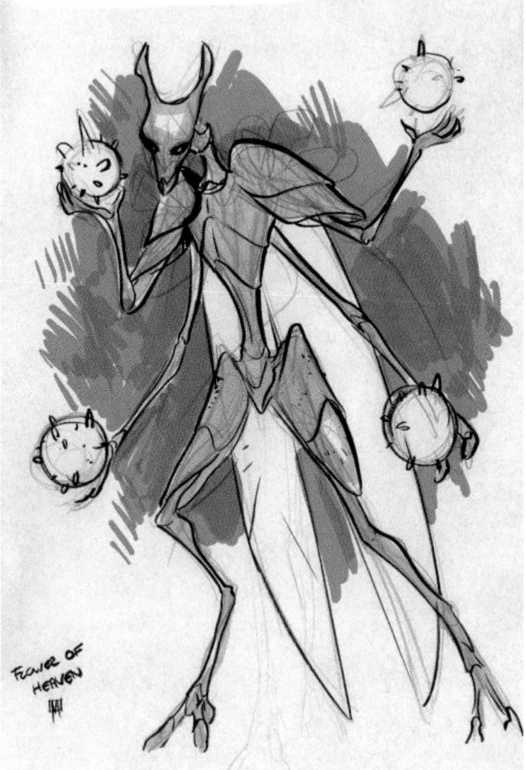
FLOWER OF HEAVEN

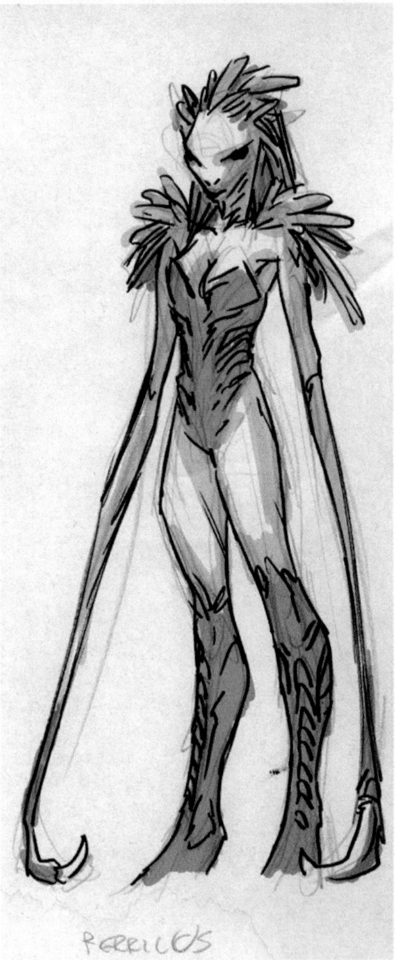

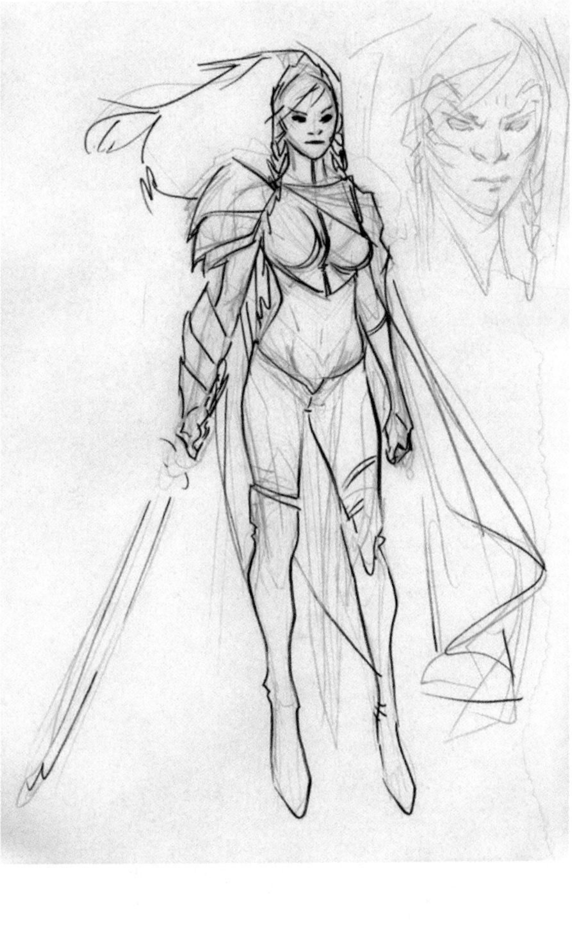

SUPERGIRL

ISSUE #6 UNUSED COVER BY MAHMUD ASRAR

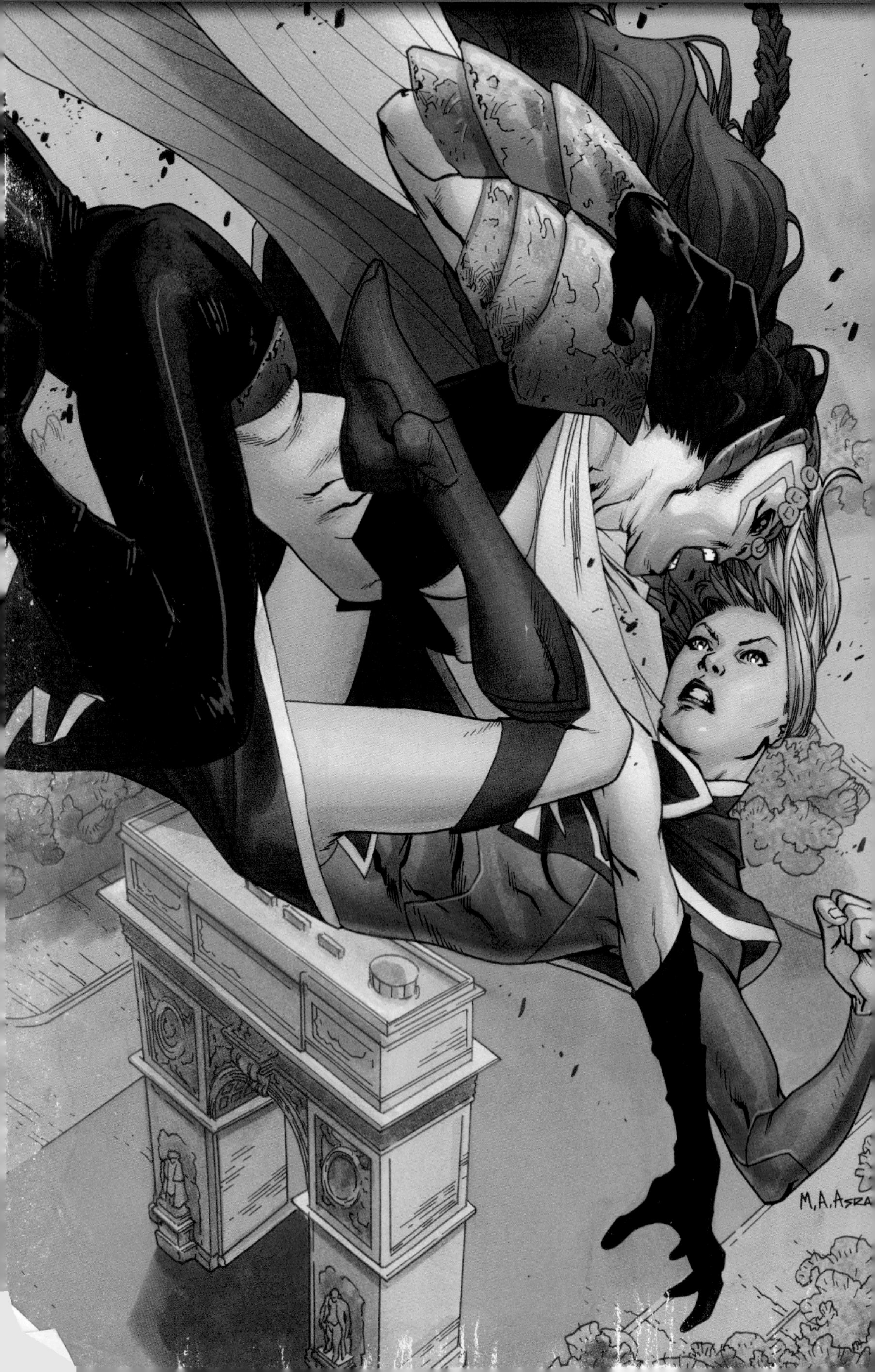
M.A.Asrar